B-Square Publishing Company

Other Novels by WILSON BAKER, JR. (a.k.a. WG Goldstein)

"Class Reunion is a heart pumping rush from start to finish. You won't know who the bad guy is until the last sentence of the last paragraph of the last page of the last chapter of the book." -Sam Foster, Tampa, Florida

"Suspense filled novel that is extremely hard to put down. Baker (Goldstein) has a hit! A must read for any avid reader."
- Jason Childs, Bowie, Maryland

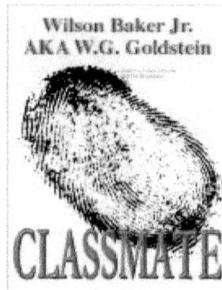

"Impressive in scope and depth. Once again Baker (Goldstein) gives you a story with a beginning, middle and end. A story with a plot that has a motive means and opportunity, Things that have been lost in today's writing." – Christine Smith Jacksonville, Florida

Revenge Has No Expiration Date
By
Wilson Baker, Jr.
Who writes as W.G. Goldstein

Dedicated to:
Morgan State University

One ($1.00) dollar will be donated to:
Morgan State University National Alumni Association
By B-Square Publishing Company
From the sale of this book.

Also by
Wilson Baker, Jr.
Who Writes As
W. G. Goldstein

Class Reunion
ISBN: 0-9672756-4-4
§
The Roommate
ISBN: 0-967256-5-2
§
Classmate
ISBN: 09672756-6-0
§
Searching For A Star
ISBN: 0-9672756-7-9

PUBLISHED BY
B-SQUARE PUBLISHING COMPANY
8020 Pink Azalea Court
Windsor Mill, Maryland 21244

This novel is a work of fiction. The characters, names, incidents, dialogue and plot are the products of the author's imagination or are used fictitiously. Any resemblance to actual persons, companies, or events is purely coincidental.

Book design by Darrell W. Baker

Library of Congress Cataloging-in-Publication Data Applied for
ISBN: 978-0-9857668-9-4

Acknowledgements

From concept to publishing, a lot of skilled and dedicated people devoted their time and energy to complete this book. I could begin to name each and every one of the individuals that took part in this effort, which I should do, but there are too many and some whose names I don't even know. Still, it must be said, and these two words are not descriptive enough to tell how I really feel, but for all of you who helped me: Thank you.

Revenge Has No Expiration Date

Chapter 1

The Night of: Jacksonville, Florida.

People ducked for cover, but it didn't matter. Glass, steel, and metal fragments tore through the hot June air indiscriminately, and anything in the path of the shrapnel, human or otherwise, fell in its wake. Those within 100 yards of ground zero were probably dead even before they heard the noise.

It was as close to a war zone as most people would ever know. Fireballs reached two football fields into the sky, the flames followed by a blanket of smoke. The blast shook the entire Bay Street area and the blaze that followed burned hot and red! Everything within a five-block radius instantly went up in flames.

In the distance, the sounds of emergency equipment began to echo over the ear-shattering noise of the blast even as secondary explosions began to go off, the heat from the fire igniting underground gas lines.

People stood horrified blocks away. Tourists at the Landing put down their drinks and sat frozen in place. Not knowing what had happened, no one knew what to do. It was like the earth opened up and a gust of flames came up as the devil spoke through the fire, "I'm here to get you!"

Three elements are needed to start a fire: air, a combustible material, and a source to begin the fire—a match, flint, spark, or lightning, anything that combines the other two elements. Every element was there for this fire to burn and burn well.

Fire Engine Company 54 from the Bay Street Fire Station was the first to arrive at the scene. The Fire Chief exited his vehicle, and for several seconds, he froze in place on the side of the massive fire engine. His eyes transmitted to his mind, and his mind confirmed, that he had never seen any destruction in his career that prepared him for what he was looking at.

—

The United Kingdom, Scotland, the Day Before.

In a villa on the coast of Scotland east of Glasgow near Edinburgh, a tall, athletic, well-built man dressed in a 19th century-style smoking jacket and smoking a Ben Wade pipe stood in the study of this classic home. He looked out of the bay window of his study at the shipping vessels as they passed through the narrow channel below headed into the North Sea.

His attention was taken from this majestic view when he heard a voice from his computer: "You have mail."

Still puffing on his pipe, he walked over to his computer and clicked the mail icon to view his double encrypted email message. The message read: "Ten million dollars transferred to your Swiss account. Balance to be sent upon your confirmation of completion of operations."

The man created a new file folder and labeled it Seventy-One. The man then clicked the attachment icon and downloaded the attached file into the newly created file folder.

Seventy-One was probably the most skilled contract killer in the business. He was always successful, never a dissatisfied customer. He worked on all sides. The British, Soviets, Americans, even the Mafia. He had no allegiance other than to the price of his service. The man with the numbered name had never even been seen, let alone caught. There were no pictures on record, no fingerprints, no voice pattern. He never killed the same way. Sometimes he killed with a rifle, from great distances, but always with a different caliber, and sometimes with a knife. He had even killed with his bare hands. No two contracts had been carried out in the same fashion.

Interpol didn't even know what race he was. The only identifying trace anyone had was that an email message would be sent to a W.C. Baker confirming that his payment had been forwarded to a Swiss numbered bank account. Once Interpol attempted to monitor the whereabouts of everyone they could identify with the name W. C. Baker. Their efforts proved to be fruitless.

After downloading the file, Seventy-One turned on his laser printer and began to print the dossier. While the archive was printing, Seventy-One walked over to his stereo cabinet and turned on his compact disc player. Mozart's "Adagio Clarinet Concerto in A" began to play, filling his study. He then walked to his whiskey cabinet, pulled out a bottle of 20-year-old brandy and a large brandy snifter, and poured himself a drink. By this time the dossier had finished printing. Seventy-One placed the document in a folder and seated himself in a large chair positioned at this massive 18th century-style desk.

For several moments, Seventy-One closed his eyes, put the glass of brandy up to his nose, and relaxed while inhaling the aroma of the brandy. He then took a sip of brandy and set the snifter on the desk.

Seventy-One then carefully read the dossier. After Seventy-One finished reading the file, he laid it down on the desk and began to make notes on a white legal pad. Several hours passed, and after filling up all the pages of four legal pads with drawings and notes, Seventy-One spoke to himself in a whisper. "It can be done."

He then sat back in his chair, refilled the empty three-quarter snifter, and sat quietly in the darkened room. The daylight had gone, and it was late evening. The only light in the study was from his desk lamp. After several moments of quiet reflection, he got up from his chair, walked to his computer and sent a one-word encrypted return message: "Accept."

—

Little Havana, Miami Florida, the Morning of.

It was early Saturday morning, and a steady drenching rain, much needed in the Miami-Dade County area, was coming down. Over the last two years, the hurricane season had been mild, which resulted in the water tables measuring extremely small for this time of the year.

Not paying any attention to the heavy rain, the two men walked out of a rundown office building, the headquarters of the Movement for the Independence for Essequibo, MIE.

Neither wore a jacket, not even a hat, and both had a fiercely determined look on their faces as they opened the trunk of the waiting Mercedes-Benz parked at the curb of the headquarters. Each of the men placed a large bag into the trunk of the waiting vehicle.

One man closed the trunk and took a seat on the passenger side of the car next to the driver. The other man occupied the seat in the back of the car where he could see the driver's face in the rearview mirror. The Mercedes-Benz pulled away from the curb, quickly accelerated, and headed in the direction of the interstate and the Florida Turnpike.

As they picked up their turnpike ticket and accelerated to turnpike speed, the man in the backseat, still viewing the driver in the rearview mirror, spoke.

"Aún no entiendo por qué debemos proporcionar nuestro debe armas y municiones para el entrenamiento?"

The man seated beside the driver replied. "Krish, we have been over this 100 times. If they give something, we have to give something. This is not up for discussion any longer, and also, from this point on, we only speak English!"

With a frustrated look on his face, Krish turned his head toward the window and looked at the passing orange groves in a dark stare. "I understand completely, Ranuel, but I do not like the Americanos controlling our destiny."

After several minutes, Ranuel replied, "We would not have this opportunity if it were not for the Americanos." The Mercedes-Benz continued north on the Florida Turnpike.

The road they traveled, formerly known as the Sunshine State Parkway, was re-designated the Ronald Reagan Turnpike. It is a north-south toll road that runs 312 miles through 11 counties in the Florida peninsula from US Route 1 in Florida City to Miami, Fort Lauderdale, and West Palm Beach, paralleling Interstate 95 to Orlando where it crosses Interstate 4, its northern terminus at Interstate 75 near Wildwood. The turnpike opened in two stages between 1957 and 1964. The first phase is the mainland, a 265-mile route from Golden Gables intersection north of Miami to Wildwood that carries the hidden designation as State Road 91. The second step, 48 miles long, is called the Homestead Extension of Florida's Turnpike. Completed in 1964, this section carries the hidden designation of Florida State Road 821 from Florida City through the suburbs of the west and north of Miami and connects to the mainland four miles north of the Golden Glades Interchange.

After about an hour and a half of driving, the rain stopped, and the sun came out; it was evident why Florida was called the

Sunshine State. A brilliant bright sky, clear for as far as you could see, forced the passengers to relax and brought down the tension level that had built up during the drive.

The Mercedes pulled into a rest stop and stopped at the gas pumps. Ranuel and the driver got out of the car and walked into the mini market type store. The driver went to the counter where a kid of 17 or 18 was sipping on a big gulp soda while staring at the in-store video monitor.

The driver handed the clerk three $20 bills for a fill-up on pump four and walked out of the store and back to the gas pump. Ranuel wandered around the store until he found what he was searching for, a prepaid cellular telephone. He took the phone to the store clerk and laid it on the counter. The clerk scanned the phone and declared the cost: $87.39. Ranuel handed the clerk five $20 bills. As the boy took the money, the kid said, "You know, you automatically get 20 hours of service. After that, you can buy hours in increments of 10, 20, and even 40 hours. If you want to do text messaging you will need to purchase the smartphone model, but we are all out of that one. We will probably have some in next week. That's the one that I have, and man it is sweet." He handed $12.61 back to Ranuel, who was just about to say keep the change when it hit him that he didn't want to leave any trace of evidence to remind the kid that he had been there. He figured that it was probably not often that someone left a tip, so Ranuel took the money and walked out of the store and to the Mercedes.

The driver was still filling the Mercedes as Ranuel got back to the pump. He asked the driver to pop the trunk open because he wanted to get something out of his bag. The driver reached inside the car door and opened the trunk. Ranuel unzipped his bag and pulled out a small black notebook and closed the trunk. He then walked around to the passenger side and got into the car. He opened the prepaid cell phone and inserted the battery and the memory chip. He then checked to see if he needed to charge the phone. The phone showed only a 20% charge. So he pulled out the charger from the box that the telephone came in and inserted it into the cigarette lighter and into the phone. The screen on the phone indicated that it was accepting the charge. Ranuel then turned his attention back to the black notebook. He began thumbing through the pages. About halfway through the book, he found the page that he was looking for, a page containing a list of 20-25 telephone numbers. As Ranuel was using his fingers to scroll down the numbers, the driver got in and started the engine. Ranuel turned to the driver and, while pointing, said,

"Pull over there and park. I need to make a few calls, and I want to ensure I have good reception."

When the driver parked the car at the location where Ranuel ordered him to go, Krish reached his hand across the front seat of the car and touched the driver's right shoulder, snapped his finger, and opened his palm. The driver reached into the glove box and pulled out a cigar then placed it into Krish's free hand. Krish got out of the back seat, walked to the rear of the car and sat on the trunk. He looked at the cigar, carefully reading the name as if he were verifying the quality and the authenticity. Krish then unwrapped the cigar and carefully holding the cigar in his left hand, crumpled up the wrapping and threw it to the ground. He then placed the cigar between his lips, closed his eyes, and rolled the cigar around in his mouth. Krish bit off a small piece of the tip of cigar and spit it on the ground, then pulled out a lighter and while lighting the cigar, closed his eyes and took an enormous draw. Tilting his head back, he exhaled the smoke through his nostrils and his mouth. As he brought his head forward, he looked across the rest area parking lot and saw a Florida State Highway Patrol car pulling into the mini market. Krish reached into his shirt pocket, pulled out a set of sunglasses and placed them on his face. The Florida State Trooper parked his cruiser and went into the mini market to get a cup of coffee.

Back inside the car, Ranuel looked at the screen on the phone and saw that it read 70% charged. He turned the phone on and dialed the first number that he had selected from the little black book. While the phone was ringing, Ranuel watched the minute hand on his watch. The phone rang three times, and precisely before the fourth rang, someone answered the phone but didn't say anything. Ranuel said only, "In route!" Then he quickly ended the call.

Ranuel dialed 10 more numbers, repeating the exact same process, each call answered precisely before the fourth ring and his response restricted to one and a half seconds. After Ranuel had completed the last call, he took a handkerchief out of his hip pocket, unplugged the phone from the cigarette lighter, got out of the car and walked over to a trashcan. He then proceeded to take the battery out of the phone, remove the memory chip, wipe the phone clean of all fingerprints, and smash the phone on the edge of the trashcan before discarding. He then took the memory chip and walked to a different trashcan, broke the chip in half and threw it in the can. Ranuel then got in the Mercedes-Benz as Krish jumped off the trunk of the car, threw the cigar to the pavement, and took his seat in the back of the car. The car pulled away merging back into the turnpike traffic. Ranuel looked over his shoulder while speaking to Krish. "See my friend, everyone has arrived in the country. Everything is going as plan. You see the Americanos have not betrayed us. They can be trusted."

—

Washington, DC, four hours before.

Wallace C. Barker, or WC as he liked to be called, found himself standing in front of a display counter looking at diamond rings. He was in a very exclusive jewelry store in the Georgetown section of Washington, DC. With only four hours to spare before he had to be at Ronald Regan Airport to catch a plane to Jacksonville, Florida, Wallace was shopping for a wedding set.

"The Four C's," Wallace kept repeating in his head as he stared into the jewelry display cabinet. The cabinet contained row after row of some of the most beautiful and exquisite rings one could imagine.

"Cut, color, clarity, and carat weight." His focus shifted to this one tray that was filled with rings containing marquise-shaped stones

A feminine-sounding male voice broke Wallace's concentration. "I can see that you have been thinking about this for some time."

Wallace very slowly raised his head. WC made eye contact with the tall and fragile gentleman who appeared to be in excellent physical condition. He had come out of nowhere and was standing on the opposite side of the counter looking down at Wallace.

Wallace said to himself, "I'm six-one; so he must be, six-five, maybe taller. Probably doesn't weigh any more than 150 to 170 pounds, though." Continuing to size up the clerk, he thought, "The guy probably knows some martial arts, but his balance is all off, and so he either doesn't practice enough, or he just started his training and only has a white belt. In his late twenties, maybe early thirties, I would say."

This guy must spend at least a hundred bucks a week on manicures. His nails and hands look better than Eve's though I better not let Eve hear me say that." The store clerk's suit matched the ambiance and exclusiveness of the shop: tailored, white linen shirt with Wall Street-type accessories.

From Wallace's Special Forces training, his instinct was to pick up any details that would give him an edge, any edge in any situation.

"Obviously, you have a reason for saying I look like I've been at this a while? Can I ask you why?" Wallace smiled and waited for the sales clerk to respond. Wallace could see from the expression that appeared on the sales clerk's face that he had thrown the clerk off of his sales game plan.

"You seem to have a higher level of confidence and experience in diamond selection than most men who come into our store alone. I would even go so far as to guess that you have been married more than once."

Wallace took a step back from the counter. Was it so obvious? How could anyone just look at someone and tell that he had been married before? Was he walking around with something stamped on his forehead that says loser?

The store clerk, now leaning on the display counter with his elbows and looking up at Wallace, said, "The marquise-cut rings you are looking at are of the highest quality, and very few first-time buyers even consider that particular shape. Most men who come in by themselves just look at the round-shaped cuts. Would you like me to take that tray out so you can have a closer look?"

Wallace was still reeling from the fact that the store clerk had guessed that he had been married before and got it right.

"Why, yes, I would like to take a closer look. Thanks for asking."
While the store clerk was unlocking the cabinet and taking out the tray, he gave Wallace a big smile.

"This is your lucky day. We don't have many, but today marks the second day of our discount sale on these unique rings."

After placing the tray on the top of the cabinet, the clerk took out a pair of white cotton gloves and slowly slipped them on. He then brought out a jewelry loupe, a velvet ring size stick, and a jeweler's mat.

"I'm so excited that you have your eyes on these unique rings. They are so exquisite. Let me point out my favorite and we can see if we have the same taste. I so hope that you don't mind."

Before Wallace could reply, the store clerk picked up one of the most beautiful rings on the tray and placed it on the sizing stick, then pointed to the exact place where he wanted Wallace to hold the stick without touching the rings.

Wallace reached across the counter and, putting his hand exactly where the sales clerk directed, took the sizing stick. "Now tell me the truth: Doesn't that just take your breath away?"

Speaking to himself, Wallace said, "This is really getting weird. This is one of the rings that I had my eye on."

"I must agree; this is an exquisite ring." Thinking for a second, Wallace picked up the loupe and began to examine the ring closer.

While Wallace was looking through the lens of the loupe, the store clerk said, "I must say, you do look familiar. Were you at our office in Cape Town, South Africa last June during our buying trip?"

Wallace didn't reply.

"Maybe at our annual New York showing? I meet so many people in this line of work, but I'm sure if we had met you would remember."

Still holding the sizing stick in his left hand, Wallace placed the loupe back on the display counter. The store clerk broke into Wallace's thinking process.

"I'm sorry I didn't introduce myself. My name is Melvin."

The store clerk then reached out his hand to Wallace. As they were shaking hands, Wallace replied. "My name is Wallace, but please call me WC." The store clerk began to grin, sounding like a teenage girl as he made direct eye contact with Wallace. "What does WC stand for? Let me guess: wow and crazy?"

Wallace didn't reply and turned his concentration back to the ring. After a few seconds, Wallace said, "Now, what is your recommendation for a band to complement this ring?"

Folding his arms in utter joy, Melvin burst out, "You do like it! I was so hoping that you would. But just as I said when I first saw you looking at this selection, I just knew you displayed the confidence of a man who knows what he wants. I have just the band she would die for. Hold your breath for just another moment and I'm sure that you will appreciate the wait. It will only take me a minute." Pointing to another counter, Melvin then said, "I have to step over there."

—

Jacksonville, Florida.

It was the third Saturday of the month and one week from being the first month anniversary of Chris Martin's promotion to Fire Chief. Chris was in charge of Fire Engine Company 54 of the Jacksonville City Fire Department, which consisted of two fire engines, an extended ladder engine, and an emergency medical team. The station was a 50-50 unit. Half of the people who made up the unit were professional firefighters and the other half were volunteer firefighters. Unit 54 was one of the oldest fire companies in the department, and Chris Martin was the youngest Chief to ever hold the position.

A third generation fireman, he stood frozen as he scrutinized the situation. Slowly he began to formulate a course of actions. Within microseconds, his reflexes started to take over his fears.

His hand trembling, he reached for his microphone. "Control, this is 5-4, on station!" The control center quickly replied. "Acknowledge, 5-4! What's the situation?" the dispatcher shouted back.

Receiving no immediate response, the dispatcher shouted into the microphone again, "What in the hell is going on over there, Chris? I felt the explosion over here!" It was uncommon for the command dispatcher to deviate from radio procedure and express any sign of concern, emotions, or fear during an operation.

Chief Martin sensed the concern in the dispatcher's voice, but the seconds were too precious to fill his mind with this deviation from procedure. He figured he'd deal with it later. As he ran toward the fire, he reached for his microphone and began to bark out orders, directing his fire teams to the precise point where he wanted them to engage the fire. The point where the Fire Chief leads his units to engage a fire is the point where the battle with nature begins, and thus the first order in attacking a fire is the critical order.

Chief Martin's confidence rose as he turned to see that his men were attacking the inferno in standard form and just as he directed. His biggest fear when he took over the company was that, because of his youth, the men would not think he had the experience to handle a big one. But he could see that his first command made sense to them from the way that they reacted.

Martin's youthfulness overcame his uncertainty, and he began to direct his men to work on containment. First, attack and then contain. Attack and contain.

His radio sounded off. Suddenly Chris remembered that he had not gotten back to the dispatcher with a situation report.

"Dispatch, this is the 5-4 command, over."

Chris waited, focusing on the fire and contemplating what he would request from the dispatcher. The silence was broken when the dispatcher shouted, "Go ahead, 5-4."

It was becoming clearer and clearer to Chris. He had attacked the fire properly, but the three units he had with him at the scene were doing little to contain the fire, and so he had to request assistance.

"Dispatch, we need backup, over."

"Roger, 5-4. Backup is on the way, over."

Standard procedure requires that once a second fire unit has been dispatched to the fire, all hospitals within a 15-mile radius must be notified that an emergency situation exists. The city police had also analyzed the situation and were diverting traffic from the emergency area.

"I was in the neighborhood and thought that I would stop by." Chris snapped his head in the direction of the sound of the voice. Standing beside him on his right was Fire Chief Gayle Rivers of Engine Company 1-1 off Myrtle Avenue. He also saw her fire company beginning to engage the fire.

"Glad you guys got the call, Gayle." After a brief moment of eye contact, both Gayle and Chris quickly turned their attention back to the fire.

"A hell of a way to start your new job, Chris, but everything you've done so far is by the book." Gayle's statement was reassuring to Chris.

Gayle Rivers was one of the most senior fire chiefs in the Jacksonville Fire Department. Gayle received her initial training while she was in the Navy. In fact, she experienced fighting two major ship fires, both at sea and one of the two during a typhoon. Chief Rivers was born in Jacksonville, did a couple of years at the community college, and then joined the Navy. When her enlistment ended, she came back home and joined the fire department.

"Yeah, but I guess I had to get the big one sooner or later. What do you think?" Both, still analyzing the fire stood quietly in thought.

"I believe this is major, and you better go code red." While reaching for his radio microphone, Chris said to Gayle, "I think that you're right. I'll put the call in now!"
It took less than two minutes for an additional five fire companies to arrive at the scene. The mobile emergency command center was set up, and the Jacksonville mayor's office was notified.

—

North Jacksonville, Jacksonville, Florida.

In a new gated community, the telephone rang. Debra Webb walked across her kitchen and answered the phone.

"Hello, Mayor's hotline."

"Debra, this is Joe." Joe Singletary was Director of Jacksonville's Emergency Preparedness Reaction Team. "Sorry to disturb you, but we have a situation I need to brief Bubba on." Debra smiled. Of all the people who worked directly with her husband, Joe was one of the people Debra saw as the most loyal to her husband.

"Joe, no problem. I'll get him. He's out by the pool catching up on his reading." Debra pushed the hold button on the telephone and then pressed the intercom button.

"Bubba, Joe is on the special line. I think you better take it." Debra paused for a second to hear his response. "OK, honey. I'm on my way." Debra left the kitchen and walked into the study. There she turned on Bubba's desktop computer; she also then turned up the sound on three televisions. One was set to CNN, one to MSNBC, and the last to an all-news local television station. She then proceeded to turn on a citizens' band radio and a police scanner.

Bubba Webb's study served as his home office and his personal command center. Even from home, he could keep up with anything that was taking place in and around Jacksonville, Florida.

Bubba came into the study, laid a folder down on the table, and walked over to Debra to give her a big smile and kiss her. Then he said, "Thanks, honey. Do you think it's serious?" Debra looked around the room, double-checking everything to ensure that she hadn't missed turning something on or turning the volume up.

"I think it's more serious than political, Bubba. Joe had his serious voice on rather than his political one."

In Bubba Webb's world, everything came down to three possibilities: serious with no political implications, purely political, or severe with political implications.

Bubba sat down at his desk, put a set of headphones on, smiled and pushed the button on the telephone.

"Joe, how the hell are you doing? Tell me what's up?

"I'm okay, but we got one helluva mess over here. A five-alarm fire. All engine companies are on alert, and, at least, four engine companies have responded. No reports of casualties, but I'm sure we are going to get our fair share. Property damage will probably top 20 to 50 million. But the good news..."

Bubba Webb interrupted Joe. "Good news? You have good news?"

"Yeah, Bubba, I think there is an upside to this. The fire is on the west side of Julia Street and all of the damage at this time goes from west of Julia Street to Jefferson."

A big smile came to Bubba Webb's face. "Please tell me that it covered from Bay to Ashley Street?"

Joe continued, "That's right, Bubba. It did. It looks like the fire took out every joint in the area." Joe paused for a second. "The only downside is that it took out that church that's a designated a historical site."

Bubba cut in again. "Joe, how many TV crews are there?"

Joe told Bubba to wait while he stepped out of the back door of the Mobile Command Center with the remote headphone and looked around the yellow taped area. After a moment, he replied to the Mayor's question. "Surprisingly, Bubba, I only see two. But that's about right for this part of town."

Bubba thought about what Joe said and shook his head in agreement. "I just finished talking to the Fire Chief, and he said that it will probably be another hour or two before they get this thing under control. I'll give you updates as usual and let you know if you should come out."

"The first sign of any casualty or any loss of life, call me immediately!"

Joe's tone changed as he replied, "Mr. Mayor, I understand exactly and will call you instantly when the situation changes."

A brief silence came over the phone line. "Thanks, Joe. I appreciate that. I know I can depend on you."

—

Jewelry Store, Washington, DC.

Wallace didn't hold his breath; he just looked at his watch. The airport was 45 to 50 minutes from Georgetown in perfect traffic conditions, but this was Washington DC where perfect traffic conditions don't exist, ever. So Wallace knew he had to keep track of time, but he also knew that he was about to make the biggest decision of his life and did not want to do it as if under the gun.

This time, he wanted to get it right. "Everything starts with the ring," he told himself.

Wallace had gone through this process two other times, neither marriage worked out. As a matter of fact, he proposed over the telephone the first go-round and later bought the ring and band, but in his second marriage, he didn't even officially propose. One day they were walking through a mall, walked into a jewelry store and walked out with wedding bands. It was almost like another shopping trip to the mall.

Things were different now. Wallace was more settled in his life and in his career. He loved developing computer software, and now that he had moved into the program and project management position, he could utilize all the leadership and managerial skills that he had acquired while he was in the military.

Although he had left the regular army, he was still in the Reserve and commanded a Special Forces A-Team. He knew this might be a sticking point when he asked her to marry him because of his duties in the reserves still required him to do a lot of traveling, many times to parts of the world he couldn't speak about.

In a sense, being away on long missions, while on active duty probably caused his first marriage to go south. The second was somewhat similar. The question was always the same from both wives one and two: "What do you do when you go away?" But the answer was always the same too: it is classified. And so he couldn't say.

Just a week ago he and his team had returned from a sneak-and-peak mission, what his men called such forays in Southwest Asia. His Reserve Special Forces battalion received a lot of missions like this. A team would fly into an area of operations commercially as businessmen. The stated purpose of their business trip when authorities asked was to verify certain things for a possible business deal to take place at some unspecified future date.

The team was actually verifying information, anything from the time of day that the area had the most congested traffic patterns to road construction that was ongoing to verification of an individual's daily routines.

As a matter of fact, it was on Wallace's second mission as the team commander when he thought he saw his old roommate, Harry Paxton, the thought that came to him out of nowhere as he stood before the glass case in a jewelry store.

Wallace's team was handling a group of men serving as taxi cab drivers. These people spoke several different languages. It's amazing the conversations that take place in the backseat of a cab, especially when the people in the cab believe that the driver does not speak their language. These particular drivers manned routes that took them to selective embassies, their passengers mostly second and third-tier embassy personnel, people who would talk about their jobs and bosses to vent their frustration. These people would know enough of the local language to give directions to the cab driver and then revert to their mother tongue to conduct their conversations.

Assuming the driver did not speak their language, they would inevitably begin to talk about office stuff, most of which was not classified but a word here and phrase there in many cases provided verification for other information the team was investigating.

Wallace was on his way to meet one of his drivers when the cab that he was riding in came to a traffic stop. Out of the right corner of his eye, Wallace saw a man with a full beard who was dressed as an Arab, but he noted the man had the same height and build as his old roommate, Harry Paxton.

When Wallace was on active duty, he was stationed at Fort Bragg, and he and Harry were in the same Special Forces Battalion the last year Wallace was on active duty. Wallace recalled that Harry grew a full beard once for the purpose of going on a mission in the Middle East, and the man Wallace watched crossing the street in front of his car had a beard groomed in the same fashion as Harry's. Wallace could tell that the man sensed he was being watched, and when he finished crossing the street, the bearded man turned his head and made direct eye contact with Wallace before vanishing into the crowd. The contact was so quick that it left Wallace feeling unsure if it was really Harry, but it was enough for Wallace to keep that sighting in his memory. He was shaken from his reverie by Melvin's return.

"Now that didn't take long, did it, WC? I am confident that once I open this box, the sight of this ring will give you more pleasure than anything that you have experienced in your life." With a giggle, Melvin then said, "I guess I should say almost anything in life." Melvin opened the box.

Wallace looked at the wedding band, then picked up the loupe and holding the ring box up to the lens of the loupe, conducted his examination of the band. He then placed the wedding band on the sizing stick. Once again using the loupe, he did a second review but, this time, looked at the two rings as a set.

Wallace slowly placed the sizing stick and the rings back on the mat. And then he stared at the rings glittering against all of the black velvet backgrounds. Wallace slowly raised his head. "Melvin, I think you have outdone yourself. I'll take them."

Clapping his hands in excitement, Melvin replied, "I just knew it. I just knew it. I could tell by your sophistication that you have the most exquisite tastes, and that lady of yours will be the happiest woman in the world. Let's step over to that counter and we can conclude the sale."

As Wallace followed Melvin to the closing desk, Melvin looked over his shoulder and said, "With the discount, this set should come to $32,233.10." Wallace pulled out his credit card and handed it to Melvin as he walked behind the counter.

Melvin completed the paperwork, wrapped the wedding set, and reminded WC he had a lifetime warranty. "It's been a pleasure assisting you in making your selection. I hope you have a wonderful wedding and a long marriage, but if things shouldn't work out, come and see me."

Wallace shook Melvin's hand and said, "Thanks for your help, but, this time, I think I have it right. Have a great day."

Wallace immediately looked at his watch. "I have just over an hour and 50 minutes to get to my gate," he thought as he headed for the door.

Wallace was fortunate. Traffic congestion was minimal, and he made it to his gate with 20 minutes to spare before they began boarding. He pulled out his cell phone and made a call.

"Hi, honey. We should start boarding in the next 5 to 10 minutes, so I'll see you in about another hour and 20 minutes."

The voice on the other end replied, "Sounds great, lover. I'll be leaving the Landing in about 10 minutes and will meet you at the airport. Everything is packed. All we have to do is grab a bite to eat and get on the road."

"Wonderful. I'll see you when we land. Love you."

—

Home of Henry "Bubba" Webb, Jacksonville, Florida.

To look at Henry "Bubba" Webb, especially after you talked with him, your first guess would be that he grew up in Florida, did his schooling in Florida and, except for a stint in the military, probably had always lived in Florida. You would be wrong, entirely wrong.

The truth is, Henry B. Webb was from Maine. His family was extremely wealthy, and Henry got just about anything and everything he wanted as a kid. After high school, Henry got an athletic basketball scholarship to attend one of the state universities in Florida. Because of Henry's high school grades, the scholarship required him to go to summer school before the semester he was scheduled to begin at the University. This was Henry's first trip to Florida, and except for changing planes in Atlanta, this was his first trip to the South.

When Henry arrived on campus, it was a match made in heaven. Henry Webb fell in love with Florida and everything that came with it. In fact, Henry wanted so much to blend in and be accepted as a local that when he started summer school, he told everyone his middle initial stood for Bubba rather than Bernard. From that point on, Henry Bernard Webb was Henry Bubba Webb or Bubba Webb, but mostly he was just Bubba.

During his years at the University, Henry played on two championship basketball teams. He was not a starter, but as the sixth man on the team, Henry was known for putting in a solid performance when he did get into the game.

After graduation, Henry got a couple of professional basketball offers but turned them down. He chose to attend law school, and he went home to Maine and to State University's School of Law. After finishing law school, Henry "Bubba" Webb immediately returned to Florida, passed the Florida Bar, and got a job with the state. Eventually, he made his way to Jacksonville, and for the last 15 years, Jacksonville had been his home.

Six years ago Bubba became the District Attorney for Jacksonville, Florida, and Duval County. He received a nomination to get the judgeship for the Eleventh District Judicial Court, but he turned it down. Most people thought he turned it down because he wanted to run for office, and not long after turning down the offer, he did.

Just after Bubba's second year at State, he met Debra. One of Bubba's teammates brought Debra to a fraternity party; the teammate had a little too much to drink at the party, so Bubba escorted Debra back to her apartment. That was the beginning of their relationship.

Initially, when people saw Bubba and Debra on campus they thought it was only one of those overnight things and would soon fade away. It was not uncommon for Bubba to be seen on campus with several different girls during the basketball season. However, once the season ended and people still saw Bubba and Debra together, they knew that there might be more to this relationship than previously predicted.

Debra was from Jacksonville with a middle-class upbringing and a strong religious background. She was an education major, and Debra had a dreamer's goal: to make a difference in the quality of teaching in the South. Bubba Webb and Debra were not the two people you would pick to be made for each other, but about two years after they graduated from State, they were married; and after more than 25 years together, two grown children and two winning campaigns, they were still going strong.

Debra had reached success in her own right. Her goal of trying to make a difference in the educational system in the South never changed, and as the principal of a middle school, she had taken on the system and proven that changes could be made.

Joe Singletary and Mayor Bubba Webb have been together since the early days of the Mayor's public office career. In a sense, Joe Singletary was like the old saying "always a bridesmaid and never a bride." Beyond being the Director of Jacksonville's Emergency Preparedness Reaction Team, Bubba Webb placed his political life in Joe Singletary's hands.

Joe managed Bubba's first run for office, which was a seat on Jacksonville's City Council. The race for city council was the warm up for the mayor's race that came the next year. Joe's political savory was natural; it was almost like he was the head coach for an NFL team. The only thing that Bubba disliked about Joe's organization and strategy was that it cost money. Lots of money! Joe ran a first rate campaign that got the results that Bubba wanted, however, and this level of professionalism built a deep friendship, along with a high degree of loyalty between them.

Chapter 2

Jacksonville Mobile Emergency Command Center.

    At the command center, Joe Singletary put down his hot cup of coffee when he saw the city's Fire Chief walk into the control center. The activity came to a halt in the control center as everyone anticipated receiving new directions from the Chief.

    Chief Paul Ferguson had a unique background. When he graduated from high school at the age of 17, he enlisted in the military and retired after 20 years of military service. The Chief returned to Jacksonville, took the firefighters' examination, attended training, and joined the Jacksonville Fire Department. Between his years in the military and the fire department, he earned a bachelor's degree and a master's degree. Now 50, he rose to the position of Fire Chief five years ago.

    He was a quiet man, but whenever you were in his company you could sense his confidence and leadership ability. Paul stood there now, calm and showing no emotion, as he read the status boards and analyzed the situation maps.

    The mobile command center is just that. A facility built into an 18-wheel van structure that contains the latest in communication and computer technology. The facility enables the Mayor's emergency reaction team to make real-time decisions and recommendations at the scene of an emergency. Joe Singletary walked over to situation board where the Fire Chief was standing and reached out his hand. The Chief turned to Joe and grabbed Joe's hand and elbow at the same time. "Hello, Joe. How the hell are you doing?" Before Joe could respond, the Chief quickly turned his attention back to the situation board.

    Paul Ferguson took a deep breath and said, "Ladies and gentlemen, I concur with your status report presented on the board. Continue the good work. Our fire companies should end this emergency in the next two to three hours. Thank you again for your hard work."

    The Fire Chief smiled and left the command center, and Joe continued to look at the situation board. Meanwhile, the fire had totally engulfed four city blocks. The section of town where this disaster had occurred was due for a facelift, but the city planners had not envisioned the changes taking place in this manner.

This section of Bay Street had vacant shops, rundown bars, pawn shops, and abandoned houses. However, the area was also home to the US Federal Reserve Bank, Federal Court House, and what everyone referred to as the Federal Building because it was occupied by several federal agencies, such as the IRS, FBI, and INS. The area was also known for drug activity and prostitution. In a way what had happened solved one of Jacksonville's problems.

The fire was still far from being brought under control. Fire Chief Ferguson called it right when he said that his fire companies still had about two to three more hours of work before the fire could be brought under control. Joe thought the most surprising thing was that there had not been any reports of loss of life yet. However, the casualty figures would be going up, he was certain, because there were several reports of missing and unaccounted-for people, but still, that no one had reported a fatality seemed quite miraculous.
Joe Singletary called the Mayor to give him an update. "Bubba, have you talked to the Chief?"

"Just got off the phone with him. In fact, that was the second call I got from him this morning. I'm pretty satisfied with his report."
Joe, still looking at the situation board, said, "Yeah, I think they have handled everything as well as they could have. An indication is that none of the television stations sent out one of their mobile vans. Each sent a two-person camera crew, but nobody sent out a team to stay on site. This whole thing is actually getting little coverage."

Joe paused to take a look at the casualty broad. "I just looked over at the casualty broad, Bubba, and still, no fatal injuries have been reported. I don't think that this can keep up, but no news is good news."

Bubba replied, "That's a given. If we can go through this without a fatal casualty, someone has done a great favor for the city. However, the odds are that will not happen."

The Mayor paused, his attention focusing on the television monitors in his home office. "Joe, I'm just spitballing now, but could this be a terrorist attack?"
What the Mayor said, at first, surprised Joe Singletary, but his job as the Directory of Jacksonville's Emergency Preparedness and

Response Center was to think in multiple directions. The two most key buildings in the blast area are both federal buildings. One, in particular, is a US Federal Reserve Bank. This building being knocked out of operation is going to have a ripple effect on a multitude of financial transactions up and down the east coast, stretching as far as Dallas even up to Chicago, until the system can be re-adjusted. Even a system of adjustments taking as long as 4 to 6 hours could possibly mean economic losses soaring into the millions of dollars

"Hold on Bubba, what you are saying could make a lot of sense. I'll have the police chief contact the FBI and the Office of Homeland Security and have them check this out as a possible motive for the explosion."

"Okay, Joe. Anything else you think I should know? If that's it, just check with me if anyone gets killed or based on your own good judgment as regards to what you think I need to know or get involved in." Joe's reply did not come for several seconds, which was beginning to make the Mayor feel a little uncomfortable, but then he finally heard Joe's voice.

"Sure thing Mr. Mayor. Sorry for the delay, but I was watching the situation status board. They were updating it, and that took my attention away for a second."

"No problem, Joe, you were just doing your job. Talk to you later." Saturdays were typically a very busy day for the Mayor. However, for some unknown reason, on this third Saturday of the month, only one telephone call had interrupted the few quiet moments Bubba could spend at home with his wife.

The Mayor and his wife had only recently purchased their home. The driving force that led to them buying this house was that he wanted to stimulate development and growth in this area of Jacksonville where growth had slowed.

Leaving all of the communications and monitors on, Bubba walked out of his study and back into their kitchen where Debra had prepared a snack for them to eat. "Sit down and have something to eat before we leave for the awards ceremony." Bubba walked to the refrigerator, pulled out a bottle of mineral water, and sat down at the kitchen table.

Debra began to say grace, and while saying grace, she looked up at Bubba to see whether he was taking part. Bubba saw Debra

22

staring at him and immediately lowered his head and participated in the blessing of the meal. "Bubba Webb, Bubba Webb, what am I going to do?"

Not responding to his wife, Bubba smiled and said. "Thanks, Honey. What ceremony are you talking about?" Debra took a bite from her sandwich and looked across the table at her husband. "Bubba, if your head were not screwed on your shoulders, you would forget you had one." Debra got up and walked over to the refrigerator, pulled out two bottles of mineral water, and sat back down at the table.

"The installation of the new President of the Daughters of the American Revolution."

Bubba stopped in the middle of taking a bite from his sandwich. He was looking at Debra while holding food in his mouth. Then he gulped it down, took a drink of mineral water, smiled and said, "I'll bet that is going to be a lot of fun." With a grin on his face, he said. "Do you think Mark and Peggy will be there?"
Debra stood and began to clean up the table. "Probably so, Bubba, since Peggy's mother is the person being installed as the new president."

This was an election year, and what Bubba Webb wanted more than anything else was to have the second term. As odd as it may appear, the Daughters of the American Revolution had contributed significant money to Bubba's first campaign, and this was no time to disappoint major contributors, he thought. The other thought in Bubba Webb's mind was that the Daughters of the American Revolution had the reputation of being an important factor in the selection of a nomination to head the party for the next presidential election.

Bubba's grin changed to a smile, then he said, "I hope Mark brings my driver. He has had it since we played golf at that new course up in St. Augustine. Remember? That was the weekend when you and your book club attended the book fair down in Gainesville." Debra closed the dishwasher door and looked across the kitchen at Bubba.

"Was that the time when the car broke down while we were trying to cross that bridge?"

Bubba got up from the table and walked across the kitchen to his wife. "Yeah, that was it. By the time the patrol car got to you with the tow truck, you guys were so drunk the patrolman had to drive each of you home." Debra turned away from him and walked into their bedroom. Bubba followed.

"By the way, I'll probably leave the ceremony a little early." Bubba was standing in front of his closet. He began taking suits out and laying them on the bed. After he had put three outfits on the bed, he placed neckties next to each suit.

Debra walked across the room and looked down at her husband's selection. "Bubba, you really should wear your blue suit. You seem a lot more conservative in it than the one you have in your hand." Bubba looked at Debra, nodded his agreement, then put the other two suits back in his closet.

Bubba finished dressing and walked back into his study to check the monitors while Debra was sitting at her dressing table fixing her hair. In the study, Bubba took a look at each of the monitors and was contemplating calling Joe Singletary before they left for the ceremony. But after listening to the police and fire scanners, he concluded that if the situation had changed, Joe would have contacted him.

Debra called out to Bubba that the car had arrived. "I'll only be a minute."
Bubba turned off all of the monitors and joined Debra in their living room. They left the house to get into the Mayor's limousine.

Henry Bubba Webb loved living in Florida and loved Jacksonville even more.
Mostly known for its favorable weather, Florida has been characterized as the Sunshine State. In fact, however, the weather can vary tremendously from the Panhandle down to the Keys. Florida is also described as a place where senior citizens, the most influential lobbying group in the United States, can choose to live in a gated condominium community and stretch their retirement savings.

Florida is also home to several professional sports teams: one professional basketball team, two hockey teams, two professional soccer teams, two baseball teams, and three national football teams.

Because of its favorable year-round weather, a significant source of Florida's revenue comes from the tourist industry. People from all over the US and abroad are attracted to the sandy beaches, tropical climate, marlin fishing, Daytona Beach stock car and formula car racing, and, of course, Disney World. When world travelers think of Florida, the picture that is formed in their mind's eye is represented by the cities of Daytona Beach, Orlando, Tampa, Miami, and the Keys. Jacksonville, located in the northeast part of Florida, comes to most as an afterthought.

Jacksonville is the largest city in the United States as measured by land mass. It is the home to one of the Jaguars professional football team. A transportation hub, with rail systems, three interstate highway systems merging at the city core, an international airport, and the third major shipping port in the United States with facilities for ships to be rebuilt or refitted ships.

However, Jacksonville is overshadowed by Atlanta, Georgia and Memphis, Tennessee, as far as most people are concerned. Jacksonville has always been the little city of the South that you would pass through and forget.

Chapter 3

Arlington, Virginia.

Roy Benning occupied a three bedroom, two and a half bath condominium with underground parking just off Duke Street, a newly renovated building. He was able to obtain a lease through some connections in the Agency where Roy was Desk Chief of Central American Operations. Benning had more than 25 years of service for the CIA. He was a career professional and very proud of the work he had done in the service of his country.

He was finishing his third cup of coffee and was sitting in his kitchen thumbing through a magazine while occasionally glancing at a stack of folders he had brought home from the office to work on. Each folder had a label attached which read "unclassified." He was trying to find an excuse not to dive into this paperwork.

Roy grew up in Council Bluff, Iowa where his parents owned and operated a Best Western Hotel. Roy Benning was recruited into the Agency directly from the University of Iowa, where he had taken a degree in English and become fluent in Spanish and German. Having a fancy for languages he was able to pick up Arabic and Swahili soon after joining the company. He would often joked with his closest friends that the secret to his success in the Agency was the fact that he could read and write.

Roy was, in fact, the epitome of the CIA field agent in appearance: not too tall and not too short, just the right size and build to enable him to fit in anywhere and not be noticed.

Just as Roy was reaching for one of those folders, his BlackBerry started to ring. Looking at the number on the phone he knew that the caller was from the Agency.

"Director Benning, we just picked up a news flash off of a local television station that a fire followed by explosions has occurred in the area around 400 West Bay Street in Jacksonville, Florida." Roy knew the address. It was the location of Agency Field Office.

Holding his BlackBerry to his ear, Roy Benning stood up from his kitchen table and walked to his kitchen window to take in the view of the Potomac River.

"What time did you say this news flash came in?" Roy looked at his watch and the clock on his microwave oven as the voice on the phone responded to his question. He thought to himself, it's only been about five to ten minutes since they saw that feed. I wonder why I haven't received a call from Karl Mansfield.

Roy Benning responded, "See if you can get Karl Mansfield and ask him to give me a call. Oh, also contact the Flagler Center. I know it is closed on the weekend, but give it a try anyway."

Roy picked up the folders from the kitchen table and walked into his study. In the back of his mind, he was still concerned that Karl Mansfield had not called him.

▬

Jacksonville Mobile Emergency Command Center.

With a diet soda in his hand, Joe Singletary walked over to the situation board in the big emergency command center trailer. As he was looking at the board, he was thinking of all the things that could be done to improve the area of town that was affected by the fire, which had engulfed over an eight-block area. What was really beneficial to the city was that two of the major buildings within this field were the US Federal Building and the Federal Reserve Bank.

Joe's attention swiftly shifted to another board reflecting casualties. It appeared that the emergency workers and firemen had found their first victims, four unidentified bodies. Joe knew that he would be calling the Mayor sooner or later; this was just the first sign that a call would be needed.

Joe's eyes and attention shifted to another board with a heading that read "projected casualties": between 11 and 25 deaths from the fire and explosions and a possibly another 15 or so injuries. As a matter of fact, a few people in the command center were taking bets on who could come closest to the actual number of bodies and casualties that would be found. But what Joe was witnessing was the real-time transformation from pure speculation to actual deaths. Joe decided that rather than calling Mayor Webb at this time, he would send him a text message to alert him to the current development.

As Joe finished typing a message on his telephone to the Mayor, an iPad was handed to him, and a young aide said, "We just got this in from the GSA in Washington." The General Services Administration, or GSA, was the federal agency that served as the landlord for the majority of all federal government buildings. If you wanted to know about any piece of federal government property in the world, all you had to do was contact the GSA and talk to the appropriate person. Joe didn't bother to read what was on the iPad but just listened to the aide.

"The GSA said that the federal buildings here had two security guards on duty and two cleaning teams made up of 10 people each in the Federal Reserve Bank there were two cleaning teams, again 10 people on each side and a total of four security guards."

Before the words had finished transmitting through the air, Joe Singletary shouted, "Change our projections to 50 to 65 deaths and keep the injuries the same."
Joe redirected his attention back to his BlackBerry and the text message that he was preparing for Mayor Webb. He updated the text message and estimates of casualties and asked for the Mayor to give him a call before he left the ceremony he was attending. After he had finished typing the text message Joe shouted," If we have not done so already, prepare a list of all the names of the building owners in a 10 block radius of the Federal Building. Please include the property tax status and whether or not their taxes are delinquent or current. You can reach me on my BlackBerry. I'll be out taking a look at the damage."

Joe grabbed a hard hat and his mobile radio, opened the door of the trailer, and stepped out into the smoky sunlight. The command center was set up in the early morning of the third Saturday of the month. Since then, Dawn had broken, and the Florida sunshine was beaming down on Joe's beloved city of Jacksonville.

When the emergency started, only two news vans were covering the fire. The number had grown to seven. As Joe read the station letters on each of the vehicles, he didn't see any of the national networks. Four of the local channels were affiliated with CBS, NBC, ABC, and Fox, which meant that they had to develop a good story for the majors to run it and place it on national news.

Joe's eyes squinted against tears running from the irritation of the smoke-filled air. It was an eerie scene, something like a science fiction movie. Gray and black smoke filled the air everywhere with

28

the sprinkling of sunshine dotting through as a gentle breeze kept the smoke flowing.

Joe had two choices: he could either take one of the four-wheel-drive SUVs or take a look at the damage from the sky using the Command Center helicopter. The command center was located one block west of Main Street on the corner of Laura and Adams. From this location, he could see the fire line of yellow tape where the police and fire brigade had established their command post up at Julia Street. Joe wasn't interested in receiving a dog and pony show briefing but wanted to make an actual site assessment of the damages before the insurance investigators started pumping up the numbers, and so he decided he would take the helicopter. Joe signaled for one of the SUV drivers to pick him up.

Joe was still standing outside the emergency command center facing in the direction of the fire, watching the physical activity for blocks away at the fire brigade command when the vehicle arrived. Joe opened the door and got into the passenger seat, smiled and said to the driver, "My name is Joe. What's yours? And how are you doing this smoky morning?"

The driver didn't respond, but Joe could see by the expression on the driver's face that she was not used to the city's professionals caring about the well-being of city employees. With a no-nonsense look own the driver's face, she then pulled away from the emergency command center, made a left turn, and headed in the opposite direction from the fire.

Joe quickly said, "Before we get too far down the road, let me tell you where I want you to take me: the city's heliport. I need to get an aerial view of the fire." The driver quickly made a right turn and headed in the direction of the city's heliport, which was located very close to the police station.

Then suddenly out of a cloud of tense silence, the driver said, "My name is Shirley. How are you doing this morning, sir?"

Joe turned his head to the driver with a big smile on his face and said, "I'm doing great. Thank you for asking."

It was less than a 10-minute drive to the heliport, and as Shirley turned the SUV into the parking lot, Joe said, "Pull the vehicle over here, and I'll walk the rest of the way."

Joe had radioed ahead and alerted the heliport that he would be coming and wanted an aerial tour of the fire area. The pilot was in

29

the cockpit with the helicopter running. Shirley stopped the vehicle in the exact spot where Joe directed. Joe stepped out of the vehicle, closed the door, took one step in the direction of the helicopter, and stopped. He came back to the SUV door, leaned his head in, and said, "Shirley, pick me up at this same location in one hour."

—

Fort Lauderdale, Florida-Hollywood International Airport.

United Flight 987 was scheduled to depart in five hours, and international travelers had to arrive at the airport a minimum of three hours before the departure time. With one stop, the flight was scheduled to arrive in Rio de Janeiro, Brazil around 8:00 AM Sunday morning.

Wallace C. Barker and his girlfriend, Eve Harding, had driven from Jacksonville Friday night so they could have a good night's rest before the 14 and a half hour flight to Rio. They had planned this trip for months.

Although they worked for different defense contractors, their duties, and the complexity of the software and firmware they were developing for the army entailed that they see each other daily.

It wasn't very long before they were dating. However, within six months of the beginning of their relationship, Eve, who had a master's degree in electrical engineering, made the decision to leave the fast-paced life and lucrative salary of a software engineer and become a teacher. She relocated to Jacksonville, Florida, and became a chemistry teacher in the Jacksonville public school system.

He never questioned Eve's decision to leave the corporate software world, but the fact she resettled in Jacksonville, Florida, was somewhat of a puzzle to him. Wallace never brought up the subject concerning Eve's decision to relocate to Jacksonville, however, because he didn't see it as a major obstacle to the relationship. Sterling Business Machines, SBM, had an office located in Jacksonville, which required Wallace to fly there on business trips.

Eve was born in Washington, DC, but grew up all over the world. Her father worked for the government, and they lived in places like India, Pakistan, Germany, and even Korea. Up to this point in their relationship, Wallace and Eve had not gone into any depth about their family background but just spoke on the subject in bits and pieces.

Oddly enough, Wallace was born and grew up in Jacksonville, graduating from high school in Jacksonville; but after high school he left and never looked back.

In spite of Eve's move to what had been his hometown long ago, their relationship continued to grow. In fact, it was at the point that Wallace was seriously considering popping the question, and he had planned this trip to finalize his decision.

WC and Eve selected a hotel for the night that was a 20-minute cab ride to the airport. They were traveling extremely light, each with a carry-on bag and one suitcase. WC and Eve made a pledge to each other that they would leave technology behind and just relax and enjoy themselves for the next 10 days, and so no laptops, iPads, or tablets.

When they arrived at the hotel, they made arrangement for a cab to pick them the next morning. Just as they have planned, when they finish breakfast the morning of their departure a taxi was waiting to take them to the airport.

There was little traffic that time of the morning, and so the drive to the international terminal at the airport took less than 20 minutes. Wallace quickly stepped out of the cab, got their two suitcases out of the trunk and turned them over to a porter standing at the curb. The porter immediately said, "What airline Sir?"

While taking his carry-on bag out of the backseat of the cab and while Eve looked on, Wallace said, "United Flight 987." Eve paid and tipped the taxicab driver and quickly joined Wallace on the sidewalk. They walked into the terminal.

The porter took them to the economy class line for United Airlines. Wallace handed him a $20 bill and said thanks. He gave Wallace a big smile and said,
"Thank you, sir. Hope you have a safe and pleasant trip." Wallace turned his attention to checking his pockets to see if he had everything: passport, tickets, American Express travel checks and cash. Eve calmly stood next to Wallace.

Eve was tall, five-eight, and in high heels nearly six feet. She had one child who was a graduate of the United States Naval Academy, a fighter pilot currently stationed with a carrier group in the Mediterranean. She was in excellent physical condition. She ran two to three miles each day, and only two weeks before this trip Harding had finished a half marathon. She wore a sundress with sneakers and no socks today. In anticipation of the humidity, her hair was pulled back and tied. She wore a sun visor with the Jacksonville Jaguar logo that matched her dress along with very stylish sunglasses.

They had planned to leave on this trip the third Saturday of July because Wallace had just finished his two weeks of Army Reserve summer camp training. He had also finished delivering the last of the software products that he was developing when he and Eve met. So this was perfect timing for him.

The timing of the trip also worked well for Eve. The school was out for the summer, and her book club did not meet in July and August.

As he looked at the passenger check-in sections to his right where the line formed for the business and first class passengers, Wallace got the feeling, he recognized someone he knew. There weren't very many people in the line compared to the economy class, and among those in line, Wallace noticed this gentleman who reminded him of his old roommate.

Eve sensed something was amiss and reached for Wallace's hand. "Is something wrong, Lover?"

Wallace turned and looked at Eve, smiled and said, "I just saw someone over there that reminded me of someone I knew some time ago."

The United counter clerk motioned for them to come forward. Wallace and Eve handed the United clerk their passports, WC set their bags on the scale and started their check-in. The check-in only took a few minutes. They got seat assignments and boarding passes and headed for security. Eve led the way, and Wallace walked directly behind her. As they walked, Wallace looked over his shoulder one last time, trying to confirm if he had seen his old roommate.

The gentleman he had spied in the first class check-in line had an athletic build and was wearing a polo shirt and a suit a half size too large as if he was trying to conceal his actual height and weight. He received his boarding pass and walked toward security. The man wore a Panama style hat and glasses with lens almost as

32

thick as the bottom of a coke bottle. The man, who was traveling on a Canadian passport, quickly moved through the security checkpoint and went directly to the United Airline's business and first class lounge to wait for his flight.

Wallace and Eve strolled through the terminal. Because of the early hour, most of the stores were still closed, but a few were just starting to open. Eve's cell phone rang.

"Well, good morning my little lieutenant. It's so sweet of you to call your mother. I love you too. I know, I know. You never have any time to talk to your mom. Is everything OK? Where are you now? I understand. You can't tell me. Love you!" Eve kissed the cell phone and placed it in her purse.

As they passed several more shops, they walked in silence. After arriving at their gate, they took seats to await boarding.

Eve spoke first. "You military people are all alike. Always silent. So much secrecy. I can't stand it." Wallace didn't respond to Eve's outburst. He didn't know what to say, and so he felt it would be best to keep quiet.

Passengers on United 987 boarded the plane from two doors. First and business class boarded through the front cabin door and economy class through the middle door. The man who was traveling on the Canadian passport entered the first-class section of the plane and occupied seat number 4.

WC and Eve entered the plane through the middle doors of the aircraft for economy class. Their seats were in the second section of the aircraft, numbers 231 and 232. The 777 economy section was configured with eight seats across set-up: two seats, an aisle, four seats, an aisle, and two seats. Seat's 231 and 232 were in the middle section.

Eve took the inside chair. Wallace took two books out of their bags and then placed their carry-ons in the overhead compartment. WC handed both of the books to Eve as he took his seat. The flight attendants came around and passed out pillows and blankets. When the flight attendant came to Wallace's row, he asked for a second set of pillows for him and Eve. The flight attendant smiled and handed Wallace two more pillows. Wallace pulled his cell phone from the case and was just about to place it in airplane mode when it rang. Looking at the face of the phone he saw Felix. Eve also saw Felix's face on the phone and smiled.

"Hello, Buddy! So glad you called. We are on the plane, and I was just about to send you a text message and turn the phone off. What's up?'

WC and Felix first met when Wallace joined SBM. They instantly bonded with the respect they had for each other as professionals, and their bonding had since grown into a lifelong friendship.

WC and Felix were both programmers at the beginning. Felix, a 100% certifiable geek, super nerd, and probably one of the most brilliant programmers at SBM had been with SBM for at least two years when he and Wallace first began to work together.

WC quickly moved through positions of increasing responsibility, from assistant software build design lead to design lead, and with added training, certifications, and courses, he built up his resume and became a project manager.

However, programming, which was Felix's passion. Felix was so respected for his software brilliancy that he worked across SBM's massive company lines. If any SBM project were having any type of trouble with software, Felix would be called in. Felix was authorized unlimited access to any software project within the company. The standard joke around the company was that only God had a higher security clearance than Felix.

"WC, I just wanted to catch you before you and Eve got on the plane and headed for your vacation. I got the inside scoop from a couple of pals over at DOA that acceptance testing is going great. As a matter of fact, they said that it was 100 for 100. It looks like we may have another bonus check coming before the end of the year. Really could use it because I'm planning on buying another server so I can get more into BYOD security and…

"Felix, I want to hear about the testing and your plans for Bring Your Own Device security, but I must get off the phone before they close the doors." WC had to cut him off because Felix would spend forever telling anyone about the next big thing in software. "Oh, oh, sure Buddy. You guys would never be together if it weren't for me, you know. Have a great trip, and I'll see you when you get back."

"Thanks for calling, Felix. I'll call you when I get back in the States." WC and Eve looked at each other and smiled, and they shared a laugh as WC turned off his cell phone.

First-class and business-class travelers are treated much differently than those that are flying economy class. They should be because they are paying as much as two to three times more than the people sitting in the back of the plane who are going to get off the aircraft at the same location as the first- and business-class passengers.

The flight attendant came to each of the passengers in the first- and business-class sections and handed them a hot towel. Then each was offered their choice of a variety of tropical juices or a glass of champagne. The man who wore glasses with lens that look like the bottom of coke bottles asked for a glass of champagne and wanted to know if he could get the *London Times, New York Times,* and *The Herald.*

"Certainly, sir," the flight attendant said with a smile. She walked up to the galley and returned with copies of the requested papers.

Chapter 4

Arlington, Virginia.

Roy Benning continues to surf the channels for news concerning Jacksonville and the ongoing fires. Unlike the Agency, he didn't have access to local networks within the Jacksonville viewing area and so he had to settle for the major networks, which for their own reasons had not picked up the story.

Roy made a decision to send an email to the director just to let him know that a fire had occurred in the location of their office in Jacksonville. His next thought was to give Karl Mansfield a call just to make sure that nothing had been compromised. On second thought, Roy decided not to give Karl a call and to just wait until he or the Agency made contact with him. Roy walked into his bedroom where he changed into his running shorts, T-shirt, and sneakers.

Roy laced up his running shoes, grabbed the armband for his BlackBerry along with his headphones, punched in his security code, closed and locked his front door and started down the hall to the elevator. As he was walking down the hall, he put his BlackBerry into his armband carrying case and strapped it to his upper left bicep. He plugged in his headphone jacks and opened his musical app.

After pushing the button for the elevator, Roy placed one of the earpieces in his left ear, letting the other hang down. The elevator came, and Roy stepped inside and pushed the button for the first floor.

Even though Roy was no longer a field agent, he continued to practice most of the crafts of the trade that kept them alive while in the field. Roy always varied his schedule, for example. Some days he would take the elevator. Some days Roy would walk down the stairs. Likewise, some days he drove to work and some days he would take the Metro and bus. He always avoided establishing a routine. When the elevator stopped at the first floor, Roy pushed the button for the basement. He stepped out of the elevator into the basement and took the stairs back up to an exit.

Roy never really liked running, but when he started his career with the Agency, on his first training day on the farm, in fact, he discovered that he and only one other person recruited into the class did not have a military background. Military people are accustomed to physical training, and the core of their physical training is running.

His training class consisted of himself and 22 other recruits. Sondra Kristin was the only female in the class and the only other person who did not have a military background. Because of that fact, Roy and Sondra connected. Both Sondra and Roy pushed themselves to learn how to run, and eventually Roy began to tolerate the sport. Most people view running as an exercise or sport that you just do. However, real running involves an understanding of both the mental and physical aspects of the game and how you and your body fit into the overall dynamics of the activity.

Of the 23 people in the class, only seven completed the course and were placed in the field. Sondra and Roy were among those seven. Unfortunately, Sondra's career with the Agency only lasted three years. Doing an operation in Somalia, she was killed when an exchange with a trusted source went bad.

Roy didn't have a set running route. He would just set his watch for either a 20 minute or 30-minute timeframe and continued to run until the alarm went off. He went through his stretching routine, preparing his muscles, then started out.

It was a bright and sunny day on this the third Saturday of the month in July. The heat and humidity were just right for running, and so Roy was glad that he made the decision to come out now rather than waiting until later in the day. He took in the scenery, the sun reflecting off the buildings and the windshields of automobiles as he passed them. He could feel more shock in his lower ankles and knees and made a mental note to purchase a new pair of running shoes. After several minutes of running, his thoughts shifted to work.

Roy currently had 41 agents on assignments throughout Central and South America. Of course, this was far fewer than operations going on in Southwest Asia, the Middle East, Europe, and the Balkans. He had a major operation scheduled to kick off in the next 45 days.

When Roy was promoted to take over the desk of Central and South America, his colleagues patted him on his shoulder, said congratulations, then walked into the corner of the room and began to talk about them behind his back. South America is not a hotbed of activity, nothing close to the Middle East, Africa, or South West Asia, so you hardly ever heard or saw anything in the media concerning South America except for in areas like Florida. In states like Texas, California, and other border states with Mexico, the news is mostly about how immigration from Mexico will have an effect on the state but nothing about South America.

As Roy came to a busy intersection, his thoughts shifted to watching the traffic while jogging in place. When the traffic signal changed, he looked both ways just to make sure that one last car wasn't trying to beat the light, then continued his run, increasing the pace.

—

Jacksonville, Florida.

Joe Singletary opened the door of the helicopter and took the passenger seat. While he was fastening his seat and shoulder harness, the pilot handed him a headset. Joe put the headset on and said, "Test, test. Can you hear me?"

The pilot gave Joe a thumbs up and said, "Roger that. Where would you like to start, sir?"

As the helicopter slowly began to lift into the air, Joe responded, "Why don't we work our way from Main Street west, then circle around the fire and go from south to north. Let's say from Water Street, flying over the central area back as far as Ashley Street. That should give me a pretty good assessment of how wide the fire area is, and maybe, if the smoke should clear, I can even see some of the damage." The pilot acknowledged Joe's request and instantly switched to the radio air control frequency.

"J, A, X, Flight Air Control, this is City Chopper 6. We are lifting off on an east to west heading from Main Street, then doing a 360 from the center of mass over affected area from Water Street south to Ashley Street north. Estimated flying time 30 minutes. Over!"

The pilot heard through his headset. "This is J, A, X, Flight Air Control acknowledging flight plan. Please stay within authorized ceiling. You are cleared for lift off. Roger out!"

The helicopter smoothly lifted off made a sharp banking right turn and headed in the direction of Main Street. The helicopter followed Main Street until it was almost over the emergency command center. Then it banked to the left and started west in the direction of the fire.

Joe's thoughts flashed back to when he was a door gunner on a Black Hawk gunship. Joe only did one enlistment in the army, and he never served in any combat operations. A lot of people thought that was strange because Joe was stationed at Fort Bragg, the home of the Airborne, Special Forces, Delta Force, and Special Operations—often referred to as the 911 of the world. Yet the aviation unit he was stationed with was assigned to the base headquarters, and Joe and his Unit would move only if the entire headquarters were deployed overseas. For Joe's four years on active duty, the entire Headquarters only deployed in sections, never as a full unit.

The pilot gained altitude so that the copper would be flying over the smoke. As the plane was going up above the fire, Joe could feel the heat even if he couldn't see the flames because of the smoke. It was obviously a hot burning fire.

Even above the smoke, visibility of what was going on below was almost impossible. However, Joe figured that because he could only see smoke and no flames, the fire was almost under control just as the Fire Chief had predicted.

The pilot gestured to Joe and pointed to a pouch beside Joe's left leg. Joe reached down opened it and pulled out a set of binoculars. By this time they were directly above the fire, but Joe couldn't see much more using the binoculars because of the smoke. What he really wanted to confirm was the total area of damage that the city would have to rebuild.

Joe was pleased that he didn't see any other helicopters in the air. The mobile command center must be doing their job, he thought. News camera crews feel that they don't have to play by the rules. Anything to get the story first, which was frequently more dangerous for others than for the crew itself. He made a mental note to give a "that-a-boy" to his air traffic control coordinating team once he returned to the mobile emergency command center.

They were just about to make a turn and head in the north-south direction over the fire when Joe heard a voice come through his headset. "Joe. Joe Singletary, this is Jacksonville command. We have the Mayor on the line. He's trying to reach you. Is this a good time for us to patch the call through to you?"

Joe spoke back into his mic, "Command, go ahead. I can talk." Then Joe heard the voice of the Mayor.

"Joe, this is Bubba. How does it look from up there?"

The helicopter started to the south to north leg of the flight plan as Joe replied, "Well, Bubba, there is so much damn smoke up here we really can't see a thing. I guess I can say that the affected area is just as we stated earlier, but what I can't tell is how much damage there is down there." As the helicopter was crossing over the spot where the Federal Building was located, Joe picked up a smell in the air. He turned and, while looking at the pilot, grabbed his nose. What Joe was breathing was the burning of human flesh.

"Well, Joe, I'm headed back over to City Hall. I am just leaving that installment ceremony for the new President of the Daughters of the American Revolution. A good-old bunch of girls, bless their little hearts. I think I stayed long enough and shook enough hands so that everyone was pleased with my presence. Matter of fact, and for the life of me, I can't remember her name, but the executive treasurer told me to give her a call next week. Jerry made a note to remind me about that." Jerry was Jerry Clark, the Mayor's Community and Public Relations Director.

"I also told Jerry that I want to have a press conference by 2:00 concerning this fire." As Joe listened, he could tell that the handshaking and backslapping at the installation ceremony had fired up the Mayor with some new ideas. From the enthusiasm in Bubba's voice, it wouldn't be long before they would be having a planning session. Joe continued to listen as the Mayor said, "Jerry has already started to contact other agencies such as social services, the Red Cross... Damn, I even told him to get the Boy Scouts if he thought it was necessary. We'll wait for you and the Fire Chief and Police Chief to get here before we meet, and then after that, we'll have the press conference. But I still want to shoot for 2:00 if you think that is possible."

The helicopter had flown just about a block north of the Federal Building when an explosion erupted below, sending building debris, flames, and gaseous fumes over 2000 feet into the air. The helicopter was spun to the left, and the pilot compensated, but then there was an explosion behind them in the engine compartment, and the helicopter started to lose altitude.

The pilot started shouting over the radio, "Mayday! Mayday! We've been hit by debris and are going down! Mayday! Mayday!"

Joe sat frozen, staring at the pilot. The helicopter began to plunge toward earth spinning 360°, blazing fire coming from the rear of the chopper, somewhere around the engine.

People on the ground heard the explosion even at the mobile command center, and there was a rush of bodies out of doors to see what had happened. All that was visible was a bright red flame glowing through the smoke as the sound of sirens from emergency medical team vehicles and fire engines rose into the air. Everyone standing in front at the command center stood in frozen disbelief, hoping that the ball of flames falling to the ground was not the helicopter carrying Joe Singletary.

Chapter 5

Florida Turnpike.

The Mercedes-Benz exited the turnpike and proceeded in the direction of Orlando. It was passed midday, and so Ranuel suggested they pick up some sandwiches. They located a Burger King and went through the drive-through, purchasing burgers, fries, and milkshakes, paying cash. They parked in the parking lot and consumed their burgers. Each took turns going into the men's room to relieve themselves.

When everyone was back in the car, Ranuel nodded to the driver to proceed. Once they were back on the interstate headed north on I95 in the direction of Daytona Beach, Ranuel said that he needed to check in and provide an update on their status. The driver pulled off at the next exit. The exit sign read Longwood. He saw a BP Mini-Market service station and pulled up to the gas pumps.

Just as before, both the driver and Ranuel got out of the Mercedes-Benz and walked into the mini market. The driver went to the counter to purchase fuel, and Ranuel wandered around the market until he found the prepaid mobile telephones. The driver and Ranuel paid with cash. As Ranuel exited the store, he carefully looked at the large parking lot, checking for any police cars.

When he reached the car, the driver was pumping gas. Krish had fallen asleep in the back seat. Ranuel sat in the front passenger seat, opened the prepaid phone, plugged the phone into its charger and into the lighter to build up the phone's battery power to make his calls. He then pulled out the book containing the numbers. When the driver finished filling up the car, Ranuel pointed to a parking space and the car was moved. Ranuel again made the calls in the exact way and manner that he did before, and then he disposed of the prepaid phone in the same way. "I'm finished. Let us proceed," Ranuel said.

After a few blocks, they saw the sign that read Interstate 95. The Mercedes-Benz took the ramp for I95 North toward Jacksonville.

—

The MIE (Movement for the Independence of Essequibo)

Little known to most Americans is a 56,000 square-mile region, which is roughly the size of Florida, that has been in international dispute for more than 180 years. The two countries contesting this territory, Essequibo, are Venezuela and Guyana. Like many other areas of South America, from colonial history accounts it is clear this area changed hands many times. In fact, during the period of exploration, four countries held ownership of this area: Spain, France, the Netherlands, and Britain.

Guyana, formerly a Dutch colony in the 17th century, became a British possession in 1815. After receiving its independence from the United Kingdom in 1966, Guyana began to express its intention of asserting claims in the area west of the Essequibo River. However, Venezuela also claims all of the areas west of the Essequibo River. Venezuela argues that the Essequibo is the natural border between Guyana and Venezuela and that this was established in an arbitration proceeding that Great Britain took part in.

The conflict was stirred up when the stakes were raised. The media reported that Exxon Mobil Corporation, in partnership with Roy Dutch Shell, began exploring for crude oil off the coast of the disputed Essequibo. A much smaller and poorer country than Venezuela, Guyana asked the United Nations to settle the dispute. Venezuela calls the area a "reclamation zone," but in practice, it functions as Guyanese territory.

The Essequibo is an area of rolling savanna and remote jungle that in fact shows few signs of Venezuelan presence. Guyana sees it as crucial to their economic future due to its reserves of minerals, gold, diamonds, and bauxite.

At one time the US was eager to exert its influence in the hemisphere and brashly championed the Venezuelan stance. Then the thought of an independent Guyana under a socialist government created fear of a second Cuba in the US's backyard. But the most compelling reason for the US shift was the actions of the former President of Venezuela, Hugo Chavez.

The Movement for the Independence of Essequibo, or the MIE, is made up primarily of groups from both countries, a small splinter group from the Union of Oil Workers of Venezuela, or

FUTPV, and a similar splinter group from Guyana, the Public Service Union, or GPSU. Because of feelings of disenfranchisement by their respective parent organizations in each country, similarities slowly brought them together to form the MIE. Their collective goal is to create an independent country in the state of Essequibo. Currently, the MIE leadership consists of three individuals with a committee of six representing different sections of Essequibo. The three primary leaders must agree on all decisions, and if there is a disagreement between the three, the committee of six will break the deadlock. Members of the MIE have developed a preliminary constitution that no single leader will be determined until the country can have free and open elections. Its' not clear whether or not the MIE has any other hidden agenda beyond establishing a democratic state with free elections. With the prospect of becoming an oil-rich independent country, along with the other mineral reserves, the country of Essequibo would have an economic base equal to or greater than most of the countries in the southern hemisphere, with the US also being a friendly and supportive ally.

—

Congressional Golf Course, Washington, DC.

Bo Brooks walked out of the shower and headed to his locker to change. He was very pleased with himself. Bo played 18 holes and shot a 78. He and a group of friends get together on the third Saturday of the month and played golf at the Congressional Country Club Golf Course, but he had not been able to play in nine weeks.

After three years his application for membership had been endorsed, and a year later he was approved for membership. Bo was able to meet with golf buddies this Saturday because one of his business trips was canceled.

As Bo moved through the locker room, his thoughts continued to flashback to the course and how accurately he placed his shots on the green. Bo said to himself: the short game is the key.

Two business trips ago, before he left, he purchased one of those putters that you can unscrew and put in your suitcase. He took the putter with him on both trips, and each night in his hotel room he would practice putting for an hour in the morning before he went to work and an hour at night before he went to bed.

Bo Brooks worked for the FBI, assigned to the Anti-Terrorist Threat Unit-Information and Cross-Referencing Section. Any crime that may have FBI jurisdiction, even before the jurisdiction is determined, Bo's team would fly to the location where the crime took place and gather data. They would then take what they found back to FBI Headquarters and cross reference the information to other known terrorist attacks to see if any connections existed. Every ounce of information would be broken down into its smallest element. Their objective was to look for patterns that suggested the signature of a given terrorist or terrorist group.

Access to the database extends to all Law enforcement agencies and intelligence gathering agencies as well as to the Department of Defense. Interpol and the intelligence services of foreign countries that are aligned with the United States in the fight against terrorism can also access the data. The unit that Bo worked in was not an investigative unit but more of an information gathering and analysis unit. Bo liked to refer to his job as connecting the dots.

The Anti-Terrorist Threat Unit-Information and Cross-Referencing department are located in the J. Edgar Hoover building in Washington DC. Ten agents make up the team. The unit was organized shortly after 9-11. At first, they would deploy to locations in two-person teams, but the demand for their services built up so quickly that now each member of the team is deployed singly to a crime scene. Bo had been with the unit for seven years, and the team chief and a couple of the guys were some of the original members of the unit. The department's area of responsibility is everything within the Continental United States plus Puerto Rico and the Virgin Islands. This area of responsibility is very loosely enforced, in fact, some of the team members had been on assignments in the Middle East, and Joe had been on one job in Europe.

The locker room was beginning to thin out as Bo turned the corner and headed down the aisle to his locker. It was going on 6:00 pm and many of the lifelong members of the club had changed into the traditional blue blazer with khakis and were going upstairs to have drinks and cigars before they met their wives for dinner.

Bo opened his locker and began to dress. After putting on his T-shirt, shorts, and trousers, he sat down on the bench and started to put on his socks and shoes. His mind shifted to the evening. He had a date, the first date he had been on in a long time. A new member of the team had a sister who was having a birthday party. Bo didn't know the team member's sister, but the team member and his wife knew that Bo was single and wasn't involved with anyone, so they invited Bo to the birthday party. Bo knew at the time that the intent was for Bo to meet the sister, but the electricity just wasn't there, and Bo was just about to leave the party. But as he was giving his goodbyes, thank you, and saying I had a great time, another guest was leaving. His team member's wife asked Bo if he would escort the lady to her car, and Bo agreed. The car was parked less than a block away from the apartment building, but as they strolled, a connection was made. Bo knew that he would be going on the road the next morning, but they agreed that when Bo was back in town or between trips, they would meet for dinner. That time had arrived, and Bo was eagerly anticipating how the night might develop.

Bo finished putting on his shoes and stood up, and while reaching for his shirt, his cell phone went off. Bo had hesitated before he reached for his phone because he knew it would probably be an assignment on the road. Bo's instinct was correct. It was a text message from the office: "Incident occurred in Jacksonville, Florida. Airline ticket in your name at BWI Thurgood Marshall Airport. Southwest airline flight number 631 departure 9:00 PM. Hotel reservation Jacksonville Marriott. Hertz rental car reserved Jacksonville airport counter.

Bo looked at his watch. He had about two and a half hours to get back to his townhouse and then drive over to the Baltimore airport. After Bo had finished dressing, he proceeded out of the club to the parking lot. He wondered why they had booked everything through BWI, but he assumed the flight he was on was probably the only one that would get him out before tomorrow. Bo's next thought was that Jacksonville is the home of Sawgrass Country Club, the birthplace of the Tournament Players Club Network, one of the PGA's major golf tournaments. Bo made a decision that he was going to take his clubs just in case an opportunity presented itself and he was able to play at least nine holes.

Bo threw his golf clubs into the back seat, got into his car and placed his cell phone in the voice activated cradle. He started the engine and pulled out of the Congressional Country Club parking lot onto River Road and headed in the direction of 495. Bo owned a townhouse in Silver Spring, Maryland, that was within walking distance of the Silver Spring Metro Train station.

Most days Agents Brooks would take the Metro to the Hoover Building for work. Bo decided that since it was Saturday, he would take River Road to 495 and take the Beltway around to 29. With a little luck, he should be able to reach his townhouse in about 20 minutes.

Once Bo reached 495 and got on the Beltway, he voice activated his cell phone: "Hi, it's me."

The voice on the other end of the call quietly answered, "Hi. I'm not at all surprised that I would be getting this call. Margaret warned me to be prepared for many disappointments." Margaret was Bo's teammate's wife.

Bo was really surprised and at the same time pleased to hear the disappointment in her voice. She sounded so sincere, and in a strange sense, she was expressing the same frustration that he felt. "I'm headed to Jacksonville, Florida. Once I get on the ground, I'll be able to determine how long I will be."

Before Bo could say anything else he heard, "That's fine. I understand. Call me when you can. Have a safe trip and be careful."

Chapter 6

Jacksonville Mobile Emergency Command Center.

"Somebody tell me what happened! Talk to me! What happened?" Bubba Webb shouted into the headset of his telephone. He reached across the front seat of his limousine and grabbed his driver's shoulder, yelling, "Get me to that command center as fast as possible. I have to find out what happened!"

The driver accelerated, turning on blue flashing lights along with a siren. As the Mayor, Bubba did not like the image of being led around town by a police escort, and so he had blue emergency lights installed behind the front grill of the car as well as an emergency siren. To make sure that everything fell within the city's ordinances, Joe Singletary had recommended that the emergency lights and the siren get approval from the city council. Surprisingly, the city council did not fight the Mayor on this recommendation and gave their permission for the Mayor to have the lights and sirens installed.

Bubba was hoping for the best, but he knew that all the sounds that he heard on the phone pointed to one conclusion that the helicopter crashed. The Mayor was on 95 headed north. They had just passed over the J Turner Butler exit, so they still had about 10 to 15 minutes before they crossed the Main Street Bridge. The Mayor sat back and refastened his seatbelt. Then he called Jerry Clark.

"Jerry, where in the hell are you? Joe Singletary was up in that damn helicopter flying over the fire, and I believe that the chopper has crashed." The Mayor then realized he had gone to Jerry's voicemail, and so he concluded his message with a request that Jerry meet him at the emergency command center. Bubba ended the call and began to think about his friend.

Joe Singletary was in his second marriage. He and his first wife were college sweethearts who got married two days after they graduated. They made a charming and loving couple that Bubba thought would be together for the rest of their lives. But 18 months into their marriage, while getting an annual physical, Joe's wife found out she had a very rare form of cancer that was untreatable. They got several second opinions. Joe and his wife even flew over to Switzerland to find out about an ongoing clinical study. All of the

48

answers were the same. Within 11 months from the diagnosis, she passed, and Joe became a widower at the young age of 24. Joe was devastated and threw himself into his work nearly every minute of the day. While Bubba's career was progressing on his rise to becoming Mayor, he could call Joe anytime of day or night, and Joe was there to listen to his crazy ideas and provide the planning to make those ideas into reality.

The Mayor's limousine driver, an off-duty police officer, paid an extra stipend to drive for the Mayor, continued to accelerate, sometimes reaching 85 miles per hour as cars in their path got to the side of the road in response to the lights and siren. Bubba continued to think about his friend, reflecting on the main events that had molded Joe's life.

Nine years after Joe's first wife died, he and Bubba attended their second national party convention. The convention was in Chicago, and this was the first time either of them had been in this part of the country. Although this was their second national conference, they were still neophytes among the seasoned political bosses. Joe insisted that they must attend every meet-and-greet, handshaking, pat-on-the-back cocktail party, breakfast, lunch, or tea that they could. Many of the meetings and caucuses were by invitation only, and of course, there were the meetings that only a few people even knew about—those were the ones that Joe and Bubba hoped they would one day be able to attend.

It was next to the last day of the convention, and they had gotten less than four hours of sleep after a caucus on restricting the import of oranges and grapefruits into the United States. But they got up, showered, shaved, and left the hotel for a 5:30 AM breakfast meeting.

The Mayor's thoughts were interrupted for a moment as he noticed his limousine was now passing cars like they were picket fences. The Main Street Bridge was in sight so it would be only minutes before they arrived at the command center. Bubba's thoughts then returned to Joe.

When attending those meetings at the Convention, Joe and Bubba would never sit together. They would split up with the strategy of doubling the number of contacts they made by not seating together.

The auditorium where the breakfast was being held was just about full when Bubba and Joe arrived. The breakfast was assigned seating, and Bubba was seated very close to the head table. He took this as being a sign that maybe he was moving up in the party's ranks. Joe was sitting in the back of the room at a table very close to the entrance. At this breakfast was where Joe met Helen. There was only one day left to the convention, and for the next 24 hours, the only contact that Bubba had with Joe was either through a quick cell phone call or a text message.

It wasn't until they were seated on the airplane headed back to Jacksonville that they were able to talk. Their conversation didn't last long, however, because shortly after the plane took off, they both fell into a deep sleep and did not wake until the aircraft touched down at the Jacksonville International Airport.

They got back into Jacksonville from the convention on the third Saturday of the month. Debra met Bubba at the airport, and Joe picked up his car at the long-term parking lot and drove home. The next morning around 10:00, Bubba was awakened by a telephone call from Joe. Bubba could sense the excitement in Joe's voice, a sound he had not heard for some time.

About two years ago, Bubba and Debra purchased a cabin up in the hills of Massanutten, Virginia, their getaway place. Joe said that he was going to take a week off to recuperate from the convention and asked if he could use the cabin. Without hesitation, Bubba said yes and gave Joe directions on how to pick up the keys from their caretaker, who looked after the cabin and prepared it for use before they came. That week that Joe stayed at Bubba's Massanutten, Virginia Cabin was the beginning for Joe and Helen, and 14 months later they got married in a ceremony held in Bubba's office at City Hall.

As Bubba's limousine crossed the Main Street Bridge, his driver picked up the microphone on a two-way radio located in the car. "Command Center. This is J.A.X. Car one. We should be at your location in the next couple of minutes. The Mayor requests a full update on the situation and the status of Joe Singletary. Over." No reply came from the command center. The driver repeated his transmission, but once again the radio was silent.

Bubba's limousine made the last turn, and they could see the mobile command center. There was a lot of activity taking place, and in the distance. They could see the flashing lights of two medical emergency vehicles speeding away. As the limousine pulled to a stop and the Mayor opened the door to get out of the car, Jerry Clark came running in their direction.

"Get back in the car! Get back in the car!" Jerry was waving his hands as he called out to Bubba. Jerry opened the passenger door and leaped into the backseat of the car seating himself beside Bubba. "We've got to get over to the hospital! They are taking them to Shands!" The driver pulled away from the command center and drove in the direction of 8th Street, where the emergency room of the hospital was located.

Bubba grabbed Jerry's arm, squeezing it, and said in a calm tone, "Has anyone called Helen?"

"No, we thought that you would want to be the one to do that," Jerry answered the Mayor's question in a high pitch and excited voice. Jerry's shirt was covered with perspiration. It was very easy to tell that Jerry had been very close to the crash because of the smell of gasoline and smoke coming from his clothing.

The Mayor looked at his cell phone and then turned back to Jerry. "This is what we will do. Helen is probably still at that installation thing along with Debra. You call Helen and tell her I will be calling her in a few moments. I will call Debra and tell her to go to Helen and await my call from the emergency room with what information we have at the time. Then get a police escort to bring Helen and Debra to the hospital."

Jerry reached into his shirt pocket and discovered that he had misplaced his cell phone. "I've lost my phone. I've lost my cell phone!" The limo driver quickly said we can patch you through using the mobile radio. "Make it happen!" Jerry shouted.

Meanwhile, the Mayor contacted his wife. Debra answered her cell phone with "Hello, Honey. Is everything all right?"

The Mayor quickly replied, "No, I'm sorry to say this couldn't be anything further from being good. There was a helicopter crash, and Joe Singletary was in the copter. They are taking him to the emergency room at Shands. Find Helen and stay with her. I'm headed to the emergency room now and will call you as soon as I find out any information. Jerry is sending a police escort to bring both of you to the hospital. I'll call you back as soon as I get more information. Love you!"

Debra said, "Love you too," and as she hung up she scanned the room looking for Helen. She spotted Helen just as she was pulling her cell phone out of her purse.

—

Arlington, Virginia.

Roy Benning completed his run, returned to his condominium, took a shower, changed into sweatpants and a T-shirt, and sat in his home office at his computer station. He began eating a leftover subway sandwich, a cold beer sitting on the table.

Roy was reading his backlog of Unclassified email messages while eating. He selected, read, flagged and deleted messages. Two words continued to float around in his thoughts: "Think ahead. Think ahead."

One thing that the current Director of the CIA regularly drilled into each of his Desk Chiefs was to think ahead and stay in front of the situation. Look at every possible scenario and plan in anticipation of what could happen next.

Roy completed going through his emails then clicked on another link, and after providing a retina, fingerprint, and voice scan and password, opened his classified calendar. Even though this calendar was still encrypted with binary numbers on calendar dates, it still gave him a clear idea of what lay ahead of him in the coming months.

His attention turned from his computer monitor when he heard the word "Jacksonville" coming from his television. The 7:00 PM news was on, and Roy swiveled his chair in the direction of his TV monitors, reached for his remote and turned up the sound. On the television screen, a female reporter was standing in front of what appeared to be a large trailer.

She said, "About two hours before midnight a fire erupted in the downtown section of Jacksonville, Florida. At this time, little is known about the circumstances that led to the fire starting, but at least, a 10 block area has been consumed by the blaze. Several casualties have been reported, but there is still speculation that more losses can be expected. There is an unconfirmed report that a massive explosion occurred in the vicinity of the Federal Reserve Bank located here, but once again, this is an unconfirmed report.

"Also, a bystander at the site of the fire said that they saw an observation helicopter crash after being struck by debris from an explosion. I stress that there has been no official confirmation from either the emergency command center or the Jacksonville Mayor's office that a helicopter has been involved in a crash. We will stay with this story as it progresses. This is Kyle Martin, WZXL, Channel 4 coming to you live from the fire scene here in Jacksonville, Florida."

Roy turned back to his computer and began typing an email message to the Director of the Agency. "Fire confirmed via 7:00 television news broadcast at our Jacksonville office. As of this email no communication with any of my people at our J.A.X. location. Will keep you updated."

After finishing, he clicked the send button on his computer and reached for his BlackBerry. He pulled up Karl Mansfield's cell number and dialed it. After the fourth ring, he was switched over to voicemail. "Karl, this is Roy, give me a call as soon as possible with the update on the fire situation. Talk to you soon. Roy."

Next, he dialed Karl's home telephone number, but once again his call went to voicemail. He thought it was a little strange that it was almost 9:00 PM and no one was home at Karl's house. But it was a Saturday night, and so maybe they were out for dinner or taking in a movie or something, he reasoned.

Roy then looked up Nancy Mansfield's number in his cell. Nancy was Karl's wife, but she also worked for the Agency. Karl and Nancy had been married for only two years. Nancy was in charge of training for Roy's desk. She joined the Agency as a field agent and after a year in the field requested a transfer to Training. She and Karl met when he had to go for an annual certification. When Roy asked Karl to be his deputy, Nancy moved with him to Jacksonville and became the Central and South America Desk Training Officer.

Being out of contact with his agents working in the field was somewhat of a typical situation. Roy could remember times, even since he had been at this desk when one of his agents had not provided an update on his status for over 10 days. What also eased his anxiety level was the fact that he could always jump on the commercial flight or even request an Agency plane to fly him to Jacksonville so that he could see what was going on for himself.

The last number that Roy looked up on his Blackberry was Elkin Ardila, Karl's number two in Florida. Elkin was asked to go Black, undercover, for the next operation: Fertile Ground. Roy dialed Elkin's number.

"This is Elk. What's up, Roy?"

Roy Benning breathed a sigh of relief that he was able to finally reach someone in his Jacksonville operation. "Elk, can you provide me with an update on what is going on in Jacksonville?" There was a slight pause before Elkin replied.

The Agency provided BlackBerry cellular phones to all field agents that were modified with unique encryption for all incoming and outgoing calls, emails, and texts. These phones were even equipped with double ciphers and a self-destruct mode if an Agency BlackBerry was lost or stolen.

"I have been out at the Plantation since noon yesterday. Everything is set up for the trainees arriving with the advance party tonight. So I haven't had any contact with Karl or anyone at the Flagler Center. Has anything happened to compromise Fertile Ground?"

After listening to Elkin, Roy was beginning to wonder if he was making more of the situation than it really was. There were really only two pressing issues. If the office at the Jacksonville downtown location had been consumed by the fire, being that it was a Saturday, all of the classified information should not have been compromised because it was in the safe. That is if all of the office protocols had been followed when everyone left the office Friday.

The second issue was that Elk was to make the first contact with the trainees coming in on Fertile Ground and that operation seemed to be secure and on track. The only loose end was to hear from Karl so he could confirm no classified material had been compromised.

So, with a very calm and pleasant tone, Roy replied, "Elk, there seems to be a major fire in progress where the office is located in Jacksonville. I've been trying to reach Karl, both on his BlackBerry and at home, but I haven't had much luck. I also reached out to Nancy as well. Of course, I left voice messages, but as of this hour, no one has returned my calls. When was the last time you spoke to Karl?"

Elkin told Roy he was driving on Florida State Road 21 but saw a fast food restaurant just ahead. He pulled into the parking lot to continue the conversation without any distractions. Elk was playing his compact disc when he received the call from Roy, and he now reached for his radio and switched back to the satellite radio network and pushed the preset button for CNN.

"Sorry, Roy, but as I said, the last contact I had with anyone was yesterday; and quite frankly I just haven't had any time to check the news in the last 24 hours. All my focus has been on getting everything set up for this operation."

Roy could understand perfectly what Elk was talking about. He had played the role of being the primary go-between on many operations when he was an agent in the field. Before Roy could say anything Elk continued. "I'm only about a 45-minute drive into the city, so let me head in and take a look around and see what's going on and try to contact Karl. I just turned my satellite radio on to CNN, and nothing has come over while I've been sitting here. Wait... I hear something now." Elk stopped speaking to listen to his car radio.

Roy liked Elk's suggestion, but he added, "Elk, if you are unable to run into or contact Karl, maybe he and Nancy are out at a movie or something, give me a call back at midnight. I need confirmation that all of the classified material was secured when they closed the office last night."

Elk finished listening to the CNN news report on the fire in Jacksonville. "Roy, it sounds like it is a mother of a fire. I understand perfectly everything you said, and I'll give you a call before midnight if I don't reach Karl. If I do, I'll have him call you ASAP."

Roy felt better now that he had contact with one of his people in Jacksonville. "Thanks, Elk, and I will be looking for a call from you or Karl later tonight." He ended the call and laid his BlackBerry back on the desk. He picked up the bottle of beer from his desk, but it wasn't cold any longer. So he walked into his kitchen, poured the beer into the kitchen sink, tossed the bottle into the trashcan, and then went to the refrigerator for another beer.

As he closed the refrigerator door and opened the beer, he leaned back against the wall and began to replay his talk with Elk.

After rethinking everything that had been said in the conversation, Roy concluded that the most important issue was confirmation that all the classified material was secure. If any piece of classified material were discovered due to the fire, it wouldn't matter whether or not it was an ongoing operation or a previous operation, the mere fact that it would become common knowledge that a major CIA office was located in Jacksonville would be something that the Agency just couldn't stand for.

The CIA's Central and South America Desk for Clandestine Services had been headquartered in Jacksonville for well over 50 years, and the office's operations went back to before the Cuban missile crisis. It was the command center for all of the activities during the Bay of Pigs and the Contras network operations. In fact, money paid to Manuel Noriega, the Panamanian strongman, came from the Agency's account at the Federal Reserve Bank located in Jacksonville.

Since 9/11 operations had expanded with the opening of the Flagler Center. It was determined that Jacksonville was a perfect location to position such a strategic and significant intelligence service because it was the last place that anyone would think of.

Even a major training facility was built less than 40 miles from the downtown office. Most people have heard of the Farm, the CIA training facility located near Williamsburg, Virginia. However, little is known about the Plantation. The CIA needed a location where they could train indigenous personnel from Latin America on the trade craft skills necessary to be an effective intelligence field agent. The Agency first looked at locating the training center at Doral Beach near Miami where the United States Army Southern Command (SOUTHCOM) is located. The next potential location was the US Army School of the Americas (SOA) when it was based in Panama. The SOA was a combat training school for Latin American soldiers. This location made the Agency short list until the army relocated the SOA to Fort Benning, Georgia. The Agency's planners viewed Fort Benning just like SOUTHCOM: it was too big of a signature.

Jacksonville slowly emerged as the most ideal location and thus the Plantation was created at the Florida National Guard Training Center at Camp Blanding.

The Plantation is a black training facility where the Agency conducts train-the-trainer instruction to indigenous foreign personnel. Most of the trainees are from South and Latin America.

Emerging from his thoughts, Roy said out loud, "I will not let that happen on my watch." He finished his beer, tossed the bottle into the trash, turned the kitchen lights off, and walked to his bedroom.

Chapter 7

Jacksonville International Airport.

Southwest flight 631 touched down shortly after 10:40 PM. Bo Brooks was seated in business class, so he was one of the first to exit the plane. After picking up his bags, he went to the Hertz counter and got the keys to his rental car, a Ford Taurus. Bo picked up the car, changed his BlackBerry to the GPS app, and pulled out of the parking garage as a lady's voice from his BlackBerry GPS directed him to the Marriott Hotel.

This was Bo's first trip to Jacksonville, and what little he knew about Jacksonville had to do with the football team and Sawgrass.

The office of the FBI in Jacksonville was small in comparison to cities like Mobile Alabama, Atlanta, and, of course, Miami. However, during the civil rights era, the Jacksonville office had a relatively large caseload, including many common cases with the offices in Mississippi, Alabama, or South Georgia. More recently the office workload was almost a balance across all areas of federal investigation and crime fighting.

FBI Agent Brooks' concentration shifted away from the voice of the lady giving him directions to wondering whether or not he had ever worked with any of the agents assigned to the office in Jacksonville during his career with the Agency.

Up until he was appointed to his current job, all of his assignments had taken place in the DC-Philadelphia corridor. He was a most surprised person when he received a call that he was to be interviewed for the Anti-Terrorist Threat Unit-Information and Cross-Referencing Section. The Information and Cross-Referencing Section falls under the Terrorism Division. His work in the DC-Philadelphia area was in the Public Corruption Division, Government Fraud.

Fraud cases take a long time to develop, and Bo had seen agents in this division start a case at the beginning of their career and retire from the FBI with the case still open.

It was sort of odd how he found out that he had passed the interview and would be joining the Information and Cross-Referencing Section. It was a week after Bo was interviewed and he was working out of the Philadelphia office. When he arrived at his office on a Monday morning, he had a telephone message from a guy with the Bureau's relocation section asking that he return the call. He opened his email, and there was an email from the same section with an attachment, a relocation package for Washington, DC. Bo called the guy at relocations to find out if there was some type of mistake, and the guy said, "No. If you are FBI Agent Bo Brooks, then you are moving to Washington, DC. Fill out the paperwork and email it back to me by close of business tomorrow and start packing!"

Bo relocated and purchased his townhouse in Silver Spring, and it was a Friday before the third Saturday in August when he parked his car in the underground parking garage at the J. Edgar Hoover building and was waiting for the elevator to come down when his attention was directed to a female agent walking toward the elevator. There were strict rules at the Agency concerning fraternization between Agents, but as Bo watched her walking toward him, his only thought was that this was a very attractive lady. As she got closer, their eyes made contact for a flicker of a second and Bo's instinct signaled that maybe a connection had been made.

Simultaneously, they gave the professional greeting, "Good morning," followed by a controlled smile. The elevator door opened, and Bo gestured for her to proceed. This was the last day of his first week at the Hoover Building. He was still getting lost trying to find the bathrooms and locating the office supply room.

His mind was racing, trying to think of something to say to break the silence of the elevator ride. Finally, he said, "I was thinking about trying out one of the new Smith and Wesson .50-cal automatics. Have you fired one?"

The female agent slowly turned her head and looked directly into Bo's eyes, and with a smile that lit up the elevator, she said, "Is that the best pickup line you could think of?"

The elevator stopped at that moment, and she exited with the smile still on her face. The smell of her perfume filled Bo's nostrils as he watched the swaying of her hips. Bo memorized the floor number.

For several weeks, Bo attempted to schedule his arrival at the office at the same time he had encountered the female agent. He also took it upon himself to go down to the floor where the lady got off the elevator to stroll around to see if he could run into her again. It wasn't long before his workload increased, however, reducing the amount of time he had available to look for the missing agent.

Several years passed and Joe was flying back from a bombing to DC on a chartered Agency Gulfstream with a group of agents. Joe and the officer that he was sitting by on the plane had developed a level of friendship, which made Bo feel comfortable about asking him a question. Joe described the female agent he met during his first week at the Agency. The Agent turned his head away from Bo and started staring at the back of the seat that was in front of them. Bo could barely hear him whispering several names through his lips. Then he suddenly said, "Faye. Are you talking about Faye, Faye Cook, Faye Cook-Little?" Bo raised his head and looked around the cabin of the plane to see if anyone had heard that outburst from the agent.

After Bo was comfortable that no attention had been drawn to their conversation, he whispered, "That could be her. This is the closest I've come to connecting the name with a description."

The agent whispered back to Bo quietly because he knew that he would be concerned about someone overhearing their conversation. "I'm pretty sure that is her, and at the time you were reassigned to the Hoover Building, the floor you said she got off at was only occupied by investigative agents from the Bank Robbery Division. There were only two females in that section around that time. One was already married, and if you made any move or said anything to her, she was the type to turn you in for sexual harassment. The other woman was Faye, a Super Agent, who had a reputation for being the first one to go through the door. All the guys in that division really respected her and said that she was a joy to work with."

It took a while for Bo to take in what he had heard. He was pleased that his perception was matching the lady's reputation. "What happened to her, because I have been on that floor a thousand times and I have not run into her again?"

Once again the agent sitting beside Bo turned his attention back to staring at the back of the seat in front of him. With an uncertain facial expression, he said, "She was promoted and reassigned to either the Miami-Dade office or possibly Jacksonville. I'm not certain which."

—

Shands Hospital's Emergency Room, Jacksonville, Florida.

As Bubba Webb's limousine was pulling up the driveway to the hospital's emergency room, his car was besieged by newspaper reporters and cameramen. Cameras were flashing, video cameras were rolling, and there was no doubt that the story about the helicopter crash and the fire downtown was making headline news. "I never knew there were so many reporters in Jacksonville. I can't remember seeing any of these faces at our press conferences. Jerry. Is this a sign that you are looking for a raise?" Bubba said as he was stepping out of the car.

Bubba Webb barely took two steps when microphones were shoved in front of him, and questions were shouted at him from all sides. The police were doing their best to make a pathway for Bubba and Jerry to get into the emergency room. Bubba walked at a moderate pace, making eye contact, moving his head from side to side but maintaining a solemn expression.

Jerry was a master of these situations. He always had the perfect mannerisms and facial expressions, always the right words with the exact impact to say at the right time.

"Please stand back. The Mayor will be making a statement shortly. We will be having a press conference back at the mobile command center. Thank you very much for coming to see our citizens. The Mayor will be giving you an update after he speaks with the doctors in the emergency room." He this very calmly and with the right inflection, and he repeated his statements over and over until he and the Mayor had passed through the doors of the emergency room lobby.

The Mayor and Jerry were met in the hallway by an attendant and were immediately escorted to a triage area. This area had a nurse's station, where three nurses, two female and one male, were behind the desk. The male and one of the female attendants were seated at the counter and the other woman was standing at a file cabinet with her back to the Mayor. She turned her head toward them as they approached the station. All were dressed in the same color scrubs. Two hallways intersected at the corner of the station the Mayor was walking toward. The hallway to the right proceeded through an open doorway, and above the door, a sign read: To X-ray. The doors were closed to the left entrance, and the sign above that door read: To Operating Rooms 111-123.

The doors opened from the direction of the operating room, and a figure came out dressed in a surgical tunic, surgical mask, and cap. As the person walked toward the Mayor and Jerry, he was taking off rubber surgical gloves. "Good evening Mayor, I'm Dr. Jo, and the physician on-call here tonight. First of all, I'm sorry to have to tell you this…"

At those words the Mayor stood frozen in place with solid eye contact, his thoughts hanging on every word.

"The pilot of the aircraft did not survive the crash due to the injuries he received. The other gentleman, Mr. Singletary, survived, but your friend is in very critical condition. He has compound fractures of both of his legs, and we know that two of his vertebrae, the L4, and L5, are cracked. There is possibly more damage to his spine, but we won't be able to tell until some of the swellings have gone down. He also has two cracked ribs, one of which punctured his left lung. We also believe that he has a concussion. We operated on both legs, setting the bone, and we have stabilized him; but once again, we probably won't look at his spine until the swelling is down. He is resting comfortably but is in critical condition. The next 24 hours will determine if he will pull out of this. I wish I could give you better news, but he was involved in a severe crash."

Bubba Webb sighed with relief that his lifelong friend, though in critical condition, was still alive. "Thank you very much, Dr. Jo. I can't tell you how much I really appreciate you taking time from your tremendous workload to give me that very detailed update on both of the citizens of our beautiful city. I would greatly appreciate if you would provide a similar update to Joe's wife, who will be arriving here in a moment." The Mayor reached out and shook the doctor's hand. He started to turn to leave, but hesitated and turned back to the Doctor. "Please, Doctor. It goes without saying, but if my office can do anything, do not hesitate to contact me. I'm available 24/7." The doctor replied that he would.

Bubba proceeded to shake everyone in the room's hand, introducing himself and asking each how long they had worked at the hospital and lived in Jacksonville, what section of Jacksonville they lived in, and if they were a fan of the Jaguars. All of this was going on while Jerry Clark was writing down detailed information on the emergency room doctors, obtaining any information on the names of anyone who had contact with Joe Singletary and the pilot. The Mayor had established a standard procedure of sending out personal thank you letters to everyone involved in any type of emergency situation. No detail was too small. Firemen had received letters from the Mayor thanking them for rescuing a cat out of a tree.

The Mayor and Jerry Clark were entering the lobby when Bubba's wife and Helen were making their way through the gauntlet of reporters. Bubba walked directly up to Helen and embraced her, reaching out to hold his wife's hand while he consoled Helen.

"Everything is going to be okay. Joe is a very tough and determined man, and he will pull through this. The doctors are doing everything humanly possible. Come this way, and you can speak with them for yourself."

Meanwhile, at the Marriott, Bo Brooks was parking the rental car. As he opened his car door so he could get his bags out of the trunk, the thick smell of smoke blended with petroleum and a gaseous smell permeated the air. Bo gathered his bags from the trunk of the car and started walking into the lobby of the hotel. Just as the automatic door was opening, he did a quick about-face with a startled look on his face. He said aloud to himself, "Is that the smell of gunpowder? I think I'm smelling gunpowder." He turned back around and walked into the lobby.

—

Elkin Ardila had to park several blocks from the fire scene. The police were forced to extend the safety zone after the explosion. It might have been due to the air being filled with the smell of smoke and burned bodies and because of the possibility of more explosions going off. The smoke and the smell of burning bodies put Elk automatically into survival mode as he moved to the outskirts of the fire safety zone. He had worked many missions for the Agency in Afghanistan and deep in Iran, and so he was no stranger to moving through a crowd unnoticed.

It took Elk 20 minutes to determine that both the Federal Building, where his office had been located, and the Federal Reserve

Bank were leveled. From his current location just beyond another yellow taped-off area, he could see the emergency command center. There was a crowd of mobile news satellite vans with their antennas stretched upwards to the heavens. Elk decided to make his way over and see if he could pick up any information. He was less than 50 feet from the trailer and just outside of the restricted area when police began to push the crowd back because the Mayor's limo was pulling up.

Once the reporters identified the car, it became a race to get as close to the car as possible. Elk blended into the rush and picked the pocket of one of the reporters for a pad and pen and another for a press badge, and by the time he reached the Mayor's car he had all the tools of the trade to enable him to look just like another reporter attempting to get a story.

Jerry Clark was the first to emerge from the limo. It looked like a scene from a motion picture unfolding, Bubba Webb stayed in the car just long enough to raise the anticipation of the reporters to the point of wondering if the Mayor was there, which would have served as a whole new story line. Then suddenly he stepped out of the car.

Once the Mayor got out of the car, Bubba gave the typical 360-degree spin so all of the cameras could catch a shot of him. He then joined Jerry Clark at a set of microphones positioned in front of the Mobile Command Center.

Jerry did a quick introduction for the Mayor, and then the Mayor began to speak: "We are very saddened by the events that have taken place today. Fire is an unknown beast that can come at any time or any moment, but I have the utmost confidence in our emergency preparedness plans, and I'm entirely satisfied with the way that all of our departments have attacked this situation in a total team effort. Fire personnel, hospitals, police, social services, and all of the agencies and departments working behind the scenes are acting as one to ensure the safety and the protection of people and property of our Jacksonville community. I will now turn the mic over to Jacksonville's Fire Chief, Chief Ferguson. He will give you an overview of where we stand."

—

Interstate 95, Florida.

The Mercedes-Benz was on Interstate 95 North about 20 miles outside of Jacksonville. Ranuel said to the driver, "We need to take one last stop before we reach the Beltway. Find somewhere we can park, and I can make my calls." The driver saw a sign that read outlet mall, pulled off and parked among the many other cars there so their drivers could take advantage of the discount sales. Just across the street from the mall was a 7-11 convenience store. Ranuel exited the car, leaving the driver and Krish behind, and crossed the street. At the 7-11 he purchased a prepaid phone, again paying cash. After returning to the car, Ranuel pulled out his black notebook and began to make his calls.

But unlike the previous calls, on the very first ring of the first number that he dialed someone answered. "Change of plans. Meet me at Whitey's at Doctors Inlet on the Island." Elkin Ardila held his cell phone to his ear waiting for confirmation that the caller understood the message.

Finally, he received the acknowledgment that he was waiting for: "Understood. Will meet you at the rendezvous point, Fleming Island."

After hearing the acknowledgment, Elk quickly ended the call and turned his prepaid phone off. Then he left the Mayor's press conference and started for his car. As Elk made his way through the crowd that had gathered, he knew he had to report back to Roy Benning. He pulled out his BlackBerry.

"Roy, this is Elk. Did I wake you."

Roy Benning had in fact fallen asleep in his bed while he was looking at the television. "No, Elk. I guess I was just resting my eyes, but I was expecting your call."

Elk, still walking at a moderate pace but being very cautious of his surroundings, started to give his summation of the situation in Jacksonville. "It's pretty bad here. I can tell you for the fact that our building is gone. The whole Federal Building has been leveled. It also appears that the Federal Bank has been demolished. My guess is that the ammunition we were storing in the basement somehow got ignited. It was scheduled to be moved to the Plantation tomorrow. That is probably what caused all the damage. At this point, the locals know it was a major explosion, but it's probably still too early for them to determine what caused the explosion and where the explosive material came from. I've contacted the people from Fertile Ground, and we are meeting at our other rendezvous point at Fleming Island. They were scheduled to come through tonight and pick up the first supply of ammunition before they went out to the Plantation. I think what I have to do now is get those guys stashed away and then come back to town tomorrow morning and see what I can find out about what the authorities have found in their initial investigation."

By this time, Roy Benning had gotten out of bed and was walking around his bedroom absorbing Elk's report. From Roy's years of experience, he knew that Elk was taking the proper course of action. What he had to do was to stay ahead of the situation, and his most immediate thought was to contact the spin doctors at the Agency to provide appropriate answers to satisfy the media.

"Thanks, Elk. I appreciate that update. Have you heard anything from Karl?"

Elk thought for a minute. "While I was en route, I gave him a call, but it went into his voicemail; and since surveying the situation here, I haven't had a chance to call him back. I'll try again after we finished talking."

Roy didn't like loose ends, and not hearing from Karl created a loose end. "Okay, Elk. Thanks again for the update, and as soon as you hear anything from Karl let me know or have Karl give me a call. "

Meanwhile, back at that outlet parking lot off of Interstate 95, Ranuel, still holding the cell phone in his hand, stared out across the parking lot, processing the information he just received. His thoughts raced through every step of the plan as he tried to figure out any move that they had missed, any move that they made that may have compromised their position.

The silence in the automobile was broken by Krish. "Something has happened. What has gone wrong?'

"Shut up, Krish!" Ranuel shouted. "I'm tired of your whining. Our plans had anticipated something like this, and we must rendezvous at one of the alternate backup locations. Everything is still all right." Ranuel quickly made nine other calls speaking just one word: "Halt!"

He then turned to the driver. "Take us to Doctor's Inlet located on Fleming Island. Once you get us on Fleming Island, I'll give you the address we want you to take us. The driver started the Mercedes-Benz and slowly exited the outlet parking lot and returned to Interstate 95 North toward Jacksonville.

Back in Arlington, Virginia, it became a long night for Roy Benning. Immediately after talking with Elk, he went back into his study and filed situational update reports, alerting all relevant Agency sections to the situation in Jacksonville. He also contacted the IT section to find out the last time that Karl or Nancy logged on to their computers from within the Jacksonville office. This would also be cross-referenced to the last time that they used their key cards to enter and exit the office. Knowing this information would give Roy an idea if either of them was in the building during the fire.

An alert went out to Agency personnel in Jacksonville informing them of the situation and to stay in place until they received further notice. Roy did not want anyone to show up at the building on Monday and be caught on camera by some news agency. He knew that an inventory would be made to account for every square foot of office space and who occupied that space and what it was being used for. Since the FBI maintained an office in the same building, Roy figured that the spin guys would put the ammunition and the firing range on them and, maybe, just perhaps, no one would go deeper. At least, that is what he was recommending in his report.

—

Jacksonville Mobile Command Center.

After the press conference, Jerry Clark assembled key city department heads in the command center briefing room. The meeting room filled up very quickly because, first, the department heads brought all of their key people to ensure they would be able to answer any unexpected questions that could come from the Mayor. Bubba Webb had a reputation for being incredibly detailed, allowing for every part to be uncovered.

The mood in the room was solemn. Joe Singletary was a popular administrator and was well-liked by almost everyone. Jerry was just about to start the meeting when a hand went up. The person was recognized, and a voice spoke from the back of the room: "Jerry, can you give us an update on the condition of Joe and the pilot?"

After looking down at his notes, Jerry raised his head and looked around the room. "I can tell you that the pilot didn't make it. That information has not been released to the press. We are contacting his next of kin and plan to bring them into the hospital before we release his name and details of what happened. I'll let Bubba give everyone an update when he comes in. He's outside on the phone with the hospital trying to get an update on Joe's condition." Just as Jerry finished, the Mayor entered the conference room and walked directly to the head of the table and took a seat beside Jerry.

"How is everyone?" the Mayor said as he sat down. "I know that a lot of you have been here since early morning, and so the first thing I'd like to say is that I really appreciate all that you do for our city in such situations. I just got off the phone with the emergency room doctor about Joe's current condition. Everybody knows me, and you know I cut straight to the bottom line." Bubba Webb paused for a moment and looked around the room, giving the effect that he was looking everyone directly in the eye.

"As I look around this room, I can see that most of you have been with me from the beginning. Therefore, you know how close Joe Singletary and I are. Joe is like a brother to me. As a matter of fact, a lot of you can remember some of the things he has done for us. For example, Mary over there. He drove her to the hospital when her water broke just before having her first baby." Then Bubba pointed to the rear of the conference room. "Charlie, Charlie Kelly, I know you remember that, two years ago during the hurricane, the wind picked up blowing poor Charlie into the St. Johns River, and everybody knows what happened next." He paused for a long moment. "Joe jumped in and pulled Charlie out." Pausing again, the Mayor scanned the room, then said, "His condition is serious. At present, he is in critical condition, and the doctors told me that the next 24 hours will determine what will happen next." Bubba's eyes were tearing up, so he stopped for a moment to clear his throat. "Let's have a moment of silence for each of us to say a prayer that my lifelong friend and our fellow co-worker pulls through this, and while you're at it, please also say a prayer for support for his wife, Nancy." After a few moments of silence, he said, "Amen!"

The Mayor sat down and looked at Jerry to start the meeting. Jerry looked down at his notes and said, "All right, we'll start with Fire Chief Ferguson."

The Fire Chief rose from his seat and walked to the situation board. But just as he was picking up the laser pointer and about to turn around to start his briefing, Bubba Webb blurted out, "What was that damn explosion and what caused it!

Chapter 8

Whiteys, Doctor's Inlet, Fleming Island. Whitey's

Elkin Ardila parked his car a few yards from the entrance into   Whitey's. He wanted to check everything out before he walked in for his meeting. He was glad that he did because he noticed two cars that his instincts told him were out of place. Elk pulled out a set of binoculars from his glove box, took a look and wrote down the tag numbers. He contacted Langley with his BlackBerry and ran the car tags.

The full name of the rendezvous point, located at Doctor's Inlet on Fleming Island, was Whitey's Fish Camp. The camp consisted of a small restaurant that sold some of the best seafood on the island. It was well known that people as far as Palatka and even Gainesville drove over to Doctor's Inlet to eat at Whitey's, many ordering their most famous dish, fried catfish with hush puppies.

Besides the restaurant, there was a dock where small to medium-sized fishing boats could be rented and a trailer park that consisted of about 20 trailers also available for rent. Through an alias, the Agency had contracted six of the trailers for seven months to house personnel training at the Plantation.

Elk's BlackBerry rang, and before the second ring Elk was speaking with Langley. "OK, they are clean. Thanks." Elk put his phone away and checked his 9mm and both of his backups, a .38 revolver and 380 automatic. His car was set up so the inside light would not come on when he opened the door, and as he stepped out he gently closed the car door, making as little noise as possible.

Walking toward the entrance of Whitey's, he counted all of the vehicles in the lot and on the curb: twenty cars and trucks along with three motorcycles. He checked his watch. It was half past midnight, and it was evident that the restaurant, at least, the bar portion was still going strong. Elk was close enough that he could hear music, a country and western band with a singer. Just before opening the door, Elk closed one of his eyes, his firing eye, so that when he entered he would have one eye adjusted to the darkness of the bar.

After stepping through the door, Elk surveyed the room, checking for exits and any hidden entrances, such as an office or a storage closet. A scantily dressed woman walked up to Elkin holding several menus and a pad and said with a weak smile, "Would you like to have dinner? Our kitchen is still open."

Elk smiled back and asked to be seated in a booth away from the band.

"I would have never guessed you were the type that didn't like music," the hostess said, looking Elk up and down. "Follow me, handsome. I have just the table for you."

Elk followed the lady to a booth on the far side of the room away from the music. He took a seat where he could see all of the exits and the front door.

"Jenny will be your waitress. She'll get your drinks and take your order. If you feel like you want to dance, you can ask for Margie. That's me." Her smile was a lot more cheerful as she turned and sashayed back to the front of the restaurant.

The protocol for the rendezvous was as follows: when Ranuel arrived he would remain outside and make a call from his prepaid phone; Elk would answer the call and let Ranuel know that he was already inside the restaurant and direct him to the table where he would be sitting. Elk pulled his prepaid phone out of his pocket and laid it on the table. Just as he set the cell phone down, a tall and also scantily dressed blonde approached his table.

"Hello, handsome. My name is Jenny, and I will be your waitress. Would you like to start off with a drink or did you have something else on your mind?"

As Elk was about to order, his cell phone rang. Elk quickly said, "I'll take a Dewar's on the rocks and a Budweiser." Jenny wrote the order down, smiled, and started for the bar. Elk answered the cell phone and gave Ranuel the location to the booth where he was seated. The protocol also dictated that only Ranuel and Krish should come in for the meeting, leaving the driver in the car to act as a lookout.

Elk's full attention was on the entrance. He saw Ranuel and Krish enter Whitey's. They stood in the doorway for a few seconds to obtain their bearings. Ranuel was in the lead as they walked across the floor toward Elk's table. Elk stood and greeted them, and everyone took a seat in the booth. Elk on one side of the table with

71

Ranuel and Krish sitting on the other side. By this time Jenny was back at the table with Elk's drinks.

"I guess the rest of your party has arrived. What can I get for you, gentlemen?" Ranuel asked for a beer and Krish ordered a double shot of tequila.

Once Jenny had left their table, Elk began to reassure Ranuel and Krish that nothing had gone wrong with the execution of Fertile Ground and that the only problem that they had was that the building where the training ammunition was stored blew up due to a fire in Jacksonville. Because the Agency was moving the ammunition in small amounts, it would take a week to replenish the full supply of ammunition.

"In the meantime," Elk said, "you gentlemen must be starving. "You've been on the road since this morning, so let's order some catfish and hush puppies. Jenny returned to the table with their drinks and took their orders for dinner.

Elk could sense the lack of trust from both Ranuel and Krish. After their initial greeting, neither had spoken a word. They didn't even respond when he told them about the ammunition. He was certain he would get some kind of reaction from that, but he didn't. The Agency only had ten weeks to whip these guys into fighting shape as a cohesive combat unit before they left to execute operation Fertile Ground. Ten weeks was cutting it really close. Now, with a week delay, it would be an even tougher job to prepare them to do the job ahead.

But the biggest obstacle facing Elk was that it was common knowledge throughout Central and South America what happened to Brigade 2506 and how the CIA betrayed them during the Bay of Pigs invasion of Cuba. In fact, the Central and Latin American Desk wanted Fertile Ground to become the operations that would right the wrong of the Bay of Pigs.

"OK, gentlemen. After we enjoy this meal, I'll get you settled in your trailers so you can get some rest before we start tomorrow."

—

Marriott Hotel Jacksonville.

After checking into his room and taking a shower, Bo Brooks sat on the side of his bed with his laptop open. The faint sound of the Jacksonville television news announcer could be heard in the background describing the scene at the fire.

Bo was checking his emails when he saw the subject title "Welcome to Jacksonville," an email from the local FBI office. "Welcome to the FBI First Coast Office. Will meet you in the lobby for breakfast at 0800. Agent in Charge, Faye Cook-Little."

A smile came across Bo's face. "I guess he was right. She is in Jacksonville. I wonder if she remembers me. It's been over four years since that day in the elevator, and she probably has gotten married. I wondered if she ever tried to find out who I was or sought to look me up in the directory. I guess she couldn't have done that if she didn't know my name. Well, I'll find out tomorrow." Bo put his laptop away, set the alarm on his BlackBerry to wake him up at 7:00, and went to bed with thoughts of the morning meeting with Faye.

—

Galileo International Airport Rio de Janeiro.

After 14 hours and 20 minutes flying time, WC and Eve's flight touched down in Rio. Wallace hadn't thought about the strange sensation he'd had when he thought he saw his old roommate Harry Paxton while checking in at the airport in Fort Lauderdale. Throughout the flight, Wallace and Eve just enjoyed each other's company, laughing and talking about how much fun they intended to have during this vacation. They agreed: no serious talk, just laughter along with the joy of being together. Wallace thought to himself that he had not laughed this much for such a long time, and he wondered, "Could this really be real?" This was so much different than either of my first two marriages. Eve was different. Reflecting back, he realized he was a lot different now too, a few years older and much more mature. It was only a few days after their Honeymoon when WC had to leave for airborne school and jungle operations training followed by Ranger school. After the nine months of training, he and his first wife were only together for about three weeks when he was called out on his first deployment. In fact, over the first two years of marriage, he was deployed 70% of the time, and he could never tell her where he was going or when he'd be back. In fact, in many cases, he didn't even know where he was going until airborne.

There were so many arguments that many times he didn't even want to come home because he was aware that, sooner or later, she would start with the questions about where Wallace had been and what he was doing while away. It didn't matter how many times WC attempted to explain to her that the work he was doing was Classified and that he could not disclose to her or anyone what his job entailed in the places that he and his team were deployed.

He looked over at Eve, staring at her. "What?" she said. "Is something on my nose?" Wallace said no and kissed her. She giggled and said, "You're crazy."

"Welcome to Rio de Janeiro," came the voice over the plane's intercom. "The local time is 9:20 AM. Please keep your seatbelts fastened until we reach the terminal." Once the light went off, and the announcement was made that they could exit the plane, Wallace pulled their bags from the overhead compartment, his excitement dampened waiting for the passengers in front of him and Eve to leave the aircraft.

In the business section of the plane, everything moved much faster. As the man with the glasses stepped from the aircraft into the Trans walk, he removed his reversible jacket and turned it inside out, then changed his glasses to a different style frame. After quickly passing through customs with his Canadian passport, he headed to baggage claim to pick up his luggage. As he picked up his bag, he took off his jacket, changed glasses to shades, and put on a baseball cap for going through immigration.

Wallace and Eve finished going through customs and reached the back of the line for immigration as the man with the glasses, Seventy-One, was exiting into the main terminal. That same sensation that WC had at the airport in Fort Lauderdale reemerged just as Eve touched Wallace's shoulder.

"Lover, I knew it was going to be hot here, but this is a little more than I expected." At that moment, Wallace spotted the figure of the man he had seen in Fort Lauderdale moving swiftly beyond the immigration stations. "Honey, it's not the heat it's the humidity. Give yourself 24 hours and it will feel just like you are back in

Jacksonville," Wallace replied, keeping his sights on the man moving away from the immigration checkpoint.

The entire country of Brazil was on a heightened security alert. In 10 weeks, on the third Saturday in September, the Chiefs of State for Venezuela and Guyana were to meet in Brasilia, the capital of Brazil, with the expectation of signing an agreement that would put to rest the issues regarding the disputed region of Essequibo. Oil deposits had been confirmed in the area, and this agreement would ensure that both countries shared in the development and, hopefully, the future returns.

The negotiations were starting in two weeks in Rio de Janeiro. Each of the countries' respective heads of security arrived in Rio de Janeiro that morning to personally oversee the process of working with Brazilian officials, the planning for the protection and safety requirements for both the negotiation teams and if everything went as planned, the signing of the agreement in Brasilia. Both Teams were staying at the same hotel on Copacabana Beach, the Sofitel.

Wallace was sparing no expense for this trip. Using the money he had received from his bonus for bringing his last project in on time, within the contract specifications, and within budget, the sky was the limit. He had booked a suite for them at the Belmond Copacabana Palace located on the Copacabana Beach.

As WC and Eve cleared immigration, Eve said, "WC, that man over there is holding a sign that has your name on it."

Wallace grinned and said, "The hotel sent a car to pick us up."

Seventy-One moved through the airport lobby looking for the lockers. He found the lockers and stood in front of the one he was searching for. He pulled a key from his pocket and opened locker number 71. Seventy-One took a large duffle bag out of the locker and replaced it with his suitcase. He then reversed his jacket and put on a different cap along with new sunglasses. Seventy-One reclosed the locker and went in search of the men's room, not just any toilet but a specific one. He found it just about mid-way across the vast terminal. The sign read: Toilet, Room Number 71. This particular toilet was in a dead zone so none of the security cameras and the terminal could observe anyone going in or coming out. As he got closer to the door of the toilet, Seventy-One pulled a set of rubber gloves from his pockets, put them on, and opened the door. He checked to see if he was alone and then went into one of the stalls.

When he stepped out, he had changed into a set of coveralls with the words "Roofing Maintenance" in both Spanish and English on the back. He still had the rubber gloves on as he left the toilet and headed for the parking lot. From inside the coveralls, he pulled out a parking ticket that read "Section A-7, Row 1." Seventy-One followed the signs until he saw Section A, coming to a stop at parking station 71. Here he pulled out the keys to a panel van. Four different styles of the ladder were strapped on the top of the truck. He unlocked the van and placed the duffel bag in the back, then shook the ladders to see if they had been tied down thoroughly. He then proceeded to check under the vehicle, inside the engine compartment, and inside the cab of the van looking for bugs or any type of tracking device.

After being one hundred percent satisfied that there was no tracking or listening devices in the truck, he got into the driver's seat and pulled out a GPS from the glove compartment. The GPS had already been preset to a location. He attached the GPS to the window and pulled out of the parking garage. The GPS indicated that from his present location, it would take approximately 58 minutes to reach his destination.

Meanwhile, Wallace and Eve followed the limousine driver to the curb where the car was parked. When they took their seats in the back of the car, they found a bottle of champagne and two glasses along with grapes, caviar, cheese, and a variety of crackers. Eve's excitement blossomed as she looked at Wallace and said, "Is all of this just for us?"

Wallace was impressed also. "Nothing but the best for my Honey."

Wallace poured both of them a glass of champagne while Eve spread caviar on several crackers. "I hadn't had caviar since I was a little girl when my father let me have a bite of a cookie that he had spread with caviar."

Wallace hesitated for a second, thinking to himself, "That's the first time I've ever heard Eve say anything about her father."

WC then handed a glass of champagne to Eve and said, "Let's make a toast!"

She replied, "That sounds like fun. Go ahead."

As they touched their glasses together, Wallace said, "Here's to six days and a wake-up of fun in the sun and beautiful nights." They both took a big drink of their champagne. Wallace placed his glass down and reached for another cracker spread with caviar.

As he picked up the biscuit, Eve said, "Now I want to make a toast."

Wallace placed the cookie back on the tray, picked up his champagne glass and looked at Eve.

"Here's to six days and a wake-up to fantastic sex and passionate moments."

Eve giggled, and Wallace's eyes opened wide, then he winked and said, "I'll drink to that!" He took a sip of his champagne and leaned over to give Eve a passionate kiss.

The driver opened the door, and as he was climbing into the driver's seat, he said, "Your bags are in the car, and everything is taken care of. It will be about a 58-minute drive to Copacabana Beach. Please relax and enjoy yourself." The driver then slowly merged into traffic headed for the Parkway that would see them to their hotel destination.

Wallace and Eve settled into the comfort of the soft leather seats. Wallace had his arm around Eve, and she was leaning on his shoulder. It wasn't long before the flight, and the two glasses of champagne made Eve fall fast asleep in the comfort and safety of WC's arm.

As Eve slept, her thoughts drifted back to the occasion when she was first introduced to caviar. Just a little girl, it was also the time she could remember being with her grandmother and grandfather. Her mother, grandmother, and grandfather were having some type of celebration. Eve's mother later told her that the party was because her granddad had gotten a promotion in the Navy. In her mind, she could see her mom, grandmother and granddad laughing and enjoying each other. Her grandfather called her his "little copilot." Eve remembered that he spread a small amount of what she thought was something like jelly onto a cracker. "Take a bite of this, my little copilot, and let me know if you like it." In her flashbacks, she couldn't remember if she liked the taste or not. The only thing that mattered was the fact that her daddy asked her to try it. "I like it, granddaddy. May I have another?" He would always give her anything she asked for. Eve snuggled in closer to Wallace as she fell deeper into her sleep, feeling safe and warm, just as she could remember being held by her grandfather.

Holding Eve, Wallace felt more relaxed and could feel the stress and anxiety of the pressures of being a project manager in the competitive information technology world of Sterling Business Systems slowly passing out of his system. His thoughts and his eyes were fixed on the scenery and this lady who was giving him some of the happiest moments that he could remember.

Wallace began to compare the traffic in the hustle and bustle of the Rio, which they were passing through, to the many places that he had been: Nairobi, Kenya, Jakarta, Indonesia, Cairo, Egypt, and even Bangkok, Thailand. They all seemed to have very similar traffic patterns. Taxicabs, small cars, big cars, limousines, carts being pulled by little men and the occasional donkey or some type of beast of burden pulling a wagon overloaded with vegetables, fruit, or some type of goods headed to the marketplace.

Eventually, WC's thought turned to his old roommate, Harry Paxton. He couldn't escape that sensation that he had seen Harry not once but twice, including the gentleman he saw moving away from the immigration station at the airport. But he knew that Harry Paxton was dead. However, he reminded himself, he was only going by what he was told. WC never saw a body or a death certificate, just a one paragraph obituary in the *Washington Post*. Wallace's mind drifted back to when he first met Harry Paxton.

At the time, Wallace was still on active duty, a first lieutenant assigned to Fort Bragg, North Carolina. He was the assistant team leader of a Special Forces A-Team. It was a training exercise. Four teams had been deployed by C-130 aircraft to the jungles of Panama. Wallace's Team Leader did not come on the training because he and his wife were having their first child. This made Wallace the guy in charge of the team for this task.

It was 0-dark thirty, and the operation was an E and E, escape and evasion. This was their sixth day in the jungle, and it had been raining, almost continuously for all six days that they had been in the bush. The training was scheduled to go for two more days. They had a total of eight days to reach their target destination.

Wallace's team reached the Chagres River just about the same time Harry's team did. Unknown to Wallace, Harry's team was less than 100 meters upstream from Wallace's position. It was close to midnight.

Even before WC reached the river, he could hear the rushing of the river water. From his map, he saw that the Gatun dam was very close, and he knew that water fed into the Chagres from the Gatun whenever they opened the locks of the dam.

This procedure, the opening, and closing of the locks would happen several times during the day. From the sound of the currents, Wallace was reasonably sure that the dam locks were probably open. This meant the currents in the river would be moving 3 to 4 times faster than when closed.

When Wallace's team cut through the last portion of the jungle before reaching the river, WC's thoughts were confirmed. Even in the dark, Wallace could see rapids moving swiftly downstream. The river was too wide to build a two-rope bridge, and it was too deep to forge across. The only option was to fabricate poncho rafts.

Wallace's team had been together for a little over a year, and this was not their first training exercise that Wallace was serving as the Team Leader. They knew and respected Wallace and were very confident in his leadership ability. Wallace broke the team down into three groups, four men per group, two strong swimmers with two weak swimmers. From other water exercises that the team had gone through, everyone knew that Wallace was the most powerful swimmer of the team. Wallace made the decision that his Raft would be the last one in the water. This made sense to everyone because, if anyone got into trouble in the water, Wallace would be in a position to help them out.

Wallace's thoughts were interrupted when Eve repositioned her head and body, placing her head on Wallace's lap. The limousine was at a dead stop, caught in the morning rush-hour traffic.

Wallace said to the driver, "You have traffic jams in rush-hour traffic just like we do back in the states."

The driver, looking at Wallace in his rearview mirror, replied, "I'm sorry, *señor,* about the traffic, but believe it or not, this is the quickest and most efficient way to the hotel. Once we get through this, we will be on the open road, and you will get a chance to see our beaches."

Wallace answered, "No problem. I'm in no hurry. I'm on vacation." Wallace's thoughts quickly went back to the situation that started his friendship with Harry Paxton.

Wallace was kneeling on the bank of the river with a flashlight that had a red lens on it checking the map. Looking across the river to get an orientation of what the terrain was like where he wanted his team to land, he could hear Master Sergeant Kupchak in the background motivating the team. "Make sure everything is tight and snug. We don't want any fuck-ups when we get in the middle of that damn river. You know how the lieutenant hates doing paperwork."

It didn't take the team long to put the poncho rafts together. "Lieutenant, we are ready for you to inspect the Rafts," Sergeant Kupchak said.

Wallace replied, "I'll be over in a second." Wallace took one more bearing and walked over to his team, checked each of the rafts, and then gathered the team together. "Ok, we will be shooting for that tree line over there." Wallace pointed across the river and paused for a moment, giving his men time to focus on the spot. "Sergeant Kupchak will take the first group, and Sergeant Mason you are the second group. I have the third with Williams, Morris, and Rivera. Watch everyone's six. Remember I hate paperwork, so get to the other side. Any questions?" Each of the men looked at each other and back to Wallace, making direct eye contact. "Ok, let's do this."

The team entered the water, and when Wallace got his raft into the water, he knew instantly that they would miss the mark that he had directed them to shoot for. The current was moving twice as fast as Wallace had estimated. Although they were making some headway, the current was still pushing him further downstream.

The team was almost halfway across when Wallace heard Sergeant Kupchak shout, "Debris! Look out for the debris!"

A second voice also shouted, "Debris!"

Just as the second voice shouted, someone yelled, "It's a log! Look out!" Wallace turned his head to the right, but it was not a log Wallace saw but the silhouette of a man's body rushing past him. Wallace turned loose of the raft and started swimming as hard as he could to catch-up to the body that was moving swiftly downstream. He reached out his hand as far as he could reach and grabbed some part of the man's clothing, probably his pants leg. Wallace then pulled the body close to his, put his arm across the man's chest, rolled over on his back and started doing the frog kick in the direction of the other side of the river. Wallace couldn't tell if the soldier that he was carrying was dead or knocked out. His only thought was to reach the other bank.

Wallace swam to the bank and pulled the soldier out of the river. He fell down to his knees from exhaustion, but he quickly sprang back up to check on the condition of the man he saved. He found that the soldier was not breathing and immediately began to give mouth-to-mouth resuscitation. The soldier's body shook and began to cough and spit out water from his lungs. Wallace then rolled the soldier over and began to pound on his back. After several minutes, the soldier started to breathe on his own. He looked up at Wallace and said, "Did you pull me out?"

Wallace stood up and helped the soldier to his feet. Wallace was relieved that the soldier seemed to be okay and also that it was not one of his men who had gotten dragged down the river. "Yeah, I'm the guy. What's your name, soldier?"

Having regained most of his composure, the soldier said, "Harry Paxton. Lieutenant Harry Paxton. What's your name?"

Wallace reached out his hand, and while they were shaking hands, Wallace said, "Lieutenant Wallace Barker, but you can call me WC. We need to get moving, so we can get back upstream and rendezvous with our teams."

Eve lifted her head off of Wallace's lap, saying, "Are we there yet?"

WC smiled and said, "Take a look at the beaches." The car was paralleling the beautiful beaches of Rio. The morning sun was sparkling off of the crystal Caribbean blue water.

"I feel like I just woke up in paradise," Eve said. Shortly after that, the limousine pulled up in front of the lobby of the Belmond Copacabana Palace.

After following the GPS directions and maneuvering through the congestion of Rio, Seventy-One stopped his van in front of a massive church in the south zone of the city. After parking, He pulled out a clipboard, got out of the truck, and walked over to a security guard who was standing close to the front of the church. He showed the guard the clipboard and the guard directed him to an office just inside the church. Once again Seventy-One showed the clipboard, and on it was a work order for repairs to be made on an inside section of the roof. The man took Seventy-One to an elevator and told him that the elevator would take him up to the fourth floor and from that point on he had to use the stairs. Seventy-One thanked the man and went back to the van, where he picked up the duffle bag and a ladder and put on a tool belt. He reentered the church and proceeded to the top section of the church.

Once Seventy-One reached the last floor of the cathedral, he used his ladder to carry his duffel bag into the top part of the tower.

Here Seventy-One opened the duffle bag and laid out the contents of the bag: a pad that had the itineraries of the two heads of security for Venezuela and Guyana, a set of high power binoculars, a GPS range finder, telescopic sniper scope, the three sections of a Barrett M82A1 sniper rifle, a small box of Raufoss NM140 MP, .50 caliber ammunition, a killer stand and a small acoustic HD player.

Seventy-One turned on the player, which issued simulated sounds of a person working in an attic. He then walked over to one of the ventilation louvers which were positioned on the side of the building that was facing the beaches and the Sofitel Hotel where both delegations were staying.

About 50 meters to the left and right of the canopy were two security guards on each side. Seventy-One looked at the pad. The men's itineraries called for both of the Security Chiefs to meet at that location to have drinks and get to know each other before the talks began. They were scheduled to meet on the beach in 20 minutes. He quickly assembled the sniper rifle and attached it to the stand, screwing it down tightly. He then took the rangefinder to accurately calculate the distance, then carefully repositioned the tripod and adjusted the scope to compensate for the wind velocity and curvature of the earth

The distance to his potential targets was a little over 2100 meters, within the range of the Berretta M82A1. Seventy-One's favorite sniper rifle was the McMillian Tac-50, but since he was traveling on a Canadian passport he didn't want to leave any loose ends that might be tied together, and the McMillian was made in Canada.

Wallace and Eve checked in and were escorted to their suite. The room was just as they had expected: a large sitting area, a separate bedroom with a king-size bed, a large sliding door to the balcony overlooking the beaches, and a large Jacuzzi and shower in the bathroom. They decided to change into their beachwear, have a light lunch, and head for the beach. To their joy, they found out that they could have their lunch brought to one of the cabanas on the beach.

It was a beautiful day, the sun bright but not burning, a fresh tropical breeze flowing across the beach. WC and Eve selected a cabana that was positioned such that they could see the coastline with the Sofitel Hotel to their left and the fabulous resort hotels populating this beautiful beach to their right.

Just after their lunch was brought to them, Wallace noticed the canopy just up the beach along with the security guards. "Look up there, Eve."

Eve leaned forward from her recliner and said, "Where?"

Wallace replied, pointing in the direction of the canopy, "Just look up the beach. Don't you see the security guards? A celebrity of some type must have reserved a special place on the beach. They shoot a lot of motion pictures here, you know, those James Bond-type of movies."

Eve lay back on the recliner. "Well, if they take any videos of us tonight, I can tell you our movie will be rated R."

Wallace thought to himself, this was a much different Eve than the computer programmer he met on the government project. This was the third statement she made revealing a different and stimulating side of her. "Okay then, let's go take a dip in the water so I can feel all over your body to see if you're in shape for filming tonight." They both laughed and took off running to the water. Eve was wearing a two piece red swimsuit befitting of her athletically built body, and her hair was pulled back and tied.

Meanwhile, Seventy-One checked and double checked his calculations. Once the two heads of security reached the canopy, he was to wait until they were in a position such that he could terminate them with just one shot. The ammunition that he was using could easily pass through one victim and into a second. Then he could follow up with two shots, one into each of the targets to finish them off. The silencers that he was using along with distant wood assured that no sound would be heard other than that of falling bodies.

This would be the first time that the two heads of security of both countries had met. They'd had many telephone calls and conference calls leading up to this day, however, and each knew that there was a lot on the line for the future of their respective countries. They had shared intelligence that there might be two outside groups that may try to do something to derail the meetings.

Many thought that allowing only two months to finalize the document was not enough time. But everyone knew that it was a third power pushing for everything to move as quickly as possible. There was no hard evidence, but the most likely group pushing for this meeting and for an agreement to be signed consisted of the oil companies and possibly the United States.

From all indications, the tests and analysis of the deposits lying off the coast of Essequibo and inland showed that there was potentially enough oil to supply the southern hemisphere with petroleum products for the next 100 years.

Seventy-One never questioned why his employers wanted his victims to be terminated. He had established his pricing many years ago, and he set the price high enough to assure that only governments or the extremely wealthy, including the occasional underworld figure, would have the means to pay his price. All of his clients paid on time, placing the money in the proper currency as instructed. Once he had experimented with changing the type of money he wanted to be paid in, but this resulted in his margins fluctuating too much, so he discarded that practice and only accepted payments in US dollars. He resolved that if the client were willing to pay his price, the client would have looked at every option possible before making a decision to reach out to him. Thus, Seventy-One considered himself the last resort, his customers having exhausted all other means to solve their problems.

Seventy-One alternated between the telescopic sight on his rifle and the binoculars to observe the activity underneath the canopy on the beach. It looked like the waiters were finishing up setting the table for lunch for the two chief security officers. It appeared that only one server would remain under the canopy to provide service. Seventy-One made the decision that if the waiter were still there when he made the shot, the waiter would have to go down also. He wanted everything to be wrapped up as tightly as possible when he left the scene.

The Chiefs of Security met beside the pool to provide a very brief photo session for several selected news organizations, but they did not take any questions from the reporters. After the photo session, they casually began to stroll toward the beach.

They were about the same height, the Minister from Venezuela a little taller at perhaps six-one. Both of the men appeared to be in good physical condition with muscular builds with little or no fat. They were almost to the canopy when they stopped one of the gentlemen pulled out his wallet, and it appeared that he was showing pictures of his family. They continued to walk then, finally reaching the canopy. They first walked over to the table that contained the assortment of food for them to consume, then to the table that held the alcoholic beverages along with mineral waters and juices.

Meanwhile, Seventy-One was following their every move through the sniper scope. His round was loaded into the chamber, and he was waiting for the right moment to pull the trigger.

The skillset distinctive of a real professional killer is detailed planning, before, during, and after the job; but above anything else, that skillset includes patience, especially to wait for the shot.

Both of the Chiefs of Security finally took their seats at the table. The man from Venezuela sat at the table with his back facing Seventy-One's gun sights. Across the table, sitting directly in front of him was the Chief of Security for Guyana. They could not have sat more correctly aligned for Seventy-One's shot.

Seventy-One took a deep breath and focused on his first target, then exhaling half of his breath, with hardly any motion or muscle movement, gently, lighter than the brush strokes of Leonardo da Vinci painting the Mona Lisa, squeezed off the first round.

With the exact same precision, body control and breathing, he then gently squeezed off the second and third shots.

The muzzle velocity for a round fired from the M821 is 853 meters per second. In less than 2.5 seconds the first round hit the Chief of Security of Venezuela, exiting his heart and entering the chest of the Chief of Security for Guyana.

The second shot penetrated the rear of the skull of the Chief of Security for Venezuela, passing through the upper cranium and penetrating directly into the eyes of the man from Guyana. The third shot was a head shot to the waiter, a small entry wound in the front of the skull, but when exiting the rear of the skull the bullet exploded the rear portion of the head, spraying bone fragments, flesh, and blood over the back canvas of the canopy.

Seventy-One took a few seconds to see that there was no movement from his three victims, then he checked quickly to see if the security guards on either side of the canopy hadn't noticed anything. They had not.

It took Seventy-One exactly seven minutes to repack his duffel bag and pick up the three spent shells. In another three minutes, he was down the ladder and in the elevator. When Seventy-One reached the first floor, he walked into the office and informed a clerk behind a desk, in perfect Portuguese, that Seventy-One was finished for today but would return no later than the end of the week, once Seventy-One obtained a panel he needed to complete his work. The clerk never looked up from her work, and while still looking at her computer screen said, "OK, we'll see you when you return."

Seventy-One re-strapped the ladder to the van and proceeded to a parking garage near the Carioca Subway Station. He parked the van in the lowest level, then took the ladders off of the top of the truck and placed them inside the vehicle. He pulled the magnetic signs on both sides of the van and placed them in the back of the vehicle. Seventy-One then got into the rear of the van and changed into very casual clothes, jeans with polo shirts and sandals. After thoroughly wiping everything down, he set an explosive to go off in 48 hours to give him more than enough time to get far away from the area.

Then he made his way to the subway station and eventually to the closest bus station, where he bought a ticket, paying cash, to Brasilia. It would take the bus several hours to reach Brasilia with all of the local stops that it must make along the way.

Once he reached the bus station in Brasilia, he took the local bus to a back alley hotel where a room had been reserved for him under an alias. Using a Brasilia ID card, he checked into the room. In the room, there was a suitcase and a change of clothing hanging in the closet. There was also an airline ticket along with a United Kingdom passport.

Seventy-One shaved, took a shower, and changed into the new clothing. He then checked out of the room and took a cab to the airport. At the airport, he caught a commercial flight, business class to New York. Once the plane was in the air, Seventy-One asked the flight attendant for a brandy and newspapers, two local and two international.

Chapter 9

Jacksonville, Florida Marriott Hotel restaurant.

"That area is still designated a hot spot simply because the fire is still too hot, and the fire investigators will not let anyone into the area until they can be sure that the fire is completely contained."

Agent Bo Brooks sat across the breakfast table from Agent Faye Cook-Little of the FBI's field office in Jacksonville, Florida. The agent that he had talked to on the flight back to Washington was right. Faye had been reassigned to the Jacksonville office with a promotion.

Bo was completely mesmerized by her. Faye was professional, there was no nonsense and total attention to detail, she seemed to have a great sense of humor. Mostly he noticed Faye appeared to have been keeping herself in excellent physical condition and was, even more, beautiful than when he first saw her in the Agency underground parking lot at the Hoover building.

They had been sitting down for breakfast going on 20 minutes, and Bo had not yet seen a sign she remembered him from Washington and their short elevator ride. He wanted to bring up their meeting, but he didn't think that this was the right time.

Agent Faye Cook-Little continued. "I've worked with the lead fire investigator on a couple of other bombings that happened out in the County. He's good, and the type of guy who leaves no stone unturned. That said, I don't think we will have access to the crime scene until possibly Wednesday. Do you think you can hang on that long?"

Bo wondered if she thought that he was looking at her breasts. "I plan to stay as long as needed. My goal is to collect information that we can put into our terrorist database to see if anything connects to any other threats in the world."

Faye's cell phone was constantly going off, signaling text message or alerts. She even had two calls come in but quickly tapped her mobile phone, sending the incoming calls to voice mail. She paid no attention to the distractions, and to Bo's surprise, appeared to be entirely concentrated on their conversation.

Bo continued. "The bottom line: what I do is just data collection and storage. On some of the cases, the anti-terrorist guys will ask me to do some searches, but that is very rare. In today's environment almost anything will trigger one of the guys from our section to be on the road."

Bo and Faye finished their breakfast. Since the Jacksonville FBI office was located in the Federal Building, the staff temporarily didn't have a place to work. The General Services Administration was finalizing temporary office arrangements, but that would not be completed until Wednesday. So for today, all agents were assigned to field duty.

"Well, I guess this is all we can discuss today. Do you have any questions?"

At first, Bo thought about asking her if she had any plans for dinner, or maybe asking her to recommend a good place for him to eat, but he put those thoughts away and decided to ask a work-related question.

"Yes, Agent Cook-Little, I do have a couple of questions." She was placing her notepad and reference material back into her briefcase and looked over at Bo.

"Do you have a casualty count, and also, when I parked at the hotel last night, I could smell gunpowder mixed in with the smoke so was there an armory located in any of the two government buildings?"

"I'll answer the second question first, which you probably already know the answer to. Yes, there was an armory. Our office is located in one of the buildings, and we have the standard allocation of weapons and ammunition. As far as the casualty count, the unofficial information that I have is that we are probably looking at between 50 to as many as 70 people who may have been killed by the fire and the subsequent explosions. Which is a relatively high body count, but it could have been more if the fire would have started earlier in the day or in particular on a weekday. I guess, in a sense, the city was relatively lucky in that the fire probably started somewhere between the hours of 11:00 PM and 3:00 AM."

Bo contemplated her response. "With it being a Saturday, why were so many people still in the building?"

"Splendid question, Agent Brooks. Both government buildings had two cleaning teams on that night consisting of approximately 10 people per team. So our count is 20 per building right there, and with one supervisor of the teams for each building, that brings our count up to 42. That's the majority of the people who were killed. The other bodies belong to the security guards and individuals who were on the street, mostly homeless, within ground zero of the blasts."

Bo paid for their breakfast, and they walked into the main lobby of the hotel.

"Well, Agent Brooks, thanks for the meal, and if I find out that we can get into the site earlier than Wednesday I'll give you a call. Meanwhile, I'm going to the range and try out that new Smith and Wesson .50-caliber automatic."

Faye smiled then strutted away, leaving Bo standing in front of the check-in counter of the hotel with his mouth open, speechless, as he watched her walk out of the lobby and into the parking lot.

"She remembered me. She remembered me." Bo went after her and caught up with her just before she reached her car. "Hey, wait a minute." Faye stopped and turned, facing Bo. She looked into his eyes and took two steps toward him.

"You remember me. You remembered that day we met in the parking garage of the Hoover building." She was still smiling and still looking into Bo's eyes as he went on. "You don't know what I've been doing to locate you."

"OK then, take me to dinner. I'll be by to pick you up at 7:00," Faye replied. "I have to go to my son's school and talk to his teacher about how he is doing in math. See you at 7:00, and I hope you like seafood." Faye didn't wait for an answer. She just started for her car. Bo stood in the parking lot watching her as she got into the car and drove away.

—

Langley, Virginia.

Roy Benning was going through personnel files after finishing a conference call with the Deputy Director of the Central Intelligent Agency, the DDCI, and a couple of his assistance.

The IT section had confirmed that both Karl and Nancy Mansfield's cards were swiped at 6:45 PM, the night of the fire. According to the log they were the only two CIA personnel in the office during the fire. All other staff had swiped out, the last person swiping out at 6:33 PM.

The network servers at the Jacksonville office went out around 3:00 AM the next morning and no signal at that time indicated that either of them had swiped out before the servers went offline. At this point, they could only assume the fire department and or the city had turned off all power going to all the buildings in that area as part of standard procedures.

Roy's primary task at this point was to realign his office in Jacksonville with personnel changes. He decided he was going to move Billy Mills up to Acting Chief of Branch for the Western Hemisphere Division, and after he got confirmation from the locals that Karl and Nancy got caught in the fire and were dead, Billy would move from Acting Chief to Chief.

Billy was the most senior agent, and he had been working in that office for the last five years and had an enormous amount of field experience throughout Central and South America. Elk was Chief of Branch 7 and handling the Fertile Ground operation, currently the largest operation in that division. Roy didn't want to move him from an operation of such significance. The other two choices that Roy could consider were Patrick Jefferson and Khristy Newborn, both outstanding Agents with excellent field experience. Roy made his decision to move Billy to the position.

Andrea, Roy's administrative assistant, walked up to his desk and laid a sticky note on his telephone. "The Directorate for Plans, Clandestine Service wants you to call her at 11:00." Andrea stood in front of the desk waiting for Roy to read the note.

Roy looked up. "Bring me the operational files on Fertile Ground."

Roy felt that most of his colleagues looked at his desk as a safe place to wait for retirement, but Fertile Ground was going to change all of that. He kept going over in his head that this is not going to be like the last time. The last time the South American desk had any amount of notoriety was the Bay of Pigs invasion that went disastrously wrong and costs his predecessors their jobs. They had left the Agency in disgrace. Roy Benning was determined that Fertile Ground would make amends for what had happened during the Bay of Pigs in planning and execution.

"I figured you would be asking for them. So here they are. You have about two hours before the call. You want me to hold all of your calls until then?"

"Yes, and I'm going to move Billy to Chief, but I haven't decided on anyone I can replace Nancy with."

"Roy, you really think that they both got caught in that terrible fire?"

Roy leaned back in his chair rubbing his eyes with both of his hands. He hadn't had much sleep, and his mind was working on overload trying to ensure that he didn't have any loose ends.

"Our security check-in log indicated that they were in the building and never checked out. So, unless there's a flaw in our security network… Unfortunately, they were both consumed by the fire."

Andrea thought for a second, then said, "So, are you ready for me to get Billy on the phone?"

"Yes, go ahead and get Billy on the phone so I can give him the word in his new position."

Billy Mills' entire career with the Agency has been with the Central and South America desk. He had been given several opportunities to run his own field operation, but he turned them all down so he could operate in the area of the world he had grown to love and admire. Billy and his wife, Cathy, were both from Arkansas. Cathy was an airline flight attendant, and they met while Billy was traveling for the Agency. Billy was flying to French Guiana with a stopover in Paramaribo, Suriname. They met in the hotel lobby while checking in. Billy tripped over Cathy's luggage, which she had set down behind Billy at the check-in counter. Cathy offered to buy Billy a drink, and after dinner that night they met in the hotel's lounge for drinks.

Roy heard Andrea's voice through his telephone intercom. "Billy is on the secure line."

"Thanks, Andrea."

Roy pushed a button on his phone. "Hello, Billy. I guess I don't need to ask how you are doing."

"Morning, Roy. The locals still haven't put out any information about casualties or missing people as of yet. But I guess it's still a little bit too early in the investigation to start releasing those types of details."

Looking down at the jacket cover of Billy Mills personnel file, Roy replied, "Billy, you're right, but I'm still proceeding on the factual information we have that both Nancy and Karl were still in the building during the fire." Roy paused for a moment. "I've been on the phone with the Director and the DDCI, and I recommend that the position should go to you. Both agreed with me. As a matter of fact, the DDCI said, and this is almost word for word, that if I had recommended anyone else, he would have been utterly shocked. That tells me that everyone at the Agency holds you in as high regard as I do for what you have done, not only for this agency but for our country as well. Congratulations, Billy, you are now the Acting Chief and in charge of operations in Central and South America."

Billy Mills hesitated for a moment. "Roy, what about the DDP. You didn't say that she had given her approval for me to take over as Chief."

"No, I didn't Billy. I'm scheduled to talk with the DDP at 11:00 this morning, but I'm certain she will not have any qualms about you being elevated to that position. After all, if the DCI and the DDC have no problem with it, and I'm the Chief of Operations down there, she can bitch all she wants to, but she will just have to get over it." Roy stood up and walked to his dashboard table.

Billy replied, "I see what you are saying Roy, and it makes perfect sense, but as we all know, the DDP has a memory like an elephant, and I had a run-in with her several years ago about operations in French Guiana. I know you know my record, and so you probably have seen the remarks that she put in my jacket..." Roy cut Billy off.

"Billy, let me stop you right there! Don't try to do my job. I'm the guy who will have to pay the price at the end of the day." Looking at his dashboard, he pulled up Fertile Ground.

"Now let's talk about Fertile Ground and where we stand."

"Roy, I'm in my car headed to the Flagler Center. Elk and all the guys are to meet me over there. I think Elk should be in on this discussion. I can tell you this. He met with Ranuel and the advance party last night and put them to bed in the trailer park over at Fleming Island."

Roy was now looking down at the screen-like desk and saw the checkmarks indicating completion of a phase of the operation.

"I think you're right, Billy. Let's set something up for 1900 tonight. One last thing. Have they completed sanitizing Karl's house?"

"Yes they have, and I'll forward the confirmation email to you after we finish talking."

"Okay then, Billy. Congratulations. I know you'll do an excellent job for me. Speak with you at 1900 Hours."

Roy still had about an hour and a half before he had to be on the conference call with the DDP. He was confident that he could handle any objections that she may have concerning his placing Billy in the position as Chief. But what was of a larger concern to Roy was keeping the lid on any possibilities that a CIA presence existed in Jacksonville.

Looking at a spreadsheet containing every operation being run out of the Jacksonville office, he knew that, if any of this were to get out, Jacksonville would no longer be the sleepy little Southern town on the bypass headed down to Disney World and Miami.

Billy Mills and Roy Benning completed their conversation. Billy looked at his watch and then at the digital clock on his car's dashboard, confirming he was only about 15 minutes from Flagler Center. He was crossing the Fuller Warren Bridge, and his thoughts shifted to who would be attending the meeting and how he was going to announce to everyone that he had taken the position of Chief, and the office would be reporting to him.

The Flagler Center was a secure, state-of-the-art off-site location away from the downtown Jacksonville office. The Center served a variety of purposes. It was a safe house for up to four people, each in their own apartment and living very comfortably for extended periods of time. It also provided for 100% secure communications to any location in the world. The Center was also totally fortified and could withstand almost any type of conventional bomb blast. Finally, it had a state-of-the-art computer system that was 100 percent secure.

Billy's thoughts moved to what he was going to say to the team. Everyone knew him, but the toughest thing would be telling the office staff about Karl, who had held the position for six years, and Nancy dying in the fire. Karl had led the team through some rough times, but he always ensured that everyone received the proper recognition for even the most insignificant role they had performed in an operation. Karl was a stickler for promoting a team-effort environment. In a nutshell, Karl was a professional who knew the value of attention to detail.

But what complicated the situation, even more, was that Billy had to break the news that two comrades had fallen. Nancy was also a valued member of the team, one could say even more so than Karl. As the Chief of Training Nancy knew everyone's skillset, how qualified they were to be in their current position as well as if they had the technical training qualifications to move to a higher position, which would mean a promotion. But just like Karl, Nancy was a professional and any weakness or strengths that she knew of concerning an agent were only discussed with the people who had a need to know.

Billy cursed to himself as he came to a stop at the traffic light two blocks away from the Flagler Center. Someone on the team would definitely ask him whether or not a star would be put on the wall at Langley for Karl and Nancy. He should have asked Roy before he finished the call, but it didn't cross his mind with so much on his plate, especially the kick-off of operation Fertile Ground.

While sitting at the light, he gave Roy a call but went into his voice mail. Billy left a message asking Roy to give him a call with the answer to his question.

Billy continued the final two blocks to the Flagler Center where he pulled out his cell phone and swiped it over the security eye at the gate so his barcode could be read. The buzzer sounded, and the security gate opened to let Billy into the parking lot of the center.

—

Copacabana Beach, Rio de Janeiro.

As Eve and Wallace gathered their things and left the beach, Wallace took a quick glance in the direction of the dignitaries who appeared to still be having lunch under the canopy. From Wallace's vantage point, it looked as if both the gentleman heads were down as they were talking to each other. The security guards appeared to be doing just what security guards are supposed to do, looking for outside threats while letting their clients have their privacy.

As Wallace and Eve were walking through the lobby of the hotel toward the elevators, Wallace said, "I need to stop at the hotel shop to pick up some batteries for my camera." While Wallace surged through the store for the batteries, Eve walked over to the newsstand. Wallace finished paying and joined Eve, who was holding a Brazilian newspaper in her hand, and it appeared to Wallace that she was reading it.

"Honey, I wasn't aware that you knew Spanish."

Eve was startled when WC walked up on her. She thought he was still at the counter paying for the batteries. She quickly gathered her composer and said, "Lover, if you only knew all the things that I am capable of doing and the things that I plan to do, it would probably scare you half to death." She then smiled and kissed Wallace on his lips.

As they were walking out of the hotel shop, Wallace had a puzzled look on his face as he tried to interpret her statement. They reached the elevators, and as Wallace pushed the button he said, "Well, do you speak Spanish or not?"

Eve looked up into his eyes and smiled. "What are you talking about? Let's just have fun and enjoy ourselves."

When Wallace and Eve got back to their room, WC ordered another bottle of champagne, a platter of fruit, squid, prawns, oysters, and scallops. They took a long shower together, alternating the cold and hot water. After the shower, they got into the Jacuzzi. Wallace was playing a playlist from his iPad, a collection of music featuring some of the jazz greats.

Feeling the effects of the long flight, the sunbathing and the swimming on the beach, Eve was falling asleep in the Jacuzzi. So Wallace picked her up in his arms, stepped out of the tub, and carried her to the king size bed. Wallace gently laid her down on the bed and began to dry her off. He then took out of his bag a bottle of massaging oil that he then heated in the microwave for a few second.

With Eve lying on her stomach with her body still damp from being in the tub, Wallace began to pour drops of heated massage oil onto her upper shoulders and down her back just to her waistline. Eve's body responded to the scent and the warm oil as Wallace's masculine hands firmly but so gently moved up and down her back, with each movement coming closer to the curvature of her hips and buttocks. She softly moaned with each second of pleasure, absorbing the tantalizing feeling of relaxation uncontrollably taking over her body.

Then, suddenly, with a movement quicker than a Japanese wrestler, Eve moved her body around and wrapped her voluptuous legs around Wallace's waist, and they engaged in romantic and passionate pleasure.

—

Doctor's Inlet, Fleming Island.

The bright Florida sunshine was up and sparkling over the waters of Doctor's Inlet. Ranuel and Krish sat on the side of their beds in the trailer that Elk had assigned them the night before. Both in their shorts, Ranuel was shirtless, and Krish had a T-shirt on. Neither man had slept very well. Still, in silence, Krish reached over to the chair where he had laid his trousers before going to bed and pulled out a cigar. He found out that he had misplaced his lighter and walked across the room to the dresser to pick up a pack of matches. He lit his cigar as he walked back to his bed and took his seat facing Ranuel. The silence in the room was broken by an outburst from Krish.

"I've said it a thousand times. You trust the Americanos too much. They have no commitment to what we are trying to do. You actually think that they believe in our cause, in what we are willing to die for. I had said it before we left home. The Americanos cannot be trusted. I do not understand what it will take for you to get it through your head."

Ranuel sat silently on the side of his bed looking down at his hands and feet. Frustrated, Krish stood up and began pacing the floor. A double knock was heard on the trailer's door. Both men looked toward the door, then quickly hastened to their beds. Ranuel pulled a Smith and Wesson 9 mm automatic from under his pillow and Krish a Browning 357 magnum revolver from his. Simultaneously, they pointed their weapons in the directions of the door. Finally, they heard the familiar voice of Elk.

"Will you guys let me in?" Ranuel walked to the door and opened it while Krish kept his gun aimed at the entrance. Elk walked in slowly, immediately sensing the tension in the room and that both men were holding firearms. "Hope boys slept well last night." He paused a second to get a response. After no response, Elk calmly walked to the only chair in the trailer and sat down. With their firearms in their hands, Ranuel and Krish perched back on the beds. With a nonchalant smile on his face, Elk carefully watched each of the men as they sat down and laid their guns beside them.

"I have some good news and some even better news. I won't ask you which you would like to hear first because everything is all good." Once again Elk waited for a response, and he also made eye contact with the man. Neither said anything.

"First, we are back on plan. We had a load of training ammunition flown into the Plantation last night so we will be able to start training immediately. This means that we can stick to our schedule and have you back into your country just as planned. The other good news is that as of 2:00 AM this morning all of your men have arrived. We have put them in trailers, and they are resting as we speak. From everything that they told us as they were coming in, everything went as planned." Elk paused for a moment to see if he was going to get any type of reaction from either man. Once again no response.

"I contacted our people and gave them a status report, and they should have already provided an update to your people." Now he was looking directly at Ranuel.

"So as I said, all the news is good news, and we can now start your training at the Plantation today just as the plan we negotiated dictates.

A smile appeared on Ranuel's face, but Krish just continued smoking his cigar without any appearance of appreciation for the news."

Ranuel noticed that Elk had a large envelope tucked under his arm. "Elk, what do you have in the envelope?" Elk pulled the envelope from under his arm and began to open it.

"We have six minivans in the restaurant's parking lot. Here are the keys to the vans. You have already agreed that the six drivers have and will carry the U.S. driver's license and IDs we provided. The vans are all gassed up. Remember, you will only fill up the vans at the Plantation. You cannot stop at any of the local gas stations or minimarts. Oh, just one more thing…"

Abruptly jumping into the conversation, Krish blurted out, "We will keep our part of the agreement as long as you Americanos keep your part. Understand, Elk. Everyone throughout Latin and Central America knows how the CIA left Brigade 2506 on the beaches of Cuba to be killed or to rot in Cuba's jail for the rest of their lives."

Ranuel stood up and got between Krish and Elk. "Calm yourself, Krish. Everything will be okay. I am sure that the Americans, especially the CIA, will live up to everything that they have agreed to. Isn't that correct, Elk?"

Slowly and calmly Elk stood up from his chair and walked toward the trailer door. He reached out his hand to open the door then turned back to Ranuel and Krish.

"We have contracted with the restaurant to feed you and your men. Breakfast will be from 0800 to 0830. At exactly 0845, ensure that all of your guys are in the vans so we can depart for the Plantation in time. After this morning, all meals will be at the Plantation." Elk left the trailer, closing the door behind him.

—

Jacksonville, Florida, Marriott Hotel Restaurant.

Bo Brooks lay on his bed staring up at the ceiling. He was rubbing his head and wishing that he had an Alka-Seltzer for a headache he was experiencing.

As if speaking to the room, he said out loud, "She didn't come, and not even a text message, email, or telephone call." He waited in the lobby of the hotel until about 7:45. Then he wandered into the lounge where they had a piano player. He started out with coffee. After the second cup of coffee he considered calling Faye, but as he thought about it, he didn't believe that it would be such a good idea. After he had finished his second cup, he asked for a beer, then a second. By this time the piano player was playing some type of jazz, Bo was on his third beer and added shooters.

Bo closed the lounge down because he remembered that the piano player came over, and they talked about football followed by fishing and finally golf.

Bo pulled himself up and sat up on the bed. He was now staring at the television.

"If she really wanted to go out with me, she would have taken the initiative and contacted me. Maybe something came up at the office, and she was assigned to a new case. That type of thing happens all of the time." Then he remembered that she had a son and that she said she was going to his school to check on him. That was a surprise because in the conversation he had on the plane trip back from Boston, the agent he was talking with didn't say anything about her being married. It had been several years since they met at the Hoover Building, he reminded himself, and so it's very possible that she got married somewhere in between the elevator ride and yesterday, had a child, and got divorced. "Maybe something happened to her son, and that is why she stood me up."

Bo got out of bed and walked over to his laptop. "I better check my emails and see if she sent me anything." After logging in, he found no messages from Faye. Disappointed, he decided to see if he could get a tee time at a local course and take it out on his golf balls.

"After last night, everything is strictly business. I'm here in Jacksonville to do a job, to gather evidence from the fire and blast, catalog the findings, and place the information into the database."

Bo had enough time before his tee-time to shower and have breakfast. As he was leaving the hotel's restaurant, he checked his cell phone to see if he had received any messages. There were none. After throwing his golf bag into the back seat of his rental, he punched in "Fleming Island Golf Club" on his GPS and starting listening to the lady for directions.

Chapter 10

Jacksonville Mayor's Office.

Bubba Webb was seated at his desk, his administrative assistant standing next to him and handing him documents, pointing to the location where his signature was required. "I wish we had a better way of taking care of some of this routine work. Why is it that every month I must sign the exact same documents from the previous month to keep the city running?"

Mildred, the Mayor's administrative assistant, held the same position for the last five mayors. Each year she would say that this was the last year, that she was going to retire once the current mayor completed his term, but year after year, mayor after mayor, she always came back. It was common knowledge at City Hall that the city of Jacksonville could not properly operate if Mildred retired.

"And each month you say the same thing. Bubba, and guess what, we will be back at your desk, you sitting there and me standing here handing you the same sheets of paper for you to sign so the city can keep running." A quick knock was heard at the door, and Jerry Clark rushed in.

"Sorry to disturb you, Bubba, but I have something that I think you'll like to hear." Jerry stopped in his tracks and looked at Mildred. "Oh, hello Mildred. How are you doing this morning?"

Mildred didn't look up or acknowledge that Jerry was there. She didn't like people just barging into the Mayor's office. Her rule of thumb was that, if you wanted to see the Mayor, you had to come to her and be placed on his calendar. This was the proper way of running the office and would ensure that the Mayor stayed on schedule.

Bubba, on the other hand, liked to think of his operation as a freewheeling open-door policy for normal operations. If you had a problem that called for the Mayor's input, he wanted all of his staff to feel comfortable coming to him for his guidance. Sure there were times during each day when Bubba would lock his door and tell Mildred that he did not want to be disturbed unless it was Debra or a city emergency, but mostly, he maintained precisely that open-door policy.

"Sure thing, Jerry. I'll be with you in a second." Still looking down, concentrating on the paperwork he was signing, he said, "Have a seat over there, and I'll be with you as soon as I finish signing these documents for Mildred."

Jerry walked over to the Mayor's staff meeting table and laid a folder on the table. Rather than sitting down, Jerry walked across the room to the window.

The Mayor's office was designed with wall to wall, floor to ceiling one-way windows that could be seen out of but not into. The view from the Mayor's office was breathtaking. Just about everything that makes Jacksonville the city that it is could be seen, including the Landing, transportation networks, the sporting complex, and the port authority. Jacksonville, the city in waiting to become a city, as Bubba liked to say.

Bubba signed the last document and handed it to Mildred. She placed it in the folder. "Thank you very much, Mr. Mayor. I'll leave you now so you and Mr. Clark can have your discussion." When she reached the door, Mildred turned and said, "Mr. Clark, when you have an opportunity, please review official office procedures, and, this time, read the document concerning the proper protocol to follow to discuss matters of importance with the mayor." After giving Jerry a look so sharp that, if it were a knife, would kill, she left the room and closed the door behind her.

Both grinning, Bubba and Jerry walked to the conference table. "I don't know what I would do without Mildred running this office. She is probably the most valuable person in all of City Hall," Bubba said.

As they were sitting down, Jerry said, "Bubba, I couldn't agree with you more. Mildred is a true professional and someone I really admire.

"Well said, Jerry. Now, what do you have to show me?" Jerry opened his folder and set several pieces of paper in front of Bubba side by side. Bubba picked up one of the papers, press releases. At first, Bubba looked a little puzzled. He then picked up the second press release, read it, and then the final one. Bubba looked at Jerry not saying anything. He then stood and walked to the window. After that, he walked to his desk. All the while Jerry sat at the table with a big smile on his face.

The Mayor opened a lower drawer of his desk and pulled out a folder, laid it on his desk, and walked back to the conference table with several news clippings in his hand that he had taken from the folder. He put the news clipping in front of Jerry. Jerry looked up at the Mayor. "I know what these are without even looking at them. These are the only three news reports that you got when you won the office of mayor."

Bubba slowly sat down at the table. "That's right, Jerry. Only two of the local papers carried the story and one in Orange Park. I made none of the State circulated newspapers, not in Atlanta or Mobile. Hell, I didn't even get in the Savanna, Georgia newspaper, and nationally the word Florida wasn't even mentioned, let alone Jacksonville." They both sat in silence.

"But, Mr. Mayor, this is a game changer. Here we have three press releases, one each from the top news agencies in the world: API, UPS, and hold onto your britches, Reuters. It doesn't get any better than this. Just read some of these articles."

Jerry read aloud: "The Mayor of Jacksonville, Florida has executed a crisis management program the way an emergency management program is supposed to run."

Bubba Webb leaned back in his chair. He stuck his chest out, absorbing the words Jerry was reading. The grin on his face grew larger and larger the more Jerry read.

"It was very clear to see that Mayor Webb is not a micromanager – he has selected and placed the right people in the proper job for an emergency to be handled correctly."

While Jerry continued reading, Bubba Webb got up from the table and took out a set of keys to unlock a cabinet. He then took out two large glasses and a bottle of 10-year-old Kentucky bourbon and brought it back to the table. Bubba poured two finger shots into each glass. He then pushed one of the glasses over to Jerry.

"Jerry, I think that this calls for a toast."

Jerry shook his head and stood up. "I agree, Bubba, and it's five-o'clock somewhere in the world."

They raised their glasses and Bubba Webb said, "Here's to our next stop, Washington DC, and my next job, President of the United States of America."

—

Langley, Virginia.

Roy Benning dialed the secure extension for the DDP.

"Hello, Roy. I see that it is probable that Karl and Nancy died in the fire. Do you have any more on that?"

Roy, staring at his phone, replied, "No other confirmation. The locals are still securing the site with the fire department taking the lead. We do have confirmation that the FBI field office and an agent from Washington are on site, but the fire department has not opened the location as of yet. Also, ATF has a presence there as well."

"I hope you had the foresight to have Karl's home sanitized."

"Yes, ma'am. All taken care of." There was no answer from the DDP. It seemed an eternity to Roy before she responded.

"I hope you haven't made a recommendation as to who will replace Karl. If you have any plans to recommend Billy Mills, forget it! I will not support a proposal like that, and I plan to make my position known to the Director when we meet this afternoon. I've worked with Mills before, and he is not up to the tasks that we need to be accomplished in that office, especially with operation Fertile Ground kicking off."

Roy Benning was sitting at his desk clenching his fists, holding back the response he really wanted to say.

"Roy, I want to know if we are on the same page with your recommendation for the replacement for Karl's Position."

Forcefully Roy responded, "No, Madam DDP, we are not on the same page!"

Before Roy could finish, the DDP broke in. "Actually, Roy, I was hoping that you would say something like that. That is foolish, you know. Since I've been in this position, I never thought that you had the balls to be in charge of a desk. Even when I reviewed your personnel jacket, you have always had assignments that did not require you to make the tough decisions. The Central and South America desk has been nothing but an embarrassment to the Agency as far back as the Bay of Pigs. Yes, that's right, the Bay of Pigs. That office couldn't even sell drugs so we could fund the Contra operations. Roy, your performance appraisal will be coming up in about six months. If you do not reconsider this decision, all of this will be noted in my recommendation on your next PA and be placed in your personnel jacket. I have a more important meeting to go to. This discussion has ended!"

Roy placed the telephone receiver back in its cradle and sat in silence. He was only able to replay the conversation with the DDA for a few seconds when he heard Andrea repeating his name.

"Roy. Roy. Roy, are you OK? Billy Mills has been trying to reach you. He left several messages. He wouldn't discuss what he needed even after I asked him."

Still staring at Billy Mills' personnel jacket lying on his desk, Roy reached for his telephone and punched in the preset button calling Billy. While the phone was ringing, Roy was saying over and over in his mind, "The Director and DDCIA have both concurred with my recommendation for Billy to have the job. The Director and DDCIA have both agreed to my proposal for Billy to have the job. The only thing that I need to do now is to be patient and let the oversight committee battle this out. His call went into Billy Mills' voicemail.

"Sorry, I missed your call, Billy. I have to go out to Quantico for a meeting so send me a text or email if it can't wait until you, Elk, and I talk this evening. Speak to you later."

━━

Jacksonville, Florida Mayor's Office.

Bubba Webb was reading minutes from the city council meeting when his private line rang. He picked up the phone and said, "Hello, Honey. Are you using that new cell I got for you?"

"No, Bubba. The damn thing has too many bells and whistles. I'm just beginning to get familiar with this one to the point I know what I can and can't do and no longer feel like I'm mentally challenged every time I make a call."

Bubba stood up from its desk and walked to the window. "But Debra, you asked me to get you the phone. So what I'm hearing is that I got you something you told me to get for you and you are not using it."

"Bubba Webb, we been married all this time and you still don't know me. So never mind. What I'm actually calling about is that I just left the hospital. Joe's condition hasn't changed. They have him in a medically-induced coma to ensure that his body has a better chance of accepting the antibiotics they have going into his system to fight any infections around his broken bones."

Bubba cut in. "How is Helen?"

"I guess as well as can be expected. I'm headed over to Helen's house now to get a change of clothes and some items for Helen. She hasn't left the hospital since the accident. Some of the girls from the book club are going to the hospital this afternoon to be with her. I will probably stay fairly late myself, so make sure you get something nourishing to eat and not a lot of that junk food you like. When do you think you will be able to go to the hospital?"

Bubba walked to his desk and brought up his calendar on his computer screen.

"I plan to stop by first thing in the morning before I come into the office. Today I'm pretty jammed up, and I still have to meet with the longshoremen, and you know how that goes. So I won't be able to squeeze it in today because I would like to stay a while. As you know, Jerry has been providing updates to the media."

"Okay then, I have about 10 more minutes before I get to their house if this traffic holds up so I should be back to the hospital in about an hour to an hour and a half. Love you."

"Love you too."

Debra Webb was moving through traffic and began to think about her book club and if all of the members were aware of Joe's condition. She sent out an email and text message on behalf of Eve Harding, the president of the club. Eve was vacationing in Rio de Janeiro, before leaving Eve said that she would not be checking any messages while on the trip. Debra thought to herself that it was probably best not to reach out to Eve while on vacation because it would probably spoil the whole trip. Knowing about the condition of Helen's husband and how critical his condition would only make Eve worry and be upset.

Eve and Helen were close friends. As a matter of fact, Eve was the one who asked Helen to join the club. She could remember the club meeting when Eve brought up inviting new members to join. For some reason, Gracie Black did not think it was such a good idea, but Eve was able to make her see the light.

She really didn't realize how close Eve and Helen had come together as friends until the time Helen shared with her that she, Joe, Eve and that guy she was dating, WC or something, met for dinner with Nancy and Karl Mansfield at the Crown Crab. It was shortly after that Helen told her about Eve bringing up the possibility of Nancy Mansfield joining the book club.

Debra punched in the security code at the gated community where Joe and Helen Singletary's home was located and proceeded to drive to their house.

Using her cell phone from the hospital, Helen turned off the security alarms at the house and unlocked the front door. All Debra had to do was to enter the house, go to the bedroom, and pick up the items that Helen had requested. ` Debra had been to their home over a million times. Joe and Helen were two of Debra and Bubba's oldest friends.

Debra picked up the items and placed them into a travel bag. While walking back to her car, her thoughts shifted to Bubba. Joe and Bubba's friendship went back a long time. Bubba hid his feelings behind humor and jokes, even suppressed feelings more when it was someone really close to him. I know Bubba was hurting inside, Debra knew, and probably fearful that he may lose his friend.

—

The Plantation.

The Plantation is located at Camp Blanding Joint Training Center, Florida. It is the primary military reservation and training base for the Florida National Guard, both the Florida Army National Guard and certain non-flying activities of the Florida Air National Guard. The installation is located in Clay County near the city of Starke. The site is 73,000 acres and includes Kingsley Lake. It also hosts other Reserve, Army National Guard, Air National Guard, and some Active Components training for the U.S. Armed Forces.

Additionally, the camp serves as a training center for many ROTC units, both Army, and Navy. Jacksonville University and

University of South Florida NROTC Battalions conduct their week-long orientations at the camp each August before the college semester starts.

The camp also hosts the Audie Murphy field training exercise where Army ROTC units from more than a dozen Florida, Georgia, and Puerto Rican universities gather to conduct a five-day field problem focusing on small-unit tactics, land navigation, and leadership development every April. Camp Blanding is the primary training site for most of the Florida National Guard's military units and the main combat arms brigade, the 53rd Infantry Brigade of the Florida Army National Guard. It is also home to the headquarters and support companies of the 3-20th Special Forces Group, the 211th Infantry Regiment, and the 2-111th Airfield Operations Battalion (AOB) Aviation Regiment.

In the 1970s, an expansion program began to upgrade post facilities, and in 1981, the Department of Defense redesignated Camp Blanding as a class "A" military installation. It was at that time when the Central Intelligence Agency began looking for another clandestine training location other than the Farm.

Ranuel rode in the lead van. Krish was following in the last van of a six-vehicle convoy. Each car carried 11 men, in all 66 totally committed people to creating a free and independent country of Essequibo. These men would be the trainers of hundreds of their dedicated countrymen and women to organize and possibly fight for the freedom of their newly formed country.

The agreement was that the Agency would provide a train-the-trainer program. The training would provide all the necessary classes and techniques necessary, not only to organize for what was ahead but also to establish the foundation required to govern and have a sound economic development model ready that would allow the country to grow.

The 66 men would be broken up into training groups for economic and financial development, a political organization for forming a democratic would be cross-trained so at any time, any one person would be ready and trained to take the place of another in a seamless transition.

The full training program would last nine weeks. Once their training was completed, the men would return to Essequibo and separate into four groups. Twenty Patriots would deploy to Northern

Essequibo, 22 in Central portion of the soon-to-be-formed country and 20 in the southern part.

The operation in the central part of the country would serve as the command and control center for the movement. The remaining four trainees would travel to the US and eventually meet with the MIE political leaders and key organizers of the movement in New York.

As Ranuel was taking in the scenery of the Florida countryside, his thoughts began to shift to Krish. He and Krish grew up together and were boyhood friends. Both their fathers were fishermen, and as boys, they would help their parents on the fishing boats. But just as boys always do, they would have fun diving and fishing whenever they could break away from the tedious work of helping with the catch.

Krish always seemed to have an instinct for when some type of danger was approaching. Many times they would go diving in areas that were plentiful in coral and the sponge fish that they could bring up and sell to tourists. Diving in these areas was extremely dangerous due to the high concentration of sharks. On more than one occasion when they were diving, Krish saved his life by alerting him to a great white shark that had identified him as a future meal.

Ranuel would ask Krish, "How did you know that the shark was behind us?"

Krish's answer was always the same. "I don't know; I just knew." There were other times when things were just about to happen, and Krish would warn everyone.

As they grew older, Ranuel did a year at the University, but Krish continued to help his father. It was just after Ranuel became involved in the movement that he ran into Krish at a café. They hadn't seen each other for several years, but it did not matter. The bond between them was still there.

Krish came to the next movement meeting and quickly became fully committed to the cause. What intrigued Krish most about the movement were the possibilities that their next country could become similar to one of the oil-rich countries like the UAE.

Within the MIE, Ranuel was identified as an organizer and natural leader, and so it was a no-brainer to everyone when he was selected to lead this initial training group. Once Ranuel received the word that he was to lead the team, his first choice to assist him was

Krish. He knew that Krish would be that one individual who would question everything to ensure everything was being done properly.

Just like Ranuel, Krish's parents were born in Essequibo; but even though Krish had never formally admitted to it, Ranuel found out that Krish had relatives from Cuba and, at least, one, possibly two, had taken part in the Bay of Pigs invasion. Although never confirmed, one had been killed on the beach, and the other was later captured and placed in prison for life without a trial. He eventually died in prison. The Chief of Staff of Brigade 2506 was Ramón J. Ferrer Mena. Krish's full name was Krish J. Ferrer Mena. Ranuel figured that this was the main reason that Krish would always reference how the CIA had abandoned the Cuban freedom fighters on the beaches of Cuba.

Krish had a knack for seeing things from a different perspective than most of the people on the team, and Ranuel was wondering whether or not his friend was sensing the beginning of a betrayal by the Americanos. At this phase of the operation, there was really nothing for them to gain. Essequibo had not yet become a country, but more importantly, until they became an independent nation recognized internationally and by the United Nations, they would not be able to declare full and lawful ownership to all of the country's natural resources.

Once this happened, it would mean that all that had been discovered, not only on land but also in the jurisdictional waters that belonged to the country, the country would become vulnerable to multi-national takeovers. So what could Krish be sensing that he was not?

The truck and the convoy came to a stop in the city of Starke, the last town before they reached the Plantation. While waiting for the traffic light to change, Ranuel noticed a fruit stand that was set up on the side of the highway. It was very similar to the ones in his own country. A couple of wooden boxes with two or three wooden planks laid across them served as a table. Baskets of a variety of fruits, including mango, pineapple, and watermelon, were almost the same as if he was home. The light changed, and the convoy continued.

Ranuel looked at his watch. It was just about time for him to check in with the group. When the movement started, the founders made several pledges, one being that reaching the objective of an independent new country should be the only reason that motivated anyone to join and follows them. They did not want one individual to become larger than the cause. The reason an individual would want to join would not be due to the leadership of one person.

The MIE was organized into groups, referred to as leadership groups and identified as Government, Recruitment, Defense, Education, and Health. Each group consisted of five leaders. All decisions and or courses of action must be voted on by the five leaders in the group. Majority rule would determine the course of action they would take. In the situation where two members would vote one way, and two would vote a different, the fifth voter would determine the course of action to be taken.

Once the country was formed and a constitution established, free and open elections would be held to elect a two party Parliament followed by presidential elections.

Just as before, Ranuel pulled out his prepaid cell phone and began to make his calls. The routine was the same. The phone rang three times and on the third ring, someone picked it up. If everything was proceeding according to plan, the person answering would immediately disconnect from the call. All total, there were 25 calls that he had to make. Each call represented, checking in with either a primary group or subgroup of the MIE. If everything went according to plan, the 25 calls would take approximately 25 to 27 minutes. Ranuel was on his twenty-third call with only two more to finish up this check in when he heard a voice say, "Divert to Bravo Plan. Call at 2300 Zulu."

Ranuel almost dropped the phone. He immediately ended the call, pulled the battery and sim card out of the phone and began to destroy the phone by pounding it on the dashboard of the truck. Then he threw it out the truck window onto the payment so that one of the following vehicles would run over it.

Something had happened. This was probably what Krish had been sensing and could not put his finger on, Ranuel decided. Ranuel looked at his watch as the convoy was passing through the first gate into the Plantation. He had about eight hours to purchase another prepaid phone and make the call to Group 23. Protocol dictated that the call must be done on time at the exact moment indicated in the message.

Ranuel's dilemma was that the convoy was just about to enter the training area of the Plantation. Because training would be all day that meant Ranuel could not purchase another prepaid cell phone until he left the Plantation later tonight.

What could have gone wrong? What could be about to happen? Ranuel began to go through worst-case scenarios. All 66 trainers were here at the
Plantation, just as the plan had called for. To his knowledge, all 66 trainees made the trip without any problems or incidents. Some entered the US through Miami, others New York. A few came in from Canada with others flying into LA and then traveled across the country by bus to Jacksonville.

There were 25 calls that the plan called for him to make to verify that everything was going as planned. Although the MIE consisted of four leadership groups plan checkpoints, depending on the mission, there could be as many as 50 unit inspections. The Defense Group made it a point to never give anyone any indication of how large or how small the MIE membership was. A small size could signal to the Americans that they were weak.

His van, which was the lead van, was slowly approaching the main checkpoint for entry into Camp Blanding. There were three cars ahead. The sign over the entrance to the camp read 100% Identification Check, Security Level 5, have your Photo ID ready."

Here they were, about to enter a US military installation, 66 foreign nationals attempting to enter a military base, all with illegal documentation. This would be the ideal time for the entire operation to be brought to an end.

The guards at the gate were fully armed. As the cars ahead of Ranuel were cleared and signaled to move ahead, Ranuel noticed that several other armed security police came out of an office building and started walking toward the check-in point at the gate. The van stopped at the security checkpoint. The guard stepped closer to the truck, then signaled to the other guards that were walking toward the checkpoint. Suddenly, a white pick-up truck with lights flashing pulled in front of the van. Guards jumped in, the directed the convoy to follow them. All the vehicles moved out following the pickup with its lights flashing.

All six vans followed the white pick-up truck that led them deeper into the installation. After about an hour and several miles, the pick-up pulled into an area that consisted of four building. One was vast like a gym, and the other three were about the size of a classroom or mobile trailer.

A man walked out of the building that looked like a gym and to the van that Ranuel was riding in and introduced himself. "Hello, my name is Mike Robinson. Have your men get out of their van and join me in the gym."

Ranuel entered the gym first. It was set up in an auditorium with a stage on one side of the room, rows of chairs at the far end, and a table set up with what appeared to be military camouflage clothing on it. They were directed to take seats. As they took their seats, writing pads with pens were passed out to each man.

Mike along with four other men walked up and took seats on the stage. Mike then stood with a microphone in his hand and tapped on the microphone to test to see if it was on.

"Good morning, my name is Mike Robinson, and I'm your senior trainer. Each of the gentlemen that you see on this stage will be training you in different stages of your program." Ranuel and Krish were seated on the last row. Ranuel had not had the opportunity to tell Krish about the call.

—

Jacksonville, Florida, Marriott Hotel.

Bo Brooks was standing in front of the mirror in his hotel room tying his tie. A sharp pain passed somewhere between his temple, shooting to the back of his head. His thoughts flashback to that last tequila shot that he had last night before coming upstairs and falling into bed with this clothes on and falling fast asleep.

He still had not gotten over being stood up by Faye. Conversation, body language, and that beautiful smile… Nothing added up that gave him any indication that he would be stood up for dinner that night. But Bo had made a conscious decision that it was not meant to be, and from this point on it would be purely business, strictly professional between them.

From his emails, he found out that the Jacksonville FBI office had temporarily relocated to Orange Park. The address was someplace off Blanding Boulevard not far from the naval airbase.

But there were no emails from Faye to indicate why she stood him up. Bo finished dressing and headed downstairs.

"Agent Brooks." Bo had just stepped off the elevator and was passing the front desk when he heard his name called. "Hello, Agent Bo Brooks. My name is Agent Harris, and I'm with the office here in Jacksonville. I came over to escort you to the crime scene."

Bo stood there, not making eye contact with Agent Harris because he was looking for any signs of Faye being present. He didn't see her, and for a second, he thought about asking if she was supposed to meet them at the crime scene just to find out why she wasn't there.

"Oh, good morning, Agent Harris. Glad to meet you. Have you had breakfast? If you haven't, I think we still have enough time to grab a bite to eat."

Harris reached out his hand, and while shaking Bo's said, "Thanks very much, Agent Brooks, but we don't have a lot of time. We're having a meeting with several different groups. I'll explain it in the car while we drive." Agent Harris then led Bo out of the lobby of the hotel and into the parking lot where his vehicle was waiting.

As they pulled out of the Marriott parking lot, Harris began to bring Agent Brooks up to date on the investigations concerning the Federal Building and the Federal Reserve Bank fire. "We are headed to the Federal Reserve Bank. I guess I should say the site where the Federal Reserve Bank once stood because it is nothing more than rubble now. Once we reach the bank, we will be meeting with agents from the ATF, Department of Homeland Security, investigators from the Jacksonville Fire and Rescue Department, the Jacksonville Police Department, US Marshals, and, of course, us. The big issue is jurisdiction. At first, everyone thought that authority rested with the local authorities, in particular, the Jacksonville Fire and Rescue Department followed by the Jacksonville Police Department. But all of this turned upside down because the two most important buildings that were damaged belong to the federal government. Somewhere within the last 12 hours, all the other letter groups have been bringing their people into Jacksonville to help with the case." Bo sat in silence while Agent Harris continued with the update.

From the Marriot, it was about a 25 to 30-minute drive to the Federal Reserve Bank. Bo continued to listen carefully to everything that Agent Harris was saying. When Harris turned onto I95, Bo asked his first question. "Have the forensics people found where the fire started?" Agent Harris turned his head and took a quick look at Bo.

"Officially they have not said, but I have an inside source who works with the fire department, and he told me that they believe it started at a gas meter line in the underground parking garage of the Federal Building."

Agent Bo Brooks thought to himself that, wherever the start point of the fire, that is where he needed to take the maximum amount of his pictures. For the remaining portion of the drive to the bank, Bo pulled out a notepad and began making notes.

Agent Harris pulled up to a police boundary line of yellow tape. A city police officer signaled for the car to stop. As the police officer was walking toward the car, Agent Harris and Agent Brooks pulled out their badges. They showed them to the police officer as he was walking toward their vehicle. The officer signaled to another officer who was standing closer to the tape to raise it, then told Agent Harris to proceed.

As Agent Harris's car got closer to the bank, Agents Harris and Brooks saw a group of about 20 people walking away from the rubble of the Federal Reserve Bank headed toward the Federal Building. Agent Harris pulled the car to the curb and parked. "That's the group we should be with," Bo replied, "I think you're right." Both men got out of the car and jogged to catch up with the group.

The group was being led by a woman with a vest that read FBI on the back. Standing beside her was a man with a vest that read JFRD Fire Investigator. Bo whispered to Agent Harris, "Who is the agent talking?"

"Oh, that's Agent Albright. She is forensics, and the guy next to her is Terry Jackson from the Jacksonville Fire and Rescue Department. He is the fire investigator and probably one of the best in the business." The group came to a stop in what was the underground entrance to the Federal Building Garage. Agent Bo Brook started taking pictures of the destruction. They were waiting for some hard hats to be brought over before going down into what remained of the underground garage.

"OK, we will have to be very careful going down to where we have identified the spot where we believe the fire was initiated."

Hard hats were issued to everyone in the party, and they began that treacherous climb down into the garage area of the Federal Building. Maneuvering over and under twisted steel, cement bowlers and glass, it was a lot harder than most of the people in the party thought it would be. Taking over 28 minutes to reach the spot.

"As you can see, this is what remains of an automobile that evidently parked directly in front of the gas meter on the wall. You can see the remains of the gas meter and where the inlet pipes were attached. We won't be able to remove the car until the corps of engineers comes in and gets this area better stabilize." Agent Albright pointed her flashlight in several different directions, and then a question was asked.

"Agent Albright, as far as you know, were there any other automobiles in this location?"

Before Albright could respond to the question, Terry Jackson, the fire investigator from the Jacksonville Fire and Rescue Department began to answer the questions. "JPD was able to get to the building's backup server and access the security file. According to the card-swapper, there was only one car remaining in the garage at the time of the fire. The building security guards and cleaning team all park their vehicles on the street. Please hold your remaining questions until we get back on the street. This area is still not safe, so let's cautiously make our way back to the top."

Climbing out of the garage seemed to be more hazardous than going in. One ATF agent slipped and twisted his ankle. Fortunately, he was still able to climb out of the garage under his own power.

As the last person in the investigative party climbed up the ladder, suddenly the ground started to rumble. A voice shouted out. "Get the hell out of here! Run!"

Everyone ran in different directions. Agent Harris and Bo Brooks ran back in the direction they had left the car. The sound of rumbling grew louder and louder. The foundation of the Federal Building was collapsing, and they could see the asphalt splitting across the parking lot and along the street. It was turning into a foot race, every one of the agents running as fast they could to reach safety.

Agent Harris got to the car first, jumped into the driver seat and began searching for his keys. Bo Brooks was not far behind, but when he reached for the door handle, he found it locked. While pounding on the car door window, Agent Brooks looked in the direction of the Federal Building and could clearly see the remaining portions of the building caving into the ground just at the spot where they had descended into the garage. The cave-in was spreading into a sinkhole, pulling in other burned out adjacent structures.

Agent Harris finally found his keys, started the car and opened the passenger door. Brooks climbed in, and with rubber burning, Harris did a quick U-turn and headed for the yellow police tape boundary. Appropriately driving past the yellow tape was like passing into a safety zone. The ground collapsing gave rise to a massive wall of dust and debris.

"Harris, I don't know if it's just me, but I would say that we were very lucky to get out of that underground garage when we did. If one more question would have been asked, our names would probably be mentioned on the nightly news." Agent Harris pulled the car to the curb and stopped. He got out and walked to the trunk of the car and pulled out a jacket. He frantically worked his way into the pockets of the jacket and pulled out a partially empty package of cigarettes along with a lighter. Agent Harris lit the cigarette, then sat on the curb shaking like a leaf. Agent Brooks got out of the car, walked over to a nearby tree, unzipped his trousers, and relieved himself. He then joined Agent Harris sitting on the curb. Agent Harris's composure was coming back.

"I stopped smoking a couple of weeks ago, but I keep one in this jacket in the trunk of the car just in case I run into a situation like this." Harris took one last draw on the cigarette, then threw it to the ground and rubbed it out. "You been in any gun battles, Agent Brooks?"

Agent Brooks was still sitting on the curb. He looked up at Harris. "I've never had to discharge my weapon since I've been in the Agency. However, I did get caught up in a gun battle at the Serena Hotel in Kabul Afghanistan."

Both Harris and Brooks were silent for a moment. Harris spoke first. "How in the hell did you get into that situation?" Bo stood up.

"I was sent in to verify some information we had about a new type of explosive triggering device." The men just stood there looking back at the destruction left behind after the collapse of the remaining structure of the Federal Building. By this time, emergency units and the fire department were back on the scene.

"Well, I guess there is nothing more we can do here. I'll take you back to your hotel."

"I think you're right, Harris. Let's go."

—

Jacksonville, Florida Fire Station 21.

Jerry Clark parked his car in the parking lot of Fire Station 21 on North Julia Street. Before stepping out of his car, he checked his Blackberry for any messages that might have come in while he was driving from the Mayor's office. There were no new emails, which was good because he wanted to concentrate on what was foremost on the Mayor's agenda.

This afternoon Jerry had scheduled a press conference for the Mayor, the objective to update the public on the status of the investigation surrounding the Federal Building and the Federal Reserve Bank fire. Jerry got out of the car and walked to the building. He was here to meet with Terry Jackson, the city fire investigator assigned to investigate the fire.

This was Jerry's first time coming to Fire Station 21. The building served as a fire station but also housed several different offices of the Jacksonville Fire and Rescue Department. One of these departments was Fire Investigation.

Jerry walked in and stood on one side of a counter that was about waist-high. On the other behind the counter were four people, all sitting at desks, all wearing fire department uniforms and working on their desktops. No one looked up to acknowledge that he was there, so Jerry figured that there must be another person whose job was to meet walk-in visitors.

Finally, Jerry said, "Good morning, I'm Jerry Clark from the Mayor's office, and I'm here to speak with Terry Jackson."

One young man who was sitting at the desk that was the farthest away from the counter shouted out, "She stepped out for a minute but should be back shortly. Have a seat, and she will be with you as soon as she returns."

Jerry saw five chairs on the opposite side of the room. He walked over, pulled out his Blackberry, and took a seat.

"Hello, may I help you?" Jerry was finishing an email on his Blackberry when he heard the voice. Since he was the only person in the waiting area, he was sure that she was talking to him. While walking to the counter, Jerry was putting his Blackberry back into his pocket but became transfixed by the young lady standing on the other side of the desk. Jerry had heard the expression Southern belle, and he knew whoever created that expression had this beauty in mind. When Jerry was about two feet from the counter, her smile opened up, and it was like the room became brighter.

"I'm sorry I had to keep you waiting. How can I help you?"

With his best smile on his face, Jerry attempted, to say something but nothing came out. He took a deep breath, and still smiling, he said, "You really took my breath away. My name is Jerry, Jerry Clark, and who may you be?"

With a twinkle in her eye, she replied, "Marybeth. Marybeth Ferguson." Jerry took two steps back still smiling.

"Did you say Ferguson is your last name?"

"Yes, my father is Paul Ferguson, Fire Chief of Jacksonville."

Jerry thought to himself that this could get complicated if he continued to pursue the course of action he was on. "I'm from the Mayor's office, and I'm here to see Terry Jackson." From the tone of Jerry's voice, Marybeth knew that the mood had changed to all business.

"Terry is on the fourth floor. Sign in and you can go straight up." Marybeth laid a sign-in book on the table and handed Jerry a pen. He filled out the essential information on the book, then pushed it back to Marybeth. She looked at the paper and said, "Follow me, and I'll show you which elevator to take."

As Marybeth and Jerry were walking to the elevators, she asked, "Did you hear what happened to Terry and those other investigators at the fire scene this morning? From what I was told the ground and all of the foundation of the Federal Building just collapsed around them. That had to be a very scary situation." They reached the elevators and Marybeth pushed the button and turned to face Jerry. "Mr. Clark, do you have a business card?"

Jerry Clark took out his wallet, pulled out one of his business cards and was just about to hand it over to Marybeth as he asked, "Why do you need my card?"

She was looking up into Jerry's face, and they made eye contact. "Well, I need something to write my telephone number on, and you can't give me a call unless you have my number, right?"

Jerry handed her the card, and she wrote her telephone number on the back while giving Jerry one of her best smiles. She gave the card back to him as he stepped into the elevator. "Terry's office is the last office on the left down the hall. Call me." Jerry looked at the back of his business card as the elevator doors closed.

When Jerry reached the last office on the left, the door was open. Jerry did a quick knock on the door and walked into the room. He saw a middle aged man sitting behind a desk reading the screen on his computer. The man looked away from his monitor and said. "What can I do for you?"

"Hello, my name is Jerry Clark, and I'm from the Mayor's office." The gentleman stood up from his desk. He had on navy blue trousers, a white shirt with a name tag that read Jackson and gold lieutenant's bars on the epaulets of his shirt. The shirt was dirty with the smell of smoke and fuel.

"Mr. Clark I've been expecting you. Someone called yesterday. Looks like you could use a cup of coffee?"

Jerry and Terry Jackson left his office and walked down the hall to a coffee station. "Go ahead and help yourself. We drink a lot of that stuff around here."

Terry Jackson had a reputation for being one of the top fire investigators in the state of Florida. In fact, it was very common for Terry to receive invitations from all over the United States to come to training conferences and speak on the subject. Almost every wall in his office was covered with plaques and certificates of achievement. They sat down next to each other in Terry's office.

"I guess Mayor Webb wants to know exactly where the city stands in regards to the fire." Sipping on his cup of coffee, Jerry just shook his head. "With all my technical and professional instinct, I would bet my entire paycheck against a donut that the fire was started by some type of combustion originating from an automobile. The combustion was so powerful that it ruptured the gas line and set off a chain reaction throughout the gas piping system. The fact is, however, until we can fully analyze that car, all of this is only a theory. The larger problem is that it will probably be months before the area will be safe enough to attempt to pull the car out. By that time, the integrity of what evidence is left will be useless." Terry stood up and while walking back to his desk. "The short answer is that we don't have *jack shit* until we can check that car out."

Chapter 11

Shands Hospital, Jacksonville, Florida.

Debra Webb parked in the visitor's parking lot grabbed the bag with Helen's change of clothes and headed to the hospital. There were two mobile news vans with a scattering of reporters and media people hanging around the entrance. As Debra approached the main entrance, she was recognized, and the reporters moved in to attempt to obtain anything for a story.

Before the first mic came within speaking distance, Debra was yelling out, "No comment! No comment! All information will come from Jerry Clark of the Mayor's office!"

Two police officers approached the developing crowd. They formed a path so Debra could pass through and enter the hospital. As luck would have it, an elevator was waiting, so Debra rushed in and hit the button on the fifth floor where Joe Singletary's room was located. As she exited the elevator, she could see Helen and Gracie Black sitting in the waiting area, Gracie holding Helen's hands.

Gracie saw Debra first. "Hi, Debra."

"Hi, Gracie. I am so glad you could come over." Debra embraced Helen and handed her the bag. She then turned and hugged Gracie. Debra turned back to Helen. "Helen, are you going to change in Joe's room?"

"Yes, I'll wash up a little and try to do something to my face. I must look like a mess. I would hate for Joe to wake up and see me like this."

Helen left Debra and Gracie in the waiting room and walked the few feet to the room where her husband was resting in a medically induced coma.

Shands Hospital is an 852-bed hospital that has 142 intensive care beds. Shands is a Level 1 trauma center and a leading organ-transplant hospital. Joe Singletary was placed in a private room on 24-hour monitoring with the doctor on call if anything changed in his condition.

"Well, how are you holding up, Mrs. Webb?" Debra sat down, and Gracie Black continued to stand.

"I'm all right, Gracie, really I am. It's Bubba I'm worried about. Joe is one of Bubba's oldest friends. They mean everything to each other." Gracie sat down next to Debra. For several moments, they didn't speak.

"I was thinking, Debra. Has Helen had anything to eat? I mean real food other than what's in this hospital?"

Debra quickly answered, "Forget it, Gracie! If you are about to say let's take Helen someplace where she can get something to eat, you must have some type of death wish. She plans to stay here for as long as it takes to find out that Joe is out of danger."

"Yes, I think you're right, Debra. I don't know what I was thinking. I would do the same thing, and I know you would do the same thing if Bubba were in there. Let's get some coffee."

Gracie Black and Debra Webb started for the elevator so they could go down to the hospital cafeteria. "Debra, have you talked to Nancy Mansfield?" Debra took a few moments to reply.

"You know, Gracie, I've left a couple of messages on her cell phone and, at least, one message on her home phone, but she hasn't called me back. I really had not thought about it much until you brought it up."

"For the life of me, Debra, I really don't know why Eve ever asked Nancy to join the book club. She never reads the books, and she always comes across like she has so much to do, and she's so important. She only has that little old civil service job, but one would think she was some type of special James Bond type secret agent." They purchased two cups of coffee and a cup of tea. The tea was for Helen.

"But, nevertheless, Gracie, she still hasn't called me back, and one of the messages I left was about Helen and Joe being in the accident." Debra and Gracie were back on the elevator headed for the fifth floor.

"By the way, were you able to reach Eve? I guess she is having the time of her life in Rio. I've never been to Rio, but I hear the beaches are fantastic, and the nightlife is 24-7. You know she flew down there with that guy from Maryland that she's been dating. I can't remember his name, some type of computer geek."

"His name is Wallace Barker, and yes I know that they were flying down together, but Eve didn't tell me. Nancy did. We ran into each other at the mall and had lunch together, and that is when it came up. Nancy and Eve are a lot closer than you would think."

The elevator reached the fifth floor, and as Gracie and Debra were exiting the elevator, they immediately saw that a lot of activity was taking place in the area of Joe's room. Walking down the hall, they slowly picked up their pace when they realized that people were frantically running in and out of Joe's room. As they got closer, two nurses were almost carrying Helen out of the room and back to the waiting area. They assisted in setting her as comfortable as possible. Helen was crying uncontrollably. Debra reached out to try to stop one of the nurses, but the nurse ran back into Joe's room. Gracie walked over to Helen, sat down beside her, and put her arms around her. Debra looked at Helen crying and then looked back in the direction of Joe's room, then back at Helen. Then suddenly Debra ran into Joe's room.

As Debra moved into the room, one of the physician's assistants stopped her and said, "Ma'am, you have to leave so we can do our job. Someone escort this lady out of the room and back into the waiting room."

A nurse dressed in surgical scrubs grabbed Debra's arm and said, "Please come with me." She escorted Debra out of the room. As the door closed behind them, Debra said, "I'm the Mayor's wife, and you must tell me what has happened to Joe?"

Once Debra and the nurse were out of Joe's Singletary room, the nurse said, "Mr. Singletary came out of his coma and was hemorrhaging. He has some very severe internal bleeding, and we are about to operate to try to locate the origination point of the bleeding to bring it under control. So please go back to the waiting room and continue to comfort Mrs. Singletary. It would be greatly appreciated. Once the doctor stops the bleeding, she can stabilize the patient. She will then be out to talk to the patient's wife."

—

Rio de Janeiro, Brazil.

It was the somewhat public knowledge that the Chiefs of States for Venezuela and Guyana would meet in Brasilia in two weeks. What was one of the best kept secrets, however, was the signing of the agreement concerning the disputed land of Essequibo.

124

Venezuela's oil is responsible for 95 percent of the country's total export revenue, contributes about half of the central government's income, and is responsible for about a third of the country's gross domestic product. In short, Venezuela's dominant oil industry, helmed by the state-run petroleum company, is a hungry monster that must be fed. Even a share of 50% of the projected oil production of Essequibo would go a long way to feeding that oil monster.

In Guyana, the economy is based on agriculture and mining, notably of gold and bauxite, and the principal cash crops are sugar and rice. The signing of the agreement would bring more diversity to the economy and ensure a foundation for the creation of jobs for future generations.

When Venezuela and Guyana were searching for a location to have the historic agreement signing, they wanted a site that would be symbolic but sends a statement to the global community of the economic power developing in Central and South America.

Jointly, the ambassadors from Venezuela and Guyana reached out to the Brazilian government and presented a proposal for Brazil to host the signing of the agreement. The primary selling point was that Brazil, Venezuela, and Guyana share a bond in that their countries surround Mount Roraima, considered to be the oldest geological formation was known, some elements dating back two billion years.

However, what sealed the deal was that the agreement between Venezuela and Guyana signed in the capital of Brazil would symbolize the economic coalition of the three most powerful countries in South America, a moment of such significance that every country in the world would jump to provide their highest dignitaries to witness the signing.

Venezuela's oil reserves already exceeded that of Saudi Arabia, and with this agreement, Guyana would make Venezuela, even more, powerful as a world petroleum giant. Guyana would not be far behind, and based on all projections, the country would be one of the top ten oil-rich countries in the world. Brazil would end up having two energy-rich super powers as allies, giving Brazil the subtle but powerful leverage to expand its cotton exports.

The signing of the agreement between Venezuela and Guyana over the disputed region of Essequibo would be quickly followed by economic and trade agreements, national defense agreements, and a mutual coalition agreement on health, education, and the environment between the three countries.

The ambassadors laid out their proposal very carefully, tactically, and strategically; and the government of Brazil accepted the proposal and agreed to the signing being held in the capital of Brasilia.

The security and bodyguards were over 100 meters on either side of the beach from the location where the two Chiefs of Security were having their working lunch. There was also a Brazilin Navy Patrol boat moving up and down the beach waving off any boats that may come within range of the meeting location. The third layer of security was a military helicopter flying as eyes in the sky over the meeting site.

Although the luncheon meeting had lasted well into the early afternoon, it was not unusual for this type of high-level first get-together to last a long time. The head chef of the Sofitel hotel had laid out a buffet of delicacies that would satisfy almost any taste and setting. To complement the food, the highest quality of the vintage wine, spirits, and other beverages were also placed under the gazebo for the ambassadors' pleasure.

The head chef looked at his watch and directed one of his maître D's to go to the beach to ensure that everything was in order and to see if there was any need for additional services.

Chapter 12

The United Kingdom, Scotland.

"Welcome back, sir. I trust that you had a most rewarding and pleasant journey. I'll take your bags, sir. Will you require a bite to eat?"

"No, but thank you very much, Higgins."

Higgins, Seventy-One's most trusted valet, greeted him as he pulled his vintage Austin Healey to a stop in front of his estate.

"Just a brandy will do very nicely before I retire, Higgins." Seventy-One handed the keys to the car to a second gentleman who was assisting Higgins.

"MacFits, have the timing on the Healey checked tomorrow please."

MacFits quickly and in a military manner replied, "Certainly, sir. First thing in the morning, I will, sir. Yes, I will."

As Seventy-One was walking up the steps, he looked over his shoulder. "Oh, by the way, MacFits. How are the wife and that new son?" MacFits was just about to drive the car away to the garage. He quickly stopped the car and got out and stood at attention.

"Thank you for asking, sir! The Mrs. is during wonderfully, and the newborn, my son that is, is doing as fine as ever. I'll be sure to tell the Mrs. that you spoke of her."

Seventy-One smiled at MacFits, taking in the proudness of a new father.

"Very well then, Mr. MacFits, you may carry on." MacFits hopped back into the Austin Healey and drove the car off to the estate's garage.

"Higgins, do I have much mail?"

"Just a bit, sir. Everything is in your study, just as you wish."

"It is always good to come home. How has the weather been?"

"A little warmer than last season, sir."

Seventy-One entered his study as Higgins took his bags into his bedroom.

"Good night, Higgins. That will be all."

"Good night, sir. Sleep well."

Seventy-One entered his study, walked over to his stereo system, and turned on his music. The brandy bottle and snifter were in position on his desk just as Higgins had said. Seventy-One poured the 10-year-old brandy into his glass and sat down to go through his mail. Seeing nothing unusual or urgent in his mail, Seventy-One turned his attention to his computer. He logged in using an encrypted browser system and began to check his email. Seventy-One had a total of one 171 email accounts, each account representing a different contract. He also had a total of five bank accounts associated with his work. He was mainly checking on his Cayman Island account ending in 1451. A casual smile came across his face when he saw that the payment for his last contract had been deposited by the agreed upon terms. "I must have Higgins remind me tomorrow to set up an appointment to meet with my banker and my solicitor," he said out loud. Seventy-One took a sip of his brandy and casually sat back in his chair.

"I love doing business with these guys. They always know what they want, money is never a problem, and they don't dillydally about the details and pay on time."

Seventy-One moved his mouse to another folder on his computer and clicked to open it. The folder title was "operational plans." His thoughts were still lingering on his last contract and how efficiently it had turned out, but he then began to ponder working with some of his most frustrating customers. One such disappointing deal was when he worked for the Institute for Intelligence and Special Operations, more commonly referred to as the Mossad.

Most of the contracts that Seventy-One received were referred to as far-reach contracts, which means the customer has a target located in an area, specifically a country where they have little to no present operational structure or field agents working. They want a target to be neutralized with extreme prejudice to send a particular message. On the individual contract he was remembering, the Mossad had a presence in the country, but they knew that if they utilized their own resources, their field agents would be exposed. The Mossad contracted with Seventy-One to execute the job.

From the beginning, there was one complication after another. Seventy-One's skill set requited that he work alone, but the Mossad handler in the field wanted to run the operation like they were developing a software program with an operational kickoff meeting followed by in-progress review meetings coupled with tons of text messages, conference calls, and emails.

Still looking at his computer monitor, Seventy-One took another sip of brandy, but his thoughts were still consumed by his experiences working with the Mossad.

The target, in that case, was a notorious Middle East terrorist who had received credit for over 17 bombings, one of which was the attack that killed a desk chief of the Kidon, an elite group of expert assassins of the Mossad. The Kidon wanted to make the hit themselves, but government politics dictated that the hit must come from an outsider. The Kidon had attempted three hits on the target previously, but in all three cases, the attempts not only failed but ended in disaster with the loss of some of their most experienced field agents.

Seventy-One's plan called for him to move into position and have a 30-day window to execute. The Mossad, however, wanted a much quicker execution. The debate over this and other options of the plan went on for weeks. At first, Seventy-One did not care because he increased the cost of his services each time there was a delay.

Many terrorists, especially bombers, like to keep their identity and knowledge of their movements very secret; but this particular target was just the opposite. He considered himself a ladies man, and he loved to gamble. The reason he could be so bold was that he had surrounded himself with the best security and bodyguards' money could buy. But payment was only part of the equation. The bigger reason he was so protected was that each member of his security team was loyal to the cause, looked up to, and even idealized the bomber for his boldness and courage. His security team was also unique in that they maintained an intelligence gathering section and monitored any chatter going over the network and social media that may indicate a possible attempt on the bomber's life.

Seventy-One grew frustrated with the Mossad bureaucracy and made the decision to execute the plan in a different fashion, on his own terms. He found out that the bomber loved sleeping in hotels that offer waterbeds. For some reason, waterbeds were his thing.

Next Seventy-One obtained information as to what location and what hotel the bomber would be staying in on his next trip.

Seventy-One bribed the desk clerk to place the bomber in a particular room. Before the bomber checked into the hotel, Seventy-One entered the room disguised as a maintenance worker and drained the water from the waterbed into the bathtub. He then refilled the water bed with a flammable liquid. He also disconnected the sprinkler system and the smoke alarm in the room.

It was about 2:00 AM when the bomber and two lady friends returned to their suite after a night of gambling and dancing. When Seventy-One was confident that they had gone to bed, he fired a .50-caliber incendiary round through the balcony window and into the water bed mattress, which exploded, completely burning up the bomber and his two female companions.

The Mossad was very pleased with the manner and precision in which the contract was carried out. However, they did not like the fact that Seventy-One had broken away from their very careful oversight and gone it alone. At first, they refused to render payment, but after close to three months of name-calling and insults, cash was deposited into Seventy-One's Swiss bank account, which also included the reimbursement of interest for the delay.

Seventy-One initially said that he would never work for the Mossad again. However, 10 days after he had received his payment. He accepted another contract. This time, the Mossad gave him full authority to plan and execute the contract as he saw fit. He finished his last sip of brandy, logged off his computer, and took the short walk to his bedroom.

—

Langley, Virginia.

The United States intelligence community consists of some 16 government agencies. These agencies work both independently and collaboratively to gather the intelligence necessary to conduct foreign relations and national security activity. The 16 agencies report to the Office of the Director of National Intelligence within the executive branch.

Most commonly known members of this group of 16 are the CIA, NSA, the branches of the military and Homeland Security. The lesser known agencies that play significant roles in intelligence gathering are the Drug Enforcement Administration (DEA), the National Geospatial-Intelligence Agency (NGA), and the National Reconnaissance Office (NRO).

Regular meetings are called by the Director of National Intelligence, and all agencies are required to attend. Before that meeting, the eight leaders of the CIA have a dinner meeting that crosses all lines of the Agency, their focus on the past, present, and future operations. The dinner meeting is attended by the Director, Deputy Director, Executive Director, Deputy Executive Director, Directorates of Intelligence, Science and Technology, Nation Clandestine Service and Support.

This month's dinner meeting was held on a Wednesday night. The Director and the DDP, or Directorate of Plans and Clandestine Service, were at the buffet table selecting what they would place on their plates.

"Try some of that crab dip. It's splendid."

"I think I will. It should help me with my cholesterol level."

"Mr. Director, you are in better shape than most of my field agents. Didn't you just finish running in the Marine Corps Marathon?"

"You know what they say, once a Marine always a Marine. It doesn't look like you are eating a lot tonight yourself?" The DDP looked down at her plate.

"That's right, sir. I'm trying to cut back. You see I bought this very expensive dress about a year ago, and the other day I wanted to wear it to work and am almost too embarrassed to say that I had to change my mind about what I would wear to the office that day. So, since then, I've cut back on my portions, and I'm back in the gym every day, on the treadmill and lifting weights." The Director gave a pleasant smile.

"How do you think the Nationals will do this year?"

"I'm sure that they will be in the playoffs, but I actually follow the Redskins." As they were walking to their table, the Director shifted the subject.

"The report I received said that Fertile Ground was running smoothly. I always say that the beginning of an operation is the key to a successful operation. If the Operation starts smoothly, it will end in the same fashion."

"I understand, Mr. Director, but as you know, when I was given the opportunity to take over our clandestine services operations, I inherited all of the current desk chiefs. Of course, one will be retiring in October, and so that will solve one of my problems, but I would like to make some changes and replace them with people I know I can depend on. But since you brought up Operation Fertile Ground, Roy Benning is one of those desk chiefs I believe does not have, and I'll be frank, the balls to do the job. When I reviewed his personnel jacket, I didn't see where he had any experience at any desk where you had to push the limits. He has always held a position in locations that were safe." The Director started to walk away from the DDP before she could finish what she was saying.

When he was a few feet away from her, he stopped, turned back to the DDP, and said. "Let's wait until Fertile Ground has finished and then we'll talk about personnel changes. Oh, by the way. How did that other matter that was scheduled to be executed in your area work out?"

The DDP smile and said with assurance, "Fully completed, Mr. Director, with full compensation paid to the contractor."

"Remember, he is one of our most valuable assets. We trained him ourselves, so he has a firm understanding of how we work and what is expected. Glad to hear it went smoothly. Keep up the good job, and give my personal regards to your team."

"Please provide me another moment, sir, to discuss with you the personnel changes I would like to make." The Director walked closer to the DDP.

"Another point," the Director said as he approached the DDP. "How are your people holding up in Jacksonville with the loss of Karl and Nancy Mansfield? We gave full approval for Roy to place Billy Mills in that position without a probationary period. You do realize that I have complete oversight and final approval authority for all Positions." The tone of the Director's voice said it all.

"I understand correctly, Mr. Director, but I will bring this subject up again at the conclusion of Operation Fertile Ground. Just one last point and I'll let you get to your meal. I plan to recommend that both Karl and Nancy Mansfield's names be placed on the memorial wall." The Director realized how close he was standing to the DDP and took a step back.

"I guess this could be somewhat similar to Nels Benson and the work he was doing with Brigade 2506 back in '61 with the Bay of Pigs. I'm sure that if you have it written up from that perspective, it would probably have a better chance of approval." The Director smiled and walked to his table, and the DDP returned to hers.

—

Meanwhile, in Roy Benning's Office.

Roy was halfway through a conference call with Billy Mills and Elkin Ardila. "So, Elk, what do you think of the men that Ranuel assembled for the training."

"Roy, as you know you can't tell much from the first day. Today they received their equipment, books, and clothing and training centered on conditioning and map reading. After we wear them down with tonight's five-mile road march, we will see how they rebound with the classroom instruction tomorrow."

"Very well, then. I think everything has started off in good order. All of my reports thus far have reflected that. I'm sure that they have reached all the way up to the Director. Is there anything else that we need to discuss?"

Billy quickly replied. "Yes, Roy, there is one thing. What about putting in a recommendation for Karl and Nancy's names to be placed on the wall?"

"I'm glad you brought that up. I made a note to myself to start writing up the recommendation tonight when I get home. The example that I'm going to use is Nels Benson, who was killed in a training accident at the training site for Brigade 2506 in Retalhuleu, Guatemala, as we all know that assignment was managed from this desk back in '61. I think that this is a similar situation, but I'll give it 100%, and we'll see what happens."

Chapter 13

Belmond Copacabana Palace Hotel, Copacabana Beach.

Wallace woke up. The bright Caribbean sun was shining through the windows and reflecting off the mirrors in the room. He and Eve slept with the balcony sliding doors open to take in all the mild but humid sea breeze air. They enjoyed the moist air because it made them sweat. The sweat acted as a welcome lubricates between their hot bodies.

He looked at the clock on the night table next to their bed: 9:23 AM. Eve was out of the bed, and at first, WC thought that she was in the bathroom. He gave himself a good stretch. He could feel muscles that he had not felt in years. They had not been out of their room since coming from the beach the day they arrived. He and his lover had engaged in almost continuous lovemaking over the last 24 hours.

Everything they needed was delivered via room service, including appetizers of squid, and oysters, lots of oysters, avocados, and of course chocolate. Eve loved chocolate, and it was like the more she ate, the greater the passionate moments that were produced.

A smile of pleasure and relaxation crossed Wallace's face as he looked up at the ceiling fan and reflected on the joy he and Eve had enjoyed together over the last several hours. Eve was open to receiving pleasure at the most intimate places on her body, and to returning pleasure in a similar manner. The intensity that she received from him was the intensity that she returned.

What moved their lovemaking to higher levels of the most intense orgasms was the fact that both Wallace and Eve were in excellent physical condition. They made love on the bed, on the balcony with Eve lying on her stomach on the table in the 4:00 AM moonlight, in the Jacuzzi, in the shower, standing up and in the missionary position lying on the floor. Their desire for touching each other's bodies had moved to new encounters coming full circle in their union.

As Wallace rolled over in bed, he laughed as he felt the sting of the scratches on his back. He could still hear Eve's screams of pleasure when climaxing when they were on the balcony, in the shower, and the Jacuzzi.

In his mind's eye, he could still see the facial expressions as she climaxed into his arms. There are no words to describe the look on her face except satisfaction. He could feel that he satisfied every sexual urge that Eve's body demanded.

In between their lovemaking they would engage in pillow talk, leading to petting, to foreplay and ultimately penetration, deep penetration. Wallace realized his reflections were beginning to arouse him.

"Eve, lover, how long are you going to be in there?" There was no reply. Wallace looked at the clock again and got out of the bed. Once again he laughed to himself as he wrapped a towel around his fit body. What amused Wallace was that he had not had on any clothes since they came from the beach the day they arrived. He tapped on the bathroom door, and the door moved open. Eve was not in the toilet. Wallace turned and looked around the room. On the dresser, he saw a piece of paper, a note from Eve. "Gone for a run. Meet you at the pool at 10:30 for a late breakfast." Wallace looked at the clock. It was 10:15. He rushed into the bathroom for a quick shower so he could put on his swim trunks and meet Eve down at the pool.

When Wallace reached the elevator door, he looked at his watch. It was 10:30. As Wallace was riding the elevator down to the lobby, he said out loud, "That wasn't Spanish that Eve was reading in the hotel store; it was Portuguese. The national language of Brazil is Portuguese, not Spanish."

Wallace exited the elevator and started for the pool. There was an inside pool and an outside pool, but he was sure that Eve would be at the outside pool.

The pool area was not as crowded as Wallace had anticipated, but still, he was glad that he came down to the pool when he did. Having a late breakfast is a desire anyone on a tropical vacation. Partying and dancing into the wee hours of the morning, sleeping late and then stuffing yourself with the delicacies of a delicious buffet breakfast is always on every tourist's list of things to do.

As he walked into the seating area, he did not spot Eve. His concentration was on getting a table as close to the pool is possible, which he was successful in doing. After securing a table, he went to the buffet and returned to fill the table with cups of coffee and glasses of water and juice to ensure that he marked off his turf. The aroma, followed by the taste of the first sip of the dark, delicious Brazilian coffee, was a moment in itself. Wallace took a second sip and again started looking around the area for Eve.

He looked at his watch, and it read 10:55. It was not like Eve to be late for anything. He stood up from his chair to get a look out toward the beach. There she was, about 100 feet away and walking toward the pool area. She was talking on a cell phone. Wallace quickly sat back down at the table. His mind was racing back to the conversation they had about totally cutting themselves away from technology while on vacation so that they could just enjoy each other's company and really get to know one another other.

"Maybe an emergency came up at home, and it was imperative that she make a call," he thought. "Oh my God, I hope it wasn't anything bad about Tony." Tony was a naval pilot and Wallace knew that if anything tragic has happened to Eve's child, she would be devastated. "But we said that we were going to keep our cell phones in our luggage. I don't understand why she would break the pledge we made to each other? In fact, it was her idea about putting all the electronics away so we could totally concentrate on each other."

Wallace could now see Eve walking toward the area of the pool where he was seated. She had not spotted him but had ended the call and put the cell phone away. Wallace stood up and waved to Eve. She saw him and, with that beautiful smile, acknowledged that she saw him. She waved, then began to jog toward his table.

When she was close enough, she jumped into Wallace's arms. With surprise, Wallace caught her and swung her around. Eve gave Wallace a deep passionate kiss. After the kiss they were holding each, smiling and staring into each other eyes.

"Lover, I had such an incredible run." Slowly they let each other go, and Wallace seated Eve at their table. "I ran on the beach, even left my running shoes in the room so I could feel the sand between my toes. The spray from the water and the sea breeze was so invigorating that I must do it tomorrow."

Eve was talking a mile a minute. Wallace just sat there smiling and amazed by how radiant she looked in the midday sunlight.

"Have you ordered, lover?" Eve opened the menu and was drinking a glass of water at the same time. "I'm so hungry I probably could eat you if there were an apple in your mouth." Wallace chuckled and opened his menu.

"Come to think of it, I'm pretty hungry myself."

"What are you having? I think I'm going to order from the menu rather than the buffet. I am going to order big since it is so late in the morning and I probably won't eat until dinner tonight. I think I'll have the Western omelet, hash browns, hold the wheat toast, yogurt, fruit, and more coffee. What about you?"

Before Wallace could reply, she said, "I'm going for a swim while you order the food. I'll be back before it comes." Eve quickly pulled off her running shorts and a tee shirt, disclosing her bikini. She jumped up from the table, walked the few feet to the edge of the pool, and dived into the water. Wallace just sat at the table in wonderment of how revved up she was.

Wallace signed for the waiter to come over to the table. He ordered the food, and after the waiter had placed their order, WC then called the waiter back to the table and ordered a double Bloody Mary.

Sipping his Bloody Mary and watching Eve swim in the pool, Wallace felt that he was in the middle of a dilemma. In the short period, they had been in Rio de Janeiro, two situations had come up that made him feel uncomfortable. Here he was planning to ask the woman of his dreams to marry him and give her a $30,000 ring, and he was having doubts that he could trust her. Was he beginning to have second thoughts about asking Eve to marry him because of this trust question, or was he, because of all his previous bad experiences in relationships, turning an ant hill into a mountain?

Eve seemed to be so happy, pleased and satisfied with the way their vacation was going. If he brought up his observations, he knew it could turn the remaining portion of the trip into a nightmare. On the other hand, if he did not bring up what was troubling him, his doubts would only continue to fester and at some point in the future come out uncontrollably and probably lead to the more severe argument—six on one hand and a half-dozen on the other.

The waiter came with the food and started to set the table. Wallace turned his attention to the pool to signal Eve that the food has arrived. At first glance, he didn't see he because several people were passing by. When the people finished passing, and he had a clear field of vision, she was no longer in the pool. Wallace walked closer to the pool just in case something had happened. After assuring himself that she had not drowned in the pool, he returned to his table and contemplated where she might be.

"I'm not going to stress myself out. I'm on vacation the same as Eve is. She will probably show up in a few minutes and tell me what happened. Even if she doesn't, I don't care."

WC picked up his knife and fork and began slicing his omelet, sausage, and hash brown potatoes. He caught the waiter as he was passing and asked for another double Bloody Mary.

"Why didn't you call me to let me know the food had arrived?" Wallace was chewing his meal when Eve came up behind him from a direction other than the pool.

Wallace finished and answered, "If it's not hot we can have the waiter bring you something else or reheat it. I have a Bloody Mary. Would you like to have one?" She was still wet from the pool, but Wallace knew she was not in the pool when the food arrived? "I walked over to the pool to get you, but I didn't see you. Did you leave?"

Eve started eating her omelet. While chewing, she answered Wallace, "Leave the pool? Why would I do that? Say, after breakfast let's get changed and head into the city to do some shopping and sightseeing. That will be fun don't you think." WC sat silence for a few seconds. "Why yes, that should be fun."

Wallace and Eve finished their breakfast, went back to their room, changed and came back into the lobby. They inquired about transportation into the city at the hotel concierge desk. Wallace saw a display with some brochures on it that were titled Rio de Janeiro excursions. He walked over to the table while Eve spoke to the concierge about transportation.

"Good morning, sir. Does the hotel have a shuttle bus that can take us into the city to do some shopping?"

"Oh, yes, we have a shuttle bus that leaves every 30 minutes." The concierge looked at his watch and then at a clock that was behind him. "The next bus will be loading in just about 15 minutes. You still have time to catch that bus. By the way, please be sure to take your passports and identification with you. I would also suggest that you grab your room key as well for verification that you are staying at this hotel. There seems to be a lot of commotion in the city of an unusually high presence of police and security guards. Though I wouldn't be alarmed by this sort of thing happens occasionally. More than likely it is some type of training exercise that the government is carrying out."

"So we'll catch the bus at the front entrance to the hotel, is that correct?"

"Yes, that is correct. You will see a gentleman in a red jacket. Where he is standing is where you will load the bus, and that is the location where the bus will drop you off when you return. The shuttle bus service runs every day up until midnight. Is there anything else I can do for you?"

"No, thank you very much, and have a beautiful day." Eve left the concierge and joined Wallace at the table where he was reading a brochure on a kayak river run excursion. "Eve, take a look at this. This could be fun and exciting." Wallace handed a pamphlet to Eve.

"WC." Eve reached out and grabbed Wallace hand as he was holding the leaflet. "The concierge said that there is police and security activity in the city. We should be careful and have our identification ready at any time." Wallace turned to Eve and saw the concern on her face that he had heard a voice.

"Honey, it is always best to carry your passport with you when you are traveling in any foreign country. Technically, you should check in with the US Embassy, so they are aware that you are here also. So I wouldn't make too much of what he said." They started to walk toward the exit that would lead them to the location to catch the shuttle bus.

"It is probably part of the hotel guest security protocol for the concierge to remind guests of the hotel to keep their passports with them for identification purposes. What the concierge said is just procedural."

WC and Eve reached the location where the shuttle departed. They were the third couple in the queue, but it wasn't long before enough people were waiting to fill up the bus.

"Wallace, I guess it looks like everyone had a similar idea of going into the city to shop today. I'd like to see if I can find a new purse that will match the new outfit that Tony gave me for Mother's Day. That child is so sweet and thoughtful."

The bus pulled up to the loading area, and Wallace, Eve, and the other hotel guests boarded. As the bus was pulling out of the hotel driveway, the bus driver began to speak over the bus speaker system.

"Welcome to Rio de Janeiro, if this is your first time in our beautiful country and city, I would like to thank you for coming. If this is a return trip, welcome back. My name is José, and I will be your bus driver. Once we reach the city, I will make four stops. You may exit the bus at any of these four stops. For your return to the Belmond Copacabana Palace Hotel, I will only make pickups at those same locations. At each of these sites, you will see a Belmond Copacabana Palace Hotel information booth. There will be a hotel representative at the booth from 8:00 in the morning until midnight when the bus stops running.

The hotel representatives will be wearing a red jacket so they can be easily identified. If you should have any questions while you are enjoying our beautiful city, just go to our information booth, and they will be able to assist you. The drive to our first stop will take approximately 45 to 55 minutes. After the first stop, it will take about 20 to 25 minutes to reach each successive stop. Please sit back and enjoy the drive along our beautiful coastline."

The seats on the bus were very comfortable, so WC and Eve sat back, relaxed, held each other hands, and began to take in the scenic view of the coastline as the bus proceeded into the city. This was the same route that the limousine brought them in from the airport, but neither of them could remember very much of the scenery from the beautiful coastline due to their fatigue from the long flight and drinking the champagne.

After about ten minutes of driving, Wallace noticed several police cars passing them heading in the opposite direction of the hotel. As they passed through an intersection, Wallace saw a couple of police cars along with two military light armored vehicles. Eve begins to notice the high traffic of police and army vehicles on the highway they seem to be everywhere.

"WC, I wonder if this was such a good idea, coming into the city." The bus passed another military light armored vehicle, and WC turned his head to look at the car as it passed.

"What makes you say that, lover?"

With a worried look on her face, she replied, "Haven't you noticed all the police cars and military vehicles? Something must be going on."

"Well, lover, it's just like the concierge said at the hotel. They are probably having some type of joint training exercise with the military and the police. I really don't think there is anything for us to worry about." From Wallace's experience of being in the army and taking part in military exercises in several developing countries, what he was observing was probably nothing more than a joint military training exercise being conducted.

The bus was just about 10 km from making its first stop in the town at the passenger's drop-off point when it came to a stop at what appeared to be a police checkpoint. There were three cars ahead of the bus, and the passengers on the bus could see the cops going to each car and asking for identification. The bus driver began to speak over the bus's speaker system. "Ladies and gentlemen, please do not be alarmed. There is a large military and police presence in the city due to a military training exercise. Please have your passports ready to present to the officer should it be necessary to stop. This will only take a few moments. Thank you for your patience."

One vehicle was released by the police and signaled to move on. Now there were only two vehicles in front of the bus. The police approached the second vehicle and started the same process, but this time, they asked the passengers in the vehicle to step out of the car. There were three people in the car. Wallace could see clearly that all of the passengers in the car were men and appeared to be in their early to mid-twenties. Maybe one of the men could be in his early thirties. As the police checked their identification documentation and the driver's driver license and vehicle registration, something happened that was rather strange. The police officer that was looking at the documents belonging to the driver signaled to a man standing about 25 meters away to come over to their location. The man was not dressed in a military or police uniform but in a tailored, well-fitting business suit. The man was wearing sunglasses with very dark lenses. The driver of the vehicle did not notice the man approaching them, but the other two passengers in the car did see the man in the suit walking toward them. The people started to turn their bodies such that their backs were to the man as he got closer to the car. As quickly as the man passed them, one of the men took a swing, hitting the policeman reviewing their identification; and as the officer fell to the ground, the two men took off running in the direction of the city.

It seems that no one had noticed that across the street was a military vehicle containing four military policemen who were providing security for the checkpoint. Within seconds, after the men began fleeing for their lives, the soldiers dismounted and began firing a volley of shots with their semi-automatic rifles in the direction of the men. The entire incident happened faster than turning a page while reading the morning newspaper. The Brazilian soldiers were well-trained and accurate marksmen. Both men's bodies lay on the ground in puddles of blood.   The passengers on the bus sat in their seats, frozen in terror, not believing what they had witnessed. Some started screaming with a few bursting into tears. Eve didn't flinch. She just held Wallace's hand tighter as she watched the incident unfold.

Wallace quickly moved his attention away from the man who had been shot and back to the policeman and the man in the suit reviewing the driver's identification. The man in the suit had pulled out an automatic pistol and was pointing it at the driver while the policeman forced the driver's head down against the hood of the car and placed handcuffs on the man's wrists. The police quickly put the driver of the car into a police van and took him away.

For the next several minutes no attention was being directed at the cars that were still waiting at the checkpoint. There was still one car ahead of the bus.

Finally, the man in the suit seemed to be giving directions to the police to let the cars proceed. A policeman came over to the car that was in front of the bus and directed the driver to back up and go around the car that had contained the dead passengers and the detained driver. While that was happening, the man in the suit walked over to the bus and signal to the bus driver to let him on the bus. The driver opened the bus door, and the man entered the bus. The man in the suit began to speak to the driver. Eve and WC were sitting only four rows from the door of the bus. Wallace could hear what the man was saying but could not understand the language, which he assumed was Portuguese. It was only a whisper, but Wallace could hear Eve saying, "The man is telling the bus driver to take us back to the hotel because it is not safe for us to continue to the city."

Still holding Eve's hand, Wallace turned quickly, saying, "I'm sorry, Honey, but I couldn't hear you. What did you say?"

Eve remained quiet for several long seconds. "I think we are going back to the hotel."

Wallace looked directly into her eyes and said, "You speak Portuguese. I saw you reading the newspaper in the hotel's bookstore. Why didn't you tell me that you can talk the language?" Eve turned her head away from Wallace and stared out the bus window.

"Lover, what are you talking about. I just took a wild guess as to what he was saying to the driver. Why in the world would I not tell you that I could speak Portuguese? What you're saying is so ridiculous."

The man in the suit got off the bus, then signaled for two other police officers to come over to the bus. All of the passengers on the bus focused their attention on the man in the suit talking to the two other policemen standing just outside the door of the bus. The man in the suit finished giving his instructions to the police officers, who saluted the man in the suit. Then one officer started stopping the traffic in the opposite lane, and the other officer directed the bus driver to make a U-turn and proceed back to the hotel.

The driver backed the bus up and maneuvered it into position to execute a U-turn. Everyone on the bus was still in shock and remained quiet. A few people continued to stare at the puddles of blood at the location where the two men were shot and fell to the ground. As the driver completed making a U-turn, two motorcycle police escorts pulled in front of the bus and signaled to the driver to follow them.

"Where are you taking us?" a voice shouted from the rear of the bus. Wallace turned his head in the direction of the sound and made eye contact with the gentleman. He was sitting alone in the last row of the bus. The tone of his voice and the way he phrased his words made Wallace come to the conclusion that he was from somewhere in the United Kingdom. The bus driver did not respond to the question, and once again the man shouted out, "I said, where are you taking us? I want to know where they are taking us!"

Wallace turned around and started looking in the direction that the bus was headed. "This guy in the back is making a great point. If we were just going back to the hotel, why do we need a police escort? The bus driver surely knows his way back to the hotel."

Eve quickly looked at Wallace. "Say that again, lover." Wallace turned to Eve. "Honey, the guy in the back of the bus, has a good point. We really don't know where the bus driver is taking us. Why do we need a police escort to the hotel?" Eve just stared into Wallace's face.

The motorcycle escort in front of the bus slowed, and one bike pulled into the intersection that was just ahead, stopped and signaled for all of the on-coming traffic to come to a stop. The other motorcycle escort turned on his right turn signal and made a right turn, taking the bus in a different direction away from the hotel. Wallace could see the bus driver turning on his right turn signal. The bus followed the police motorcycle escort and made the right turn.

The gentleman from the back of the bus quickly got out of his seat and ran to the front of the bus. "I demand that you tell us where we are going."

The driver looked up in his mirror and at the same time reached for his microphone. "Ladies and gentlemen, please do not be alarmed. We are headed to the district police station where you will be informed about why you have been brought there."

The man who was running up the bus's aisle stopped and at the top of his voice said, "I will require a much more detailed explanation than the one that you just gave. There is always some type of issue in these banana republics. I plan to let my ambassador know about this situation the moment I return to my hotel room."

The man then turned around and walked back to the rear of the bus and took his seat, visibly mad about the situation he and his bus passengers were in and, even more, upset about being in a situation that he had no control over.

The lead police motorcycle began to slow again, and the rider turned on his right turn signal. The passengers on the bus could see a sign indicating a police station. The bus followed the escort vehicle into a parking lot adjacent to several buildings, one of which was surrounded by a high fence with razor wire on the top. There were no windows in this building.

In the distance, Wallace noticed a helicopter coming in for a landing in what appeared to be a helipad just north of the parking lot. The police officers got off of their bikes and seemed to be standing guard at the bus. They were joined by three more policemen, all carrying semi-automatic rifles.

"Wallace, why are those men carrying guns?"

From the tone of her voice, Wallace could tell that Eve was clearly nervous. "I think we'll be OK. They probably just want to ask everyone a few questions."

Just as Wallace finished speaking, he saw the man in the suit from the police checkpoint where the two men were killed walking toward the bus from the direction the helicopter landed. "Eve, that's the same man we saw at the police checkpoint." Eve turned and looked in the direction Wallace was looking.

"I think you're right. How did he get here so fast?" Wallace told Eve about the helicopter that landed. The man walked directly to the bus. The policemen saluted the man as he came on the bus. He asked the bus driver to hand him the microphone.

"Ladies and gentleman, I'm Chief Inspector Alosio Santos Candido of the National Security Agency. We must ask each of you to be patient. We must obtain a detailed statement of what each of you witnessed at the checkpoint a few moments ago."

The bus passenger's hands begin to go up, signaling they had questions. Inspector Candido did not pay any attention to their request and continued to speak.

"As soon as we finish taking your statements, you will be allowed to return to the hotel where you are staying. You will now be escorted into a very comfortable waiting area. Please hold your questions until you are inside the building." He looked over his shoulder and while pointing at the Police Officer said, "Follow this officer into the building and bring all of your belongings."

The Chief Inspector got off of the bus and started walking toward one of the buildings when his cell phone rang. "This is Chief Inspector Santos Candido."

The voice spoke over the cell phone to the Chief Inspector. "Are you sure that you have all of the foreigners who witnessed the shooting?"

"Yes, Commandant, I'm certain. Everyone else there was locals, and they know how to keep their mouths shut because they know what would happen to them if they talk."

"Very well, then. Keep the entire group at the station until the operation has been completed, and we notify you. It is of the utmost important that the media does not get hold of this before we execute. Foreigners are more likely to call CNN or the BBC when something like this occurs. So far we have been able to keep the media out of this. That is the way we want to keep it. This is why we brought them here because, within 100 yards of this facility, all cell phone signals are jammed."

"Very well, my Commandant; we will keep them busy for as long as it takes."

Chapter 14

Jacksonville, Florida, Marriot Hotel.

Agent Harris pulled in front of the main entrance of the Marriot Hotel where Agent Bo Brooks was staying. Agent Brooks reached for the door handle to get out of the car but hesitated.

"Agent Harris, since we almost got crushed under a collapsing building today, why don't you join me at the bar and I'll buy you a drink?"

Agent Harris smiled. "If you make that a drink or two, I'll be tempted to join you."

"OK, then let's have a drink or two." Both of the FBI agents smiled. Harris pulled the car into the hotel parking lot.

When they were at the bar, Brooks said, "I'll take a bourbon and club soda, and give the gentleman whatever he wants."

Agent Harris stood staring at the variety of bottles behind the bar. "I'll take a Jamison and water with just a little ice." The two men got their drinks and walked over to a booth and sat down.

Agent Harris positioned himself so he could observe the entrance into the lounge, and Agent Brooks took the seat with his back to the entrance and began to engage in small talk such as: How long have you been with the Bureau? How were you recruited? Why did you join? Then the conversation moved to assignments and finally to the family. Harris was single the same as Brooks, but Harris had a child, a little girl. He had also been in the military before joining the Bureau. Finally, Bo felt comfortable enough to ask about Faye.

"Why was Faye taken off the assignment to assist me, and why were you assigned to take over?"

The tone of the conversation turned serious, back to business. Agent Harris sat up straight in his chair and looked directly at Bo.

"You guys in Washington really don't get it. You sit up in your ivory tower with your white shirts and your hot cups of Starbuck coffee every day. Sure you carry the latest in firearms, and you have your body armor in the trunk of your BMWs, but out here is where the shit happens."

Bo thought while listening to Agent Harris go off about how all agents who worked at FBI headquarters, when they had to interface with their fellow agents in the field, got the same tongue lashing: everyone who works in Washington has it so easy and the tough guys are in the field. The field agents do the real job, and they are the only ones who count. The Agents in Washington are just paper pushers.

"The reason Agent Cook-Little was transferred from this babysitting assignment was that she is too good an agent just to be showing you around and holding your hand. I got assigned to it because I'm just coming off medical leave. Do you know what that means?"

Bo knew what medical leave meant, but before he could answer Agent Harris continued.

"We were out on a stakeout of a known contraband dealer out off of Kings Bay. Everything went bad, and I got two just between the closing flaps of my body armor. Fortunately for me, the guy was only carrying a .32 at the time. If he had been using a 9 mm or a .357, we would not be here having this conversation."

The waitress came over to their booth to see if they needed anything. Both of the men asked for another round. Bo stayed with the bourbon and club soda, but Agent Harris ordered a Stella.

"So, if you think we have it so good in Washington, have you ever asked for a transfer to DC?" The question stopped Harris cold. He was silent and started looking around the room to see if anyone was listening to their conversation.

Then Bo ordered some chicken wings and Harris ordered a steak sandwich. They remained quiet until the waitress brought their drinks and food. Bo added it to his hotel bill.

"Well, let me ask you this, Bo. Have you ever requested a transfer to the field?"

Bo quickly snapped back, "Why do you assume I've never been in the field?' Harris finished taking a bite from his sandwich and placed it back on the plate, wiped his mouth with the napkin, and looked at Bo.

"You know something, Bo? You're right. I made an assumption that, because you are currently working in Washington, it is the only assignment you have ever had. I apologize."

148

Bo finished eating a chicken wing and signaled for the waitress to come back to the table. "Please bring me another order of chicken wings, and I will also take a Stella." Bo then turned his attention back to Agent Harris.

"No problem, Harris. That's an understandable mistake, assuming that anyone working in Washington has always worked in Washington." Bo wanted to get back to finding out about Agent Cook-Little, but before he could say anything Agent Harris started talking almost uncontrollably.

"You know Faye is a lot like me. I guess I had been assigned to the Jacksonville office for a little over five years when Faye got assigned. She always talked about working in the Las Vegas PD as an undercover narcotics agent."

Bo interrupted. "That's interesting. I thought that she had always been an FBI agent. I first met Faye while she was assigned to Washington, believe it or not, at headquarters." The news that Agent Faye Cook-Little had worked at FBI headquarters entirely changed the expression on Agent Harris's face. Harris took a sip of his beer.

"Faye is being groomed to go directly to the top. She is always the first person to go through the door and the last person leaving the crime scene, and her paperwork is more accurate than anyone I have ever worked with. But Faye is terrible in selecting the men she lets into her life. She has the most incredible tendency to get involved with total losers."

What Agent Harris said made Bo sit up straight in the booth. Bo was just about to say something when Agent Harris's cell phone began ringing.

"Agent Harris." Harris reached into his coat jacket pocket and pulled out a small pad and then a pen. He started writing something down in shorthand. "Sure, I'm on my way." He looked directly into the eyes of Agent Brooks and replied to the caller. "You sure you want me to bring him also?" Harris ended the call without answering.

Harris finished off his beer. "Did you put everything on your hotel room bill? I mean, do I need to leave a tip or anything?"

"No, I'll put everything on my travel voucher. What's going on?" Bo replied with a curious look on his face.

Agent Harris was standing up by the booth. "That call was for a full call-up of all available agents working within the state, and that means you too. Let's go."

Agent Bo Brook knew what a full call-up meant. He finished off the last sip of his beer and followed Agent Harris out of the hotel lounge. Neither spoke while walking to the car and for the first ten minutes of the drive.

A full call-up of all available FBI agents working in a state meant that something serious was happening that called for federal manpower. Brooks broke the silence. "I guess I can assume that the Agency has lead jurisdiction in this operation."

"As far as I know, we do, but what I know is limited to what I got on the call. We are headed for the airport to catch a plane to Miami."

Bo pulled out his cell phone and began to type an email message to send to his office. He finished the message just as Agent Harris was pulling onto the non-commercial side of the Jacksonville International Airport. They passed through a security gate. Both agents had to present their IDs and badges, and then the security guard at the entrance waved them through. They drove past a few warehouses and came to a stop, parking in a lot adjacent to a standard looking aluminum building.

As Bo got off the car, he could see what he thought were other agents walking toward a waiting airplane about 100 yards beyond the building. Bo followed Agent Harris into the building. The room was crowded with men and women moving in all different directions and with the utmost urgency. Agent Harris walked up to a table where a man was handing out assault equipment bags.

The man said to Agent Harris, "You look like you must be a 42 regular and boot size 11." Agent Harris nodded. The man then looked at Agent Brooks. "I suspect you are about a 42 long with the boot size of 11½."

Agent Brooks reached for the bag and said, "You must have been doing this a long time. Have you ever gotten anyone's size wrong?"

"I've only missed twice, and that was for my first two female agents. Since then, not once."

Someone with a bullhorn shouted, "Okay, stop wasting time. You'll have to change en route on the plane. We need to get moving. Let's go!"

Bo threw the bag over his shoulder and started walking toward the door with Agent Harris. It appeared to Bo that a least 50 agents were boarding the airplane.

"I wonder who the Special Agent in Charge is?" Bo made this odd statement as he was walking up the loading ramp to the Hercules C-130 Aircraft.

Someone behind Bo said, "I think Cook-Little is the SAC."

Another voice echoed, "Yes, Faye is the SAC."

Another voice also chimed in. "I heard she's the best."

Once they got on the plane, another voice spoke over the aircraft's intercom system. "We take off in zero-five. After we are in the air, you have about 45 minutes to change into your assault gear. You'll pick up your ammo when we land. There is a briefing book in your assault bags. Sit down and buckle up for the takeoff."

Bo sat down on the canvas bench of the C-130, buckled his seatbelt, and unzipped his assault bag and started inventorying his tactical equipment. Bo saw his assault weapons, a 9mm HK MP5 Sub Machine Gun, Beretta 92F 9mm, and for his backup, Colt 45 pistols. Brooks also saw body armor, tactical uniform, knee pads, gloves, glasses, body camera, and his communication set. He then pulled out the briefing binder. On the front cover were these words: Classification: Top Secret. The next page was a summary of the organization they were going after. The group's name was the Movement for the Independence for Essequibo or MIE.

———

Langley, VA., CIA Headquarters, Office of Roy Benning.

Roy was clearing off his desk and placing his classified documents into his office safe. It had been a long day, and he was looking forward to having a long run to lower his stress level, some steam, hot shower, and maybe a good steak dinner at Morton's Steak House.

Roy looked over his shoulder while standing at the safe and saw Andrea, his administrative assistant, almost running into his office. She turned his dashboard on, the TV monitor, tuning it to the South American all-news channel.

"Roy, take a look at this." Roy finished placing his classified material in the safe, closed and secured the safe, and then walked over to his dashboard.

Andrea had logged into the classified portion of Roy's dashboard to reveal a listing of operational activities that was either upcoming or ongoing. Andrea strolled to the heading "FBI operations" and pointed to an item that read, "FBI and ATF raid, Movement for the Independence for Essequibo (MIE), Date Time Group: Zero minus 24 hours out. Location: Miami, Florida. SAC: FBI Agent Faye Cook-Little, Jacksonville FBI Field Office."

"What in the hell is going on? Andrea, get hold of Billy Mills. I need to find out what is going on?" Roy turned his attention to the television monitor that was now turned on. A reporter on a South American channel said, "We have breaking news. There are unconfirmed reports, and I must stress these are unconfirmed reports, that both the Chief of Security of Venezuela and the Chief of Security for Guyana were involved in a shooting and may have been assassinated. Once again, these are unconfirmed reports. What we do know is that both men arrived in Rio de Janeiro to plan the security for the high-level meeting between both countries' heads of state at the capital in ten weeks. Both of the security ministers were staying at the Belmond Copacabana Palace located on the Copacabana Beach. Security, police, and military activity are high in that area. It is recommended that, unless you have direct business activities in the Copacabana Beach district, you should not venture into this field. Please stay tuned to this channel for further breaking the news."

For several moments, Roy just stared at the monitor. Finally, he said out loud, "Andrea, what's the name of our liaison with the FBI. Give them a call. I want to talk to whoever it is." Roy left the dashboard and walked back to his desk and logged back into his computer. He began to type up a message concerning the situation and was addressing the email to the Director of the Agency.

"Roy, I have Billy Mills on line two."

"Thanks, Andrea. I have it." Roy Benning turned away from his computer and picked up his phone. "Billy, we found a status off the dashboard that the FBI is raiding the MIE in Miami. Have you heard anything about this?"

Billy Mills was just leaving the office and was standing in the parking lot next to his car. "Roy, you're the first person to tell me anything about some type of raid. I'm just leaving the meeting with Elk and the rest of his team. They were updating me on how well the training is going out at the Plantation. I will make contact with my FBI counterpart here in Jacksonville and find out what is going on."

Roy Benning breathed a slight sigh of relief. "OK, Billy. Get on it and get back to me once you find out anything concrete."

Reluctantly Billy said, "Okay Roy, I'm on it, talk to you later." He then relocked the door to his car and walked back into the Flagler Center.

Back in the building, as he was unlocking his office door, he was cursing himself. The Jacksonville FBI office had just gone through a change of leadership and was operating under a new Field Director. His admin sent him an email with the guy's name and contact information, but he had not opened the email or transferred the coordinates to his Blackberry. To make matters worse, two meet-and-greet luncheons were scheduled and on both occasions he had canceled and rescheduled. He could still hear Karl Mansfield saying, "In case anything happens to me Billy, you need to know these people so we can have a seamless operation with all the federal forces at our disposal."

It seemed like that day had come and he didn't do the right thing like Karl had directed him to do.

After unlocking his office door and slamming it behind him. He frantically sat at his desk and began to log into his computer. After a quick search of his email, he said aloud, "That must be it."

—

Shands Hospital's Emergency Room, Jacksonville, Florida.

Debra was standing next to Helen, who was sitting and just staring down the hall in the direction of Joe's room. Debra's cell phone was in her hand, and she was trying to reach Bubba on the City Hall line, but she was going to voice mail. She had tried his private desk line too, but that produced the same results. Debra knew that Bubba was meeting with the longshoremen, and anytime Bubba met with them there would be no certainty when the meeting would end. Debra finally sent Bubba a text message asking him to contact her, telling him it was urgent.

"Did you reach Bubba?" Gracie took two steps closer to Debra because she thought Debra did not hear her; "I said, did you reach Bubba?"

Debra turned her attention back to Gracie. "I'm sorry, dear. My thoughts were on Helen. No, I didn't, but I sent him a text message asking him to call me as soon as possible.

"Eve Harding." Debra looked down at Helen. She heard the two words again. "Eve Harding."

"Helen, did you say something? I couldn't make out what you were saying. Helen stood up but was still facing in the direction of where Joe's hospital room was located.

"Helen, dear, you are tired. Help us out a little and explain what you are talking about." Helen stood up and started walking toward Joe's hospital room. Debra and Gracie walked along with her.

"Helen, please tell us what you are talking about? What do you want us to do? How can we help?" This time, it was Debra requesting.

Helen stopped walking, turned to Debra, grabbed her arms and began to squeeze them. "Helen, you are hurting me. Gracie, please get a nurse or someone to help us."

Gracie looked up and down the corridor and started walking fast to the nurse's station that was about 100 feet from where they were standing. Gracie was trying to think of what Helen was going through. Her pace changed from a walk to a run as she realized that Helen may have been having some type of psychological breakdown.

"We need some help. Our friend is having a breakdown from all of the stress of her husband being in intensive care. Please come and help her." The nurse sitting behind the counter stood, reaching for the telephone that was on the desk.

"Where is your friend now?"

Gracie quickly replied, "Just down the hall, beyond room 524." The nurse pushed a button on the telephone.

"Let's go!" They ran down the lobby to where Debra and Helen were standing.

"Helen, you are hurting me. Please turn me a loose." Helen's eyes were fiery and bright.

"Debra, when we had the blood drive, I was at registration, and all of the book club members volunteered to give blood. When it was Eve's turn, she filled out the form, and I noticed she had the same blood type as Joe."

"Mrs. Singletary, please let Ms. Webb go and come and sit down over here." The nurse was holding both of Helen's hands. The nurse spoke in a calm but firm voice. At the same time, two orderlies were running down the hall to their location. Once the attendants reached Helen and the nurse, one started taking her blood pressure, and the other pulled a small penlight and started checking Helen's eyes.

The nurse taking Helen's pulse then said, "Let's move her down to the ER stat."

One of the orderlies then ran down the hall and started pushing a gurney over to Helen's location. The three placed Helen on the stretcher and started for the elevator. Debra and Gracie stood there holding each other in utter disbelief.

As they moved Helen to the elevator on the gurney, one of the orderlies told Debra and Gracie that they would have to take the visitor elevator to the main floor and the emergency waiting room area. They said they would be able to see their friend once a doctor had fully checked her out in the emergency room.

As Debra and Gracie exited the elevator and walked toward the emergency room waiting area, neither spoke a word. It was almost like they were in a trance. They sat down and both just stared at the entrance door to the ER.

When Debra's cell phone rang it startled both Debra and Gracie. "Bubba, Oh, something awful has happened." Debra gave Bubba all of the details of their ordeal for the last hour or so.

"What do you want me to do?" Debra knew that Bubba had asked the question that way because he was still tied up in a meeting.

155

She contemplated her response. In actuality, there was little he could do. Helen was in the ER being seen, and Joe was upstairs in the hands of doctors as well.

"Neither of the doctors has provided any update about Joe, and they just took Helen in. Gracie and I are just waiting and praying everything works out."

There was a long pause with no response from Bubba, then he replied, "I'll finish up my meeting as soon as possible and then I'll be right over."

"OK, then I'll call or text your cell as soon as we hear something." Debra sat in silence for several minutes, her attention still focused on the doors of the ER.

"Gracie, you know being the wife of the Mayor of a big city like Jacksonville is like being married to a man who has a mistress. Bubba's mistress is Jacksonville, and like any other woman, she needs all the attention in the world."

Gracie reached out and grabbed Debra's hand. "Debra, always be thankful for your blessings. Just imagine if Bubba was the President of the United States."

The doors of the ER opened, and the nurse who had brought Helen from upstairs was walking toward Debra and Gracie. "We have stabilized her. It appears that she was going through an anxiety attack. Her blood pressure was elevated, and she had a very irregular pulse. We have her on an I-V, and the doctor gave her some medication to calm her. She is resting now. We will continue to monitor her and probably keep her overnight for observation. If you'd like, you can go in to see her, but for only a few minutes. Do you have any questions?" Debra and Gracie both thanked the nurse and then were shown into the room where Helen was resting.

Helen's eyes were closed as they walked into her room. Debra walked to the head of the bed while Gracie stood at the foot.

Helen opened her eyes and smiled. "I guess I'm not such an active wife. Joe is upstairs, and anything could happen, and here I have a weak anxiety attack." Debra was just reaching out her hands to grab Helen's hand when the door opened, and a woman in surgical scrubs walked into the room.

"Ms. Singletary, my name is Doctor Renfroe. I heard that you weren't feeling well. Are you feeling better now?" Helen just

156

nodded her head. "I'll take that as a yes. Good. I am so very glad to see you indicate that. Let me bring you up to date on your husband. He is stable now. We found where the bleeding was coming from. There was a small piece of metal lodged between two of his ribs. We've removed that metal, but we also found several other pieces of metal and glass that had penetrated his body from the crash. We are now 100% sure that we have removed all of the glass and metal from his body, but he has lost a lot of blood, and we must replace what he has lost. He is currently on plasma, but we need whole blood. As you probably know, your husband has one of the rarest of blood types. Unfortunately, here at Shands, we only maintain a limited supply of that kind of blood. The last time we had a patient here at the hospital who needed the same blood type as your husband was five years ago, except for two weeks ago when we had a patient who came in with a gunshot wound. Unfortunately, that patient exhausted our supply. But please don't be alarmed. We plan for situations like this. We have a request to all of the other hospitals in Jacksonville and the surrounding areas, as well as to the Red Cross and all of the private blood banks in the city, and we have also put out a nationwide alert to obtain any supply available. We can keep him in plasma for the next 48 hours, but I'm sure that we will have a supply before then. We have a helicopter standing by to pick the blood up and bring it here to the hospital. Do you have any questions, Mrs. Singletary?"

Helen tried to sit up on the bed. "Eve Harding has the same blood type as my husband. I know this because, when the book club did a blood drive, I noticed her blood type on her registration card."

Chapter 15

The Plantation, Camp Blanding, Florida.

Elk had the recruits from the MIE gathered around him after they had completed a 12-mile road march with full equipment. Each of the men had to carry half of their body weight to include their automatic weapon and backup sidearm. What this meant is that if a person's body mass were 100 pounds that man would have to carry 50 pounds of equipment. If his body weight were 200 pounds, he would have to carry 100 pounds of equipment to include his share of ammunition.

The evening temperature was just beginning to drop from a high of 93 degrees, but with the humidity, it felt like it was close to 100 degrees. As Elk looked around, the men were soaked in body sweat almost as if they were just coming out of a swimming pool.

"OK, listen up!" Elk shouted. "I want each of you to take out one of your canteens and drink the full bottle. This is one of your first lessons in survival: to keep your men in a fighting combat condition, do not to let them get dehydrated. This concludes our first day of training. We will begin tomorrow at 0600 hours, starting with physical training. Put your gear away and load into your vans to transport back to Whiteys."

The members of the MIE were enthusiastic but exhausted from their first day of training. Each man knew coming in that the training would be very intense, the days long and the night's short. Ranuel and Krish were walking among the trainees patting them on their back and providing words of encouragement. All seemed devoted to the cause and what was ahead of them.

Finally, Ranuel was able to pull Krish to a quiet spot out of ear range of the Americans so he could bring Krish up to date with the message he had received just before they entered the Plantation compound that morning.

To Ranuel's surprise, Krish didn't seem to be too upset. Ranuel was almost sure that he was going to get a tongue lashing about how he knew the *Americanos* were going to double-cross them, just as they did the Cubans in the Bay of Pigs. "I will get the men moving as fast as possible so we can get to a store where you can purchase a prepaid telephone."

Krish went to each of the men and told them that if they would hurry up and if they could get back to the trailer park early enough, they would be treated to rum and coke. This turned out to be a strong motivator, and it wasn't long before everyone was seated in the vans, and they were on their way.

Ranuel and Krish said their goodbyes to Elk and the other trainers and ensured them that they would be on time for the next day of training. On the return trip, Krish's van took the lead and the van that Juan was in was the last van in the convoy.

The first gas station and convenience store the van reached, Ranuel ordered the driver to pull over. However, the store was out of prepaid phones. He stopped at two more convenience stores with the same results. At the last shop, Ranuel asked the store clerk if he knew of a store that carried prepaid phones.

"Oh yeah, go over to the Walmart off of Route 301, and you should be able to find one there."

Ranuel typed in Walmart on his Google app and clicked for driving directions. At the Walmart, he purchased the phone, and he and his team started for Fleming Island and the trailer park at Whiteys.

Ranuel unpacked the phone and began to charge the battery. As soon as he saw a fully charged signal on the screen of the cell phone, he looked at his watch. He was just reaching the time limit to make the call.

As their procedures require, on the third ring the phone was answered. The voice on the other end of the phone gave Ranuel the code sign and Ranuel answered with the countersign. Ranuel searched his brain trying to determine if he had heard this voice before. He could not recall, but his focus shifted to what the man was saying. Ranuel ended the call by saying, "Thank you very much, and long live the revolution!"

Ranuel gave a sigh of relief. Krish's premonition had not come true, at least not yet; but there were some major problems that the MIE was facing. Ranuel ordered his driver to make all haste to get to Whiteys.

—

Langley Virginia, CIA Headquarters, Office of Roy Benning.

"Hello, Peggy. This is Roy Benning at the Agency." Peggy was the FBI liaison officer on Roy's desk.

After a short pause she replied, "Oh, Roy, I am surprised to be receiving a call from the CIA, and on our secure line no less. Something must be up. What can I do for you?"

"Peggy, I was looking at the intra-agency dashboard and saw that the FBI and the ATF are conducting an operation down in the Miami area. As our liaison, how about checking into it and getting back to me on how it was initiated, who authorized it, and most importantly to whom do I need to speak."

He could hear Peggy logging-in to find the line item Roy was asking her about.

"I see, Roy. I'll make some calls and get back to you. I guess you needed this information yesterday?"

Roy laughed and said, "You got that right. I have to brief the DDP as soon as I get an update."

"I know the drill, Roy. I'll get back to you ASAP."

It was becoming more evident to Roy that Fertile Ground had been compromised. What he needed to find out before he talked with the DDP was how it had been compromised and how much damage had been done.

Roy thought to himself that the upside was that his desk was at the beginning of the operation, and the worst-case scenario was that they could turn over the MIE people they were training at the Plantation to the FBI Task Force and just deny the entire operation. The only problem with that scenario was that, once again, the South American desk would be living up to its heritage dating back to the Bay of Pigs when Brigade 2506 was left on the Beach of Cuba. That they could not complete an operation successfully would only be further entrenched in the minds of their allies in the southern hemisphere.

Roy sent out an alert for an all-hands conference call. Most desk chiefs would just have everyone come back into the office, but Roy was not like other Desk Chiefs. He tried as much as possible to

160

respect his people's private lives and the small amount of time that they spent with their families. Roy set the conference call to take place in the next two hours. This would give him enough time to gather as much information for the meeting as he could. Roy's cell phone rang.

"Billy, did you learn anything from your source at the district FBI office in Jacksonville."

Billy was sitting at his desk at the Flagler Center. "No I have not been able to obtain any information from my source, but what I do know is that the FBI had an all-hands call-up tonight, and every agent in Florida was called in. I got this information from a bartender friend at a local drinking spot where a lot of law enforcement people hang out. Where they are going, I have not been able to get any type of confirmation." While Billy Mills was on the telephone talking to Roy, Elk walked into Billy's office.

"Roy, Elk just walked into the room. I'm going to put you on speaker." Billy pushed a button on his desk phone.

Roy paused for a second, and when he thought that he had been switched to the speaker, resumed. "OK, guys, the truth is we do not know anything for certain, nothing we can hang our hat on. I've called for an all-hands staff conference call that will take place in about an hour and a half. Let us put our heads together up here and see if we can find out what is happening. I'll get back to you after the conference call. In the meantime, make sure that Ranuel and his guys are bedded down over at Whiteys."

Billy Mills and Elk sat in the office and stared at each other, both men contemplating what their next step should be. Billy walked over to a cabinet, unlocked it, and pulled out two glasses along with a bottle of scotch whiskey and returned to his desk.

Elk gave a half smile and said with sarcasm, "I think having a drink would be a good starting point."

Billy laughed as he sat back down at his desk and opened the bottle of scotch. He poured two drinks and pushed one of the glasses over to Elk. He picked up the glass and drank it down in one gulp, set the glass back on the table, and pushed it back over to Billy for a refill.

Billy was gazing at his glass of scotch, almost hypnotized until he noticed Elk sliding his glass back toward the bottle of whiskey. Billy took a big sip of his drink, refilled Elk's glass, and added some more scotch to his drink. Elk reached across the table and grabbed his drink.

"Goddamn it, it seems like it must be some type of voodoo curse on the South American desk. I wasn't here for the Bay of Pigs, but I feel this desk will be paying for leaving those men on the beach in Cuba for as long as they have a South American office set up in Jacksonville." Elk started pacing around the room as he hit his fist into the palm of his hand. Billy, still sitting behind his desk, propped his feet up and leaned back while sipping his scotch.

"But that's not the entire story of the Bay of Pigs."

Elk stopped pacing, turned and looked at Billy. "What are you talking about?"

Billy took the last sip of Scotch, looked at the bottle and decided not to pour himself another. He looked back at Elk. "There was a lot of backstabbing, interagency squabbling, just a lot of bad blood politics that's going on in those days."

Elk walked closer to Billy's desk. "But Billy you weren't with the Agency then."

"That's right I wasn't, but just after I finished my training at the Farm, I had dinner with a couple of the trainers and one of the guys was assigned to the South American desk at the time of the Bay of Pigs. He had one too many and started talking. You see, the cold war was going on, and the country had just gotten the youngest president in history, not to mention he was the first Catholic to become president. So there was a lot of pressure on everyone." Elk didn't respond to what Billy said. He stood there, trying to comprehend, but it wasn't making any sense.

"Billy, you are holding something back. Naturally, I suspect that the guy stationed here at the time of the Bay of Pigs said something about the operation that he was not supposed to. Is that about right?"

Billy stood, picked up the bottle and glasses, walked to the cabinet and put the scotch and glasses away. Without answering Elk's question, Billy said, "I'll ride out to Whitey's with you to see if Ranuel and his men have made it back to the trailer park."

—

District Police Office, Copacabana Beach, Rio de Janeiro.

The passengers were escorted from the bus to a building that displayed a sign that read, in Portuguese and English, District Police Station Headquarters.

As they entered the door, each of the passengers had to present their passport. Wallace and Eve were close to the end of the group. From where Wallace stood he could see that as the passengers gave their passports, the police officer that was seated inspected the passports and then typed something into the computer at the desk. A few minutes passed and then that passenger was directed to move on. Wallace could see that passengers were being sent to different rooms. WC concluded that they were dividing the passengers up by nationalities. When Wallace and Eve reached the point where they had to present their passport, Eve handed the police officer hers. The policemen inspected the passport, then typed something into the computer. Wallace assumed that a search was being done to see if they had entered the country legally. The police officer at the desk completed the search of Eve's passport and handed it back to her, and just like the other passengers from the bus, directed her to a room where several other Americans were waiting.

Wallace gave the police officer his passport. The same procedure was followed. The policeman at the desk was just about to give Wallace his passport when something pulled his attention back to the computer screen. The police officer raised his hand to get the attention of his supervisor. Wallace wondered what was happening as a man in uniform, probably an officer walked over to the computer. The policeman sitting down pointed to the screen. The officer looked at the display and then back at Wallace, making eye contact and at the same time signaling for more police officers to join them at the desk. Before Wallace knew it, three men were standing behind him, each with an automatic rifle.

"Is there a problem, Officer?" Wallace spoke in a calm but irritated voice. The officer said, "No problem, sir. Please follow these gentlemen to the location where you will be comfortable." Wallace's mind was racing, attempting to think of every possible piece of information that could have come up in their database.

He didn't reply to the officer as he turned and followed his escorts. About five feet from the table, Wallace turned around. "My traveling companion was taken to that room." Wallace pointed to the place. "I need to let her know that we have been separated."

The police officer answered very quickly. "We will take care of that. Please go with your escort and soon all of this will be over."

Wallace was led down the hall in the opposite direction from where the other bus passengers were waiting. Wallace assumed that something came up on their database that indicated he was in the military and possibly, Special Forces.

Soon WC and his escorts came to a steel door. One of the men pushed a button that was on the wall next to the entrance. A small door opened, and a man looked out, then Wallace heard the electric sound of the lock being released. As Wallace passed through the doorway, he knew that he was in a much different section of the police station than where the other bus passengers were taken. Whatever came up on the computer was of such a nature they felt the need to isolate him in a secure section of the police station. Again, the only possible thing that could have appeared in their database was his Army affiliation and possibly his Special Forces connection.

After passing through the steel door, they continued a few feet and took some stairs, going two flights down to another steel door. An electric lock opened, and Wallace's escort gestured for him to walk in.

A sensor automatically turned on the lights in the room as Wallace entered. Wallace looked around the room and knew that he was in an interrogation room. His escort motioned for him to take a seat at the table in the center of the room and to sit in the chair that was facing a two-way mirror.

"Name, rank, and service number," flashed through Wallace's mine. Under the Geneva Convention Rules of War, he could only be expected to give these details. Wallace still wondered what had appeared on the computer that led to his name being identified as some sort of threat.

As Wallace sat down staring into the two-way mirror, his training kicked in, and he remained calm and relaxed. WC knew he must establish a baseline of his body language for the interrogation, a baseline of natural movements. The course of the interrogation would be prolonged if WC varied from this baseline. "I must stay relaxed, maintain minimum movement with direct eye contact," he reminded himself.

He checked his watch: 20 minutes passed. Wallace needed to go to the men's room. "I need to use your toilet." Wallace knew that a microphone was placed in the room, so he was positive that his interrogator heard his request. This also created a situation where they would not let him relieve himself unless he answered their questions. But at the same time, the process would start on his terms. "I will do something for you if you tell us what we are looking for. We'll let you go to the men's room when we hear what we want."

The door opened, and a very tall and beautiful female walked in. The scent of a pleasant but seductive perfume gently flowed through the air as the lady walked around the room to the table. She pulled the chair back away from the table so that when she sat down, her long and shapely legs were visible. Wallace thought to himself, "A beautiful female interrogator. This is going to be interesting."

"Mr. Barker," She said, making eye contact with Wallace. "My name is Officer Xoana Cardozo, but you may call me Belo. You are an American, and you make your home in Maryland. Is that correct?" One of Wallace's survival courses was in interrogation technics. One of his instructors had this Buddhist saying hanging above his door: "The key to life is not to know all the answers but to understand the questions."

Why would she ask me a question she already knows the answer to? It's on my passport. "How does it read on my passport?" Wallace said in a calm and quiet voice. Belo didn't flinch.

"Mr. Wallace, we see that you are in the Army. Do you have your military identification card?" Wallace nodded. "Can you please show it to me?" Wallace reached into his pocket, pulled out his ID card from his wallet, and pushed it across the table. Belo picked it up and walked out of the room.

"I will only be a moment." She returned and sat back at the desk, but, this time, pulling the desk up closer, not exposing her legs.

"Mr. Wallace, in that you are in the military, I'm sure that you are familiar with Interpol." Belo paused to see if she saw a reaction in Wallace's facial expression. After not noticing anything, she continued.

"We can confirm that you are in the military and a commander of a Special Forces A-Team. So some of the information I am sharing with you, you are probably aware of. Interpol has placed a worldwide alert for an international assassin who identifies himself as a number. Interpol has credited him with at least 10 assassinations in the last five years. Do you recall the murder of the CEO of a weapons manufacturer three years ago in Israel? That assassination was credited to this man, who uses the identification name Thirty-Nine. A year ago in Jordan, the head accountant for the Blood of Islam terrorist group died of an unknown poison. Interpol also credited that assassination to this man, and he used the alias Forty-Three. Most recently, our special-action section intercepted reliable communication that we believe was this same man accepting a contract to be carried out here in Rio de Janeiro. Within that communication, the name Wallace was mentioned in this context: Wallace will know." At that point, WC broke in.

"I get it. You are detaining and questioning anyone who has the name, Wallace. Do I understand you correctly?"

Belo sat back in her chair with a frustrated expression on her face. "You are correct, Mr. Wallace, but we have to investigate every lead, no matter how trivial it may be." Wallace stood up from his chair. "If that's all you have, I want to join my companion; and please provide transportation for us to get back to our hotel."

Chapter 16

United States Coast Guard Air Station, Miami, Florida.

The plane carrying the FBI field agents touched down at the US Coast Guard Air Station in Miami and taxied to an isolated area of the airfield. As the officers, dressed in full tactical gear, unloaded the aircraft, 20 vehicles awaited them.

As Bo was walking toward the cars, he saw officers from Special Weapons and Tactical (SWAT), the Crisis Negotiation Unit (CNU), the Critical Incident Response Group (CIRG) to include the Tactical Section of the CIRG. Bo was assigned to the non-tactical side of the CIRG. This suggested to Bo that this was going to be a well-coordinated assault. All of this firepower is not pulled together unless the operation is being directed from the highest level of the Agency. He and the other agents were loaded into the vehicles and moved away from the runway in the direction of a group of aviation hangars. In a few minutes, all of the vehicles pulled to a stop in front of one of the buildings.

This was Bo Brooks' first time being part of a tactical assault. He had gone through several training exercises and was familiar with the procedures, but being physically part of an operation like this was not an everyday occurrence working out of Washington. Bo thought to himself, "I guess Agent Harris has a point about what field agents are exposed to."

The Agents filed into the hangar, which was set up in an auditorium fashion. There was a portable stage with a big video display screen attached to the wall behind the stage. The chairs were arranged in theater viewing arrangement. Signs indicated where each of the assault teams were to be seated. Bo followed the crowd to the sign that read CIRG. He took a seat and looked around the room, and when his eyes reached the stage, he saw her, Agent Faye Cook-Little. She looked even more beautiful standing there in full tactical gear. Bo continued to stare, hoping she would see him, and they would make eye contact. But there was too much going on for her to pay any attention to this one agent in the crowd.

The District Director for the FBI Southern Region kicked off the briefing and introduced Faye.

"We are very fortunate to have one of our district's most seasoned agents acting as the SAC. Many of you have had the opportunity to work with this Agent on other operations and finished that assignment with some valuable lessons learned and professional experience that you will take with you through the rest of your career with the FBI. My fellow agents, I present to you the SAC, Agent Faye Cook-Little."

Everyone in the hanger stood applauding. Faye walked to the front of the stage sporting a big smile.

"My fellow agents, thank you very much and please take your seats. Over the course of this operation, I'll work to deserve your accolades. OK, let's get started." Faye grabbed the laser pointer off the table and faced the ceiling-tall screen behind her. A power point slide appeared that read; "Operation MIE."

"This operation is authorized by Directive Number 1451, Federal Bureau of Investigation Headquarters, Washington DC, date time stamp as indicated, with joint approval and authorization from the US Justice Department and the State Department." Faye stopped for a moment to give everyone a chance to comprehend the level the operation was approved from.

"Forty-eight hours ago, both ministers of security for the countries of Venezuela and Guyana were assassinated while having a business lunch on the Copacabana Beach in Rio de Janeiro. They were killed from long range by shots fired from a Barrett M82A1 sniper rifle, using Raufoss NM140 MP, .50-caliber ammunition. Because the security ministers were killed on Brazilian soil, the Brazilian government has jurisdiction in pursuing those parties and parties unknown that may be involved in this criminal act.

"The Brazilian authorities intercepted a communication that indicated the MIE contracted the hit to an international assassin that Interpol identified as 'the number assassin.' Brazil has initiated a news blackout on all media coverage of the assassination. Up to this point, the news blackout has been working, and thus, nothing has appeared on CNN, in the Guardian, or from any of the other international news networks.

"The Brazilian government contacted our State Department, State contacted Justice, who contacted us, and here we are. What we do know is that the MIE is located in the Miami-Dade area. They

168

have two locations." A map appeared on the overhead screen. Using the laser pointer, Faye pointed to a spot that was very close to the Everglades. The other location was in the area known as Little Havana.

"What we also know is that that the MIE has purchased, through legal and non-legal means, a very high volume of firearms and ammunition. I'll turn it over to the ATF to explain what they have."

The ATF agent said that the MIE had an arsenal of weapons and ammunition with the possibility of having automatic weapons as well. They even believed that the MIE had acquired at least one, probably two, RPGs and several boxes of grenades.

"For the last two days, both locations have been under 24-hour observation. The facility, which is close to the Everglades, appears to be some type of training center. The place in the downtown area serves as an office or headquarters, but an assortment of semi-automatic and automatic weapons is probably stored there as well."

The map was taken from the screen, and the next thing that appeared on display read "rules of engagement." The District Director stepped back to the microphone.

"The most valuable instruction, if not the significant aspect of any operation, are the laws governing deadly force. This includes when you can shoot, what you can shoot at, and if, in the unlikely event that a bystander or a civilian is wounded, what happens to you for injuring a civilian."

After the Director had finished reading the rules of engagement, Bo looked around the room, trying to measure reactions from the agents sitting in the hanger. As he looked into their faces, he sensed that the other Agents were well-trained and had gone through this before. The Miami Florida Dade County area is known for its drug trafficking money laundering and a host of other illegal activities that require assaults similar to what Bo was about to participate in. This was like an everyday activity for most of these guys, he realized. Bo knew that he didn't want to be the agent that screwed anything up and prove that Agent Harris was right about the field agents who worked in Washington.

Faye came back to the microphone. "Each of the assault leaders has been given your area of responsibility. We will break up into assault teams so you can get familiar with the members of your team and brief your section on their part of the operation. You have 45 minutes, and we will come back together. Once we reconvene, I will answer any remaining questions before we deploy to our respective staging areas."

Whiteys, Doctor's Inlet, Fleming Island, Florida.

Elk and Billy pulled into the parking lot of Whitey's seafood restaurant and trailer park. They were fortunate enough to find a vacant parking space that enabled them to see the entrance door to Whitey's and at the same time have a clear view the people leaving Whitey's and walking toward the trailer park.

All of the vans used to carry the MIE trainees to the Plantation were parked next to each other and very close to the entrance. Elk was pleased to see this because if any of the trainees had left the area, they had to do it on foot or someone else needed to pick them up.

Elk and Billy sat in the car for about an hour. Neither spoke. Elk kept smoking cigars while Billy was smoking cigarettes. Elk finally broke the silence. "Billy, what were some of the other things that went wrong during the Bay of Pigs operation?" Billy took a deep draw on his cigarette, held the smoke in for a moment, exhaled, and then tossed the cigarette out the window.

"The real question is what went right during the Bay of Pigs." Just as Billy made that statement, the door of Whitey's opened and several men walked out of the restaurant, taking the path toward the trailers.

"Those are some of the trainees from the MIE. They are still wearing their training fatigues that they had on today." The men were walking in small groups, laughing and talking as they headed in the direction of their assigned trailers. Several more teams came out the door, and all started moving toward the containers.

"By my count, I think that is all of them?" Billy said as he was pointing his finger, trying to count the men as they passed their position.

170

"Not quite, Billy," Elk said. "I see all of them except their two leaders. One is named Ranuel and the other, Krish." Elk reached under his car seat and pulled out a set of binoculars for a closer look at the men as they passed by.

"Elk! Look over there! Back at the door." Billy was pointing at the entrance to Whitey's. Elk turned his binoculars back toward the door and refocused so he could get a clear picture of the faces of the men.

"Okay, that's them! We have accounted for all of the trainees. I guess we can go now." Elk waited for all of the men to reach a point that was well out of sight of their car. Then he started the car and pulled out of the parking lot and proceeded in the direction of Jacksonville. While they were driving, Billy pulled out his cell phone and contacted Khristy Newborn and Patrick Jefferson. He asked them to meet at the Flagler Center for the conference call with Roy.

—

District Police Office, Copacabana Beach, Rio de Janeiro, Brazil.

Wallace was escorted back upstairs and to a room just beyond the desk where the policeman was checking their passports. The police officer opened the door, and Wallace saw Eve on the right side of the room holding her hands in her lap and looking down at the floor. The room was filled with several other people from the bus. Eve looked up and made eye contact with Wallace as he was walking toward her. She stood and ran to him and jumped into his waiting arms. She was crying and nervously shaking. It was evident that Eve was emotionally upset from all of the things that had taken place.

They had left the hotel to do some sightseeing and a little shopping and ended up witnessing two men being shot to death by the military, now they were being held for questioning by the Brazilian police.

"Okay, Honey, I'm back. Everything is going to be wonderful. We will probably be taken back to the hotel very shortly." Eve continued to hold Wallace tightly and gradually stopped crying. Wallace walked her back to the chairs, and they sat down.

"No one would tell me anything," Eve kept repeating. "The only thing they said was that you were being held for questioning."

Wallace was doing everything that he could to comfort her. He continued to repeat the same thing over and over: "I'm back, and everything is going to be okay." Gradually Eve's breathing began to settle, and it appeared that she was getting her composure back.

"WC, I'm so afraid. What are they going to do with us? We haven't done anything wrong. We are just American tourists on holiday."

In an office adjacent to where the hotel bus passengers were being held, the Chief Inspector, Alosio Santos Candido, Belo, and several other high-ranking officers from the police, security forces, and military were embroiled in a heated discussion over exactly what to do concerning the bus passengers.

"We can eliminate the American named Wallace. He is a Major in the US Army and Special Forces. It is not logical for him to have any connections with the number assassin." Everyone in the room grew quiet, no one commenting on what Belo said. A couple of seconds passed and Chief Inspector Candido spoke up.

"Nevertheless, everyone must remain here until we receive confirmation that the MIE has been captured in Miami."

A voice shouted from across the room, "Holding these people is going to hurt our tourist industry. Don't you see? Each of them will go back to their travel agency and complain about how they have been treated? This will hurt the hotels and casinos. We must let them go now!"

Another voice was heard, this time belonging to a man who just walked into the room. He was not wearing a military uniform. He was dressed very casually in a short-sleeved shirt, trousers, and very expensive shoes; but he carried himself with the confidence of someone with the authority to be there and make a statement that everyone in the room had to agree with.

"We will keep them all night if necessary. We will keep them here until we find out that the Americans have captured or killed the MIE."

Chief Inspector Candido looked in the direction of the man

while everyone turned their heads and simultaneously began to stand. The man who entered the room was Bartolomeu Donnachaidh, the head of the secret police and what was more commonly known as the Hit Squad. He never used his full name, only his first, Bartolomeu. He was the type of individual that no one dared to question.

"Chief Inspector Candido, I am placing you in charge of this operation. You only report to me. Only to me! Keep the people from the bus here for as long as it takes. I do not care about the hotels, and I do not care about the casinos. This is a matter of national security. If anyone in this room does not understand what I'm directing, you may speak up at this time." Bartolomeu looked around the room, making direct eye contact with each person. No one looked at him. They just looked at the floor.

After scanning the room, he pulled a cigar from his shirt pocket, but before he could place the cigar in his mouth, one of the officers in the room pulled out a lighter, holding it at the ready.

Back in the room where Wallace and Eve were waiting, one of the passengers on the bus walked to the side of the area where they were sitting.

"Why did they pull you aside?" The man stood tall looking down at them. All of Wallace's attention was focused on Eve, and so he didn't notice the man until he heard him speak.

Wallace looked up. "I'm sorry. Could you repeat that?"

The man, now looking a little frustrated, replied, "I said, why did they pull you aside?" Wallace stood up, looked around the room and saw that everyone had turned their attention in their direction, anticipating his answer.

"Hello, sir. My name is Wallace C. Barker," he said, reaching out his hand. "And you are?" The man took two steps back from Barker.

"My name is Hastings, and could you please answer my question?" Hasting was the same man seated at the rear of the bus who had the initial questions about where they were being taken.

Wallace shifted his body position such that he was facing the room. He wanted to be sure that everyone could hear what he was about to say. Wallace knew that this was an attempt by Hastings to identify someone in the group to blame for their current situation.

"It's quite straightforward, really. In the Secret Police database, it indicated that I'm in the Army, the US Army, and so they asked me if I was here as a representative of the military or on holiday. My companion and I are on vacation."

The man stood there staring Wallace in the face. He then turned and proceeded to walk back to his chair where he was seated. When he was about five feet from his chair, he turned and looked back in Wallace's direction. "For Christ's sakes, sir, you are a military man. Tell us why we are being held?"

Wallace walked closer to the center of the room and looked into the faces of the people. He could see the fear and frustration of not having a clear understanding of why they were being held was beginning to take its toll on the bus passengers.

"Please understand, I have no authority here. I'm a tourist on vacation with my companion. Anything that I may say now is only speculation. Today, each of us witnessed actions that were taken by the police that resulted in the use of deadly force. Basically, what that means is that everyone who was sitting on the bus can be interviewed as material witnesses for the action that took place today. Because we are not Brazilian citizens, I believe that there is some type of discussions taking place on the legal authority of the local police to proceed with questioning or if they should take us to a higher government authority."

Someone in the room shouted, "You mean this hold bloody thing is about a jurisdiction dispute?" People in the room began to mumble and talk under their breath, but with no one making any real statement until Hastings spoke up again.

"Can't they just let us make a statement? That would seem to me like the simplest way to proceed so we can all get back to the hotel."

Wallace was just about to say something when the door opened, and a police officer walked in followed by several people pushing carts that had sandwiches, bottled water, and an assortment of other drinks. Hastings spoke again before Wallace could say anything.

"If they are feeding us, this means that we are going to be here for some considerable time."

Pointing his finger at Wallace, Hasting said, "I'm sorry,

young man. What did you say your name is?" Wallace turned his attention away from the food carts, looked at Eve and back toward Hastings.

"My name is Barker, Wallace C. Barker, Mr. Hastings." Hastings began to walk toward the center of the room. "Barker, since you are a military man, you seem to have more experience communicating with these people than any of us. I vote that you act as our spokesperson, that you go to them and demand that we are released so we can go back to the hotel."

—

Shands Hospital, Jacksonville, Florida.

Gracie reached down and picked up her purse. "Debra, Honey, I must be getting home. I wish I could stay but I still have a couple of errands to run and you know I have a church meeting tonight that I must get ready for."

Debra was holding her cell phone in her lap. "I totally understand. Bubba will probably be walking through the door any minute. Those longshoremen can't keep him tied up forever." Gracie embraced Debra, then took another look at the door of the room where Helen was and walked to the elevator.

Debra sat down and punched the number to reach Bubba. Her call went into his voice mail. Just as she was about to dial another number, a nurse came out of Helen's room and walked toward her. Debra stood up. "How is she?"

The nurse smiled then reached over and held Debra's hand. "She is doing fine. Her blood pressure is back to normal, and her breathing is regular. I think the worst is behind her. Of course, she is still very much concerned about her husband."

Debra breathed a sigh of relief. The nurse turned and began walking toward the elevator. Just when she was about to push the button, Debra said, "Excuse me, but I have one other question. Have you ever had a situation where the hospital had to bring in a rare type of blood from outside of Jacksonville?"

The nurse turned and walked back to Debra. "Mrs. Webb, I've worked in this hospital for over 12 years, and this is a very unusual situation for us to not have a supply of blood, of any type. Typically we maintain an adequate supply of whole blood for just about every kind of blood known to man." Debra was listing to what the nurse was saying, growing more concerned about the situation and what the probable outcome could be.

"As a matter of fact," the nurse with a solemn look on her face continued, "I'm headed downstairs to check on where we stand to locate the blood and how soon it will be delivered. If you wait here, I should be back in less than 20 minutes." Debra smiled and watched the nurse as she stepped into the elevator.

Just as Debra was about to sit down on the sofa, she was startled when her cell phone rang. She quickly pushed the button to answer the call. "Bubba, I'm so glad you finally got away from those longshoremen so you could return my call." Debra heard a voice on the phone that was familiar to her, but it was not her husband.

"Debra, this is Jerry, Jerry Clark. Bubba wanted me to call you because he is still tied up, and it may be several hours before he can get away."

A very frustrating look came across Debra's face. She was accustomed to all of the responsibility and the directions that Bubba was pulled in as the Mayor of Jacksonville, but here was a situation that involved one of his oldest and best friends. She thought he could, at least, take five minutes to break away from his meeting and give her a call to find out whether or not Joe was going to live or die.

Debra then took a deep breath, forced a smile on her face, and replied, "Jerry, you don't have to explain. I totally understand. It's always the same old thing when Bubba has to meet with those longshoremen, debate after debate after debate. By the time my husband gets home, after a meeting with them, the only thing he is ready for is a double Kentucky bourbon."

Jerry had been with Bubba and Debra political team long enough to have an excellent idea on the situational mood swings of the first couple of Jacksonville. There was no doubt in Jerry's mind that in reality Debra was extremely upset, and the words that she had just spoken were merely politically correct.

"Be sure to pass a note to Bubba that we are still waiting for the blood for Joe. Please do that for me, Jerry. Thanks." Debra hung up.

Jerry kept the phone to his ear for a moment listening to the silence. As he slipped the phone back into his pocket, he pulled out a cigarette, taking the time to have a smoke.

The meeting with the longshoremen had moved from City Hall. They were at the Landing sitting in Ruth Chris Steak House. Although the longshoremen didn't have the political muscle they had a couple of decades ago, they still had the power to bring in a fair number of votes. In Bubba's last election, the push from the Longshoremen's Union helped Bubba pull in a little over 23% of the ballot.

Jacksonville was a transportation hub. Between 40 and 60 percent of goods sold on the east coast, either inbound or outbound flowed through the ports of the city. The human resource for the industry is the International Longshoremen's Union in Jacksonville, listed as the third most powerful union on the east coast.

Jerry finished his cigarette and walked back into the restaurant. He stood in the doorway of the private room where they were having dinner until he and Bubba made eye contact. Bubba was seated at the head of the table, with the president of the local seated next to him, and on his other side was the Longshoremen Board of Directors President. The rest of the entourage was made up of board members and principal officers of the local.

The Mayor stood up and started for the door. "That was a good one, so funny it almost made me piss in my pants. I'm going to the men's room. Please order me another bourbon and water."

Bubba met Jerry in the hallway outside of the dining room where they were eating. "How is Joe doing?" Jerry took a step back.

"They still haven't located the blood to give him a transfusion. Debra seems to be very concerned and upset, but she wants you to call her as soon as possible." Bubba Webb took a few steps away from Jerry and pulled out his cell phone.

"Hello, Honey. How are you doing? You've been over at the hospital almost the whole day. What is the status of the blood and how are Joe and Helen doing?"
The phone was silent for a few seconds.

"Bubba Webb, it's about time you gave your wife the courtesy to return her call. Helen is doing much better, but they still have her on an IV, and she is still lightly sedated. But what I am

177

really fearful of is the fact that they have not located the blood needed for Joe's transfusion."

Bubba broke in, "How long has it been since they knew he needed a transfusion?"

Debra shouted back, "Bubba Webb! That really doesn't matter if the blood still isn't here. Now do you think you can get someone to make some calls to see if that would help?"

Bubba turned around and faced Jerry. "Sure, Honey. I'll get Jerry to get on the phone and start making calls. As a matter of fact, I'll get him to go to the newspapers and television stations, and we will put a request out to the media asking anyone who has the type of blood required to come to the emergency room at the hospital. Hell, I'll even put up $500 as an incentive."

Debra smiled. "That would be so beautiful, and probably just what is needed because the hospital is only relying on typical ways of bringing in blood. Thank you, Bubba. I'll let Helen know. You better get back to the longshoremen. We'll need their votes next year."

After ending the call, Bubba placed his hand on Jerry's shoulder. "Now, Jerry, you heard what I told Debra. I want you to get on this now and see if you can make all of that social media stuff work for us so we can get the real blood over to the hospital and help Joe pull through this.

"Jerry, you have been with me long enough to know that I believe that friendship is everything. Joe Singletary is one of the oldest, if not my oldest, friend. He is like a brother to me, and I'm not saying that like a political cliché. If you were lying in that hospital in the exact condition Joe is in, I'd be doing the same thing for you."

Jerry looked at Bubba. "I understand entirely, Mr. Mayor. I'll get right on this and use every resource that I have. We'll get the blood here."

Bubba squeezed Jerry's shoulder. "I know you will Jerry. You're a good man. Thank you."

The Mayor turned and walked back into the room with the longshoremen. "Now, what did I miss? Did you guys order me another bourbon? If you did, I hope you didn't get me that cheap stuff like your union president keeps at home." The room lit up with laughter.

Chapter 17

Whiteys, Doctor's Inlet, Fleming Island, Florida.

Ranuel and Krish returned to their trailer and sat on their beds reminiscing about the activities of the day. Ranuel could see that Krish was incredibly enthusiastic about how well the men reacted to the training, that no one complained, and everyone seemed to be giving 100% throughout the day. It was evident to Krish that they had selected the right group of men to be part of this particular unit.

It was pleasing for Ranuel to see Krish in such a positive mood that he almost contemplated not telling him about the information he had received from their headquarters.

Krish completed praising the men for their outstanding work, then finished his cigar. While walking to the bathroom to take a shower, he turned to Ranuel. "After you finish your shower, you can tell me what the message was about." Ranuel agreed, but he was feeling the extent of the long day of training, and when Krish came out of the shower, Ranuel had fallen asleep lying on his bed still in his training uniform.

Krish walked over and was just about to turn the lights off when Ranuel said, "My friend, we must talk." Rubbing his eyes, Ranuel sat up on the side of the bed facing Krish.

"You have had a premonition that we would probably be betrayed by our American allies, and that still remains to be seen. But the news that I received today indicates that the betrayal may be coming from within our organization. It seems that the decision makers in New York are having disagreements concerning how the government will be formed once we announce the establishment of our new country." Ranuel paused for reaction from Krish. His friend had never really kept abreast of the inner workings of the political side of the MIE. He realized that the impact of what he was explaining to Krish may not be completely understood, so Ranuel wanted to see if Krish had any questions before he proceeded.

"You see, Krish, many things must be considered when establishing a new country. What we are being trained for at the Plantation represents only one of the many challenges that must be completed moving toward full independence. Having a strong defense force will ensure the stability of our new country and ensure that we are not overtaken by either Venezuela or Guyana. But the major obstacle that we must face is how we are going to be organized into a functioning body capable of caring for the people." Krish was sitting on the side of the bed with a very puzzled look on his face. Ranuel couldn't tell if it was from the long day or what he had said.

"I don't understand, Ranuel. Are you telling me that we are going through all this training for nothing?"

Ranuel was just as tired as his friend. "Let's get some rest, and tomorrow, when we head for the Plantation, we will ride in the same van, and I will explain everything to you."

—

CIA Headquarters, Langley, Virginia.

Roy Benning was in the middle of his conference call with his administrative staff. "You mean to tell me we are an intelligence agency, and we can't find out how the Brazilian police got their sights on the MIE in Miami?" No response came from any of Roy's staff. Then a very timid sounding voice broke the silence.

"Besides the Director and the Deputy, there is only one other person who has enough authority to keep information from being circulated within the Agency, and that is the DDP." The silence on the conference felt like someone had poured a bucket of ice water over everyone as they were getting out of a hot tub.

"Hold the line a minute and let me make a call." Roy pushed the mute button and turned to his desktop. He brought up the Agency's unclassified calendar on his computer. The DDP was scheduled to be in town. After that, he checked the "For Your Eyes Only" calendar. All of the classified and unclassified calendars confirmed that the DDP was in town.

Roy then reached for his Blackberry and pushed the number to connect to the DDP cellphone. It went to voicemail. "Madam DDP, this is Roy. Please return this call when you have the opportunity." Next Roy called the direct line to the DDP. Her admin assistant answered the phone.

"Roy, you are working rather late tonight. Why aren't you at the White House Correspondents' dinner?"

Roy changed screens on his monitor to his calendar to see if he had missed an appointment or memo and was supposed to be at the dinner. Sure enough, he had received an invitation to attend. His secretary confirmed that he would be going. "I'm just about to head over to the Hilton now."

"Well, Roy, you should see the DDP at the dinner. She is seated at table 111, about two tables from where you will be seated."

Roy looked at the clock on the computer, then at his watch. "Thanks."

Turning back to his desk phone, he pushed the mute button to reconnect to the conference call. "Everyone is over at the Hilton attending the correspondents' dinner. In fact, I received an invitation to attend. "

That same timid voice broke in. "The President's correspondents' dinner? That's big-time stuff."

Roy smiled to himself. "Well, I guess somebody must have really screwed up if they sent me an invitation." Roy cleared his throat. "OK, this is what we are going to do. If the FBI goes through with the raid on the MIE operations in Miami, we are going to cut our losses and turn over the trainees at the Plantation to the FBI. After I get off this call, I'm going to call Billy and see if his guys on the ground have any new information. In the meantime, I want you guys to keep working to find out how this thing got away from us. Any questions?"

After ending the call, Roy thought that it was somewhat odd that the DDP had not returned his call in that they were still within the first 48 hours of a new operation and protocol almost always dictated that, within the first three days of operation, anything could go wrong. So he was wondering if something else was going on in the Agency, but everyone wanted to make it seem like it was business as usual. Roy decided to check if there had been any significant pizza deliveries. Late-night pizza deliveries at the Pentagon, Langley, or the White House was a signal to the news media that breaking news was about to happen.

Roy walked into the private washroom of his office to change into his tuxedo for dinner. He decided to call Billy as he rode to the Hilton. As he was washing up, his thoughts lingered on what one of his staff members said during the teleconference. "There are only three people in the Agency who have enough authority to restrict information, and that is the Director, the Deputy Director, and the DDP."

Roy was confident that the DDP was not pleased with his choice of Billy to replace Karl, but what was even more significant was that the DDP did not think he should be on the South American desk. The realization hit him that if she had anything to do with it, she was going to see that Roy would be replaced. In the history of the Agency, this would not be the first time that an operation was sacrificed because of internal bickering and Departmental power struggles, he thought.

The more Roy analyzed the last 48 hours, the stronger the possibility existed that the way the Brazilian police were tipped off about the MIE was from within the Agency, and the person who had a major hand in providing the tip was no doubt the DDP.

Hypothetically, if the DDP had provided the name of the MIE to the Brazilian police for planning and executing the assassination of the ministers of security, the question is why?

The DDP would take such an action and jeopardize an operation that would place the United States in a position to be less dependent on oil from the Middle East.

Roy finished tying his bow-tie and uttered, "Ridiculous." Then he turned out the lights in his washroom, left his office, and headed for the Hilton Hotel.

—

Miami, Florida.

The FBI and ATF Teams began to converge on the two locations in Miami. Faye made the decision to establish the Command Center midway between the two objectives in a vacate lot across the street from a Wawa Service Station. Faye's decision was determined by where the best communication point would be for the maximum use of all resources available to her in this operation: satellites, drones, thermal and heat imaging, and in the unlikely case it was necessary, she could even call in tactical air support. The entire objective was to bring all members of the MIE into custody by any means necessary.

By the time the command center was established, they had begun to receive satellite imagery at the two locations. What they were starting to see was already causing concerns that would have an impact on how the plan had to proceed.

The plan called for simultaneous early morning raid taking place at 5:00 or 6:00 AM. At the Everglades location, FBI teams were to approach from outskirts of the Everglades, moving in from three different directions, north, west and south, leaving the easterly direction as an escape route, pushing the MIE into a trap that would be closed by the ATF teams coming in from the east.

At the downtown location, agents were to surround the building, a group of four to eight Agents approaching the building from the front to serve the arrest and search warrants.

The FBI teams found out very quickly that the movement through the Everglades was going to take several more hours than the plan called for. Many parts of the glades that the route would carry them were flooded and others infested with alligators, insects, and snakes. The movement was slow and very precise in that the operation dictated a surprise assault on the camp.

The satellite also provided laser body heat sensors that indicated there were as many as 35 hostiles located at the site in the Everglades. The location of the office in the Little Havana section of Miami suggested that there were 5 to 10 hostiles at that site. Almost all of the heat signatures at the downtown location indicated that the hostiles at that place were in the basement and appeared to be sleeping.

With the assault pushed back two to three hours, the likelihood of launching a simultaneous attack was slipping away. If they launched an attack on the location in Little Havana, they would lose the possibility of surprise at the other place. The Everglades would probably be tipped off resulting in a gun battle that could get pretty messy.

Faye had to decide if she wanted to shift to an aerial assault from helicopters in the Everglades with the ATF closing in from the east using ground transportation. An air strike would create its own set of problems, however, not to mention they still had to prepare a requisition for the aircraft, which was available at the MacDill Air Force Base, Special Operations Command (SOCOM), but the paperwork still had to be processed.

At the Command Center, a clipboard was shoved in front of Faye. "We need you to sign this so we can get the choppers from SOCOM." Faye looked at the clip while reaching for a pen from the Kevlar jacket shoulder pocket of her vest.

Before signing the document request, she said, "I want to have a Predator or Reaper on station in the next 12 hours. So add the drone to this, and I'll sign it for authorization." Faye turned her attention to the situation board. "What's the status of the teams in the Everglades?"

The FBI Teams approaching from the west progress toward their objective had been less than a mile. In fact, only about a couple of hundred yards. That's how thick the overgrowth and undergrowth of the Everglades was on the routes they had decided to take to reach the objective. Two agents had been bitten by copperhead snakes, and one agent had to be pulled out of quicksand. From the north, the team was moving at about the same rate, but fortunately, they had not experienced any casualties as a result of snakebites or quicksand. It appeared that the force approaching from the south was making the best progress.

Ideally, Faye wanted the raid to occur at sunrise. It was four hours before the sun was scheduled to come up, and both locations were showing movement activity. There was no change in the Little Havana area, but movement at the Everglades site was picking up.

"Excuse me, Agent Cook-Little." Faye turned her attention away from the situation board. A female agent was standing in front of her with that same clipboard. "Everything has been updated as you requested and an electronic request transmitted. All I have to do is get your signature, and I will fax this over." Faye took the clipboard from the agent, read through it, and quickly signed.

"What's your name and how long have you been in the Agency." The young Agent made eye contact with Faye, "Oh, my name is Peggy, and I've been with the Agency for 11 months, I work out of the Jacksonville office."

Faye took a closer look at the agent. "I work at the Jacksonville office also. Have we met before?" Faye thought for a second, handing the clipboard back to the Agent. "Yes, we did! As I recall, you were on that Little Talbot Island raid six months ago."

Peggy began to blush and feel uncomfortable, but she maintained her brilliant smile. "Yes, ma'am. We surely were both on that assignment. You were the assistant agent in charge of that operation, and everyone thought that you did an excellent job. I'm sure that this Operation will work out the same way. I just want to let you know that I'm working just as hard as I can to be as good and as professional as you are. Agent Faye Cook-Little, you are my role model, and I want to be just as good of an agent as you are."

Faye grabbed Peggy's hand. "You continue to work like you did on that Little Talbot Island raid and you will do just fine in the Agency. Keep up the good work and let's have lunch together when we get back to Jacksonville."

"Faye, we need you over here," a voice called out as Peggy, still smiling, backed away. Faye returned the smile as she turned around and walked toward the sound of the voice.

"Faye, I recommend that it's time to pull the team advancing from the west out and get them back to this location." The agent was pointing to a place on the map that was displayed on the situation board and labeled the LZ Bravo. Faye studied the area of the landing zone and checked her watch. The agent briefing Faye continued. "The first two choppers have just lifted off from MacDill and can pick that team up in the next 40 minutes."

Another voice broke in, "It will probably take that team moving in from the west about an hour to get from where they are now to LZ Bravo for the pick-up."

Faye continued to study the map. "I agree, pull the team from the westward approach and get them over to that pick-up point ASAP!"

Faye walked a few feet to the right of the situation board and began to focus her attention on the television monitors. The four screens were providing real-time viewing of the location in Little Havana. Within the last three hours, a three block area had been completely cleared of all residents, storekeepers, or anyone who could end up being an innocent bystander in the event the raid turned into a gun battle.

The people were transported to a neighborhood middle school, which also served as a natural disaster shelter in the case of a hurricane. As the people were checked in to the shelter, their cell phone numbers were taken as part of the registration process. Having the mobile phone numbers enabled the FBI to monitor outgoing and incoming calls, searching for any indication that someone was trying to tip off the MIE.

Still looking at the screens, Faye suddenly said, "I need an update on the media coverage. Where do we stand on that?" It had taken about five minutes before an agent was standing in front of Faye holding an iPad.

"Frankly, Faye, no media has shown up. No calls, nothing. Typically we will start to receive calls asking questions, but none of that has happened. I think the reason we have not received any calls from our media friends is that the word is out that the President is supposed to address the nation sometime tonight. At present, that's the big story."

A tall agent standing next to Faye replied, "OK then, and stay on top of it. Keep Faye updated if anything changes."

—

Westward Raid Approach, Everglades.

Bo Brooks was moving with the CIRG section on the western approach to the MIE location in the Everglades. A city boy, the only time Bo had seen any snakes were at the zoo, in his high school biology class, or on television. One of the agents who had been bitten by a copperhead was standing next to him. He had been bitten as they took a break. Bo had just asked him his name when he screamed out in pain.

At first, Bo couldn't imagine what had happened until he saw the tail end of the snake slithering off into the underbrush. The EMS teams rushed both of the victims away in a matter of minutes. Agent Harris told Bo that, if they could get the victims to an emergency room and extract the venom within the first 45 minutes to an hour, they both had a decent chance of surviving. A copperhead snake bite is one of the most lethal in the Everglades.

All three assault teams were being guided by national park rangers who were full-blooded Seminole Indians. They knew the Everglades like the back of their hands, but they had not been consulted in designating the routes that had been chosen to reach their objectives.

The reason given for keeping them out of the information and planning loop was to ensure the element of surprise. The concern was that the more people who knew about the raid, the higher the probability that the word would leak out.

The radio message was received to pull back and move to LZ Bravo. At first, the men thought that this was excellent news, but when they discovered they had less than 30 minutes to reach the location. That seemed an impossible task; but the Seminole Indian park rangers knew a shortcut that, if they pushed their pace hard would allow them to reach the landing zone with time to spare.

Each of the agents on the team was carrying 30 to 45 pounds of equipment and ammunition. The night air was blowing a fresh breeze through the Everglades, but after walking in stagnant swamp water for the last two hours, the conditions were beginning to take a toll on the agents. Mosquitoes were everywhere, and even using insect repellent, you could still hear them flying around your ears, trying to find a spot of skin to bite.

Southern Raid Approach, Everglades.

"Command center, this is Raider Team Three."

"Raider Team Three, this is Command Center. We are receiving you, Lima Charlie, over."

"Command center, this is Raider Team Three. Please be advised that we have reached the outskirts of the objective. We are moving into attack formation. From my location, I can see only one roving security guard walking the perimeter with what appears to be a guard dog of unknown species. The guard is armed with an AK-47.

There doesn't seem to be any movement in any of the buildings we can see from our location. Over."

Someone in command center shouted out, "Bring up their visual on the monitors."

Another voice shouted out with excitement, "Find the SAC and ask her to step back into the trailer. She needs to see this."

Faye stepped back into the command center with a cup of coffee in her hand. She walked directly to the monitors. "It's about time we got some good news," Faye said as she placed her coffee cup down on the table. The satellite feed was clearly showing the silhouettes of the FBI southern approach team in a position less than 100 yards from the three buildings that made up the MIE compound.

"Tell them to hold their position and continue to observe, and at the first sign of any increased activity, to let us know. Also, say this was a splendid job." Faye shouted from her command console, "Give me the status of Raider Team One."

The control center found out that Raider Team One, the assault team that was moving to the objective from the north, had made its' way through most of the thick jungle-like conditions and was within half a klick of the objective.

What was developing was that the assault still could be made as planned from the north and south, but the western attack, Raider Team Two's position, would be an aerial assault. Once again, Faye's primary concern was that the noise from the helicopters would take away the element of surprise. It was of the utmost importance that they give the hostiles as little time as possible to react to the assault and reduce the likelihood of a gun battle.

—

Flagler Center, Jacksonville, Florida.

It had been a long day, and after Roy had not called them back to have the conference call, Billy told everyone to go home and get a good night's sleep, and expect to have the call with Roy the next morning.

Billy and his wife Cathy lived in a gated community within jogging distance from the Flagler Center. However, on most days he would drive from South Jacksonville to the downtown office located at the Federal Building, which at this point no longer existed.

Billy chuckled to himself as he contemplated his short drive into work the next day. He could almost sleep in late and still be at the Flagler Center at the same time he would be arriving at the office downtown. After over 12 years of fighting the traffic between here and downtown Jacksonville, it took the blowing up of the Federal Building to give him a shorter commute.

Billy was sitting at his kitchen table sipping a cup of tea when his Blackberry rang. He looked at the display and saw that it was Roy.

"Roy, I let everyone go home because I figured you probably had gotten tied up. I told them that we will make the conference call first thing in the morning." An expression of disappointment came over Roy's face. "Billy, have you heard anything new about the FBI raid in Miami?"

Billy took a quick sip of his tea. "Nothing other than what we spoke about earlier today. We do know that it is scheduled to be held within the next 24 hours. But Roy, what we can't figure out is how the FBI connected the dots to the MIE."

"I have a theory, Billy, but at present I haven't fit all the pieces of the puzzle together. Hopefully, I'll be able to see whether it is a sound theory or just a figment of my imagination within the next 24 hours. But before I let you go, I made a decision as to what we are going to do if this FBI raid goes through." Before Roy could finish his statement, Billy began speaking over him.

"Roy, before you say anything, let me give you my recommendation. While we were waiting for your call, Patrick, Khristy, Elk and I had a rather frank discussion concerning our advice on how to proceed. What we think we should do is to cut our losses. At this point in the operation, there is a faint audit trail. These guys have had less than 24 hours of training at the Plantation. So we figure that what audit trail that does exist can be easily eliminated if this FBI raid goes through. I agreed with what they said, and so my recommendation is that, if the FBI executes the attack on the headquarters of the MIE in Miami, we should give up the trainees staying at Whitey's."

Roy was relieved to hear that Billy and his team came to the same conclusion regarding their course of action that he was planning on taking. He made the decision not to tell Billy at this time, but to hold off on sharing his decision for another 12 hours, until after he had talked with the DDP. So Roy didn't respond to Billy's recommendation. He just said, "Get some rest, and I'll call you in the morning."

As Roy was leaving the dinner, he was relieved that his people were backing him up with his decision to cut their losses and give up the MIE trainees. The next and most difficult part was his meeting with the DDP. She had not returned his call, and he was hard pressed to figure a reason for her not to call, especially with her being in town. If she had been in the field, that would be a different story.

The DDP was not seated at the table her Admin Assistance told him she would be seated. Nor did he spot her in the crowd. He saw the Director and the Deputy, but the opportunity did not come up for them to talk.

There was an unwritten rule within the Agency. If you are in a particular setting with other Agency members, the rule of thumb was not to be seen mingling together.

Roy arrived back at his condo. Rather than taking the stairs to his floor, Roy decided to take the elevator. It's always nice to come home, he thought to himself as he threw his keys on the table beside the door and walked into the kitchen. He opened the refrigerator door and pulled out a Blue Moon beer, walked into his home office, and turned the television on that stays tuned to CNN.

He was just about to sit down and go through his mail when the words that were being spoken on the TV entered his mind. The President of the United States had just completed an address to the nation. Roy missed the speech, but the news media were recapping what the President said.

Roy grabbed his remote, turned the volume up, and as the words were sinking in, he found out why the DDP had not returned his call. He began to shout out loud, "They did it! Those sons of bitches did it. The Middle East desk did it. They got OBL." Roy fell back in his chair and took two big swallows of beer.

A smile of ecstasy and a big grin came over Roy Benning's face. The CIA and, within the Agency, the Middle East desk, had been the butt of jokes for not being able to find, capture, or kill the most wanted person in the world.

In some ways, the Middle East desk was under a stigma similar to the South American desk; but the stigma was not as old as the cloud hanging over the people working for Roy. The President's announcement tonight erased the stigma over the Middle East desk, however. They had done what they were supposed to do.

Even though there are not a lot of daily discussions around the Agency, the history of the Bay of Pigs operation was laid in stone. The Jacksonville Florida South American desk screwed up when they made the decision to leave those people on the beach, but it just wasn't Brigade 2506 that was left on the beach.

For months preceding the invasion the CIA had contracted people to work inside Cuba, to provide intelligence to finalize the details needed for the invasion. That whole network of people was abandoned and all of the other people that the South American desk utilized to plan and set up everything, including American contract operatives, were captured, jailed, and executed by the Cuban Revolutionary Army. None of these people's names ever surfaced. To this day, none of their families knew what happened to them. The CIA disavowed any knowledge of their existence let alone any connection to the Agency and the operation. The Bay of Pigs invasion will always haunt every person who holds the position of Desk Chief of the Jacksonville South American Office from now until somehow restitution is made.

Roy sat in his chair thinking about his situation and what he had to face the next day in his meeting with the DDP. It was no doubt that the DDP did not return his call because she was in the situation room monitoring everything during the raid and giving feedback to the White House.

Both the Middle East Desk and the South American desk reported to the DDP on any type of clandestine operation. Tomorrow he would be walking into the DDP's office to try to explain how Operation Fertile Ground had been compromised and recommending that they abandon it before it became a political liability.

Roy figured that he had a strong position because the press would be running with the most recent news concerning the killing of OBL. His small operation would probably go unnoticed, except for the local papers in Miami, especially if the raid was successful and no one got hurt. Hell, most people probably hadn't even heard of Essequibo or know where to find it on a map.

The question that was still haunting Roy was why the MIE would enter into an agreement with the CIA to train them to set up their own country, and at the same time, contract out to one of the most expensive assassins in the world to take out the ministers of security for both countries.

Even while taking his shower, the question kept circulating in Roy's mind. "I could see the MIE contracting for the assassination after they had completed training and were established operationally, but they have had less than 24 hours of training.

"From all the information that we have in our files, they have some money, but not a lot of money. We have done our due diligence and screened everyone who has given them a penny within the last10 years. All the money that they have received came from private donors. We've never uncovered a funding trail that was traced back to any multi-national operation. So another question that remains to be answered is where did they get the money to pay an assassin if indeed the MIE contracted the killer?"

While Roy was stepping out of his shower, he said to himself, I wonder if the Agency contracted the hit on the ministers of security and it was authorized by the DDP so she could place her own person in my job.

The DDP was very ambitious, the first woman to hold the position, and from all of the reports that Roy had heard she was a very aggressive field agent who many said took more risks than were actually necessary. Rumor control also stated that the DDP didn't have a lot of friends in the Agency, but a lot of that was jealousy from her male contemporaries. But at the end of the day what everyone agreed on was that she always got the job done. Roy knew that she didn't care for him, or for Billy either. That was a given, but to call a hit on a foreign national was a little extreme even for the Agency.

Roy had been around long enough to have been involved in several Agency power struggles. Politics in a clandestine government organization can become putty intense.

Roy dried off, brushed his teeth, and started for his bedroom. He already knew that he would probably be analyzing his situation all night and not get much sleep, so he returned to his desktop and sent Billy Mills an email to turn the MIE trainees over to the FBI.

Chapter 18

FBI Command Center, Miami, Florida.

As FBI Raider Team Two emerged from the Everglades, they could see the three helicopters about 200 yards ahead of them from the point where they walked out of the swamp.

"Command center, this is Raider Team Two, over."

"Raider Team Two, this is command center, over."

"Command center, this is Raider Team Two. Please be advised that we have just exited the swamp and are in sight of the helicopters`. We will be ready for liftoff at your command, over."

The control center replied, "Roger, Raider Team Two, out."

Bo Brooks grabbed his canteen and poured water over his face and neck. Agent Harris, who was standing beside him, commented, "Well Agent Brooks, this is what a real FBI Field Agent does before breakfast." Bo gave Agent Harris a polite smile but just wasn't in the mood to go into a discussion on who are the toughest agents.

The Lead Helicopter Commander walked over to the men resting and drinking water. "I realize you guys just came out of the swamp, but we must go on setting you up in loading order, giving you chopper assignments and a few safety procedures."

There were three helicopters. Each helicopter would carry 12 agents. Agents Harris and Bo Brooks were placed in the group that would be flying in the second chopper into the assault.

Back at the command center, Faye was seated at the operational console, viewing the live satellite feeds from both locations when she was startled by an agent who approached as if he did not want anyone to notice and began whispering.

"Faye, we just got this in. I'm not certain what I should do with it." The agent handed an iPad to her. Faye read the email.

"Did we get anything else other than this?"

Looking puzzled, the Agent replied, "That's what's so strange. We have nothing on any activities concerning the MIE other than what is associated with this operation." Faye called over the Assistant SAC and two other senior agents.

"Take a look at this and tell me what you think." Each read the email and passed the iPad to the next agent until everyone had read the message. One of the senior officials looked at Faye as she was seated at the command console.

"Well, Faye, as you surely know, we have no resources to take care of this. My recommendation is to contact the Clay County Police Department and have them check it out, and if it is confirmed, we authorize arrest warrants, and they will take everyone into custody."

Faye looked into the faces of the other agents standing around her at the command console. "Sounds good. Give them a call and make it happen."

Then Faye checked her watch with the operational time clock. The assault was to commence at 6:00 AM sharp. "I want to have one last talk with each of the Team Leaders."

Someone shouted, "I'm bringing them up on your screen now." In less than a minute, Faye could see all Team Leaders' faces on her monitor.

Just before Faye was about to speak to the Team Leaders, someone shouted, "We have movement at the compound!" Faye quickly switched screen and, sure enough, a group of between 15 to 20 men was coming out of one of the buildings.

Another voice said, "It looks like they plan to do some physical training."

Faye quickly replied, "I don't see any of them carrying weapons."

"Neither do I. All of them seem to be unarmed."

"We have them in the open."

Faye moved closer to the monitor. Again she could not see any sign of the men holding any type of weapons in their hands. She looked at the operational clock. It was 5:53 AM, seven minutes before the raid was scheduled to kick off. From the command console, Faye shouted, "Initiate the assault. I say again, initiate the assault!"

Four agents at the downtown location in Little Havana walked up to the door of the MIE headquarters, banged on the door and identified themselves, and when there was no response, breached the door and entered the building. Another 10 agents at the rear of the building blew the hinges off the door and entered without firing a shot. Another 10 officers flooded through the front behind the first four agents who came. Within 20 seconds there were over 25 FBI agents going floor to floor in the building, handcuffing any human being inside the building.

In the Everglades, the assault team from the north and the assault team from the south began to rush to buildings. The helicopters, the assault team from the west, were in the air. Within minutes, the ATF assault team from the East had entered the compound and was making a turn into the area where men were conducting their physical training.

Faye could see everything via the live satellite feeds. Faye kept switching her console monitors from the assault at the downtown office of the MIE to the situation in the Everglades. "I need a headcount of the hostiles at both locations," Faye directed from her console.

At the Everglades, the first chopper set down and the agents unloaded and began rushing into the compound. Suddenly, between three to five men ran out of a door on the west side of one of the building. They were south of the group of agents that landed with the first drop. The command center spoke to the Raider Team Lead. "You have hostiles to your right, one carrying something that could be a rocket launcher. Over."

It was a shoulder-fired Stinger missile. The man kneeled on one knee and fired the missile at the second helicopter and made a direct fit. The 12 agents on board the helicopter, along with the crew of three, all went down in flames.

The last helicopter landed. The officers unloaded and moved on to neutralize the five men who had escaped out the west end of the building. Together, both assaults took less than 28 minutes. Twelve FBI agents and three Special Operations Command helicopters crew members were killed during the Everglades assault. No casualties were reported from the attack on the MIE headquarters.

—

Whitey's Trailer Park, Fleming Island.

Krish was the first to hear the commotion. He quickly reached for his revolver and knocked on the bathroom door. Ranuel was shaving as Krish opened the door. "Ranuel, the *Americanos* have called the police on us. Come and see." Ranuel and Krish quickly walked to one of the trailer windows and very carefully moved the curtains so they could see what was happening. They saw the police SWAT teams handcuffing and marching their counterparts toward the parking lot at the restaurant.

Ranuel quickly picked up his cell phone and began to dial numbers. Just as in his previous procedures, the caller would answer the phone, but in this case, it was Ranuel who was sending the message: "Operation compromised. Execute reprisal protocol measures. I say again, operation compromise! Execute reprisal protocol." Just as Ranuel made the last call, the SWAT team broke through the trailer door, and within seconds, both Krish and Ranuel were in handcuffs and being led away.

—

Belmond Copacabana Palace Hotel, Copacabana Beach, Rio de Janeiro.

Shortly after the break of day, the hotel guests were released and driven back to the hotel. Eve and Wallace were back in their suite soon after they arrived.

For their inconvenience, the country of Brazil agreed to pay the hotel bills, including paying for an additional three days for all of the guests who were detained by the police. They also gave each of the guests $2,000 in U.S. Dollars, plus another $1,000 dollars to be used as casino money. Each of the guests had to sign statements that they would not hold the Brazilian authorities liable for their treatment.

Most of the people from the hotel did not like signing the document, but the realization that they would be receiving an all-expense paid vacation won everyone over to accepting the deal. After signing the papers, everyone was handed $3,000 U.S. currency as they stepped onto the bus.

Once they got back into their hotel room, Eve immediately went into the bathroom and started taking a long hot shower, and Wallace began filling the Jacuzzi. While the water was running, he pulled out his tablet and was checking the internet to see if anything appeared on the web concerning the shootings. To WC's amazement, he could not find anything.

"WC, did you see anything that would explain why they held us all night?" Eve uttered as she walked from the shower to the Jacuzzi.

Wallace used all of his favorite search engines, but nothing was coming up. He even tried some of those weird sites that his friend Felix told him about, but he couldn't find anything online about any shootings that took place in Brazil. He then thought about his conversation with Belo and decided to search for an assassin wanted by Interpol, code name Forty-Three.

WC ended up on the Interpol website. Sure enough, he found what he was looking for. Just as Belo said, the number assassin was listed. No picture and no nationality just wanted for murder.

Wallace looked up from his tablet and watched Eve as she stepped into the Jacuzzi and turned the jets on and decided not to speak to Eve about his conversation with Belo. He just said.

"Funny, I can't seem to find anything that would give them the right to hold us except for the shootings that we witnessed."

After saying that, Wallace took a shower, opened a bottle of champagne, and joined Eve in the Jacuzzi. This was the last night of their vacation, and tomorrow they would be flying back to the States.

—

Jacksonville, Florida, Home of Billy and Cathy Mills.

Billy Mills was sitting in his home office watching CNN and another recap of the President's announcement on the killing of OBL. Billy and Cathy decided to do something that they had not done in some time: have breakfast together at IHOP. Checking his Blackberry, he saw the message he had been waiting for from Elk: "All loose ends have been taken care of." Billy composed a message and forward Elk's text message along with his own message to Roy Benning at Langley.

Cathy came downstairs and looked into Billy's office. "OK, I'm ready. Let's go."

Cathy got into her car first, and so Billy jumped on the passenger side and said, "After we have breakfast you can drop me off at the Flagler Center, and I'll jog home tonight. I really need to start getting into shape for the river run that is coming up."

Cathy smiled and said, "I think I'll run that this year with you."

They backed out of their garage and started down their street, passed through the gated entrance, made a turn onto their main thoroughfare, then came to a stop at the intersection. A school bus was stopped on the other side of the street, and two cars were behind the bus. Traffic in both directions came to a stop while the school crossing guard assisted high school students loading the bus.

As Cathy and Billy Mills were listening to more news on their radio about the killing of OBL, there was a flash of white light followed by a thunderous explosion. In a ball of flames, Cathy's SUV flew into the air 100 feet or more. The windows of the school bus were shattered with hot metal and glass cutting through the bodies of the children as they sat helplessly in their seats. All life within 100 feet of Cathy and Billy Mills' car ended.

———

CIA Headquarters, Langley, Virginia.

Roy Benning was swiping his security badge when his Blackberry started signaling him that he was receiving emails and text messages. Roy first checked his text messages and saw that things were proceeding as planned in Jacksonville. He pushed the button for the elevator and saw that he had received an email from the DDP. This didn't surprise him, and so he put his Blackberry back in his pocket, entered the elevator, and pushed the button to his floor.

The entire building was in an upbeat mood. People were smiling and greeting each other with "good morning." This type of date doesn't come very often at Langley. Roy knew that the DDP didn't start receiving people in her office until 8:00. It was just 6:10, so he knew, even if he were the first person on her agenda for today, the meeting probably wouldn't be scheduled until after 8:00. So he decided to put his briefcase away and go back downstairs to the cafeteria and have some breakfast.

Roy was just about to sit down at one of the tables when he looked up at the television monitor broadcasting the news, a burning school bus with several other burning vehicles in the background. Streaming below the scene, the caption read, "Tragedy comes to suburban Jacksonville, Florida community." Roy left the tray on his table and headed for his office. He stepped off the elevator to the ringing of his Blackberry. It was Khristy Newborn.

"Hello, Khristy. I just saw this scene on the monitor in the cafeteria. Does this affect us?"

Khristy cleared her throat. "Roy, I'm sorry to be the one to have to tell you this, but we're kind of sure that Billy and Cathy Mills are casualties in the explosion that took place this morning just blocks from their home. Elk is over there now trying to get as much information as he can. But we're kind of sure that their car was involved in whatever happened."

By this time, Roy was inside his office and seated behind his desk. He was speechless. In a ten day span, he had lost three of his most senior people at the Jacksonville office. Except in a war zone, it was unheard of losing people in any position in the Agency let alone so many in such a short period of time. First Karl and Nancy Mansfield and today Billy; but Cathy, Billy Mills' wife, was also gone.

"Khristy, I am temporarily placing you in the position of chief of the South American desk. I'll have to get final approval from the Director, Deputy, and DDP. I should be on the DDP scheduled for later this morning. I'm typing up an email as we speak, but I'll hold up until you guys give me confirmation as soon as you get it."

Khristy quickly responded, "Sure, Roy. I'll take over, but I don't know if I really want this responsibility. But we can talk about that later."

Roy was a little surprised to hear Khristy's response to being placed in the Desk Chief position. In some ways, Khristy was very similar to the DDP, not quite as aggressive but more than ready to hold the position she had just said she was not sure she wanted.

Chapter 19

Galileo International Airport Rio de Janeiro.

The hotel limousine dropped Eve and Wallace at the airport with more than enough time to make customs, do a little shopping in the Airport, and comfortably wait for their departure.

"I must call Tony and catch up on everything." Wallace could sense the excitement and care in Eve's voice. The connection between a mother and child is truly amazing, Wallace thought, and he smiled to himself. He tipped the limousine driver, then he and Eve started for customs.

Within seconds, after WC turned it on, Wallace's cell phone signaled that he had emails and text messages. He casually looked at the display and saw Felix's picture and decided to wait until they passed customs to respond. Eve was walking toward the line with her cell phone to her ear.

I hope she reaches her son, Wallace thought, because if she doesn't speak to him before we get on that airplane, this will turn out to be a very long and tense flight. Eve's call went into voice mail, and Wallace saw the disappointment on her face. He knew that making a comment would not help the situation, and so he remained quiet.

After customs, Eve wanted to find just the right tee shirt for Tony. Wallace wasn't into the I've-been-there tee shirt thing, and so he decided to watch their carry-on bags and catch up on his messages. As he browsed through his tablet, he saw several from email addresses were some he was not familiar with. They were government emails but from an agency that SBM was not currently contracted to do any work with. If anyone could explain why he was getting these emails, it would be Felix.

"Hi, buddy! Well, did you pop the big question?"

Wallace's lips tightened. "No, I didn't. The right moment didn't present itself, but I'll tell you all about it when I'm in the office next week. It looks like all you had to do while I've been gone was to text and email me. What's up?"

"Well, the folks around here can't decide whether or not you are a genius or just an overly ambitious project manager who went beyond the statement of work and scope of the contract." Wallace was puzzled by what Felix said.

"Remember, WC. It was about two, maybe even three or four years ago when we picked up that small contract for an agency that I cannot name to upgrade the firmware and software on this highly sophisticated fighter-bomber, and if I said the name you would have to kill me. Can you recall the contract I'm talking about?" Wallace laid his cell in his lap for a few seconds. He picked it up and said.

"I believe we were working over at Bolling Air Force Base. I think the name has changed, but yeah, I think that was it. We were working in that underground bunker. A very smelly place. Where that unknown party needed everything done yesterday. Is that the contract you are talking about?"

"You got it, buddy! Give the man a cigar. By the way, did you bring me back that box of cigars I asked for?"

WC quickly said, "What cigars? I don't remember you asking me to bring you any cigars." A long pause followed. "Of course, I got the cigars. Why would I not bring a box of cigars back for my best friend? So what's up with this project?"

After a chuckle, Felix quickly said, "Well, it seems we delivered more product to the government than we were supposed to. In other words, we went beyond the scope of the statement of work.

"What is happening now is that SBM bean counters are requesting that the government compensate the company for the work we did. From the government side, they are saying they did not authorize the work, and the government will not pay a contractor for exceeding the bounds of the contract without proper authorization."

Wallace stood up and started walking around, circling the bench he was sitting on. In the distance, he could see Eve coming out of one store and heading into another.

"I guess you cannot say over the phone what the product or products were that we delivered beyond the scope of the contract."

Felix gave a sigh over the phone. "Of course, I can't. We'll talk again when you come into the office next week. WC, I would not get overly concerned about the whole situation. Everyone at SBM knows you and the caliber of work that you do, so as of now, the only people who are really complaining about the entire situation are the bean counters. My recommendation is that next week you and I set up an appointment to talk with the program manager and sort all of this out. It is my belief that whatever we delivered that was not in the statement of work the government likes and wishes that they would have thought of it."

Wallace interrupted Felix, "Well, tell me this. If it was not in the statement of work, but we delivered it, how did they find out that they had new functionality in the system if they did not order it? I don't see how this could happen because we have in-progress reviews covering every deliverable."

It had taken a second or two before Felix responded. "It sounds complicated, and I can't go into details over this line about how they found out, but for now just know they did. WC, I've seen you work your way out of tighter situations."

"Thanks for the confidence Felix, but I guess, like always, a solution will present itself. I want you to bring up all of the software notes on every delivery we made on that contact and all of the transcripts from the in-progress reviews."

Felix coughed, then said, "I can't do that. Everything has been taken over by a review team. The software notes and transcripts from our in-progress reviews, all of that stuff has been sent over to the NSA."

Wallace was confused. He was thinking to himself, "NSA, why NSA?" It became apparent that he couldn't do too much about the situation from where he was located. He thought that, if Felix could send him the files, he would review everything as WC was flying back to Fort Lauderdale; but since that couldn't happen, he would just have to wait.

"OK, I'll just have to wait for email until I get back. I'm going to have to go. Any other reason I shouldn't come back home?"

Felix laughed. "No, but have you changed your mind about coming with me to the Wire Head computer industrial show in Baltimore in two weeks?"

Wallace wanted to say no. The Wire Head computer industrial show was the third largest technology show in the United States. WC had a love-hate relationship with those computer shows. On the one hand, it was always great finding out about the next new thing, the next big gadget in either hardware or software, from the sale presentations about how their product was going to change the world and bring prosperity to millions of people. On the other hand, it was very rare when he saw something that really excited him, however. To Wallace, software products always originated with a need derived from a customer, not someone saying you need this, here it is, you must buy it. But Wallace had not hung out with his friend in some time and computers were Felix's life and their friendship meant more to Wallace than being irritated by salespeople at the show. "I'm glad you brought that up. We probably can expense that out because actually, it is related to the work that we do."

"I'm way ahead of you, Wallace. My request is sitting on your desk. It should be the first thing you sign when you come back to work next week."

Wallace was not surprised by Felix's actions. "Sure thing, Felix. I'll give you a call before I fly back to DC. Take care."

Wallace looked around the gate area and could see that it was filling up with passengers for the flight. Eve had not returned, and he looked in the direction of the stores. WC figured she must still be one of the stores buying that tee shirt. He turned his concentration to reading his emails while he waited. He pulled out a pen along with a small notepad and began making notes.

"Gracie, we are at the airport and our flight leaves in about an hour." Eve had finished shopping and was walking back to the gate and talking to Gracie Black on her cell phone. "Certainly, I have no qualms about giving blood. Helen is a friend of mine, and so I would do anything I can to help her and Joe. Okay, I'll give you a call when we land in Fort Lauderdale. Bye, bye." Wallace looked up from his tablet. He could see the worried look on Eve's face.

"We have really been out of the loop. While we have been here, a massive explosion happened in Jacksonville." Eve began to tell Wallace the details and went into the situation about Joe and Helen Singletary. While listening and observing the expressions on Eve's face, he was picking up a sense, a feeling that he couldn't quite put his finger on. As she spoke of the bombing it almost seemed as she was enthusiastic about what had occurred, and then as quickly as you turn an egg over in the frying pan came expressions of grave concern for her friend's husband.

Wallace asked, "So you have the same type of blood as Joe. What type is that?"

Eve replied by saying, "I think I'll try to reach Tony before we board." She started walking to a more private area while dialing Tony's number.

Wallace watched her as she walked away. She had only gone a few feet when she turned around. The call had gone into voice mail, and the frustration of not being able to talk to her child was quite evident on her face. Eve sat down by Wallace, staring at the sign above the boarding gate. "We have time, so let's go someplace and have a drink." Wallace had grown tired of going through his email, and so Eve's suggestion was right on time. A few feet from the gate was a lounge.

They were seated, and Wallace ordered a champagne cocktail and Eve a tequila sunrise.

"WC, with all of the excitement we had on this trip, I don't think that we got a chance to really talk. I mean really talk about our feelings and what we want out of this relationship. I really enjoyed myself, and I enjoyed being with you. The sex was incredible, and I can't see why any of your other wives would have ever let you go. Except for being held at that police station, I think we really had an excellent time."

Wallace was extremely pleased with what he was hearing. He thought that the situation might present itself to pop the question, but then his instincts told him that there were still some issues that he felt must be explained before he could make his final decision.

▬

Home of Bubba and Debra Webb, Jacksonville, Florida.

Debra walked into Bubba's office clutching her cell phone. "That was Eve on the phone. She is flying back to Jacksonville. She has no problem being a donor for Joe." Bubba turned away from his computer monitor to look at his wife.

"That's right because we have not had much luck with what Jerry is doing. I don't understand. I was sure that, with my donating

$500 as a reward, there would be people standing in line." Debra sat down on the corner of Bubba's desk.

"I don't understand it either," Debra replied. "The one person who came forward was tested and came up positive for HIV. The poor thing didn't even know he had it." Turning off his computer, Bubba stood up and walked over to the bar.

"You didn't tell Helen about the plane caught up in the storm that was grounded. According to Jerry, it is carrying two cases of the type of blood needed for Joe. With the storm, there's no telling when it will be taking off." Debra walked over to the bar and joined Bubba in mixing a drink. "The plane is flying from some island off the coast of Hawaii. It's monsoon season out there, and that's what is holding everything up."

"No, I didn't tell her. She is not holding up well. A lot has been put on her shoulders. That would have been just one more load that I figured she just didn't need to be added to everything she is handling."

"Bubba," Debra said, changing the subject. "Tell me about that awful explosion in South Jacksonville." They sat on the sofa in Bubba's office after fixing their drinks.

"Well, Honey, there's not much to tell at this time other than what has been printed in the press, and you have seen on television. The school bus had 12 kids from Wilson High School, along with the bus driver, the school crossing guard, and people in other cars, there was a total of 29 casualties."

"But Bubba, there has to be some type of explanation as to what caused all of that to happen? Could it have been caused by someone smoking too close to a gas tank?"

"Actually, Debra, it could be almost anything. The problem we have is that our resources are stretched pretty thin. We still don't know what caused the explosion over at the Federal Building, and so we were still cleaning up that mess when, in less than ten days, we had another explosion. We have ATF, FBI, the police department, and our own Fire Department working day and night to find out what happened. Hell, Terry Jackson is the top fire investigator in the entire Southeast Region, and he's stumped. Every day I'm getting calls from CEOs of State Farm, Prudential, you name the insurance company, and I've even taken a call from some insurance company out of the Cayman Islands." Bubba paused to take a sip of his drink.

Debra put her hand on his shoulder. "Well, do you think people are holding the city responsible for everything that has happened?" Bubba took a second sip of his drink before answering.

"Honey, it's difficult to say. So far nothing has gotten out that would indicate the city is being held liable, at least as far as the Federal Building is concerned. It is an entirely different situation with the school bus explosion because school buses are contracted by the school board via the city of Jacksonville. So if something is uncovered, where the school bus missed any type of safety inspection, the driver had not been recertified, or for any number of other reasons the liability will fall on the city." Bubba thought for a second. "However, that is only if the explosion is connected to the school bus, but any halfway decent lawyer will tie some portion of the liability back to the city because that's where the real money is."

Debra looked at her watch. "It's getting late. We better leave so we can get over to the hospital and check on Joe and Helen. Maybe someone has stepped up to claim that $500 for donating blood to Joe."

When Bubba and Debra arrived at the hospital, the Mayor and his Wife first went to the floor where people would go to give blood. They were very delighted to see the waiting room full. Bubba and Debra were immediately recognized when they entered the room.

They walked to the desk, and before he could speak the nurse that was seated behind the desk said, "How are you doing tonight, Mr. Mayor? We have nothing to report on a positive match for Mr. Singletary. The people you see in the waiting room have all been tested, and we are awaiting the results. Maybe one will be a match. As soon as we have something we have been directed to contact your office." Bubba and Debra smiled and thanked the nurse for the good work, then left to take the elevator to Joe's room.

As Debra and Bubba entered the hospital room, they saw Helen in a chair beside Joe's bed. She was holding his hand and crying. Debra, thinking the worst, went to her side.

"He is just holding on," Helen said, sobering as she spoke. "They need that blood for his body to fight the infection." Debra put her arms around Helen. Bubba stood at the foot of Joe's bed, helplessly staring at his friend.

Helen, looking at Bubba, said, "I was told that a plane carrying a box of the same blood type as Joe's was being held at an airport in Hawaii for some reason. Can't you do something Bubba? Anything?"

—

MIE Compound, Miami, Florida.

The raid was a success, but at a very high cost of men and equipment. Three crew members of the helicopter and 12 FBI agents were dead, and two agents were in critical condition in the hospital from poisonous snake bites.

The raid put into custody 35 MIE personnel at the Everglade compound, 15 at the headquarters in Little Havana, and collected another 75 MIE personnel at the Fleming Island Trailer Park. Altogether a total of 125 members of the MIE were in custody and being processed for extradition to Brazil. An Air Force C17 was being fueled at MacDill Air Force Base to fly the captives there.

Faye's SUV pulled into the compound. She quickly got out and headed in the direction of the helicopter crash. At first, she was walking, but then she progressed to a run. As she ran past the last building, she could see the wreckage still burning but scattered over a 100-yard area.

The fire department was still spraying water and foam on the hotspots while the recovery teams were placing what remains that could be found the crew and passengers into body bags and stacking the bodies like food crates next to a roadway where they could be quickly placed into trucks to be transported to the morgue.

The thick smell of the mixture of airplane fuel, burning grass, smoke and human body remains filled the air. Faye stopped running as she reached the outskirts of the wreckage area marked with yellow tape. With tears running down her face, she fell to her knees as she took in the horrible scene.

"Faye, are you okay?" Another senior agent running behind Faye was trying to get her attention. "There was nothing that you could have done to avoid this. You have been around long enough to know that these things happen. There can be no blame placed on anyone's shoulders." Faye quickly jumped to her feet.

"It's very easy for you to say. You are not the Special Agent in Charge. I am. I can't send a letter to a wife, sister or mother and the children of these men and only say these things happen." She wiped her face with both of her hands,

"I won't detail statements from every team member who came in on the assault. No one will be released to leave this area until I have a full accounting of everything that happened here."

As Faye started walking back to her SUV, she could see a mobile news van pulling up in front of one of the compound houses. It was not a surprise that her cell phone rang. "Understand, we will have the media conference at the command center back in Miami."

Faye listened for a few seconds and said, "I understand. No statements to anyone. I'll see you back at the command center." Faye ended the call and got into her SUV.

To Faye's surprise, when she arrived at the command center, there were only two news vans. Once again she reasoned that the news agencies were still covering the killing of OBL, and the FBI raid in Miami would probably end up on the second page of the morning edition. This was all right for Faye because she probably would not have to explain the enormous body count.

The first face that Faye recognized was Kyle Martin of WZXL television out of Jacksonville. Kyle was one of the top investigative reporters in the state. She had won several awards, and there was even talk that she was being looked at to go national. At one time Faye and Kyle were tennis partners and won the women's doubles championship two years ago in Jacksonville.

"Special Agent Cook-Little, aren't you also handling the bombing of the Federal Building in Jacksonville?" Kyle pushed the microphone in front of Faye as she was making her way to the door of the command trailer.

"No comment! We will be making a statement shortly," Faye said as she stepped into the trailer. Once inside, Faye went directly into the briefing room. The mood in the room was depressing. As soon as she sat at the table, someone laid a folder in front of her. Faye knew exactly what the folder contained before she opened it, the casualty list, the names, and other personal information about each of the agents killed when the helicopter was shot down.

Chapter 20

Faye laid a ruler on the page and started reading the names of each agent, pushing the ruler down the page from one name to the next. Some of the Agents she knew very well and had a professional relationship with. This was the case when she came to the name of Agent Harris. Faye was the godmother of Agent Harris's little girl. Other names were people who Faye wanted to find a way to develop a relationship with, like Bo Brooks.

The number of media people had grown while Faye was going over the list of dead agents. When they stepped onto the small portable stage, the number of reporters had grown to almost 20 waiting to ask questions.

The FBI Regional Director made the opening statement, followed by the Bureau's public affairs person, then a representative from the State Department; and to Faye's surprise, a representative from the Brazilian embassy who had flown in from Washington spoke.

Just as the Bureau's public affairs person was closing out the press conference, Kyle Martin was pointed to. "Yes, Ms. Martin, your question will be the last."

"Yes, Kyle Martin, WZXL Television. Does the capture of the MIE here in Miami have any connection to the recent bombings of the Federal Building and the school bus that just occurred in Jacksonville?"

Things had been happening so fast in Miami that none of the people on the stage had been briefed on anything concerning another bombing. Their focus and only concern were closing out the operation and extraditing the captured MIE personnel to Brazil. The public affairs spokesperson quickly broke in.

"I'm sorry, but we cannot comment on any other ongoing investigation at this time. We will take that as our last question. You can pick up copies of our press release from one of our agents standing behind you."

As the group was exiting the stage, the FBI Regional Director tapped Faye on her shoulder. "I believe you were the agent handling the Federal Building Bombing in Jacksonville before we pulled you to take care of this MIE thing."

Faye nodded. "Yes, sir. I was."

CIA Headquarters, Langley, Virginia.

After completing the email to Khristy Newborn, Roy
Benning sent messages to the Director, the Deputy, and the DDP,
providing as much information as he could on the deaths of Billy
Mills and his wife in a possible explosion in Jacksonville. At the end
of the email, he said that he was temporarily placing Khristy in the
position of desk chief of the South American office. After sending
the email, he saw that he had an email message waiting for him from
the DDP administrative assistant.

"Roy, the DDP will be out of the office for the remainder of
the week. I'll reschedule your meeting once I have her new agenda
upon her return."

After reading the email, Roy left his office and took the
elevator to the DDP office.

"Good morning, Carol. I just finished reading your email,
and I'd like to call the DDP. What time zone is she in?"

Carol looked up at Roy. "Good morning to you. Fantastic
news about us getting OBL isn't it." Turning to her computer screen,
she said, "She is flying into Kabul and will be there until Friday.
Then she's going on to Pakistan. Anything else?" Roy stood
motionless until the ringing of his Blackberry pulled his attention
back.

"Thanks, Carol. I really appreciate this." Roy pulled his cell
phone out as he left the DDP's office.

"Khristy, I guess you have an update on the status of Billy
and Cathy?"

"Sorry to say I do. Elk confirmed that both Billy and his wife
were at ground zero of the blast this morning. Roy, it was so severe
that the only thing that the police were able to recover for their
identification was the VIN number of their car. They are confirming
all of this by DNA."

"Khristy, do you think that they could have been targeted?"
Khristy was slow to respond.

"Roy, from the information we have, the FBI is just finishing up the raid they made on the MIE in Miami. Fertile Ground is the only active operation we have that would have elements that would like to seek retaliation. We don't have any operations that could be tied back to anything in the Middle East. If we were working on something that had a connection to the Middle East, I would say that would be a possibility; but since we don't, I would say this was not targeted attack. Twenty-four hours from now, after more information has been gathered, we may have a different story."

Roy agreed with what Khristy was saying. But he had to ask so he would have a different view of the situation. "OK, please be sure to tie up all loose ends at the trailer park and any place else those trainees may have stopped on the way to the Plantation. Also, get a resource in Brazil to start gathering information on that shooting, providing information on how these guys are handled when they hit the country. Let's see if you can find the link to how that came to the surface."

"Sure thing, Roy. We are on top of it. In fact, Elk has already asked about going down there." Roy paused before commenting.

"Khristy, it's your call, but you may want to send a new face. Elk is known in South America, and until we have a clearer picture of this mess, we don't want to tip our hand."

"Roy, I understand what you are thinking. I'll give it a little more thought before I make a decision." Roy looked down at his notepad to see if he had covered everything.

"OK, take care and let's talk later about you holding the position as desk chief permanently."

"Okay, Roy. I'll think about it. Speak to you later." The call ended, and Roy sat back in his chair and began pondering all that had taken place.

In his entire career, he had never seen a situation like this. Two of his most senior field agents killed in two separate explosions in the same town and less than 10 days apart. Was it coincidental, just plain bad luck, or something more sinister?

The another item Roy was mulling was how the Brazilian police were directed to the MIE as the organization that contracted the assassination of the security ministers.

Next, Roy had to ensure that as little as possible leaked out about the CIA involvement with the MIE. Sooner or later it could be assumed that the CIA executed the hit on the ministers. This entire thing could get very messy.

Roy had a lot hanging over his head: two desk chiefs blown up in less than ten days, a major operation compromised, the potential exposure of the Plantation as a CIA clandestine training site, and possibly the CIA being accused of a connection to the assassination of security ministers from two sovereign countries.

Roy began to type his situation report when his secure line rang. "This is Roy."

It was the DDP on the line. "Why did I have to find out about Fertile Ground being compromised from a source other than you? It is your job to keep me updated and in the loop on all matters about any operation that is active, especially within the first 24 hours of execution of that Operation. What you have failed to do is a flagrant disregard of Agency procedures and protocol. I want a classified full report on my mail server in the next 24 hours. I have already submitted my requests to the Director to have a formal assessment of what has happened to be conducted by an Agency review board. I am also recommending that you be removed from your current position and placed on administrative leave without pay. I've contacted Khristy Newborn to be your replacement until I can find an alternative capable of cleaning up your mess. In my entire career, I have never seen such an incompetent desk chief. If I have my way, you will never have another job of any type within the CIA. If you have any balls, you will go into a closet, take a revolver and blow your brains out. You are an embarrassment to the Agency and to your country. I need that report in 24 hours, not 26 but 24 hours. Am I clear?" The DDP ended the call without giving Roy an opportunity to speak.

—

Chapter 21

Galileo International Airport Rio de Janeiro.

"We will now start the boarding of American Airlines flight number 1441, nonstop flight to Fort Lauderdale, Florida. All American Airlines Platinum Card holders, first-class and business-class passengers, you may begin boarding. Please have your boarding pass and passport ready to present as you entered the gate."

As Wallace and Eve gathered their carry-on baggage, Eve pulled out her cell phone and tapped the speed dial number to reach Tony. They started walking toward the gate. Not surprisingly to Wallace, standing beside the entrance to the ramp leading to the aircraft were Bartolomeu and Xoana Cardozo.

"Lover, it seems our friends are here to see us off." Eve didn't respond. Her total attention was hoping for Tony to answer the phone and not to go to voicemail. Just as Wallace presented his passport and boarding pass to the gate attendant, he heard Eve leaving another message for Tony.

"Hello, my little darling. I just wanted to let you know how much I love you and that I'm thinking of your safety. We are boarding the plane and you won't be able to reach me until we are in Fort Lauderdale. I'll call you the instant we land so we can catch up on all that has been going on in your life. I have a lot to share with you about our holiday. Take care, my little dear, and please try to be safe. Love you."

Eve finally noticed that Bartolomeu and Belo were standing at the entrance to the ramp. "WC, why are they here?"

Sensing a hint of stress in her voice, Wallace reached for her hand and jokingly said with a reassuring smile, "I would think that they are probably here to apologize for holding us and to see the plane off."

Eve passed through the entrance of the ramp, rolling her eyes at Bartolomeu and Belo as she walked by, more so at Belo than Bartolomeu. WC could clearly sense the envy in Eve's demeanor as he observed Eve looking Belo up and down, taking in every detail of the stunning silk suit that Belo was wearing. The obviously tailor-made suit wrapped around her body, defining her athletic built, but she was also attuned to the way Belo's beautiful dark, Brazilian eyes were staring at Wallace in such a sensual, seductive manner.

As WC followed Eve through the entrance, Belo stepped forward and gently grabbed Wallace's forearm, Bartolomeu stepping behind him.

"Major Barker, please come with us." All of the passengers following Wallace took several steps back. Passengers still seated in the gate area began to stand, directing their attention to the boarding gate, sensing something out of the ordinary was developing. Wallace's instincts and physical training were just seconds away from reacting to the aggressive move that Belo and Bartolomeu made when, suddenly, standing on her toes, Belo placed her lips to Wallace's ear and gently whispered, "Please WC, do not resist in any manner. This will only take a few moments, and you will be able to get on your flight. If you resist, Bartolomeu will kill you here, and I don't want that to happen. You must live for a time for us to be together."

Wallace relaxed. "Eve, go ahead and find our seats, and get me a glass of champagne. This won't take but a few moments."

For the first time, Bartolomeu spoke. "That was sagacious of you. Please follow me." Wallace was led away from the boarding gate.

Eve found her way to their seats. She placed their bags in the overhead storage and took the outside seat. She was clearly distraught, and the flight attendant approached her smiling. "May I offer you a glass of champagne, mango juice, or sparkling water?"

Eve made eye contact with the flight attendant. "Those people out there took my friend away. Do you know anything about it? Is there anything that I can do? Can you tell me what they are going to do with him?"

The flight attendant handed Eve a glass of champagne. "I'm sure that everything is going to be all right. These types of things happen occasionally. We haven't finished boarding, and I'm sure that he will be able to make the flight."

Eve reached out and took the glass of champagne, consuming it in one swallow. Before the attendant could walk down the aisle, Eve placed the empty glass on the tray and took two new glasses of champagne, putting one glass in the beverage holder. "That's for WC," she whispered to herself as she stared at the cabin door.

—

Jacksonville, Florida.

Khristy Newborn and her husband Pat were finishing their dinner at Market 32 on Beach Boulevard, one of their favorite places to dine. Khristy first ate at the restaurant when her book club had a luncheon meeting here. Gracie Black, the vice president of the book club, suggested the location. Two days later, in honor of Pat's birthday, Khristy brought her husband there for dinner and to celebrate.

Khristy and Pat finished their last glass of wine, then sat in silence as they drank coffee. They paid the check and asked the valet to bring the car.

After giving the valet a handsome tip, Pat closed the passenger door to their green Range Rover after Khristy stepped in, and then he got behind the wheel. He pulled out of the parking lot, merging into the light traffic on Beach Boulevard. Khristy reached for the radio and turned the volume up.

Pat spoke first. "I thought you said that you were going to turn the position down."

Khristy, not looking at Pat, replied, "In a way, I did. Roy and I were supposed to talk later this week, and my plan was to tell him I didn't want the position." Pat, coming to a stop at a traffic signal, turned his head toward Khristy.

"But how did it get to this? I like living in Jacksonville, and I don't want to move back to Langley. The environment is just not right for the kids. We've talked about this." The signal changed, and Pat pulled away as Khristy turned toward Pat.

"I know we talked about it. I don't care for Langley and the whole Washington environment either, but this could really be my chance to move up in the Agency. There aren't very many women in a position of power at the headquarters. Don't you see? I have been handpicked by the third highest person at the CIA, and even if it is only temporary, it will still be noted in my personnel jacket that I

219

was the person picked." For the next several miles they rode in silence.

"Remember, Khristy, we moved here because you said that you would have more time to spend with the kids. That hasn't worked out."

Khristy immediately said, "What do you mean by that, Pat?"

"What do I mean? You know exactly what I mean. I'll give you an example," he said as he stopped at another traffic light.

"You have not attended any of Pat Junior's concerts, and what hurt him most was when you did not go to the show where he played the solo. The most beautiful oboe solo I evey head. That was a big moment for him, and he did a fantastic job, but you weren't there."

"I'll give you another example. Sue is the co-captain of the soccer team this year, and they are having one of the best seasons in the school's history, but you haven't attended one game. Do I need to point out any other examples?"

They both sat staring down the highway. The light turned green, but it wasn't until a car horn sounded from behind that Pat pulled off.

As they pulled away, Khristy said, "Well, Pat! Someone has to wear the pants in this family. That little bit of money you make from teaching would never keep us in the lifestyle that we have grown accustomed to. Remember, if it weren't for the money that I make we would never be able to send the kids to private schools or afford the house that we live in. And please let us not forget that time when you stopped teaching and became a private educational consultant." Khristy, now leaning over the car console, was shouting into her husband's ear."

"Remember, Pat, it's because of the money that I make that we were able to pay back all that money for that damn educational software you said you had to have, and where is it now? In boxes sitting in the garage gathering dust!"

Khristy eased back into her seat as their car passed the sign saying Dames Point Bridge one-quarter mile ahead.

Jacksonville has more than 200 bridges, and the highest and most beautiful is the Dames Point Bridge. Six lanes wide, two miles long, and supported by 21 miles of steel cables, it is the longest concrete cable-stayed bridge in the United States.

Just as Pat and Khristy's car was about a quarter of a mile up the bridge, a flash of white light was followed by a thunderous explosion. In a ball of flames, Khristy and Pat's car flew into the air 100 feet, both of their bodies fully engulfed in flames. The middle and outside lanes of the northern approach to the bridge crashed into the St. Johns River, and five cars traveling in the same outer lane plummeted below. All following traffic came to an immediate stop, car after car being rear-ended, setting off a chain reaction of 25 cars colliding and running off the highway. Cars traveling on the opposite side of the bridge received a showering of glass, concrete, and blood and body parts of the victims who were caught in the explosion.

FBI Agent Faye Cook-Little's helicopter was just approaching the Jacksonville International Airport. The pilot of the aircraft said over the intercom system, "What in the hell was that over there?"

Chapter 22

Jacksonville International Airport.

The FBI Director's helicopter landed on the non-commercial side of the airport. Accompanying Faye on the flight were four agents, all from the Pensacola field office. After sitting down, they turned in their gear, got into their cars, and started their 300-mile drive to Pensacola.

Faye had a much shorter trip to her three bedroom townhome. As she was driving down I95 South from the airport back to the city, her thoughts were mostly on seeing her son; but she did drift in and out thinking about the flash of white light they saw just to the southeast of where they were landing at the airport. "The JPD will handle it, and if we have any jurisdiction, tomorrow will be soon enough to act," she thought.

Seeing home was a welcome sight, Faye thought as she pulled into her garage. Faye employed a live-in nanny and housekeeper and had texted ahead to let her know that she would be home and, if possible, to let her son stay up until she arrived. As Faye opened the door from the garage leading into her home, she looked at her watch. It was 11:43 so Faye was confident that her son would be in bed.

"Oh, Miss Faye, so happy to see you and that you are OK. I tried to keep Chris up, but as you know, he had a soccer game today, and the poor boy was so out of it, he fell asleep while doing his homework." Faye's nanny and housekeeper's sister provided the same service for Agent Harris.

"Yolanda, we must go over to Agent Harris's house first thing in the morning. I have some not-so-good news to tell you. I want to be at their home to help when her daughter gets the news about her father." Faye knew that the Agency would be sending a Family Care Team to all of the agents' homes who were killed in the helicopter crash, but because Faye had a personal relationship with Agent Harris and his daughter, she wanted to be there as well.

Faye walked into her son's bedroom and turned on a small nightlight. She stood at the side of his bed smiling, and then kissed him on his cheek. Adjusting the covers around him, then choking up with emotion as Faye walked out of the room. As she walked into her bedroom, she began to visualize what was ahead.

The next day would be a long day. Based on what Kyle Martin said, there had been a second bombing in Jacksonville while she was gone. Faye knew that Kyle could really be a pain in the ass. In looking back at the times they played tennis together, Faye thought Kyle was an incredible teammate, but Faye really couldn't stand her in a social environment. Agent Cook-Little really didn't consider Kyle a friend, in fact. But outside of Kyle's personality flaws, at the end of the day, she was a superb investigative reporter. Faye knew of at least three cases under investigation by the Jacksonville Police Department that were turned around and closed due to information that Kyle uncovered.

Faye stepped into the shower, her mind was still filled, sorting out the next day.

Agent Harris had a sister that was located in Seattle. Harris had told her on several occasions that, if anything happened to him, she would be the one who would take care of his daughter. Faye had never met her, and it wasn't often that Agent Harris spoke of her, but Faye was sure that her name appeared in Agent Harris's personnel records as the secondary next of kin.

Suddenly emotions overcame Faye and tears began to run down her face. Her thoughts shifted to Bo Brooks. She had stood him up for dinner and now couldn't understand why, not even sending him a text message to explain. A lot had taken place over the last several days. How could she have been so thoughtless, so cold? Is being a good FBI agent more important than caring about people and letting someone special into your life? Faye dropped to her knees in the shower, crying uncontrollably.

—

Shands Hospital, Jacksonville, Florida.

As the Mayor and his wife were leaving the hospital, walking toward their car, Bubba's cell phone began to ring. "This is Jerry, and I need to take this. Excuse me for a moment, Honey." Bubba stopped in the middle of the sidewalk while Debra continued to the car.

"Mr. Mayor, I hate to be the one to tell you this, but the Dames Point Bridge just blew up." The Mayor stood there, not knowing what to say but listening intently, hanging on to every word Jerry Clark was speaking.

For a second Bubba was hoping that this could be some type of prank or joke, something his longshoremen friends thought up and talked Jerry into going along with; but he knew Jerry was too much of a professional to pull any type of stunt like this.

"The fire department and all of the city's rescue squads are either in route or are on the scene now. We are setting up the mobile command center as we speak. Sir, I think you need to get over here as soon as possible."

Bubba started walking toward the car. "Of course. I'm on my way. Where is the command center located?"

"Mr. Mayor, the most direct route for you to get here is to take I-95 North up to the airport and then come over to the bridge from there, but JPD has both sides of the bridge, completely shut down. So I have the helicopter waiting for you at City Hall to fly you over."

As Bubba jumped into the backseat of the limousine next to Debra, he heard the sounds of emergency vehicles echoing in the night. "I understand, Jerry. Sound thinking. We are on our way to City Hall now. I'll see you in a few minutes."

Debra just looked into Bubba's eyes as he sat beside her and grabbed her hand. As Bubba sat down, the limousine driver turned his head to speak over his shoulder. "Where to, Mr. Mayor?"

Looking at Debra, Bubba Webb said, "Take us to the City Hall heliport, I have to fly over to the Dames Point Bridge. I was just told that we have had another major explosion, and the bridge was damaged. After you drop me off, please drive my wife home."

The driver quickly responded, "Would you like for me to pick you up back at the heliport or at another location, Mr. Mayor?"

Still holding his wife's hand, Bubba replied, "That won't be necessary, Sam. I'll get Jerry Clark to drive me home or catch a ride with one of the police cruisers. This will probably take a while."

——

American Airlines Flight 1441.

"The captain has turned off the seatbelt light. It is now safe to move about the cabin."

Eve loosened her seatbelt but did not unbuckle it. "OK, WC, what the hell happened back there? Why did those people hold you? What was that all about?" Wallace finished drinking his warm glass of champagne, then signaled to the flight attendant for a refill.

"Lover, I'm still wondering what that was all about myself. They fingerprinted me, and then they took mug shots, and that was it. After they had finished taking the pictures, they told me I could get on the plane. Someone from the airline said, 'Follow me,' and here I am. I made the flight. I think at this point that is the most important thing, making the trip."

The flight attendant brought two more glasses of champagne along with menus. "Please select from the menu. We will be starting our meal service shortly. I will return to collect your selection."

After the flight attendant had continued down the aisle, Eve returned to their conversation. "So that's all that happened in all that time that you were gone? They just fingerprinted you, took your picture, then let you go? WC, there is something that you are not telling me. Did they ask about me!?"

Wallace sat there sipping his champagne. Eve's voice was getting louder, and people were beginning to become annoyed with the outburst. He didn't want to make a scene and have some air marshal tapping him on the shoulder.

"Eve, these last few days have been very stressful on both of us. I suggest we just sit here and drink our champagne, relax, eat our meal and try to get some rest. We can sort out all this crazy nonsense out once we get back to Fort Lauderdale."

Eve looked at Wallace for several seconds, then said, "Wallace, I understand what you are saying. But if we want this relationship to last, we have, to be honest with each other, open up and tell each other about everything that has happened. I agree with you. This is not the time and the place for discussing this, but I want this to be one of the first things we talk about when we reach Fort Lauderdale."

Wallace and Eve handed their menu selection to the flight attendant. They both ordered the chicken cordon bleu. Eve put on a headset and started watching a movie. When their meals arrived, they ate in silence. After they finished and were having coffee, Eve removed her headset. "WC, I'm sorry I yelled at you. I was so afraid that you may not make the flight. I didn't know what I was going to do."

Wallace was very touched hearing Eve say this. The tone and sincerity of her voice reminded him of the woman he had fallen in love with. WC knew that, under stress, people can assume an endless list of different personalities, do and say things that they would not do or say in a typical situation. So he said, "Thanks, lover, for saying that. This will be the first thing we talk about when we get to Fort Lauderdale. I promise." Wallace kissed Eve, and she returned the kiss.

Eve pulled out her tablet and opened one of her eBooks. "I must finish this book before we get back. This is on the reading list for our first book club meeting. Khristy Newborn recommended this, and she said it is an enjoyable read." She turned on the overhead light and settled into her reading.

Wallace looked at his cell phone to see what emails had loaded while he was waiting in the airport. He was mainly searching for anything from his office. As he scrolled through his email, he became alarmed because there were so many.

He remembered he had put the automatic response on his computer, indicating that he would be out of the office and not checking email until his return. The message included the date that he would be back in the office. From the volume of emails that he saw, it seemed like people disregarded his out-of-office message. The number of emails and who they were coming from indicated to Wallace that people in the office wanted to be able to go on record saying that they had notified Wallace by email. This was a typical SBM cover-your-ass strategy.

The next thing that Wallace concentrated on was who the emails were coming from. This was the second red flag. There were emails from the computer Programmers, configuration management managers, and testers—just about everyone who made up the team working on the project Felix told him about. This volume of emails

226

and who they were coming from were an indication to Wallace that SBM was conducting some type of internal audit on the project and each of these people either had been questioned or were about to be called into question.

The third red flag that entered Wallace's thought process was when he saw emails from his SBM management chain, the people he reported to, starting with his direct report, all the way to the senior vice president of the division that he worked in.

Wallace's thoughts shifted to Felix. He didn't think that this whole matter was such a big deal. Wallace trusted Felix's judgment more than anyone when it came to developing software. However, the politics of the corporate world wasn't part of Felix's expertise. Because he was such a brilliant Programmer, he never came on this side of the conflict within the corporation. This is what made WC and Felix such a great team. Wallace had always been able to maneuver their projects through the inner office political mazes with Felix ensuring that the software they delivered met all the requirements of the contract.

Wallace felt something touching his hand. He turned toward Eve, who was pointing upward to a gentleman standing beside their seats.

"Oh, Mr. Hastings," WC remembered the man from the police station. "You made the plane."

"Yes, Mr. Barker. I saw you and your companion, and so I wanted to come over and say thank you for what you did back at the police station."

Wallace interrupted, "But, Mr. Hastings, I really didn't do anything."

"On the contrary, Mr. Barker. What you said actually provided more information and gave some rationale for what we were going through. Also, just to let you know, I still plan to file a formal complaint with our foreign office once I arrive in London. Here is my card. If you and your companion are ever in London, please give me a call. You will be welcome guests for dinner." Wallace took the card from Mr. Hastings.

"Thank you very much, Mr. Hastings. From time to time I do travel to London, and so I may take you up on that dinner appointment."

Mr. Hastings smiled. "I'll let you and your companion return to your reading. I have a movie I must watch."

Eve took off her headset. "That was really nice, wasn't it, Wallace?"

Wallace looked at Eve. "Yes, it was, and I just might give him a call the next time I have a layover at Heathrow."

Eve smiled, put the headset back on, and returned to her reading. Wallace responded to his emails.

Wallace had gotten a good idea of who was concerned about the unauthorized software delivery, and he now wanted to focus on what people were asking for in these emails, which might give him a clue as to what the disputed software was.

The first email he opened was from a Programmer that read: "Wallace, call me." The next one was from another Programmer also. "WC, will you be at the meeting with the auditors on Monday?" Another email read: "WC, people are beginning to talk. I have your back. Call me so we can meet and have a drink."

What sent the fourth red flag up was when Wallace read this email: "WC, we were at happy hour over at the Green Frog. There is a rumor going around that you stole money from the contract, and you and your girlfriend ran away to Brazil. I'm scheduled to be interviewed tomorrow for this internal audit that is going on. WC, I have two kids in college, one in her senior year, and I can't lose this job. Whatever you did can be worked out. I haven't checked, but I think you can still be extradited back from Brazil to the United States. The funny thing is that I have always admired you for being a good program manager."

"Wallace, what's wrong." Wallace turned and looked at Eve. He had drifted away, thinking about the situation he was returning to at SBM.

"Oh, nothing, lover. Just some office stuff I must get sorted out when I get back."

Eve gave him a pleasant smile. "I'm so glad that school doesn't start for another month after we return."

That's another of the endless things that I do not know about Eve, WC thought. "Do you like teaching?"

Looking at Wallace curiously, she replied, "Why, yes, I love it. Seeing the lightbulb going off in children's faces each time they find something new in the world is a wonderful experience. In this world, I have no two days that are exactly alike, and that is very exciting to me." Continuing the conversation, she now asked, "WC, have you ever thought about doing something other than developing software?"

Quickly responding, Wallace said, "I've thought about it, but I really like what I do. I like to think that I have the best of both worlds. When I analyze myself, and I cut through the Special Forces, Airborne Ranger side of my life, I'm really a geek at heart. I love technology, how it has been created and where it is going, and honestly, I feel that I am taking part in all that."

While putting her headset back on, Eve said, "It was all too stressful for me." She returned to her reading. All doubts were erased in Wallace's mind concerning the severity of the situation back at his office when he opened the email from the administrative assistant to the senior vice president of his division. Everyone in his chain of authority that he reported to had been copied on the email.

"Mr. Barker, as soon as you receive this email, you are to contact me to schedule a meeting with the SBM Contract Compliance Board of Review concerning Contract Number AF2201." Wallace put his cell phone away, pulled out his laptop, and began going through his file folders, trying to uncover a clue about the unauthorized product delivery Felix was talking about.

Arlington, Virginia.

It was the wee hours of the morning, and the lights were out in his entire townhouse. Roy Benning was sitting in his living room staring into the darkness thinking about his last conversation with the DDP. Maybe he should quit, take an early out, possibly get disability payments added on top of his retirement if he pushed the issue about the time he broke his collarbone being pushed out of a helicopter in Somalia. Roy didn't like the possibility of being characterized as an incompetent desk chief. He knew he was a lot better than that.

Nothing was making any sense, except all of the madness led back to the DDP.

Roy had placed his cell phone on the coffee table. The light came on, and it was vibrating on the table, so he wouldn't be disturbed, he had turned the ringer to mute. He looked at the cell phone and saw that it was the Director of the Agency that was trying to reach him. Roy picked up the phone and answered it.

"Good morning, Mr. Director." There was a short pause, then he heard the Director's voice.

"Roy, it sounds like you were awake. I was afraid that I was going to wake you, but I wanted to talk to you myself before you come into the office later this morning. First and foremost, please disregard the conversation that you had with the DDP, I guess it was yesterday now. You are still in charge of our South American operations and the Desk Chief. I've sent out an email to Khristy Newborn and all of the necessary people indicating that there have been no personnel changes within your office. Once the DDP and I are back in the country, I plan for the three of us to sit down and come to an agreement so that all of us are working on the same page. You have been copied on all correspondence. Rest assured, I appreciate the work that you and your people are doing, and during some tough times. Do you have any questions, Roy?"

By this time, Roy was walking around the living room with his cell phone to his ear.

"No, Mr. Director. I understand correctly. I'll reserve my questions until we have our meeting."

"Excellent then, Roy. Do you mind if I give you a suggestion?" Roy stopped pacing and reached for the living room light switch.

As he turned on the lights, he said, "Sure, Mr. Director."

Listening patiently, Roy heard the Director say, "Roy, have some tea with Honey. Anytime I can't fall asleep I make some tea and stir in Honey. It always knocks me out, and I fall to sleep like a baby. Try it."

"Thank you, Mr. Director. I think I'll try some." The call ended, and Roy shouted, "That Bitch didn't get me this time!"

Roy then reflected on the Director's suggestion. He was expecting him to say something entirely different, but the Director's recommendation showed a side of the head of the CIA that Roy had not seen before. He was pleased to know that the Director really cared about the people who worked for the Agency.

—

Shands Hospital, Jacksonville, Florida.

A smile on her face, the nurse quickly exited the elevator, then rushed to Joe Singletary's room. As she opened the door, she saw Helen kneeling beside the bed. Helen raised her head as the door opened. Helen could see the expression on the nurse's face.

"You have good news? The blood is here?" The nurse walked across the room. "Not yet, but we just got a radio message that the plane landed at the airport and a Red Cross truck picked the blood up and is en route. It has not one but two boxes of your husband's blood type."

Helen reached out, grabbing the nurse's hands. "Thank you, thank you, thank you."

Chapter 23

Jacksonville Emergency Command Center.

The Mayor's helicopter set down. The first face Bubba Webb saw was that of Jerry Clark. Jerry was standing beside an SUV with wording on the side: Jacksonville Emergency Response Unit. Jerry walked out to meet Bubba about half way to the helicopter.

"You know, Jerry, we have to find a better way to meet other than disasters." Jerry Clark forced a smile, but he knew that statement was the Mayor's style, always trying to put a positive spin on everything.

"I couldn't agree with you more, Mr. Mayor."

As Bubba took a seat in the SUV, the conversation quickly shifted to the situation at hand. "I guess this is a much bigger mess than that pickup truck that went the wrong way on the bridge."

Jerry said, shaking his head, "Mr. Mayor, the city, has never seen anything like this. We have every agency in the state on the scene. The Highway Patrol has closed 295 on both ends beginning at I95. All Southbound traffic is being routed through the city or 295 west."

The Mayor interrupted. "Casualty's, Jerry. I need to know how many people are dead. What is the body count? Jerry Clark paused for a minute, thinking about what he was going to say next.

"Mr. Mayor, we can't give you a number at this time. It is still too early. The EMCs are reviewing the video footage from the bridge cameras to determine how many cars actually went into the river." Jerry paused for a moment, waiting to get the Mayor's response. It appeared that the Mayor didn't have a question at this point, and so Jerry continued.

"The Coast Guard already has divers in the river looking for bodies." Bubba interrupted Jerry again.

"Wait a minute. Did you say that our EMCs are reviewing the video from the cameras? You mean they didn't get destroyed in the explosion?" Jerry quickly said, "No sir. They didn't. As a matter of fact, Terry Jackson stated that, with the video cameras still operational, there is a good chance he will be able to determine the exact place and time where whatever set off. Where the explosion

232

originated; and if we are really lucky, we may be able to see who set it off."

The SUV came to a police checkpoint. The policemen manning the checkpoint quickly recognized the Mayor and waved them through.

"Jerry, I think I've seen a lifetime of yellow tape in the last 10 days. I believe if I connected all the yellow tape that has been put up in Jacksonville over the last two weeks since the explosion at the Federal Building up until today, it would be enough tape to wrap around the world."

Jerry Clark looked at the Mayor. "I don't think you are too far off, Bubba."

.   About 200 yards ahead of the SUV they could see the trailers connected together making up the city's mobile command center. "There's the command center just ahead, Mr. Mayor."

"Where's the media, Jerry?'

"Good question. We came in a back way. If you take a look in that direction…" Jerry placed one hand on Bubba's shoulder, positioning him so he could look in the direction he was talking about. He then said, "You see those two additional trailers we set up? We set that area up for our press conferences. As you can understand, the media is all over this, both local and national networks."

The SUV parked in an area roped off for city vehicles, and as they were parking, Bubba's cellphone buzzed. It was a text message from his wife. "Honey, some good news. Helen just texted me that she just got news that Joe's blood was delivered by plane and two cases of his blood type are being driven by a Red Cross truck to the hospital." Bubba let out a sigh of relief.

The Mayor and Jerry left the car with Jerry leading the way into the command center. As they were walking, Jerry was pointing toward the bridge and briefing the Mayor on the situation.

"What I'd like to do first is take you to the status board so you can see all of the assets that are in play handling this situation." Jerry looked at the Mayor to see if he agreed. The Mayor shook his head.

"Another reason we are starting here is that the fire department and the explosive ordnance people have not cleared the bridge. They are still looking for any other possible ammunition that has not gone off, anything that could cause another explosion." The Mayor stopped walking and grabbed Jerry's forearm.

"So, Jerry, where are the Fire and Police Chiefs?"

"Oh, I should have pointed that out earlier. The Fire Chief is down at the bridge with the explosives team. There are several cars still burning and a shit-load of people with neck injuries from being rear ended. The Police Chief is up in his helicopter surveying the area. We can reach either one with our radios." They started walking again and entered the command center.

At the situation board, more than 200 people are projected, with injuries. The number of dead is expected to be 50 to 75. The Mayor stood frozen, looking at the projections on the board.

Jerry was standing beside Bubba as he continued to absorb the numbers on the situation board. He began thumbing through a notepad that he had with him.

"Bubba, there is something else that is sort of strange. There is no FBI or ATF presence here. No, that's not entirely correct. The people from the FBI, who handle their communication equipment, are here, but no agents let alone a Special Agent in Charge."

Mr. Mayor turned his attention away from the board and faced Jerry. "Where are they?" Jerry pointed in the direction of a table with a mass of radios and computer monitors. "I asked those guys over there, and they said that there is some big FBI operation taking place in Miami, and someone will be here in the morning."

Bubba took a few steps away from the situation board, then turned around facing Jerry. "Tell the Chief of Police that this is not acceptable. The FBI is not sending the proper personnel to assist the City of Jacksonville in this emergency situation." Jerry made a note on his pad. Bubba heard his name being called.

"Mr. Mayor, you must see this! I think some luck finally came our way." It was the voice of Terry Jackson, the city's chief fire investigator.

Bubba looked around the command center and saw Terry Jackson waving his hand on the other side of the control center, directing him to come toward him. The Mayor and Jerry made their way to Terry.

"Mr. Mayor, Jerry probably told you that all of the bridge cameras are still operational. I've been reviewing the tapes, and I'm pretty confident that I have isolated the exact point of detonation. Let me show you."

Terry signaled for the people sitting at the monitors in a small room to step out so he and the Mayor could enter. He sat down behind a console and began to maneuver a mouse. There were five large high definition color monitors positioned on the wall of the room. Terry enlarged the view on the center screen.

"Take a look, Mr. Mayor. See this group of cars headed up the bridge? In the left lane you have that white Ford Red Cross blood van, in the middle lane that green Range Rover, and on the inside lane, the guy on the Harley Davidson." Terry maneuvered the mouse. OK, now you see that green Range Rover is accelerating and picking up speed. Now it's almost two car lengths ahead of the other two vehicles." Suddenly a white light covered the monitor.

"What in the hell happened, Terry?"

Terry looked up at the Mayor. "That white light you saw on the screen was the detonation, and I believe that is what triggered the explosion."

Terry turned back to the console and cut on the other four monitors showing the pavement of the bridge caving in from the blast and sending the vehicles, entirely engulfed in flames plunging into the St. John's River. The Mayor could see 10 to 15 vehicles that were also following being engulfed in the blast, bursting into flames and trailing the cars to their watery graves.

The Major and Terry carefully looking at the video, it seemed like the green Range Rover was projected into the air first, indicating that the blast exploded two ways, up and down.

—

American Airlines Flight 1441.

It was an 11-hour flight to Fort Lauderdale with one stop for a crew change in Panama. With the Crew change, the plane was expected to land around 10:35 AM in Fort Lauderdale. Wallace figured that they should be able to leave the airport and pick up the

235

car, have some lunch and be on the road back to Jacksonville by 1:30 or 2:00. He turned back to his computer.

Wallace was getting more frustrated going through his files on his computer. He was having no luck trying to find something that would give him an idea of what was causing all of the commotions back at his company. His eyes were beginning to burn, so he closed his laptop and drifted off to sleep.

Eve was still reading her eBook, but seeing that WC had fallen to sleep, she paused for a moment to place a blanket over him. As she returned to her reading, she too began to grow sleepy, and her concentration shifted to thoughts about Tony.

Like any mother, Eve was always worrying about the safety of her child. However, Eve was part of a small group of moms who had a kid that was a US Navy aviator and flew one of the most powerful aircraft in the world at speeds twice the speed of sound.

Eve's thoughts drifted back to the day that Tony started at the Naval Academy, one of the proudest days of her life. She kissed her child along with a big motherly hug.

"I know you are going to make me proud, but above all make your great grandfather proud."

Throughout Tony Harding's life, the first day of school had always begun with some confusion. Tony's first day at the United States Naval Academy started the same way.

Standing in line with all of the hundreds of other Fourth Classman, excited but apprehensive about what was about to happen: the beginning of a college education and the first step in a life of service. After moving, what seemed to be an inch at a time, Tony reached the front of the line at the sign-in desk.

"Wait a minute. You're Tony Harding?"

Standing at attention, Tony replied, "Yes ma'am, I'm Tony Harding." The female ensign sitting at the desk looked down at the clipboard on the table, then looked up at Tony.

"Your name is spelled wrong on my list. As you know, it should be spelled Toni, for a female, but on my list, it's spelled Tony, which is the male spelling. So in reading the Fourth Classman assigned to me, from the way your name is spelled on my roster, I assumed that you would be a male. I apologize for the typographical error. We will get that corrected."

Tony quickly replied, "Excuse me, ma'am. That is the right spelling of my name: Tony."

The female Naval Officer looked up at Tony with a long inquisitive stare.

"I guess it really doesn't matter. You are in the Navy now. At Annapolis, it doesn't matter whether you are a woman or a man. From this point on, you are Harding. That's how you will be addressed as Harding, and that's all that matters. At a double-time, get over there and join your classmates."

All of Tony's life, Eve was preparing her daughter for this day. Eve paid for tutoring classes in high-level math and writing, and Tony could read and speak three foreign languages: Spanish, Portuguese, and French. When Tony was 15 she and her mother ran in their first marathon.

In high school, Tony lettered in three sports: soccer, field hockey, and cross country. Eve provided music lessons for Tony, she played piano and flute. Eve wanted her daughter to become a United States Naval Aviation Officer, the same as Eve's grandfather.

Tony was born out of wedlock, and Eve raised her daughter as a single mother. As a child, Eve was abused by her mother's live-in boyfriend. One day when Eve's mother returned from work, she caught her boyfriend in their bedroom raping her daughter. She stabbed the man 14 times with a kitchen knife, finally cutting his throat. Eve's mother was convicted of third-degree homicide and sentenced to 10 years in jail. While Eve's mother was in prison, she committed suicide. Eve was placed in foster care.

After Tony was born, because Eve had not reached majority age, they were separated. Eve did not see her daughter again until she turns eighteen. Eve worked diligently with social services and was finally able to reunite the family.

The cabin lights came on followed by, "Ladies and gentlemen, the Captain has turned on the fasten seatbelts light, and we are making our approach into Panama International Airport. Please fasten your seatbelts, bring your seats to an upright position, and close your tray tables. We will be landing shortly."

Wallace woke up as the plane was landing. "I guess this must be Panama." He yawned and stretched his muscles from the tight position he was in while sleeping. "I did some training here a few years ago."

"What did you say, WC? I guess I fell asleep too," Eve replied to WC as she stretched also. Eve then reached for her cell phone.

When she turned it on, she said, "Darn it. I don't have a signal. Wallace, do you have a signal on your phone? I want to see if I can reach Tony."

WC pulled out his cell. "No, I don't have a signal either. I'm surprised I don't have coverage here."

From the plane's intercom: "This is a change of crew stop. If you would like to deplane, please place an occupied sign in your seat and take your boarding pass along with your passport. Watch the airport monitors and listen for the re-boarding announcements for flight 1441."

"Wallace, let's get off and stretch our legs. I'm going to see if I can purchase a prepaid phone and call Tony." Wallace and Eve gathered their passports and stepped off the plane and into the airport.

Chapter 24

Jacksonville Emergency Command Center.

The sun was just beginning to rise, glittering across the St. Johns River and penetrating the remnants of smoke drifting up into the air from the remaining cars that had crashed into each other. They had not been removed from the roadway and were still burning.

Jerry Clark, followed by the Mayor, the Chief of Police and Fire Chief, entered the media trailer to begin their first press conference concerning the disaster on the Dames Point Bridge.

Jerry Clark recommended using the phrase Disaster rather than bombing, blast, or explosion. All of the Mayor's staff concurred with Jerry's recommendation, and the Mayor approved it.

Even with two trailers connected, there was not enough room for all the reporters to be inside. Jerry had speakers hooked up outside along with a monitor. The Mayor was going to use a situation screen that was set up inside the media trailer to point out what was going on and how the city was doing everything possible to stay in control and ahead of the situation. They didn't have a portable screen, and so Jerry recommended continuing with the briefing inside and taking the hit from the reporters who had to view the conference from the outside of the trailer.

When the Mayor stepped in front of the microphone, representatives from other city and state agencies were standing behind him including the Highway Patrol. Conspicuously missing was anyone from the FBI or the ATF.

In typical Bubba style, he started off by having a moment of silence for all of the victims, family members, and friends of all the people who had either died in this tragedy or were injured.

Bubba went through all of the numbers. The most shocking number was the number of bodies that the Coast Guard had pulled out of the river: "Currently, the Coast Guard had recovered 35 victims of those who went to their deaths when their automobiles plunged into the St. Johns River."

The Mayor finished going through all the numbers, projecting how long the recovery was going to last, and then he turned it over to the Department of Transportation to give an indication of road closures and how traffic would be rerouted until the bridge could be reopened. The most promising point at the press conference was that Jacksonville had already contracted for two additional ferries to assist in moving cars across the river until the bridge was repaired. The ferries were already en-route from the Virginia Beach area. Bubba came back to the microphone to take questions.

"Kyle Martin, WZXL, Channel 4. Mr. Mayor, was this an act of terrorism?" The words had not finished ringing in his ears when Henry Bubba Webb's thoughts immediately flashed back to the conversation he and Joe Singletary had the night of the bombing of the Federal Building.

"Ms. Martin, it is too early in the investigation to draw any conclusions. I'll take the next question from that gentleman in the back on the left."

The Mayor fielded question after question, answering with the same response: "It is too early in the investigation to draw any conclusions."

"Mr. Mayor, Kyle Martin again from WZXL, Channel 4. Do you think that this bombing is connected to the other attacks that have occurred in the last ten days in Jacksonville? Oh, I also have two follow-up questions." The Mayor looked directly at the reporter.

"Kyle, go ahead and ask your follow-up questions. I'll include the answers in my response."

"All right then, Mr. Mayor. Are the bombings in Jacksonville related to the FBI and ATF raid that occurred in Miami, and why is it that there is no representation here from either of those two agencies?"

Bubba looked out across the room. "I can't speak for the FBI or ATF, but what I can say is that it is too early in the investigation to draw any conclusions. I can assure you that the people standing on this stage will be following every possible lead or possible scenario to its end until we find out what caused this disaster. Thank you very much for taking this amount of interest in the city of Jacksonville and the beautiful people that live here. Please stay in contact with Jerry Clark. He will let you know the time for our next press conference."

240

Exhausted but pleased with the way all the agencies were responding to the bombing, Bubba caught a ride home in one of the police cruisers. As the police cruiser was driving over the Matthew Bridge, Bubba could already see the traffic backing up. But his thoughts were consumed with the questions asked by Kyle Martin about the three bombings being connected. Bubba sent a text message to his administrative assistant to set up a meeting with the FBI and 4:00 in the afternoon, and he said he would be at home getting some rest before he came in at three.

As he entered his kitchen, he saw Debra standing beside the refrigerator. "Have a seat, Honey, and I'll fix you some breakfast. I already have a fresh pot of coffee brewing. You can eat, take a shower, and then get some rest."

Bubba took off his coat jacket, kicked his shoes into the corner of the room, and sat down. Debra put a cup of coffee in front of him. "Thanks, Honey. It has been a long ten days. Have you heard anything more from Helen?"

Debra turned around from the stove and said, "I just got off the phone with her. The Red Cross blood truck never arrived at the hospital. She stated that they are searching for it, even called the driver's cell phone and left several messages, but he hasn't answered. Very strange."

Looking up from staring into his coffee cup, he said, "Debra, did you say Red Cross blood truck?" Seeing the reaction on her husband's face, she started walking toward the table.

"Why, yes, the Red Cross sent one of their trucks to the airport to pick up two cases of blood. Both of the cases were full of the type needed for Joe."

Bubba jumped up from the table and immediately reached for his jacket and pulled out his cell phone. He hit the speed dial number to the Emergency Command Center.

"J.E.C.C. Can I help you?"

"This is the Mayor. Connect me to Terry Jackson."

"Yes, Mr. Mayor."

"This is Terry Jackson."

"Terry, this is Bubba. On that video, wasn't a Red Cross blood truck one of the first vehicles to go into the river?"

Terry quickly replied, "That's correct, Mr. Mayor. One of the first three vehicles that went into the river was a Red Cross blood truck. What's the problem?" Bubba turned and was looking at Debra.

"I think that truck was carrying the blood needed to give Joe Singletary a transfusion."

Terry sat down at his console and began typing a message to the Police Chief asking him to run a Lojack search on the truck for verification and to cross check it with the Red Cross. Terry turned his attention back to the call.

"As you know Bubba, the Red Cross has Lojack installed on all of its vehicles. I just sent a message to JPD to have them do a trace… Wait, I have a reply. I'm sorry, Bubba, but it's confirmed. The Red Cross had already asked the JPD to do a search. It seems as if the driver took a wrong turn coming from the airport headed to Shands and ended up on the other side of the Dames Point Bridge. The driver had just called back in to say that he had turned around and was headed back over the bridge when they lost contact with him."

—

Brazilian Military Airbase, Rio de Janeiro, Brazil.

The US Air Force C17 touched down on the Brazilian military base airstrip. A fierce tropical storm was pouring drenching rain down, cooling the hot asphalt of the runway but cutting the visibility of the pilot.

With a full cargo load, the carrier transport plane skidded to a stop less than one hundred feet from the end of the runway. The pilot slowly maneuvered the massive fuselage of the plane around, then proceeded to taxi toward the airport tower.

Driving in a direction toward the C17 was a military jeep with a red and white checkered flag attached to the bumper of the vehicle but with no canvas. There were three men in the Jeep, one man standing up in the rear seat behind a machine gun and one man sitting beside the driver. He was holding a sub-machine gun of some type. All were wearing camouflage ponchos, but because of the high winds, the ponchos did little to keep the men dry.

In the distance, coming from a different direction was a convoy of 15 trucks with six escort vehicles. Mounted on all of the escort vehicles were 50 caliber machine guns. The convoy raced across the airfield to meet the plane as it taxied behind the other escort jeep. All of the vehicles and the C17 came to a stop several hundred meters out of view of the airport tower in front of a hanger. The hanger doors opened, and the C17 was signaled by one of the men in the escort jeep to taxi in. Once the plane came to a stop in the hanger, some 50 Brazilian soldiers, all armed with automatic weapons, quickly got out of the trucks and surrounded the plane.

The rear cargo door of the aircraft opened and three men began to walk down the ramp of the plane even before the ramp touched the ground. One man wore the rank of Lieutenant Colonel and was dressed in battle fatigues with an armband on his left arm that read MP. The other two men were in civilian attire, one man wearing a short-sleeved white shirt with a tie and the other man dressed in a short-sleeved polo shirt.

Once they reached the bottom of the ramp they stopped and directed their attention toward an office that was situated in the right corner of the hanger. Walking out of the office was Aloisio Santos Candido and Bartolomeu followed by Xoana Cardozo, who was referred to as Belo.

The man in the white short-sleeved shirt shook hands with Aloisio Santos Candido followed by the Lieutenant Colonel and the man in the short-sleeved polo shirt. The Colonel then handed a large envelope to Aloisio, who immediately handed the envelope to Bartolomeu, who gave it to Belo.

They then stepped to the side of the loading ramp. US Military Police began to escort the MIE prisoners off of the aircraft. Each of the prisoners was wearing an orange jumpsuit. They were handcuffed at their wrists and ankles with a long chain connecting both together. The chains around the ankles only allowed the men to shuffle.

At the bottom of the ramp, the Brazilian military quickly took custody of the prisoners and began loading the people into the back of the trucks.

Krish was walking directly behind Ranuel. They were in the middle of the group of detainees. As they were quickly loaded into the back of the trucks, Krish and Ranuel were separated. Ranuel was loaded into the third truck and Krish the fourth.

As the last prisoners stepped from the C17, the Lieutenant Colonel and other two men walked back up the ramp. The ramp closed, and the plane slowly began to taxi out of the other open doors of the hanger and to proceed to the flight line. The rain had grown more intense. Shortly after the C17 reached the flight line, it was given clearance to take off. The pilot pushed the controls forward, and the plane gathered speed and quickly lifted into the air.

Back in the hanger, each of the prisoners took their seats on the cargo benches in the back of the trucks. Their legs were shackled down and secured to the van's bed.

The prisoners' convoy commander gave one final look down the line of vehicles, got back into the lead jeep, picked up the microphone to his communication set to radio that the prisoner convoy was leaving the airbase and that he would provide periodic updates as they reached their checkpoints.

The convoy left the hanger and quickly approached the gate of the airbase. As the convoy passed through the gates of the airbase, six police motorcycles moved out ahead of them with flashing lights to provide traffic control.

All traffic was being stopped. The police motorcycle escorts leap-frogged ahead of the convoy to ensure all traffic was stopped and the way was clear. In less than 15 minutes the convoy had made what would have been a 30 to 40-minute drive in normally congested city driving conditions.

After leaving the city, the convoy proceeded west along the coast. Sitting in the third truck, Ranuel began to take a close look at the men who shared the vehicle. There wasn't one face that he recognized. They were directed by the Brazilian soldiers that, if anyone were caught talking, they would be shot, and so he did not dare ask who they were.

Krish also didn't recognize any of the men in the fourth truck. Rage and anger were bowling in Krish. In his thoughts he kept repeating, "The Americanos betrayed us, the Americanos betrayed us exactly the way they did at the Bay of Pigs with Brigade 2506."

244

The convoy made a left turn and proceeded into the mountains, driving on the road overlooking the ocean. As they drove up the mountain road, the rain intensified, along with wind gusts that were now up to 65 miles per hour.

Suddenly, from above them, rocks, boulders, and mud began to come down on the convoy. Due to the high winds and rain noise, the mudslide caught everyone by surprise. The second, third, fourth, and fifth truck, along with two escort jeeps, were consumed by the force of the rocks and debris and swept off of the road and down the side of the mountain.

The second and fifth trucks' gas tanks were ruptured, and both of the trucks instantly burst into flames as they rolled down the mountainside and into the ocean. All of the men in both of those vehicles, including the Brazilian soldiers, were dead before they hit the water. The third vehicle's gas tank ruptured, but it didn't burst into flames until it was only 50 feet from entering the ocean. As the truck began to sink into the sea, the salt water slowly extinguished the fire with the van breaking up.

The three soldiers riding in each of the two escort vehicles were killed instantly. As the fourth truck was rolling down the mountain, it took a bounce that projected the truck away from the mountain, enabling it to fall directly into the ocean without catching on fire. The impact of the van hitting the ocean shattered the vehicle, however, sending men and debris in all directions. Some of the people in the fourth truck were thrown as far as 300 yards out to sea by the impact of the van hitting the water. Krish was one of the lucky souls thrown out to sea with his chains and handcuffs broken apart from the impact.

He quickly regained consciousness and his senses of orientation such that he could see the fire from other vehicles burning inland.

Growing up as a boy working with his father on his fishing boat he had to swim in rougher waters than this. He slowly started to swim back to shore, keeping the silhouette of the fire to his left and wondering if his childhood friend Ranuel was alive.

Chapter 25

Fort Lauderdale International Airport.

American Airlines Flight 1441 gently landed at the Fort
Lauderdale International Airport. As Wallace and Eve disembarked,
Eve immediately pulled out her cell phone and attempted to call
Tony.

Wallace looked at Eve. "Lover, the signal is going to be
blocked until we get through immigration and customs."

"I know, but I still thought I'd give it a try anyway." After
clearing customs, they took a taxi to the parking lot where they left
Eve's car. They stopped for lunch and were driving on I95 North
headed for Jacksonville, very close to being on the schedule Wallace
laid out. Eve's spirits brightened when she received a long-awaited
text message from Tony.

"Mom got your voice messages. I have been working many
long hours. Logging in a lot of flight time. I have the most in my
Squadron. Promise to call you this weekend. All the things you told
me to do I've done. I want you to be proud of me. Love, Tony."

Wallace could sense the relief in Eve as she finished reading
the message. "Everything's OK?" Wallace said with a smile.

"Oh Wallace, everything is wonderful. All that I have hoped
for is happening."

The weather was humid under an overcast sky. The report on
the radio was calling for early afternoon thunder showers. The drive
from Fort Lauderdale to Jacksonville was a three and a half to four-
hour drive depending on traffic conditions. They would have to go
through Orlando, which meant they would have to deal with the
Disney World traffic and that was always a problem.

Wallace was driving, his thoughts split between thinking
about the situation at SBM and the fact he had not made a decision
concerning his engagement to Eve.

He had basically determined that he couldn't do anything
concerning the situation at SBM until he returned to the office.
Wallace was unable to find a clue from going through his computer
file folders that would lead him to discover what deliverables were
authorized. If he knew what was identified in the statement of work,

he would have a starting point for what was not allowed under the contract. But his thoughts were also with making a decision about the engagement ring he was still carrying in his pocket.

His relationship with Eve was yielding more questions than answers. As they say, six on one hand and half a dozen on the other. One minute she was sweet and caring just like when they met, but there were times on the trip when she was distance. What was more disturbing was when she just plain lied to him.

"Wallace, look at the beautiful orange groves!" Eve was taking a picture with her cell phone. She finished taking the picture and turned to WC. "My mother and I would drive down here when I was a little girl. She would tell me stories of when our family owned all of this. It's so beautiful seeing the row after row of orange and grapefruit trees lined up like they were going to be a parade." WC turned toward Eve.

"Eve, the lover, are you saying that your parents were citrus farmers?" Eve turned away from Wallace and started staring down the road.

"No, silly. Not my parents. My grandparents. At one time they controlled the entire southern market for oranges and grapefruits."

"That's very impressive. Is that property still in your family?"

Eve quickly changed the subject. "I need to call Debra Webb to let her know I'm back and find out about the condition of Helen's husband." Eve dialed Debra's cellular number.

The call went into Debra's voicemail. "Debra, I just wanted to let you know that we are back. We are headed to Jacksonville now. How is Helen doing, and, of course, Joe? Call me and let me find out if you still need me to come to the hospital and give blood?" Eve turned to WC.

"I still can't believe what happened to Joe. That was so unfortunate. I wonder if we should go ahead with our book club meeting this weekend." Eve's cell phone began to ring.

"Hello, Debra. Yes, we made it back, and it was an enjoyable trip. When we see each other, I will completely fill you in... Sure, I will definitely give blood when we reach Jacksonville. We will come directly to the hospital... No! We haven't reached Orlando. I would say in another 30 to 45 minutes… OK, I'll call you when we get to Orlando."

Debra was in her car when she was talking with Eve, headed to the hospital. After she had completed the call, she yelled at her phone to call home. Bubba was at home getting some rest.

"Wake up, Bubba. Wake up and answer the phone."

Bubba reached across the bed, first knocking the phone to the floor. After sitting up on the side of the bed, he picked it up and saw that it was Debra.

"Are you at the hospital?" Debra breathed a sigh of relief when she heard Bubba's voice.

"Bubba, listen to me very carefully,"

Bubba spoke slowly into the phone. "I'm listening, Honey."

"Eve Harding is driving from Fort Lauderdale to Jacksonville. They are about 30 minutes from Orlando. I want you to get the Highway Patrol to send a helicopter to pick her up and bring her to the hospital. Now, Henry Bubba Webb, I never asked you do anything for me, and for this one time, please don't let me down. Now you do whatever you do down at City Hall and make this happen!"

Bubba was fully awake now. "Sure, Honey. This will be no problem. Text me her cellular number so the Highway Patrol can make direct contact. I'll call you back as soon as I get confirmation."

Bubba reached for his cell phone and hit a speed dial number. "Hello, this is Jacksonville Mayor Bubba Webb."

Putting the wheels to work to arrange for an emergency pickup wasn't difficult. The Florida Highway Patrol was accustomed to responding to all types of situations. It also helped that Jerry Clark had used social media to spread the word about Joe Singletary needing blood. Because of Joe Singletary's position as the director of Jacksonville's emergency command center, he was no stranger to the Highway Patrol.

As Wallace and Eve were driving to Jacksonville, Eve's phone rang. She looked at the screen, and it read Florida Highway Patrol.

"Hello?"

"Hello, this is the Florida Highway Patrol. Is this Ms. Eve Harding?" Eve looked at Wallace. "WC, it's the Florida Highway Patrol. Yes, this is Eve Harding."

"Ms. Harding, we have a request from the Mayor of Jacksonville to pick you up by helicopter and transport you to the Shands Hospital in Jacksonville. We understand that you are currently on Interstate 95 driving north. Can you tell me the mile marker your vehicle is passing?"

"WC, they want to know what mile marker we are passing." Wallace quickly spotted the number and pointed it out to Eve. Eve responded to the caller.

"Excellent, Ms. Harding. In about 12 miles you will be approaching a rest stop. Please pull into the rest stop, and a Florida Highway Patrol helicopter will be landing shortly to pick you up and transport you to the hospital. Please keep your cell phone with you in case we need to call you again."

Wallace saw the blue highway sign after about 10 miles. "There's the sign for the rest stop, Eve, just like the patrol said." Pulling the car into the rest stop, Wallace looked around to see where a chopper would land. But it wasn't long before the helicopter was sighted, and it Landed about 100 yards adjacent to the main building.

A patrol officer exited the helicopter, walked Eve back to the chopper, and it was off.

Wallace got back in the car, pulled onto the Interstate, and headed for Jacksonville to meet Eve at the hospital. As he merged into traffic, he decided to give his friend Felix a call. They would not be talking on secure phone lines, but maybe Felix could possibly shed additional light on what was going on at SBM.

WC's call went to voice mail. "Felix, I'm back in Florida, headed for Jacksonville. I have a 10:35 flight to Reagan National, give me a call."

—

Flager Center, CIA South American Desk, Jacksonville, Florida.

Elkin Ardila was looking down at the table-top dashboard in the briefing room when Khristy Newborn's administrative assistant walked in with a very concerned look on her face.

"Elk, I haven't been able to reach Khristy this morning. This is not like her."

Jake Jefferson walked into the briefing room, and sensing something was amiss, asked, "What's up?"

Elk turned to Jake. "We haven't heard from Khristy this morning." Jake looked down at the dashboard and began to move files around, pulling up the Jacksonville Police blotter reports from the previous night.

"Look, there was that major accident on the Dames Point Bridge last night, and here is a list of car tags involved in the crash. See if you find Khristy's tag number in the bunch."

The administrative assistant placed her finger on the dashboard and forwarded the file to her desktop computer, then left the briefing room.

"Jake, you've been at this desk a lot longer than me. Has it always been like this?"

Jake gave Elk a curious look. "What do you mean, Elk?"

"I say the South American Desk can't finish an operation without totally screwing it up."

Jake walked to a coffee pot in the corner of the room and poured himself a cup. Facing the wall, he replied, "I've been assigned to this desk my entire career with the Agency, but you have a lot more seniority than me in the Agency. You tell me about your service in Southwest Asia and the Middle East. Do those desks have a better success rate than we do?"

Elk joined Jake at the coffee pot. "I guess what I am trying to figure out, Jake, is whether there is some type of jinx on this desk due to what happened during the Bay of Pigs operation."

The briefing room door opened. It was the administrative assistant again. Both Jake and Elk turned and could see that tears were running down her face, and her lower lip was trembling.

"What happened? Has something happened to Khristy?" Jake dropped his cup of coffee to the floor and raced across the room as the administrative assistant slumped to the floor.

250

Elk followed Jake and found out that Khristy and her husband Pat were killed in the accident on the Dames Point Bridge. The administrative assistant was cared for, then Jake and Elk walked to Jake's office to call Roy Benning on the secure line.

"This can't be happening; this just can't be happening…," Roy kept saying over and over again. "Jake, you guys are sure that it was her car?"

Jake and Elk looked at each other, then Jake replied, "Roy, we're sure."

"I'm sorry, I know you guys double and triple checked everything, but this is so incredible. In less than 10 days I've lost three of my most senior agents." Roy didn't speak for several moments.

"OK, this is what we are going to do. Jake, you take over running the desk. Elk, I want you to get down to the area of operations. Start in Brazil and then work your way back up to Essequibo, Venezuela, and Guyana. We're missing something about the MIE that we need to know!"

When Elk heard Roy assigning the position of desk chief to Jake, he was surprised and disappointed. Elk looked at Jake.

"Roy, I need to talk to you offline about a personal matter. What's a good time for me to call you?"

The minute Roy heard Elk ask to speak to him privately, he was almost certain of what the conversation would be about. In a sense, there had been three promotions in ten days, and it appeared that Elk was overlooked for promotion on all three occasions.

"Sure, Elk. I have a couple of meetings to attend this morning, so what about this afternoon? Let's say 2:00."

—

FBI Jacksonville Office, Temporary Location.

Agent Harris's daughter's words were still lingering in Agent Faye Cook-Little's thoughts as she parked in the parking lot at the FBI temporary location. She kept saying, "Will my daddy be back tomorrow?"

The grief counselors were trying to explain the situation to her, but she kept repeating the same thing. Faye left, letting the professionals take over. She was not equipped with the right words or proper training, and besides, she was too emotionally connected.

Faye was not surprised by what she saw when she entered the building. Most of the agents that were in the operation in Miami were given three days leave to be at home and get some rest. The office was almost empty. Faye didn't have that luxury. She had to find out whether the two bombings were connected, then file a complete report with the Director.

Faye was taking off her jacket and placing her service revolver at her desk when the office telephone rang.

"This is Agent Cook-Little. How can I help you?"

"Hello, my name is Jake Jefferson, and I work for the federal government. I'd like to meet with you to discuss the three bombings that have taken place in Jacksonville. Can we meet for a cup of coffee?"

Faye was accustomed to calls like this from local, state, or federal offices that wanted some inside information, trying to see if their office had a significant involvement in a case.

"All right, Mr. Jefferson. When would you like to meet?"

"I'm available now. I can pick you up in the front of your building."

"OK, I'm coming out."

Two federal buildings were demolished by the explosion, so she figured once the word got out she was the Agent in Charge of the investigation calls would be coming in. She also thought that she would start receiving calls from insurance companies, different banks, you name any type of organization that had a stake in any of the office space in any of those buildings that were blown up.

When Faye stepped out of her office building, a black SUV was parked at the curve with US government license plates.

"Jake Jefferson? Are you Jake Jefferson?" she asked the man behind the wheel.

"Yes, please get in."

Faye opened the door, but as she was reaching for her safety belt, she said, "Please show me your identification." Jake wasn't surprised at the request and handed Faye his CIA credentials. Faye looked them over. As she looked at the picture on the ID, she turned to Jake to see if it was him and a good likeness. The thought passed through her mind that she had seen him before. Faye couldn't pinpoint when, but his face looked very familiar.

"When you said a government agency, I was thinking more along the lines of the IRS, maybe the Department of Health. Let me guess. You believe that this was some type of terrorist attack?"

Jake quickly turned his head to look at Faye. "You have information that leads you to believe that these were possibly committed by a terrorist group?"

"Slow down, Jefferson! I think we're getting a little bit ahead of ourselves. You said three bombings. At this point in time, I only have official information on explosions. There's a difference between a bombing and an explosion. "

Jake pulled into a Starbucks parking lot. They walked in and ordered two coffees. Both Jake and Faye added sugar and cream, then proceeded back outside and sat at a sidewalk table.

Once again Faye's mind signaled that she had run across Jake before but in a different setting. They were seated at the furthest table away from the entrance.

Faye opened up the conversation. "OK, Jake… I hope you don't mind if I call you Jake?" Jake finished drinking some of his coffee.

"Only if you don't mind me calling you Faye?"

Faye gave her professional smile. "Sure, why not."

"Faye, I know your reputation, and everything that I have heard indicates that you are an excellent Agent. Some people have referred to you as the top agent in the southeast district of the FBI. That's saying a lot about your career and what you have accomplished." Jake took a couple of drinks from his coffee cup while Faye pulled out a notepad with a pen.

"Now, Faye, before you write anything down, I want to let you know that what I am about to share with you is sensitive information and, depending on the context, can easily be labeled classified." Faye picked up the notepad along with the pen and placed them back into her jacket.

"All right, Jake, I'm listening." Jake leaned forward, putting his elbows on the table, indicating to Faye that he didn't want anyone to hear what he was about to say.

"There is a CIA presence in Jacksonville. It has existed here in this city for some time. In all three disasters that have taken place in the last 10 days, the person in the position of desk chief of our operations here in Jacksonville was killed. At the Federal Building, the person who was holding the position, both he and his wife, who by the way, also worked for the Company, were working late. His replacement and his wife were killed in their car when they stopped for the school bus and the explosion that followed. Last night, at the Dames Point Bridge disaster, one of the vehicles that plunged into the St. John River was carrying the third person to be placed in that same position. I bring this information to you as a professional courtesy. If your investigation ties these three individuals together, the sensitivity of the nature of their work and the possibility of disclosing this office will get you lots of pushback. All in the name of national security."

Faye and Jake sat at the table finishing their coffee. Faye said nothing. She just looked at Jake in silence. Jake spoke first.

"I'll give you a ride back to your office."

"That won't be necessary. I need to walk and think."

Jake stood. "Very well, then. I guess it goes without saying, Faye, that we never had this conversation."

—

Shands Hospital, Jacksonville, Florida.

Wallace walked into the main lobby at the information kiosks and typed in Joe Singletary's name. The information on the kiosks read that Joe Singletary was there, but visitation was restricted, and there was no room number identified. WC pulled out his cell phone to contact Eve. He wasn't surprised that his call went into her voice mail. He walked around the lobby for a while and saw a sign that read information. Wallace explained his situation to a middle-aged lady standing behind the counter.

"Almost everyone in the hospital is aware of Mr. Singletary's situation." While she was talking to Wallace, she was typing on the keyboard that was on the counter.

"Everyone was devastated when we finally thought the blood that was going to save him was here and that stupid driver took the wrong turn and ended up in that awful explosion at the bridge." The computer responded, bringing up the information on Joe Singletary.

"Mr. Singletary has been moved to room 731." Pointing across Wallace's shoulder, she said, "You can take the elevator just behind you. We are still praying for him, so I know everything is going to work out."

—

Seventy-Five Miles outside Rio de Janeiro, Brazil.

The mudslide had taken out a quarter mile of roadway along with the six vehicles that made up the convoy. The tropical storm was intensifying, creating conditions, even more, hazardous.

The soldiers who survived got out of their vehicles and walked to the edge of the road to look down at the burning bodies and debris. They were horrified, even as they tried to figure out how their lives were spared.

The fires from the vehicles that had fallen into the water continued to burn and made an excellent reference point for Krish, his powerful arms continuing to move the rest of his body against the waves. He was steadily moving toward shore.

He wasn't keeping track of how far he had swum, but he was beginning to see the silhouettes of floating bodies. Determination, anger, and revenge were the forces keeping him alive and keeping him from being swept out to sea.

The intense rain made it hard for him to determine how far he was from the shore. Then suddenly he was swept up in a wave, and after the wave receded, he could feel the land under his body. He forced himself to get up so he would not be swept back out to sea by another wave. He ran away from the beach for another 50 feet and then fell down.

255

Exhausted, he knew he had to get up and get off the beach as fast as possible before the soldiers found their way down to the beach to assess the damage and look for any possible survivors. He also had to find shelter, a safe place where he could rest to contemplate his next move.

Krish pulled his body up and started to run away from the debris, staying just at the edge of the water so that his footprints would be washed away. As he ran, from time to time, the waves splashing against the surf line were so intense that he was almost swept back out to sea.

Krish couldn't determine how long he had been running when he saw a silhouette the shape of a boat. As he got closer, his mind's eye confirmed that it was, in fact, a dinghy.

Once Krish reached the craft, he began to inspect it to find out if the boat was seaworthy. He quickly figured out that the dinghy was a lifeboat from a private yacht. Painted on the rear of the dinghy was the name Liberty Girl. Further inspection revealed that everything was still intact for him to sail it, including the emergency box that contained flares, food, other life vests as well as the sails and oars.

Krish quickly put on one of the life jackets and began to push the boat toward the water's edge. The weather was starting to turn in Krish's favor. The rain was now a steady downpour, but the wind had died down, and there was just an occasional gust.

With a rebirth of energy and determination, Krish worked every muscle in his body to get the small boat beyond the surf and out to sea where he hoisted the little sail, which then caught the wind, taking him away from the beach and the Brazilian security forces.

Chapter 26

Shands Hospital, Jacksonville, Florida.

Wallace walked across the room to the elevators. Two ladies were waiting, and one pushed the button. The elevator doors opened, and WC stood back, letting the women step on. As he walked in, he saw that the button had been pushed to the seventh floor. When one of the ladies noticed that Wallace did not push a button, she looked at him out of the corner of her eye.

The elevator reached the seventh floor. Again, Wallace let the ladies exit first. The two women walked across the room to a waiting area and joined another woman.

Wallace stood in front of the elevator doors looking for someone he could get some information from to locate Eve. He saw the nurse's station, then proceeded to walk in that direction.

At the nurse's station, Wallace waited until the nurse sitting at the desk completed an entry on the computer.

"I hope you can help me. My companion, Eve Harding, was brought here by helicopter to give blood for Joe Singletary. My name is Wallace C. Barker, and I'm here to pick her up." The nurse stood up from behind the counter.

"Mr. Barker, do you have any type of identification?" Wallace pulled out his wallet. "Sure, here is my driver's license."

The nurse inspected the permit. "Thank you, Mr. Barker. Ms. Harding is still in the procedure room. You can have a seat in the waiting area; I'll let her know you are here."

Wallace walked back in the direction to the waiting area. The three women in the waiting area were staring at him. Wallace could sense that they were trying to figure out who he was. Just as Wallace approached the waiting area, he saw a table with magazines. WC walked to the table and began to look for something to read while he waited for more information on Eve.

WC found a magazine, then took a seat on the opposite side of the waiting area, facing away from the ladies.

Wallace could hear the women talking but could not make out what they were saying because they were talking in low tones and whispering. Then one of the ladies raised her voice slightly and said, "That must be him."

A few seconds later, WC felt a tap on his shoulder. He turned his head and saw one of the ladies standing next to him and looking down at him. Wallace stood up.

"Hello, my name is Debra Webb. We saw that you asked for our friend Eve Harding. Are you related to her?" Wallace looked at Debra and then looked across the room at the other two ladies.

"My name is Wallace, Wallace C. Barker, and yes I'm a friend of Eve. I'm here to pick her up. She is giving blood for a gentleman who was involved in a serious accident."

Debra smiled while reaching out her hand to WC. "Mr. Barker, we are so grateful to you for helping to get Eve here. We were in our last hope of ever getting a blood match to help Joe." Debra turned to the other two ladies, signaling for them to come over. Smiling, they joined Wallace and Debra.

"I want to introduce two of Eve's other friends. This is Gracie Black and Brenda Jefferson. We are all members of the same book club. That's how we came to know Eve." Wallace smiled and shook each of the lady's hands. Gracie Black seemed to be the most aggressive in trying to find out about the relationship between Wallace and Eve.

"How long have you and Eve known each other?" Wallace smiled while contemplating his response, but before Wallace could say anything, a nurse approached them.

"Mrs. Webb, I have some great news. Ms. Harding's blood is a perfect match. The doctor has just begun the transfusion for Mr. Singletary. It will probably be a while, so why don't you go downstairs to our cafeteria, grab a snack or a bite to eat, and come back in an hour or so." Everyone smiled, and Debra, Gracie, and Brenda embraced each other. Wallace turned to the nurse.

"Did anyone tell Ms. Harding that I am here?" The nurse looked carefully at Wallace.

"Oh, yes, Mr. Barker. I'm sorry I didn't mention this. We told Ms. Harding that you are in the waiting room, and she asked me to tell you to wait if it doesn't interfere with catching your flight back to Maryland."

Wallace looked at his watch. "Please tell Eve I'll wait as long as I can." The nurse smiled and walked away.

Debra Webb pulled out her phone and walked away from the group to call Bubba. "Bubba, I have fantastic news. Eve's blood is a perfect match. They just started the transfusion. I just hope it's in time for Joe to pull through this. Yes, I'll call you as soon as I find out from the doctor." Debra rejoined the group.

"Mr. Barker."

Wallace quickly interrupted her. "Please, I'd really prefer you call me WC." Debra looked at Gracie and Brenda, then turned back to WC.

"WC, I know that you have been on that highway for the last couple of hours and probably haven't had anything to eat since you got off the plane. Let us take you downstairs, and we'll treat you to something to eat." WC looked at the three ladies to see that they all agreed. They then started to the elevator for the ride to the first-floor cafeteria.

As the elevator descended, WC was pleased that he had run into some of Eve's friends. He thought that this may give him a little more insight into the woman he was carrying an engagement ring for in his pocket. Talking with them could help him in his decision process concerning their relationship.

As they stepped off the elevator, WC's cell phone rang. Wallace pulled the phone out of his pocket and saw Felix's face on the screen. "I need to take this call. I'll catch up."

Debra said OK. As they walked away while WC started to talk to Felix, Gracie Black said, "You know, Nancy still hasn't returned my call. I guess she must be out of town."

Brenda Jefferson replied, "You should call either Khristy or Cathy. They stay in touch with Nancy most of the time."

With his cell to his ear, Wallace watched the ladies turn into the hospital cafeteria.

"Felix, what's all that noise in the background? I can hardly hear you because of the noise!" Background music was blasting over Wallace's phone. "

"Kind of cool, huh? I'm working on this application where you can have any type of music playing in the background while you are on the phone talking, just like elevator music. The big difference

259

is that you can select the music based on your caller. If I know you like the Wild Hair, when caller ID identifies you are the caller, the music you like plays in the background."

"Felix, the music is too loud. The caller can hardly hear."

"I know. I still have a few bugs to work out."

Wallace thought for a minute. "Felix, I'll call you back later."

Wallace walked up to the cafeteria, and when he saw the ladies, he joined them. They were standing in the line contemplating what they were going to order. They all seemed to be in good spirits after hearing the news about the blood match and the transfusion taking place for Joe Singletary.

The ladies ordered salads and WC order a chicken sandwich along with a piece of apple pie and a coke.

After ordering their food, they all took seats at a table in the middle of the cafeteria. Wallace could sense that they wanted to find out as many details as possible about the relationship he and Eve had, so he decided to be the aggressor in the conversation and leadoff with questions about how they first met her.

It seemed that, after Eve had moved to Jacksonville, she got involved as a volunteer with Bubba Webb's first campaign for Mayor. This is how she met Debra Webb. Gracie Black was also working as a volunteer on Bubba's campaign, which led to Eve meeting, Gracie. Shortly afterward they decided to start a book club, which led to the other ladies meeting Eve.

The conversation continued to be centered on the book club and all of the beautiful books that they had read until Gracie Black said, "But WC, you haven't told us how you and Eve met?"

Wallace turned to Gracie when Debra Webb looked at her watch. "You guys continue. I'm going upstairs to check on Helen and Joe."

Wallace took that moment to say, "I'll go up with you because I have a flight to catch back to Maryland, and I'd like to see Eve before I leave."

When Debra and Wallace reached the nurse's station, they were told that Joe Singletary was stable, and his vital signs indicated his body was accepting the blood transfusion, but it would be 12 to 24 hours before the doctor was sure Joe was out of danger.

Wallace was told that Eve, extremely exhausted from the 11-hour flight from Brazil to Fort Lauderdale, had fallen asleep. Just to be on the safe side, the doctor wanted to keep her overnight. Wallace could come back the next morning to visit.

"Thank you very much for the good news." WC glanced at his watch. "But I have a plane to catch to Maryland. Can I leave Ms. Harding's car keys with you and I'll give her a call the first thing in the morning."

—

CIA Headquarters, Langley, Virginia.

It was about ten minutes until Roy Benning's call with Elkin Ardila. Roy was at his desk reading through Elk's personnel jacket. Roy was very familiar with Elk's history: two awards for valor, numerous letters of commendation, glowing performance appraisal reports, and he had the education along with all the necessary training as well as the experience. But his expertise was needed elsewhere.

The same thing that held his other supervisors back from promoting him to his own desk was holding him back now, the fact that he was one hell of an intelligent Agent, who had mastered the skill sets necessary to be successful in any clandestine environment.

Elk had the ability to get people to work for the Agency without paying them a dime. There was even a deep classified section of his personnel jacket. What this meant was that the agent made a direct action or termination of a target. A Direct Action by an agency is very rare. Most Direct Action assignments are contracted out to professionals outside the Company. Roy's desk phone rang.

"Roy Benning."

"Roy, this is Elk. I hope I'm not calling too early." Roy closed the file on his computer that contained Elk's personnel jacket.

"No, Elk. You are right on time. You said that you had something personal you wanted to discuss with me. What can I do for you?" Roy could hear Elk taking a deep breath.

"Roy, I'll come to the point. I want to be recognized and be promoted similarly to every other Agent in the Company. When I

261

was assigned to this desk, I came in with more Senior authority than any of the other people working here. In the last 10 days, there have been three opportunities for me to receive a promotion to Desk Chief. I mean, what do I have to do to get promoted? Kill every Desk Chief in Jacksonville until I'm the only man left standing?"

Roy knew that this was going to be an emotional conversation with Elk.

"Elk, you are correct. You are the most senior agent assigned to the operations in Jacksonville, and I took that fact into account in making the decision to make Jake Jefferson the current chief." Roy could still hear the heavy breathing coming from Elk.

"But Elk, you have been in the Company long enough to know that in my position I had to consider some other factors."

Suddenly Elk broke in, raising his voice, "OK, what were those factors? What stopped you from promoting me?"

"Elk, when I look at the skillset of agents working in the field from the Jacksonville operation I don't have anyone who is up to the level we need to accomplish the mission." Roy stopped for a moment.

"Sure, we have several agents assigned down there who are still honing their craft, but I think that you would agree they haven't reached the clandestine level for what is needed in the southern hemisphere."

Elk didn't answer. Then Roy continued.

"Let's do this. Go down to Brazil, look around, and find out how the Brazilian security people got tipped off about the MIE; and if you can, obtain anything about the assassination of those two security ministers. I'll start working the wheels here to get you that desk that you deserve. We'll probably start you off with a nice corner office up here close to me, and in a short while, you'll get your own desk." Roy stopped to see if he got any reaction from Elk.

"OK, then? Send your reports to Jake and copy me."

Roy could hear the reluctance in Elk's voice as he said, "All right, Roy. I'll take the assignment. I figure that it will probably take me about six weeks to three months to start the information flowing. I'll get with Jake and work out the details. But Roy, the day I get back I will be waiting to hear from you concerning that Desk Chief position."

Staring at the screen saver on his computer monitor, Roy said, "Elk, I will live up to my end. You have my word on that."

After the conversation, Roy turned to his computer, established a new file folder, and labeled it Elk's new Position. He began to copy documents from his personnel jacket that he intended to use to support his request to promote Elk to a new Position upon his completion of the assignment. Roy finished populating the folder, and then he saved the file in the non-classified section of the C-drive on his desktop.

Roy then pulled out a yellow legal pad, and his thoughts drifted to operation Fertile Ground. He jotted notes on the pad. He was trying to come up with a plausible theory on how the Operation was compromised. It was about four hours before his meeting with the Director and the DDP.

As Roy was writing, his administrative assistant walked in. Roy looked up from his pad. "Roy, I just got the word that your meeting with the Director and DDP has been changed to tomorrow morning; it will be held in the box on level-3." The box was an entirely secure conference room. "Also, you are scheduled to take a polygraph test this afternoon."

Unemotional, Roy said, "Thanks." Roy's thoughts were far away. He was developing a theory concerning the MIE. He then said, "Why is the meeting being moved to a secure briefing room and why is he having me take a poly before the meeting?" This meant that the discussion would encompass a lot more than personnel changes.

Chapter 27

Starbucks, Jacksonville, Florida.

After purchasing her second cup of coffee, Agent Faye Cook-Little sat at the table staring at the passing traffic. She had been placed in a hell of a dilemma.

CIA Agent Jake Jefferson just dumped into her lap what could be considered the elements that tied three incidents together. The dilemma that Faye was facing was this: When you start an investigation, you follow the trail of the evidence, forensic and autopsy reports, interviews and witnesses' statements, along with a whole host of other information. You use a sequential fact-finding process, and you develop hypotheses and draw conclusions as the evidence comes together. What Jefferson had just done was turn the entire process upside down and inside out. What Jefferson had also done was to tell Faye that, even if she found out that the motive for all three bombings was to assassinate CIA agents because of their position in the type of work that they were doing for the federal government, national security concerns would put a halt to the entire investigation.

If Agent Cook-Little went to the Director and told him about the meeting, he would probably look at her as if Faye had too many drinks. If the Director did believe her, she still had to get a corroborating statement from Agent Jake Jefferson. However, Agent Jefferson would not do that because he only gave the information to Faye as a professional courtesy.

The only logical course of action Faye had was to place the information Jake Jefferson shared with her in a mental vault in the back of her mind and then proceed with the investigation without opening that vault, or rather, opening it only if the evidence took her there.

Faye had consumed only half of her second cup of coffee. Faye picked it up and started walking back to the FBI temporary office on Beach Boulevard. When Agent Cook-Little got back to her desk, there was a note in the middle of her chair indicating that Jerry Clark would like for her to return his call. Faye figured that Jerry was calling to set up an appointment for her to come in and brief the

Mayor on where she stood in the investigation. Faye knew Jerry Clark, and in fact, she had his number connected to a speed dial on her phone.

"Jerry Clark here. Is this Faye?"

"Yes, Jerry. How are you doing?" Jerry was at his desk typing up a press release.

"Oh, just fine, Faye. The Mayor would like you to come down to his office to speak with him concerning the investigation of the Dames Point Bridge disaster. He also wanted to know whether or not there is any connection between the Dames Point Bridge, the fires that we had at the federal buildings downtown, and that so tragic school bus explosion. Just giving you a heads-up so you will be prepared for like you always are."

Faye was opening her desktop calendar. "You're a real sweetheart, Jerry. OK, I have my calendar open. Give me a time that's convenient for me to come."

"What about 9:00 tomorrow morning? Is that a good time?" Faye typed 9:00 AM on the next day's date. "That will work for me, Jerry. See you tomorrow."

—

Jacksonville International Airport.

"TSA Pre-check" was printed on Wallace's boarding pass. He went through security check and was sitting at gate C12 waiting for the B-Group announcement to line up. He would be loading at the B13 position, which would ensure that he got a good seat. WC's preference was to be sitting in an aisle seat just about three-quarters toward the rear of the plane.

His plan was to pull out his laptop and go through his file folders again, in a second attempt to get a clue as to what unlawful delivery was made to the government, the delivery for which SBM was seeking payment. Felix's saying that the bean counters were pushing the issue, must mean that significant money is involved with this deliverable, he thought.

As Wallace got situated in his seat, he pulled out his laptop and placed his computer bag under the seat in front of him. The

265

fatigue began to set in, and he knew he probably would not get the work accomplished that he wanted to do on this two hour Southwest Airlines flight 297 to Reagan National Airport.

WC wanted to be as prepared as possible for his meeting tomorrow with the senior vice president of the projects in question. Wallace had been working for Sterling since he came out of the military, but with Sterling so entrenched in the Department of Defense and on this project with the Department of the Navy, he knew he had to be overly prepared for his meeting.

His plane took off, and even before the aircraft reached the altitude where Wallace could turn on his laptop to begin searching again, he fell asleep thinking about his meeting at SBM mid-morning the next day.

Sterling Business Machines, or SBM, is a multinational technology corporation with headquarters in Gaithersburg, Maryland. SBM markets computer software, middleware, and firmware, and offers infrastructure and consulting services in areas ranging from mainframe computers to nanotechnology. SBM has 12 major centers located around the world and in recent years has purchased a large number of small to mid-size companies, capitalizing on the smaller companies' proprietary technology and talented but less expensive workforce.

SBM is divided into three business unit divisions, Defense Technology Services (DTS), Consulting Services (CS), and New Technology Development (NTD). Wallace worked in the DTS Division.

———

Shands Hospital, Jacksonville, Florida.

Bubba and Debra Webb were visiting Eve Harding in her hospital room while she was waiting to be released after donating her blood to Joe Singletary. Debra was seated beside her bed, and Bubba was standing. They were watching a breaking news report on the television located on the wall in Eve's room.

"This is WZXL Channel 4 breaking news. We will switch to Kyle Martin, who is on the scene at the FBI temporary office located

266

on Beach Boulevard." A brief second passed, and then the camera focused on Kyle Martin.

"This is Kyle Martin, and I'm standing in front of the temporary office of the Federal Bureau of Investigation here on Beach Boulevard. The office was relocated to this building after the explosion of both the Federal Building and the Federal Reserve Bank in the downtown area of Jacksonville. Not since the Boston Marathon bombing has a US city been held in the grip of such terror and horror. In less than ten days three separate disasters have occurred with loss of life reaching double digit numbers, and estimates of the costs to rebuild the infrastructure and the loss of property are reaching well into the billions of dollars. Through a reliable source who requested that their name not to be disclosed, WZXL Television has received exclusive reports that a closed-door meeting will be held at the Mayor's office tomorrow at 9:00 AM. The meeting will be attended by representatives from the JPD, Home Land Security, ATF, Florida Highway Patrol, Jacksonville Fire Department, Jacksonville Emergency Management Center, other agencies involved in these disasters, and the FBI. We have been told but have not yet confirmed that the FBI may be providing information connecting the three incidences together and may also compare the situation to a raid the FBI and ATF made on a terrorist group in Miami earlier in the week. This story is continuing to develop. Tune into the 11:00 news on the latest developments. This is Kyle Martin, WZXL of Channel 4 TV News."

Debra walked across the room, picked up the remote from Eve's nightstand, and turned the television off. Eve repositioned herself in bed and sat up, first looking at Debra and then at Bubba.

"My oh my, a lot has happened in our sleepy little town while I was on vacation. Is all of that true, Bubba?"

Bubba moved to the foot of Eve's bed and turned to look at Eve, but before he could say anything, Debra spoke.

"Eve, Honey, you know very well Bubba cannot talk on any official business, especially about an ongoing investigation." Bubba looked at his wife with a saved-by-the-bell expression, then turned back to Eve.

"Eve, Debra and I can't thank you enough for donating your blood to our dear friend Joe. I have a surprise for you." Bubba pulled out an envelope from his suit pocket.

"The city put up $500 to the first person who gave blood that was the match for Joe Singletary. Here is your check for $500." Eve smiled.

"This will help me cover some of my expenses from my vacation. We had to spend so much money while we were down there." Bubba gave the envelope to Eve, then walked to his wife and gave her a kiss.

"I have to get down to the office and check on something with Jerry. I won't be long." Before Bubba left the room, he said to Eve, "By the way, how is Tony doing? Navy fighter pilot, right?"

"Oh yes, and wonderful. Thanks for asking. We are supposed to talk this weekend. Tony is a pilot, but not in one of those fighters. Tony flies some other type of jet. I really can't tell one from the other. Tony always gets upset with me about that."

Bubba and Debra smiled while Bubba added, "Joe Singletary was a pilot in the Navy. He flew an EQ-6B Prowler. Man, Joe would never let us forget that. His flying days are something he will always cherish. Please give my best to Tony the next time you guys talk."

Debra smiled. "I'm going to stay here for a few more minutes, and I'll meet you at home… No, let's meet at Market 32 and have dinner?"

Bubba looked at Debra with a smile. "OK! We need a night out. I'll call for reservations."

As Bubba left the room, Debra turned back to Eve, but before she said anything, Helen Singletary walked in.

"Hi, everyone. Eve, how are you feeling?"

Both Eve and Debra turned to Helen. "I'm great. I'm just waiting for the doctor to come by and give me my release, but more important, how is Joe doing?"

Helen walked closer to Eve's bed and stood beside Debra. "It's only been about 12 hours since the transfusion, and the doctor said 12 to 24 hours before he knows for sure, but the nurse just told me that all of his vital signs started pointing in the right direction, which is a great sign." Helen began to cry. She then said. "I so hope that it's' not too late, and he pulls through this."

Debra placed her arm around Helen. "Helen, I feel splendid about this. I think that, in the not too distance future, we will all look back and see how blessed we are to have such good friends," Debra smiled and looked at Eve and noticed that she didn't smile until after they made eye contact.

Eve then said, "Debra, that was so beautiful, what you just said. I wish I had said it myself." Eve then reached over to her night table picked up a cup that contained some juice and took a sip. As she put the cup down, she said, "You know, this Saturday we are supposed to have our first book club meeting. With all that has been going on, should we postpone it and begin our reading season next month?"

Helen looked at Debra first and then at Eve. "Ladies, with Joe in the hospital, I won't be able to be there." Eve looked at Debra and back to Helen.

"Honey, I understand, but I had to say something so I could put out an email canceling the meeting," Helen quickly said.

"I'm not suggesting that you cancel the meeting. I'm just saying that I will not be able to attend." Eve got out of bed, put on a nightgown and walked to the closet. She took her clothes out of the wardrobe and started for the bathroom.

"I'm going to change before the doctor arrives. I feel much better, so I'm sure that he is going to release me. I'll keep the door open so I can hear you." Eve walked into the bathroom and left the door open.

Debra spoke. "Let me see. Brenda Jefferson was out here at the hospital last week, along with Gracie Black, and so both of them know about the meeting. Gracie said that she finished the book. I've left voice messages on Nancy Mansfield's phone. She will probably call me back the morning of the meeting, talking about how she was so busy that she didn't finish reading the book."

Helen commented, "I started reading the book, but after Joe got hurt I haven't had time to pick it up."

Eve walked out of the bathroom fully dressed and said, "Khristy gave us the title of this book. I hope she finished reading it since it was her recommendation."

Debra added, "And you know Khristy Newborn, Ms. Important, is the same way. Never finishes a book. Always

269

complaining about her workload and never having enough time for herself."

Helen added, "Nancy is the same way. Always talking about how she has to spend so much time at the office, so much to do and never having enough time for herself. But anytime you catch up to her, she is ready to go shopping."

"I tell you what, ladies," Debra said. "Let's call Cathy Mills while we are all here and see what she says about moving our first meeting to next month." Debra pulled out her cell phone and dialed Cathy's mobile number. After not reaching Cathy on her cell phone, she called her home number, which also went to voicemail. Debra left messages on both phones.

—

City Hall, Mayor's Office, Jacksonville, Florida.

After parking, Bubba Webb took the private elevator to his office. He punched the security code into the keypad and entered, turning on the lights. Bubba sat down at his desk and cut on his desktop. While the computer was booting up, he opened the cabinet door that contained his bar, pulled out two glasses along with a bottle of bourbon, then walked back to his desk.

Bubba opened a file folder on his computer that was labeled "next campaign." After the file was opened, he opened a document titled "timeline-events" and began to type. As he was typing, Bubba heard a noise and so turned his head in the direction of his office door. Jerry Clark was standing in the doorway knocking.

"Come on in, Jerry." Bubba walked around his desk to meet Jerry in the middle of his office, greeting him with a big handshake along with a hug.

"I hope you saw it on television. Kyle Martin fell for it hook, line, and sinker. It was brilliant, your idea of giving her the inside scoop on that upcoming press release. Jerry, you really know your business." A big smile appeared on Jerry Clark's face.

"Comparison to the Boston Marathon bombing was a sweet touch that made an example people could relate to."

Still smiling, Jerry said, "Thank you very much, Mr. Mayor, but with the global recognition you got from how you handled the first bombing, we needed something to build on and continue the momentum."

Bubba walked back to his desk and picked up the two glasses and bottle of bourbon. He walked across the room, and Bubba and Jerry sat down at the conference table. Jerry pulled out his cell phone and pushed it across the table.

"Look, I'm already receiving emails and text messages from all of the agencies that Kyle mentioned in her television report, asking for the room number for the meeting. It worked beautifully."

Bubba poured each of them two fingers of bourbon. Then he picked up the cell phone and began to thumb through the messages while sipping on his drink.

"All right, how do I handle the meeting tomorrow?" Jerry took out his pad and turned to a page that was marked with a post-it note.

"Now, the FBI had already set themselves up for being the bad guys for not showing up for the Dames Point Bridge incident. So my recommendation is to stay with that."

Bubba started placing the glasses and bottle back into the cabinet. "Who is the Agent in Charge for the FBI?"

Jerry Clark quickly replied, "Agent Faye Cook-Little, a very senior agent who has worked several high-profile cases for the FBI since she has been assigned to the office here. In fact, she was the lead agent in the raid the FBI and ATF conducted in Miami earlier in the week. Just a recommendation, but stay away from trying to embarrass her or to imply that she is an incompetent agent. Faye is one of the top agents, not only in the Jacksonville office but in the southeast district. She is highly respected as a professional and is very well liked."

Bubba turned off the lights on his desk, and he and Jerry Clark walked to the door.

"Jerry, be sure that Terry Jackson is present, even if we have to start the meeting late. As a matter of fact, get Terry into my office early, let's say at 8:30 so he and I can go over some things. We have to ensure that everything works for the city so we will get stuck with a small amount, and if at all possible, no money, to be paid out of the city treasury for these disasters."

Bubba and Jerry got to the underground garage and were just about to part to walk to their cars. "One last thing, Mr. Mayor. The bombings, or whatever they turn out to be, have projected Jacksonville and you to the level of national attention. We want to maintain that focus as long as we can, and if possible, until the beginning of the campaign season."

Bubba smiled and started to walk to his car. He said over his shoulder, "We will make it happen."

—

Small Sailing Boat off the East Coast of Brazil.

Krish woke with the hot morning sun beating down on the right side of his body. This is what he was hoping for, a clear sky so he could verify that the direction he was sailing was due north. The sun was burning the right side of his body, and the sun rises in the east and sets in the west and so… He went to the survival box that was in the dinghy, taking out the compass to verify his position. Krish was heading due north. A big grin appeared on his face. As long as he kept waking up with the sun hitting the right side of his body, he would be heading due north. At night, as long as the sky was clear, he would pick out the North Star to keep him on the course.

The Brazilian coastline was to his left and Rio de Janeiro behind him. Proceeding in the northerly direction, he had two more major ports to maneuver around; but to continue in this direction would lead to freedom and back to Essequibo. He had to pass the port cities of Salvador, Aracaju, Recife, and Natal and then turn to the west-northwest direction until he reached the coastline of Essequibo.

All he had to do was stay out of the shipping lanes. His boyhood experiences sailing with and learning from his father gave him the seamanship instinct and skill to do that.

Krish's thoughts were never far from their betrayal by the Americans. It was hard for him to understand how they could be so caring and sympathetic to their cause, then turn around and betray them without any regard for honesty or decency. He made a solemn vow to himself that he would get revenge, no matter how long it took. "I will kill the American who holds the position that betrayed us," he said aloud.

Chapter 28

Ronald Reagan National Airport, Washington, DC.

Southwest Airlines flight 297 from Jacksonville, Florida was starting its approach into the Ronald Reagan National Airport, and Wallace was waking up from his sound sleep.

Meanwhile, back in Jacksonville, Eve was released from the hospital and driving home. Her thoughts were consumed with Tony and their next telephone conversation. She was singing along with the music blasting from the car radio when she said out loud in the car,

"I can't wait to tell Tony that I gave my blood to Joe Singletary, who was hurt in the first blast, and this is the part that is really going to be funny, that he was a flyer in the Navy and piloted an EA-6B Prowler. Tony is going to die laughing."

Back at Ronald Reagan National Airport, Flight 297 set down on the runway and taxied to the terminal. As the passengers began exiting the plane, an announcement came over the intercom system: "Will passenger Wallace C. Barker report to the nearest Southwest Airlines counter?"

WC thought that something had happened to his luggage, that maybe it didn't make the plane and would be flying in on another flight. That had happened to him before. As he left the plane, he noticed two men he then thought were Southwest Airlines workers moving bags around just in the area outside of the aircraft's doors.

He started up the ramp, and as he got closer to the gate leading into the main terminal he spotted four men, two police officers and two men in suits. Wallace also became aware that the two men he had taken to be airline employees were following him.

When Wallace stepped from the ramp into the terminal, he paused for a second to see the reaction from the two police officers and the men in suits. They made direct eye contact with Wallace.

Their reaction was an indication they were associated with the announcement concerning him. WC walked the few steps to the Southwest counter.

"There was an announcement made for Wallace C. Barker to come to the Southwest Airlines counter.

"I'm Wallace C. Barker."

The lady and man dressed in the airline clothing at the counter were with the FBI, along with the two men in suits and the two men dressed as airline workers. The two policemen were uniform federal agents.

The man behind the Southwest counter dressed as a Southwest Airlines employee showed Wallace a badge that reads FBI. He then said, "Mr. Barker, you must come with us," and started reading Wallace his Miranda rights. Wallace was handcuffed. He remained quiet, not resisting.

WC was escorted by an entourage of federal agents away from the counter and through a side door ending up outside the terminal.

Once outside the terminal, Wallace was placed in the backseat of an awaiting black sedan. The car rushed away from the terminal with one escort SUV in the front and another one following. Wallace was familiar with Washington DC, and so it wasn't long before he could guess where they were taking him.

It took the three vehicles less than 25 minutes to reach FBI Headquarters. Shortly after they parked in the underground garage, Wallace was whisked away, and within 15 minutes he was sitting in an FBI interrogation room.

Wallace was placed on a chair, his legs shackled to the table in front of him, facing a two-way mirror. On the other side of the two-way mirror, in the viewing room, were two young FBI agents observing Wallace.

"That's him? Looks like he's in pretty good shape," the other Agent replied.

"Yea, that's him. I used to look that good back when I was in the Army. He doesn't appear to be agitated or nervous about this. The guy is not even sweating. "

The door opened to the viewing room to the interrogation room. Senior Special FBI Agent Ambrose Walker walked into the room, immediately taking a seat behind the computer that was on the table in the far corner of the room. The other two agents walked over from the viewing mirror, taking positions behind Agent Walker so that could see the screen. Agent Walker began to speak.

"Let me see if I got this. We received a request from Interpol to pick this guy up who is traveling from Rio de Janeiro back to the US and he lives in Maryland. The Brazilian secret police picked him up because he was on a tourist bus coming from the hotel and witnessed the Brazilian security forces gun down some locals. They detained him, and in the interview process, they came to the conclusion that he may be the international known Number Assassin." The agent sitting down quickly looked over his shoulder at one of the other agents but continued typing, opening multiple windows on his computer screen.

The man standing behind Agent Walker didn't say anything, their eyes are transfixed on Agent Walker as he worked at the computer. Agent Walker hit the enter key, raising his hand in the air as if he had just played the last note in a piano concert.

He stood up from the computer and said, "Now, I want you two geniuses to take a look at this." Walker backed away, so each of the agents had a clear view of the monitor.

"Attention to detail. If you really want to be successful and stay in the Agency, you have to play close attention to the details, all of the details. Take a look at this: the first thing you should notice, in Brazil, this guy presented his military ID, clearly indicating that he is a Major in US Army Reserve. From there, all you had to do was verify his military service on this screen." Agent Walker was using his pen as a pointer.

"Once you get to this screen, you can see the amount of time that he was on active duty. See this: this shows that he was active duty Special Forces, and when he came off active duty he transitioned into the Army Reserve and went directly into another SF unit. You also see that this guy has an above the level of Top Secret Security Clearance, which means that, depending on the situation, he can look at the same stuff the President sees."

The two agents continued to stare at the screen. Walker paused for a moment, smiling at the Agents. "Look, while this guy was on active duty, he served all over Southwest Asia and the Middle East: Egypt, Somalia, Jordan, Kuwait, Pakistan, Saudi Arabia, and all over the UAE. Hell, you guys probably don't even know what the UAE stands for."

The agents raised their heads from looking at the monitors, looked at each other without saying anything, then returned to staring at the screen.

Agent Walker, still pointing to the screen, said, "Now this is where everything stops, and you see this?" Walker was referring to the last entry on Wallace's record on the computer screen.

One of the agents stepped back from viewing the computer. "Everything stopped at that code number. What does that mean?"

The other Agent said, "I guess he is one of those black ops guys."

Agent Walker sat back down at the computer and began to close the open windows on the computer.

"What that means is this: first this guy is not the Number Assassin, and second, even if he was, because of national security, we can't touch him. You see, with the security level that Barker has, he must take a polygraph tests every year, and so, if Barker were doing anything dirty outside of what he does on his missions, it would have popped up."

Agent Walker finished closing all of the open windows on the computer screen. "Now, my young agents, this is what happens when you don't pay attention to detail. You spent a lot of our taxpayers' money tonight. You two geniuses authorized funding for more than eight field agents, not to mention all of the backup resources that were on alert and taken away from other duties."

Ambrose walked to the two-way mirror. "OK, you!" He pointed to one of the agents. "Go down to the night bursar's office and have an inconvenience check made out to Wallace C. Barker of $2,500." Turning to the other agent standing at attention in front of Agent Walker, he said, "You go in there and un-cuff Major Barker, apologize to him for the inconvenience, thank him for his service to our country, then take him downstairs to pick up his money. Then drive him home or to anywhere he wants to go."

The second agent started to move toward the door to enter the room where Wallace was sitting. Agent Walker grabbed the Agent's shoulder and said, "Wait!"

Looking at Barker through the two-way mirror, and then looking at the officer, he said, "I'll go in with you. This guy could tear you apart."

When they walked into the room, Agent Walker said, "Please take those off Major Barker." Senior Special Agent Walker was pointing to the hand cups and leg irons. The young agent unlocked Barker from the table and then unlocked his handcuffs and quickly backed away.

"Major Barker, I'm Senior Special Agent Ambrose Walker. With your experience, I guess you figured out why we brought you in." WC was sitting at the table rubbing his wrists.

"Let me guess. You probably got a flash message, either from Interpol or the Brazilian Authorities, labeling me as a person of interest, possibly involved with the Number Assassin, and to be on the lookout. The alert here in DC went out after I passed through TSA security when boarding my flight in Jacksonville. So rather than checking the details of the passengers through the network, you guys sent out the Marines."

Senior Special Agent Walker stood across the table from Barker motionless. "That's about right, Major Barker. On behalf of the FBI, I would like to apologize for taking you through this. This agent will escort you downstairs to the night bursar's office. We have a check for you to compensate for your time and the trouble we have put you through. Of course, you will have to sign a release."

Wallace stood up and followed the young FBI agent to the bursar's office. At a small window, he signed the release indicating that he would not file a lawsuit against the FBI or federal government, picked up his check, and let the Bureau drive him home.

While he was sitting in the back seat of the FBI car, he pulled out his cell phone and sent Eve a text message asking if she had gotten home from the hospital.

———

Jacksonville, Florida.

Eve turned into the Montevilla Housing Development and then made a right turn onto the street where she lived, Venosa Circle, a quiet neighborhood where everyone knew each other but still stayed to themselves.

The income that she earned while working in the high-tech computer industry as an electrical engineer placed her in an excellent position where she could afford almost any of the reasonably priced single family homes in the Jacksonville real estate market. With what she was making as a high school chemistry teacher, she would have never been able to afford this 3800 square foot home.

As she pulled into the driveway, her home security system cut on all of her lights in the house, also sending a live video image to the screen in her BMW. Eve could see every room in the house before she pushed the button for the garage door to open.

Eve grabbed her suitcases, and just before she opened the door that led into the main house, she turned and looked at a row of wall storage cabinets lining the forward wall of the garage. Setting her luggage down, she then walked over to the cabinets and inspected them to see if everything was in order. Standing in front of the cabinets, she quietly said in a whisper, "I'll be back, Mama."

She then picked up her luggage and entered the house. After watering her plants she went upstairs to her bedroom, unpacked, and took a long shower. After showering, she put on her nightgown and housecoat. She then turned all of the lights off in the house and sat on her bed looking at the clock on her night table.

Eve sat in the dark for exactly 20 minutes, and with all of the lights still off in the house, she then went downstairs and back into the garage to the wall cabinets. She unlocked the office's outer door, stepped into the enclosure, and locked the door behind her. She then pushed a secret panel, and the inside door opened up.

Eve stepped into a dark hidden room. She turned a lamp on, then after her eyes adjusted to the light, she turned to her right and said, "Hello, Mama."

—

CIA Headquarters, Langley Virginia.

Roy Benning got to his office even earlier than his average 5:00 AM arrival time. He was sitting at his desk going over the yellow notepad where he jotted down his theories on why and who tipped off the Brazilian authorities on the MIA.

He had not come to a conclusion, but all of the circumstantial evidence was pointing back to the DDP. His predicament was what approach he could use to say that the Deputy Director of the Clandestine Service compromised an ongoing operation by providing the name of the MIE to the Brazilian government.

Roy's administrative assistant poked her head in Roy's doorway. "You should start downstairs for your meeting, Roy." Roy gathered up his legal pad and left his office.

To enter the secure briefing room, everyone was required to first sign-in then go through a fingerprint screen followed by a retinal display.

As Roy stepped into the room, he noted that several people had arrived ahead of him. He was surprised because he was under the impression that it would be just the Director, the DDP, and himself. None of the people in the room were seated at the table. They all were sitting in the guest rows.

Roy saw name plates on the table in front of every seat. The table was capable of seating 20 people for a briefing. He found a name plate with his position title and took a seat. Roy realized that this was going to be a very high-level meeting.

After taking his seat, a man came out of the media room and stood behind the briefing podium. The door to the briefing room opened again, and people began to flow in, ultimately filling the room almost to capacity. Neither the Director nor the DDP entered the room. Roy was wondering if he was in the right briefing room.

After all of the seats at the conference table were filled, the man standing at the podium cleared his throat. "Under executive order 2080-Alpha, this meeting is called to order for Operational Working Group Crisco. Please raise your hand and state your name for the record and indicate the agency you are representing."

Roy realized that the Director had pushed him into a working group meeting. In all probability, the working group was dealing with matters about the southern hemisphere that undoubtedly had an impact on his desk.

At the Agency, a task force is a group of subject matter experts. Some CIA working groups only consist of CIA personnel, but it is not uncommon in the CIA to organize a working group across agencies that fell under the National Security Council.

It was evident to Roy that this was the case with Working Group Cisco because every Agency that fell under the National Security Council was there.

"Roy Benning, Central Intelligence Agency."

Roy had been around the Company long enough to know that he had been pushed into a bigger game. After taking the roll, the first person who walked up to the podium was from the Agency, Jackie Prat-Lewis. Jackie actually worked under Roy's group. Roy remembered that a little over a year ago, the DDP sent a request to his desk to place one of his mid-level analysts on loan to a working group. Jackie was the person who was nominated by her manager. So Roy signed the release for her to be temporarily assigned to the working group.

The way these briefings generally begin is with the most recent updates concerning the country the working group is focused on.

The room that the meeting was taking place in, three large screens were in the front of the chamber. On the main screen, the one in the center, Guyana appeared at the top of the monitor with a map of the country below.

"Good morning. For those who may not know me, I'm Jackie Prat-Lewis, and I'm the country analyst for the working group."

Jackie covered all of the standard stuff on Guyana. Her briefing actually became interesting to Roy when she said, "Guyana is a socialist country that regained strong ties to Cuba after recently signing cultural agreements three weeks ago in Havana. Next month Guyana is scheduled to sign a similar agreement with Venezuela in the capital of Brazil. With the recent discovery of offshore oil, Guyana and Venezuela will be projected to the fourth and fifth richest oil nations in the world, with Cuba being one of their biggest customers." Jackie was followed by a representative of the working group from the Department of State.

"At this time, it is questionable whether the economic and educational agreement will be signed next month in Brazil by Guyana and Venezuela because of the recent assassination of both of their ministers of security." The State Department representative clicked to a different slide showing a document.

"What we know about the paper is that Guyana will get 40% of the oil rights, and 60% will go to Venezuela. The countries will split all of the remaining oil and mineral rights within the disputed area of Essequibo, but all of the bauxite rights will go to Guyana." State sat down and was followed by the Department of Interior Mineral Management Service.

"The elephant in the room is bauxite, an aluminum ore. It is the world's primary source of aluminum, in fact. Of all bauxite mined, approximately 85% is converted to alumina for the production of aluminum metal, an additional 10% is converted to various forms of specialty alumina for non-metal uses. The remaining 5% is used directly for non-metallurgical bauxite applications." On the side screens, two slides came up with a full map, the middle screen showing Guyana, the disputed area of Essequibo and Venezuela.

"I turn your attention to the screen on your left. It displays the world's largest deposits of bauxite and where they are located and what countries lead the world in the mining and production of bauxite." The presenter, using a pointer, highlighted each country.

The first thing that Roy Benning saw was that the United States was not on the list. Only 25 countries in the world had mineral deposits of bauxite, with Australia listed as the number one country producing the mineral.

"I will now turn the mic back over to Jackie, who will go over what we are presenting on the screen to your right." Jackie came back to the podium.

"The first thing that you should notice is that, when you compare the screen on your left to the screen on your right, the countries' positions have changed. Scenario one: If the agreement is signed next month between Guyana and Venezuela, Guyana will become the number one owner of over 73% of the mineral deposits of bauxite in the world and the undisputed number one producer." Jackie pulled up another slide

"There is a second scenario. The organization known as the Movement of the Independence of Essequibo (MIE) has been making some very questionable and aggressive moves that could be interpreted as establishing a socialist form of government in the likelihood that they should come to power." Changing slides again,

Jackie showed a picture of the front of the Regent Hotel in New York City with a group of men getting out of a limousine. The car tags on the rear of the vehicle displayed diplomatic plates.

"Four weeks ago we verified that the MIE Leadership Group, in anticipation of forming their own country, met with representatives of the Russian Embassy in New York and entered into a secret letter of intent for 5% of all bauxite production to be sold to Russia. Because almost all of the bauxite that is in the 70,000 square mile area of Essequibo, the conclusion that can be drawn is that if Essequibo becomes an independent country, 100% of the 5% byproduct production of bauxite will go to Russia." All of the lights in the briefing were turned on, and a Navy captain approached the podium.

"Good morning, I'm Captain Peacock, the Project Manager for the Joker Aircraft. Those of you who have been part of this working group for the last 18 months know what brought us together is the US's development and production of laser weapons." The Navy Captain brought up on the screen a timeline of development events associated with the laser weapons.

"The US Navy has been the primary lead for the gun, and two years ago we had a major breakthrough. As you know, the development of any system is dependent on finding the balance between hardware, software, firmware, and all of the other components that are being put into the pot. The most important element of a laser weapon is to focus its energy into a spot that is small enough to heat up and damage the target. When we got to the point where we could produce the required megawatts of optical power electrically, our hardware started to break down." The Navy captain pulled up a slide that had been presented before that was labeled bauxite.

"The major discovery was that the 5% byproduct of bauxite created the perfect element to support the weapon system frame, Using that 5% to make the frame for the gun sufficiently heat resistant. As was said, the big elephant in the room is bauxite. We know that Russia is very close to solving the same problem because, if they just signed the letter of intent with the MIE, we feel that they must certainly almost be there. And the world's supply of bauxite belongs to a socialist country that has signed an agreement with a communist country."

The Navy Captain ended his portion of the briefing. As everyone began to leave the briefing room, Roy approached the Captain and introduced himself.

"Yes, the Director told me that you would be attending. So sorry to hear about Nancy." Roy was somewhat surprised.

"I can see by the expression on your face that you were not aware that Nancy was part of our working group," Roy smiled.

"No, I was not.

"Yes, Nancy was assigned directly by the DDP. She was always conferenced in when she had any input and provided her weekly reports directly to me."

Once again, the Captain Peacock could apparently sense that Roy was just getting involved with the working group and had no knowledge of what had been going on for the last 18 months.

"Tell you what. I'll authorize your access to all of Nancy's reports to me so you can catch up. Now, as I recall, you signed off on Jackie joining the group."

"Yes, I did. Jackie is one of my best," Roy said as he looked around the briefing room to see if Jackie was still there.

Captain Peacock and Roy walked toward the exit doors. "OK, then, look for an email from my office giving you the authorization for acquiring Nancy's reports and the white paper we did on Regional Destabilization." As Roy and the Captain stepped into the hallway in front of the secure briefing room, he turned to Roy.

"If we don't get our hands on a sure supply of bauxite, well, I don't want to think of what could happen."

While Roy was riding the elevator back to his office, his mind was racing for the last two hours and what he had learned. After entering his room, he went directly to his desk and opened his desktop. After opening up the security section and logging in, he discovered that sure enough, he had received the access authorization for him to read the files that Nancy had established for the working group. This data was classified at the highest level, and only if someone had a need to know would they be given the authorization to view the contents of the dossiers. Roy's attention went directly to the computer file folder labeled "white paper."

The white paper was a 213-page document that had been developed over a one-year period. Roy was reading the conclusions and recommendations of the report.

Conclusion: the scientific efforts of the Russian government toward the development and deployment of a laser weapon that could possibly be used as an offense weapon is proceeding at a developmental pace equal to or ahead of US efforts.

The working group had received credible information that had been verified by three independent sources as well as the Agency desk for European operations that Russia had discovered that the byproduct of bauxite, 5% or less, creates the perfect ingredients for building the molding for the casing frame of the weapon. An aluminum mold set up with the 5% byproduct made of bauxite could withstand the required megawatts of power for the gun to meet its maximum destructive power to destroy or neutralize any type of target at an almost infinite range.

Recommendation: In that, all bauxite mines in the US have closed, and no new discoveries have been made, it is recommended that the US proceed with strengthening its alliance with Australia and actively engage in the process of the destabilization of the bauxite mining efforts in Guyana along with regional partners Venezuela and Brazil.

Chapter 29

City Hall, Jacksonville, Florida.

The news media were staking out their locations as early as 4:00 AM. The satellite trucks were positioning themselves, raising their antennas to establish signals with local and national news outlets.

It was evident by the number of vehicles in front of City Hall that Jacksonville's Mayor's media strategy was working. Every national news agency was represented along with the Times and the Guardian newspapers from London.

Even though police cruisers were circling the courthouse all night and one stationed at the front entrance, the Jacksonville Police Department didn't begin to rope off the area leading to the City Hall entrance until 5:00 AM.

The pedestrian and normal workflow traffic started to pick up around 6:45. This was the same time that Bubba Webb pulled into his parking space in the underground garage. Oblivious to the activities taking place in front of the courthouse, the Mayor made his way to his office.

"Good morning, Mr. Mayor," greeted Mildred as Bubba entered his room. "Did you see all of the news media in front of the building? Your coffee is on your desk, and Jerry Clark and Terry Jackson are waiting in your office."

Zipping by, Bubba said, "Good morning, all. Isn't it great to be a Floridian and living in Jacksonville."

When Bubba entered his office, Jerry Clark was standing at the window, looking down at the crowd gathering below. Terry Jackson was at the conference table placing large spreadsheets in front of each of the seats. Bubba walked to his desk and checked to see if he had any messages, then looked at his computer monitor to check his schedule of activities for today. Bubba pushed the intercom button.

"Mildred, if you are not tied up, dear, could you come and take notes." Mildred was walking through the Mayor's door before he could walk to the conference table.

Everyone took seats at the table. Jerry Clark spoke first. "Mr. Mayor, how is Joe Singletary doing?"

Bubba sat back in his chair. "Debra and I had dinner at Market 32, and she said that, when she left the hospital, the nurse told Helen that all of his signs were pointing in the right direction. Debra is going there this morning, and I should have an update by lunchtime." Everyone at the table shook their heads, then turned their attention back to the spreadsheets in front of them.

"OK, Terry, tell me what I am looking at." Looking at the Mayor, Terry Jackson the fire investigator spoke.

"Well, Mr. Mayor, the spreadsheets list all of the people killed in the three disasters that took place in the last 10 days. The list is made up of a total of 132 people. The property damage varies much, of course, between disasters, but the fatalities are almost distributed equally per disaster."

The Mayor took a ruler and started moving down the list of names. He began to see some names he recognized. "I know some of these people." For several seconds, everyone in the room studied the list of names for a name that they knew.

"Bubba, remember Mr. and Mrs. Carl Goodwin?" Jerry Clark said. "He was the owner of the brick company who made the generous donation to the last campaign. I also see several of the other leading contributors to the campaign listed on the other two sheets."

Emotional, Bubba stood up and walked to one of the windows in his office and stared out at the world.

"Mildred, I want sympathy cards to be sent to everyone on that list."

Mildred quickly said, "Consider it done, Mr. Mayor. I'll have it taken care of by the end of today." Bubba walked back to the table.

"Has the next of kin been notified?" Terry Jackson pulled out a pen and pushed it over to the Mayor along with a document.

"We need your signature to release the names to the next of kin. We have had a blackout on all outgoing information on all three disasters." Bubba quickly looked over the paper, signed it, then pushed it back to Terry Jackson.

"It's getting late. We have to get downstairs to the meeting with the FBI. I need to know how much of all of this the city will be held accountable for."

A tired looking Terry Jackson rubbed his eyes and forehead. "Bubba, I can tell you that, in my professional opinion, all three disasters were triggered by the same type of device. What that device was I can't say. I mean, I have never seen anything like it. All three locations had burnt residue of a white substance that does not come up in any of the databases that I have access to. I am scheduled to have a meeting with FBI Agent in Charge Faye Cook-Little this afternoon. At that time, we will go over all the forensic evidence that I currently have. The FBI has access to more databases than I do, so maybe we will be able to find a match."

Bubba jumped up from the table. "That's good enough for now. Everything is still in the FBI's corner. Let's go down to the meeting."

Bubba, Jerry Clark, and Terry Jackson left the office to take the elevator to the first floor and the meeting. Mildred went back to her cubicle to go through the casualty lists and prepare the cards to be mailed out to the next of kin. Several names caught her attention, and Mildred picked up her desk phone receiver and pushed the preset number to reach the Mayor's wife.

"Hello, this is Debra."

"Debra, this is Mildred, I have the list of those killed in the Federal Building, school bus, and Dames Point disasters. I think I may have some unpleasant news for you."

Debra was just about to leave for the hospital to check on Joe's condition and see about Helen.

"Go ahead, Mildred. Tell me their names." Mildred took a yellow marker and highlighted the names on the spreadsheet.

"I see a Nancy Mansfield, Cathy Mills, and a Khristy Newborn. I remember their names being associated with your book club." Mildred stopped talking, waiting for a response from Debra. "Debra, are you still there?"

Debra sat down in the closest chair to where she was standing in her living room, holding the phone to her ear and trembling from the news of her friends' deaths.

"I'm still here, Mildred."

Sensing that Debra was upset, she said, "Debra, I'm so sorry to be the one who had to tell you this news. Bubba just authorized the release of the names to the next of kin and the media."

"No, Mildred, I'm glad that it was you who told me. I'll let the members know. Oh, Mildred, what about their husbands? Were their husbands also killed in the explosions?" Mildred looked at the spreadsheet. Just below the ladies' names, she saw the names of their spouses.

"Debra, I see a Karl Mansfield, Billy Mills, and Pat Newborn."

Still sitting down, Debra was already thinking about her circle of friends who needed to be notified of the death of their book club members.

"Thank you, Mildred, and tell Bubba I'll be late getting home tonight."

Debra sat in the chair thinking about the loss of her friends. They had shared so many beautiful moments together. The bond that held them together was their love of books and the joy of reading.

She looked at her cell phone, pulling up her contacts, and called Eve Harding. Debra's call went into Eve's voicemail. Debra decided just to ask her to return the call as soon as possible rather than leave such news in a message.

Debra's next call was to Brenda Jefferson. Again, Brenda didn't pick up, and Debra left the same message with Brenda. She then dialed Gracie Black.

"Hello."

"Gracie, this is Debra. I have some terrible news."

Back at the entrance of the Jacksonville City Hall: "This is Kyle Martin of WZXL Television Channel 4 News. I am standing at the door of the Jacksonville Florida City Hall building, as WZXL was the first to report on the closed-door meeting that is scheduled to take place any minute concerning the three major disasters that have occurred in this city, all within the span of ten days."

After finding out that City Hall's underground parking lot was filled, Faye had to find street parking. As she approached the entrance to City Hall, she saw the crowd and media in front of the building. She knew that somewhere between the first steps of City Hall until she walked into the entrance door, she would be faced with meeting Kyle Martin, who just had a way of getting under Faye's skin and rubbing her the wrong way.

Out of the corner of Faye's eye, she saw the WZXL satellite truck, so she knew that Kyle was there. What she had to do was to proceed at an angle up the steps to avoid Kyle spotting her, she thought, but it did not work.

While on-camera, Kyle Martin saw Faye and said, "I see the Federal Bureau of Investigation Special Agent in Charge of all three disaster investigations is approaching City Hall now." Kyle, followed by her cameraman, walked on an angle toward Faye to intercept her before she could reach the City Hall door. Other news anchor persons saw Kyle moving toward Faye, so they joined her in the pursuit.

They caught up with Faye when she was just about halfway up the steps of City Hall. The first mic pushed into her face was held by Kyle Martin.

"Special Agent Faye Cook-Little, is it true that the reason you are arriving late to this meeting is that the FBI and ATF raid on the terrorist group, the MIE, which you were in charge of and took place in Miami two days ago, is linked to the bombings here in Jacksonville?"

Faye stopped, making direct eye contact with Kyle. "No comment."

Kyle fired back. "Well, then, Agent Cook-Little, can you explain to the citizens of Jacksonville why you are late to a meeting that you are about to chair?" Faye stopped, looked around at the cameramen and news people and microphones positioned in front of her.

"These are ongoing investigations. I cannot make any comment concerning any investigation that is still in progress."

Several JPD started breaking up the crowd of media people that had surrounded Faye, opening a path for her to proceed up the steps and enter City Hall.

When Faye entered the closed-door meeting, all eyes turned to her and followed her as she took a seat at the table. Terry Jackson was just finishing going over the casualty list. He then informed those gathered that the Corps of Engineers had certified that the foundations were stable enough that demolition of both of the federal buildings and all of the surrounding buildings in the disaster area could begin. The Corps of Engineers would have final verification on the status of the Dames Point Bridge by the end of the week.

The city's commercial office presented a report that insurance claims and estimates for the total cost of rebuilding the area where the federal buildings stood had already reached $1.1 billion, and he was projecting a similar figure for the Dames Point Bridge. The good news was that the city was heavily insured for an endless list of different types of disasters that could possibly hit the city.

The Jacksonville city council had authorized this over insuring of the city, mainly because of the high military concentration in the Jacksonville area, including the Jacksonville Naval Air Station, Navy Station Mayport, and Camp Blanding Joint Training Center.

The Controller ended by saying that their primary concerns centered on the possible lawsuits that could be filed against the city.

The city's legal counsels presented that they were receiving calls from insurance companies and law firms from as far away as the west coast and London, and they reported that two Atlanta firms had established temporary offices in Jacksonville, and three more were looking for office space. Everything, they said, was going to hinge on the first report released by the FBI.

Mayor Bubba Webb stood up. "I think we are at the appropriate time for Special Agent Faye Cook-Little to give us an update on the ongoing FBI investigation."

Faye stood up, and the sense in the room was as if everyone was holding their breath. "For those of you who do not know me, I'm Special Agent Faye Cook-Little. I'm heading the investigations of the three disasters that have occurred. I have five agents working with me, and we have temporary offices set up on Beach Blvd. We have the same telephone numbers that we had in the Federal Building location. I have a forensic team flying in from Atlanta that I will be picking up this afternoon, and we have a meeting scheduled with Terry Jackson. I must remind you that this is an ongoing investigation and at present, I can't provide any information that the FBI has identified as being sensitive. Are there any questions?" Hands went up all over the room.

Wilson Baker, Jr. Revenge Has No Expiration Date

Jacksonville's financial officer was followed by the city's legal counsel, but Agent Cook-Little kept to her first statement that it was still an ongoing investigation. The Mayor went around the room one more time asking each of the agencies that were represented if any had additional information to present. The next meeting was then scheduled to take place in one week at the same time.

As the meeting was breaking up, the Mayor asked Jerry Clark to see if he could get Faye to meet with him in his office.

In the Mayor's office, he said, "Faye, have a seat." Faye looked around the Mayor's office, then turned back to the Mayor.

"Thank you very much, Mr. Mayor, but I'm running late to pick up our Forensic team from Atlanta. Jerry Clark said that you wanted to speak to me." Bubba looked at Jerry, then back to Faye.

"I would greatly appreciate it if, when you are ready to release information concerning your report, you will give this office the courtesy of speaking to us first, before the report's released." Bubba paused, looking into the eyes of Agent Cook-Little to measure her reaction.

"You see, Faye, a flood of lawsuits could very well bankrupt the city. I feel that the more information I have if something like that begins to happen, the better I will be able to prepare the city to meet those challenges." Fays looked at Jerry Clark and back at the Mayor.

"Mr. Mayor, your request is duly noted, and I will take it into consideration." Faye then shook the Mayor's hand and left his office.

—

Sailboat off the Coast of Guyana.

A smile was on Krish's face. He could see the shoreline of his country. He had spent four days at sea, and everything had gone in his favor: the seas, the wind, his food and water supply. All the things that he had been taught by his father came back, and he thought, it was just like riding a bicycle.

His thoughts were focused on formulating a plan, an idea that he wanted to implement to obtain revenge on the Americans for luring them in and then turning them over to the Brazilian government. He had not figured out why they had been given to the

292

Brazilian officials rather than to Guyana or Venezuela authorities, but nevertheless, the Americans had betrayed them, resulting in the death of many of his comrades and his best friend. Someone was going to die.

By nightfall, he should reach Anna Regina, the fishing village on the Atlantic coast northwest of the mouth of the Essequibo River where he was born and where his father taught him how to sail, fish, and fend for himself. He laughed to himself because Anna Regina was no longer referred to as a village but designated a town and had a population of about 12,000 people, and it was now the capital of the Pomeroon-Supenaam region of Guyana.

Ranuel was also born in Anna Regina. He and Ranuel first met while attending the Anna Regina Multilateral School. After Multilateral School, Ranuel enrolled at the Essequibo Technical Institute. It wasn't until years later that he and Ranuel ran into each other at a cafe' up in Bartica.

After he got some rest, he would go to Ranuel's parents and tell them the news about his death. Once he had done that he would have to seek out the families of the other members of the movement who had joined him and Ranuel and traveled to Florida to receive their training and to suffer their ultimate betrayal.

Krish had been extremely cautious, staying as close as possible to the shoreline while staying out of the fishing areas and shipping lanes. He had only seen a few fishing boats, and in every case, they were sailing away from him.

The Guyana Navy was small, and at that most of the time, their ships were in need of repair and not seaworthy.

His plan was to hide the boat after he landed in Anna Regina. He could use it to sail up the Essequibo River to Bartica. The headquarters of the movement was located in Bartica, and he must report in and provide the details of what had happened but also find out why everything had fallen apart.

There were so many questions circling in Krish's head. In the movement of which he was a part, just as in most movements, some people were pro-MIE and others who were for continuing the status quo.

Since the government of Guyana had thrown a bone off the table and designated Anna Regina as a regional capital, many felt that real change was being made. However, there was still no change in Guyana and Venezuela's mining of the natural resources within this 70,000 square mile area and not paying the workers decent wages for their efforts.

The natural resources of Essequibo were the main reason the MIE was formed and sought out help from the Americans. With the Americans betraying the movement, what would be the next steps for the Movement for the Independence of Essequibo?

As night fell, Krish was slowly sailing in closer to the shore. Finally, he began to hear the sounds of his little town. Soon he was picking up familiar smells too, of cooking fish, rice, and black beans. His eyes began to fill, and the tears ran down his face, and his thoughts shifted to his friend Ranuel and how they would not be able to enjoy any more moments together drinking rum and eating freshly cooked fish.

Krish maneuvered the small boat into a hidden cove not far off of the Essequibo River.

Moving quietly in the dark, he made his way to his cousin's house. After the death of Krish's parents, his older cousin was the only family that he had.

He was greeted with surprise but a warm welcome. After hugs and kisses, he was given the opportunity to bathe and provided a change of clothes, after which he sat down to eat with his cousin and his cousin's wife. As they ate, they told Krish about the soldiers coming into the city searching for anyone who was associated with the MIE. There were rumors that the MIE were responsible for assassinations of some high officials of the Guyana or Venezuela governments in Rio. The situation surrounding the stories of killings wasn't clear, and no information was being broadcast on the news. They warned Krish that he had to be very careful, especially if he traveled to Bartica.

Krish asked if they knew if any members of the movement had been arrested. They had not heard of any movement members being taken into custody by Guyana security forces. His cousin assured him that it would be safe for him to stay with them for a couple of days, but it was routine for the security forces to come looking searching the city every three or four days.

Krish was so happy to be home with friends, but because of the exhaustion of being at sea for the last four days, along with his stomach being full of fish and rum, the need to get some rest was overtaking him. He collapsed on a small cot and drifted off into a sound sleep.

—

Flagler Center, CIA South American Desk, Jacksonville, Florida.

Jake Jefferson was sitting at his desk reviewing Elk Ardila's field operational plan. Elk had more experience in working in Central and South America than any other agent working out of the South American desk. Jake had spent some time in the field, but as soon as he met the minimum requirements to move away from the field pressures, he quickly jumped at other positions.

Elk's operational plan indicated that he would fly into Brasília, Brazil's capital and sign into the American embassy as an Economic Officer on temporary assignment to gather information on mining and road building operations throughout the country. From Brazil, he would use the same cover working out of the embassies in Guyana and Venezuela.

What was interesting to Jake was a footnote on the plan. Elk indicated that all of the members of the MIE he had interfaced with had not gone underground. He had made contact with them, and they were scheduled to meet with Elk in Bartica once he got to Guyana.

Jake's desk telephone rang. "Hello, this is Jake Jefferson." It was Roy Benning calling.

"Hello, Jake. I just wanted to check with you on whether you had a chance to go over Elk's plan?' Jake looked at the folder containing the program.

"Why, yes, I just finished reading it. The footnote was sort of strange. I would think that everyone in the MIE, especially back in Guyana, would have gone underground."

Roy quickly replied, "I would think so, but in the last two hours I've learned a lot about the operation that was at a need-to-know level. So that is part of the reason for my call. When can you fly up here?"

Jake turned to his desktop calendar. His experience made him sense that the meeting must be on something classified concerning Fertile Ground.

"I probably could fly out tomorrow. I'm sending Brenda back home to Chicago for a couple of days to check on her parents. She is scheduled to fly out tomorrow and will probably stay until Thanksgiving."

Roy thought about what Jake said. It made sense. All of the three previous desk chiefs and their wives were dead. It appeared that anyone who held that position ended up being targeted in a bombing. All had been killed in the last 10 days, but there was no tangible evidence supporting a theory that they had been targeted.

"That makes great sense Jake, and I'll be expecting you the day after tomorrow."

Jake hung up, turning his attention back to Elk's plan, but before he could start his telephone rang again. On the caller ID, he saw that it was his wife.

"How's the packing going?' Jake could hear his wife sobbing. "What's wrong? Brenda?"

"Jake, why didn't you tell me? I just finished returning a call to Debra, and she said. I guess this is why you are sending me to Chicago, isn't it?"

"Brenda, we can't have this conversation. You know I can't discuss this." Jake could hear the emotion in his wife's voice. He knew how much she enjoyed her book club meetings, especially being in a setting with other women who were in or had spouses in the Agency.

"Brenda, I have to go now. I'll leave the office early, and we'll discuss this when I get home and on the way to the airport."

On the other side of town, Debra Webb was pulling into the Shands Hospital parking lot. Her cell phone begin to ring. On the screen display, she saw that it was Eve Harding, and she pulled to a stop in a vacant parking space.

"Eve, I'm so glad that you called me back. While you were gone, we had such horrible things happening here. Besides the bombing that injured Joe, there were two others. I'm sad, to say that…"

"Nancy, Cathy, and Khristy are dead along with their husbands."

Debra pulled her phone down from her ear and looked it, wondering how Eve knew.

"That's right, but how did you know that? I guess you must have talked to Brenda Jefferson. I told her only an hour or so ago. I'm so upset." Nothing was heard on the phone for a few seconds.

"Why, yes, Debra, this is so troubling. We have basically lost half of our book club members. Have you told Gracie?"

Debra was now walking up to the main entrance of the hospital. The reporters were gone from camping out at the main door, shifting their attention to City Hall and the morning meeting. Debra was pleased to see that she did not have to run the gauntlet of microphones being shoved into her face, reporters asking for a comment on Joe Singletary's condition.

"Eve, the thing that I loved about our club was that we had such a small intimate group that we were able to open up and actually share how each of us really appreciated what we were reading. Debra stopped at the elevator and pushed the button.

"Well dear, I'm at the hospital. I'm just about to get onto the elevator to go up and see about Joe and check on Helen. I'll give you the news on how they are doing. I'll try to call you when I get home tonight."

"Very well, Debra. Just call me tonight."

To Debra's surprise, when she got off the elevator she saw Gracie Black sitting in the waiting area.

"Gracie, you didn't tell me that you were coming over." Gracie stood up. She and Debra embraced.

"Well, after you told me the news about the girls, and you said that you would tell Helen when you came over, I just thought that I would come over too." Debra took a step back and smiled.

"That's so sweet of you. Have you seen Helen?" Gracie sat down.

"No, I haven't, but the nurse said that she was taking a shower to freshen up. I have asked about Joe." Just when Gracie finished saying that, coming from the direction of Joe's room, she heard Helen's voice.

297

"Hello, everyone. I am so glad to see you. Joe is doing much, much better. All of his vital sign have improved, his skin color is coming back. He's not out of the woods yet, but the doctor is very encouraged by his progress."

Helen, sensing that Debra and Gracie were not sharing her good mood, said, "Something is wrong. What is it?" Debra reached out for Helen's hand.

"Come over here and let's sit down." The three ladies sat in the waiting room area.

"Helen, that's fantastic news about Joe. We were all praying that the news would be good. But we have to tell you something about our Book Club members."

Debra explained about the deaths of their members, then said, "I called Eve and Brenda and left voice messages, and then I was able to speak with Gracie. Brenda called me back, and I told her. Just after I talked to Brenda, Eve returned my call, but she had already spoken to Gracie, who told her."

Gracie Black interrupted. "Wait a minute. I haven't talked to Eve. As a matter of fact, I haven't spoke to Eve since she got back from her trip."

Everyone turned and looked at Gracie.

—

Jacksonville's Fire Investigations Unit, Terry Jackson's Office.

Terry was walking out of the break room with a cup of coffee in his hand when he saw the elevator doors open on his floor. Stepping off of the elevator was Agent Faye Cook-Little along with two men and a female behind her. Terry was sure that these must be the forensic people that she had spoken about in their morning meeting with the Mayor. Terry waited in the hall until they reached him. Then extending his hand, he said, "I guess we meet again, Faye. We just saw each other a little over two hours ago. These must be your people from Atlanta."

Faye shook Terry's hand and introduced the agents standing there with them. Terry then said, "We'll have to take the elevator to the basement floor. That's where our lab is."

Terry Jackson had everything all arranged in his lab, including spreadsheets covering every piece of evidence that had been recovered. Faye and her forensics team went through each page of Terry's report along with the spreadsheets documenting each item that had been retrieved from each of the disaster scenes, line by line, asking, and even sometimes firing, questions at Terry.

They had been working for about an hour when the Jacksonville Chief Coroner walked into the lab. "Sorry I'm late, but I had to testify at a murder trial."

No one looked up from their work. Terry quietly said, "Doctor, your pile is over there," pointing to a pile of documents on the table. "We are on page 79, body positions at the scene of disaster number two."

Faye looked at her watch and turned to Terry. "It's getting late. Let's drive over to each of the disaster's locations before it gets too dark." Terry agreed.

The first location they went to was the Dames Point Bridge. Repair of the bridge had already begun, the first contracts having been awarded the day before. Except for the first 100 yards on the northbound side of the bridge, it looked like nothing had happened.

The bridge had been approved by the US Army Corps of Engineers as entirely passable for two-lane traffic on the left side of the bridge. So traffic was flowing with one lane going north and one lane south, and barriers were placed in the middle lane for safety.

As Faye and her team from Atlanta checked out the damage, Faye saw the WZXL mobile television truck pull up to the bridge and park just beyond the yellow crime scene tape. Faye said, "I just finished talking to that bitch this morning." Terry Jackson turned in the direction where Faye was looking.

"How did she find out that we were coming here?" Terry pulled out his radio and contacted the two police officers who were providing security at the end of the northbound ramp leading up to the bridge.

"This is Terry Jackson of the Jacksonville Fire Investigation Department. Do you read my transmission?" Terry could see from where he was standing that both police officers reached for their microphones.

Terry heard the sound of a voice come over the radio. "Go ahead. Terry. This is Wil Frazier."

Terry knew Wil Frazier.

"Wil, can you see that television truck up just ahead of your position? No news or media are to be allowed beyond the tape." Wil Frazier turned his head to see the vehicle.

"We see them, and that's the word we got from the captain also. No news or media people beyond the tape. We'll take care of them if they try to proceed. Out!"

The FBI forensics team from Atlanta was taking picture after picture. One of the members of the group shouted, "Let's get moving to the next site before we lose the sunlight." Everyone piled back into the Fire Department van and headed for the location where the bus exploded. As the truck pulled away from the bridge, the WZXL news truck followed.

The Fire Department van pulled into the second disaster area, and the forensics team exited. One of the members of the group quickly walked across the street of the yellow taped area to the location where Billy and Caty Mills SUV had stopped for the school bus. It was as if he had spotted something from the van as they drove up. Faye saw the gentleman and followed, knowing that the Forensic Agent probably saw something that made sense to the mystery of what had occurred. When the Guy reached the location of Billy's SUV, he kneeled down on one knee.

"The blast originated here. See how this white substance began to spread from this point outward. The bomb or whatever triggered the explosion was in the vehicle stopped at this spot. Looking at this area, I can see that the damage after this was because of secondary blasts that were started by whatever caused this vehicle to explode."

All heads turned in the direction where they parked the truck.

"Agent Faye Cook-Little, it looks from here that you guys must have found something at that location?" They could see the news camera pointing directly at them and knew that it must have picked up a few shots while they were taking pictures of the ground.

Terry Jackson yelled, "Back away from the disaster scene." Two JPD patrol cars pulled up behind the camera team and escorted Kyle Martin and her team out of the area.

The forensics team took double the number of pictures at this location as they took at the bridge. Everyone gathered around Terry Jackson and Faye.

"We've decided that there is little need to go to the federal buildings. When the ground collapsed, the area where we think the blast originated was covered. What do you guys think?"

Each of the team members looked at each other. The team member who spotted where Billy's SUV was located spoke up. "I have a feeling we should still take a look at that entire area."

Faye looked at Terry and said, "By the time we get back to downtown Jacksonville we will have about an hour of daylight remaining. So let's get going."

Chapter 30

Montevilla Bartram Park, Gated Community, Jacksonville, Florida.

Eve Harding, who was in her kitchen making breakfast, hung up the telephone after talking to Debra Webb. Eve was retracing the conversation she had with Debra. As Eve started walking to the refrigerator, the phone rang. She looked at her caller ID. It was WC.

Eve answered the phone. "Hello," Wallace replied. "I just wanted to call and see how you are doing this morning?" Placing the telephone receiver under her chin, Eve walked back to the refrigerator and took out a bottle of orange juice.

"Oh, Wallace, I'm so glad you called. I was just thinking about you. I was planning on calling you after I finished breakfast to see how your flight went."

Before Wallace answered, his thoughts went over his experience at the airport and at the FBI Headquarters.

"Honey, I really couldn't say because I slept all the way back. I fell asleep when the plane took off from Jacksonville, and the next thing I knew, I awoke when the plane touched down in DC."

Smiling at Wallace's response, Eve put slices of bread in the toaster, then looked at the clock on her stove.

"I guess we were both a little tired after that long flight back to Fort Lauderdale," Wallace cut in.

"How is your friend's husband doing?"

"I just finished talking to Debra Webb; she said that all of his vital signs are pointing in the right direction, but it's still too early to tell if he is going to make it. Are you going into work today?"

Wallace smiled to himself. "Yes, I'm sitting in our DC traffic now. I'm on the Beltway, just about two exits before I get off." Eve sipped some orange juice and repositioned the telephone receiver under her chin.

"You know Tony is calling me this morning, so I'm trying not to keep the line tied up. I'll call you tonight after you get home."

Disappointed that the conversation was ending Wallace said, "Sure, call me tonight if you have a chance. I'm just about to get off at my exit. Take care and tell Tony I said hello and I hope we will meet one day."

"I will, lover. Take care." Eve hung the receiver up and continued to drink her orange juice.

Her thoughts begin to shift to Tony. She looked at the calendar that was hanging on the wall. It was almost two years to the day when Tony was at the Naval Air Station in Pensacola. Tony would write her, sharing that she was at the top of the class and thanking her for pushing her to join the Civil Air Patrol and learn how to fly.

Upon graduating from the Naval Academy, Tony Harding chose aviation and reported to the Naval Air Station in Pensacola, Florida for preflight indoctrination. After receiving all of her flight training, Ensign Harding earned her aviator's wings of gold and went on to her mission–specific training in radar and electronic intercept warfare systems officer.

Eve began to think of situations that Tony shared with her, like when she was training in Pensacola. One time was when a flight instructor said, "Hey Harding, there is nothing in your personnel file that indicates that you have had any aviation training. Either you are lying, or you catch on to this stuff quicker than any Ensign I've trained, and I've trained many Navy aviators in my 15 years of service."

In the Navy's efforts to avoid concentrating all of its east coast fleets at the Naval Station Norfolk, VA, it moved an amphibious ready group to Naval Station Mayport. The group consisted of the USS New York, USS Fort McHenry, and the Nuclear Aircraft Carrier USS John F. Kennedy. Flight Officer Ensign Tony Harding got assigned to the Kennedy Aircraft Carrier. Everything was falling into place just as Eve wanted.

Tony continued to excel in all aspects, as a pilot, and as a Naval Officer. It wasn't long after Tony joined the Aircraft Carrier Kennedy that it deployed to the Mediterranean. Eve wanted Tony to stay overseas for as long as possible but at least for three years.

The telephone rang again. Eve looked at her caller ID and saw that it was Tony's number. Positioned beside and connected to the phone was a small black box with a silver metal switch protruding from the side of the box. There were no other distinguishing features about the box. Before picking the telephone receiver up, Eve pushed the silver metal switch, and a small red light bulb began flashing. Eve grabbed the receiver and spoke.

"Hello, my little darling. It seems like we haven't talked in such a long time."

"Hello, Mother. Did you push the switch?"

Smiling, Eve replied, "Yes, Honey, we are secure."

—

Washington, DC.

Wallace turned off his cell phone and shifted his concentration to the traffic. As he maneuvered his car to the exit lane, his thoughts lingered on his conversation with Eve. WC still had not decided about asking Eve to marry him. It dawned on him that he had never visited Eve's home in Florida, that he had never set foot in the door.

When they first met, Eve was living in Maryland in a townhouse community. Over the two years they had known each other, while they were dating before she moved to Jacksonville, he had spent many times at her house with Eve visiting Wallace's townhouse as well. After she left the high-tech company she was working for and moved to Jacksonville, over the three years that she has been living there, Wallace would travel to see her, but they always met someplace other than Jacksonville.

They would meet in places like Vegas, the Poconos, Reno, or New Orleans, or Eve would travel to Maryland. At the time, Wallace didn't see it as strange, mostly because each time they planned to meet someplace there was always something going on, like a jazz concert, skiing, even a sporting events. With Wallace trying to make a decision concerning the future of their relationship, however, the last three years were taking on more meaning.

Wallace pulled up to the security gate at SBM and presented his ID badge, but he noticed a change in the processing procedure at the gate. Rather than just looking at the ID badge, the guard took Wallace's Badge, then stepped back into the guard room. Wallace could see that the guard was looking at the computer screen. She then typed something on the keyboard, walked back to Wallace's car, and handed him his ID badge.

As Wallace pulled away from the security gate, looking in his rear-view mirror, he saw that the guard did not follow the same procedure with the next two cars.

WC cruised around the crowded company parking lot until he found a vacant spot, parked, and walked into the building.

SBM has many locations in the Washington-Baltimore corridor, all associated with contracts the company had won. The SBM Gaithersburg's complex was the largest. This complex consisted of three buildings. The tallest building was 22 floors, which was the corporate headquarters. The other two were 15 levels each; one was Wallace's division, DTS.

Wallace swiped his ID card at the security desk; immediately he began to get an uneasy feeling. He spoke to the security guard seated behind the information desk just as he had done so many times before.

"Hello, Maxine. How are you doing this morning?" The security person behind the counter did not reply. She just raised her head from the computer screen and stared at Wallace as he walked past. WC stopped at the elevator, pushed the button, then turned around. Now both of the security guards at the information desk were staring at him. Wallace smiled at them, and after the elevator door had opened, he stepped in and pushed the button for his floor.

Wallace could assess that there was tension in the air, but it was confirmed as he stepped off the elevator onto the 11th floor and started walking toward his office. On all days, except for weekends and holidays, when Wallace stepped off the elevator, there was a continuous sound of keyboards clicking, chatter, and random loud conversation coming from the break rooms.

As Wallace walked toward his office, the entire floor slowly grew to a quite whisper. Passing by work cubicles, he gave his morning smile along with his trademark greetings, receiving in return a casual look with no response but mostly people were trying to look the other way or make it seem like they were concentrating on their computers. Just before Wallace reached his corner office, he approached his administrative assistant's cubicle. Alice was not there. Wallace was not surprised. He stopped at the cubicle and checked the file box where Alice would leave any messages for him, and he noticed a cup of tea sitting on Alice's desk. Seeing the cup of tea on the desk was a good indication that Alice was in the building. In the box were only two messages. WC stood at the cubicle reading the notes.

One message was from the administrative assistant to the DTS Senior Vice President, and the other was from the manager WC reported to, Leola Rogers. Both of the messages said just about the same thing: drop by my office when you get into the building.

Wallace swiped his ID badge on the doorjamb of his office to unlock it and walked in. On his desk was a pile of mail and the message light on his telephone was blinking. WC was just about to sit down when he heard a voice from the doorway.

"Welcome back, WC." Wallace looked up. It was one of his lead software programmers. Wallace smiled, and the developer quickly said, "Stop by my cubicle when you get a chance, and by the way, did you get my email?" The developer immediately left without waiting for a response.

As Wallace was turning on his desktop computer, his telephone rang. He quickly picked up the receiver. It was another programmer who worked in his department. Wallace greeted the caller. "This is Barker."

"WC, man are we glad that you are back. I know you will have a lot going on today, but I just wanted to tell you that we met at the Green Frog, and we all have your back." Wallace looked up from his desk, and Alice was standing in his office doorway. Wallace waved his hand for her to come in then said to the caller, "Many thanks for your support. I'll call you back." Wallace looked into Alice's eyes. "How are you doing?"

Alice smiled. "I'm OK WC, but the real question is how are you doing? How was your vacation? Did you pop the question? Are you getting married?"

Alice had been his administrative assistant for the last four years. Married with three kids, Alice's husband was a police officer who worked in the undercover narcotics division of the County Police Department.

Wallace responded, "We'll talk about that a little later. I'd like for you to set up a meeting with the entire group." Alice sat down in the guest chair in front of WC's desk and began taking notes on a yellow legal pad. "I'd like the meeting to be the first thing after lunch. Please include all of our off-complex people; they are to be skyped in. Next, find Felix so he and I can talk. I'm going up to see Leola, and after I get back, you and I will catch up." Wallace walked out of his office to the elevator.

Leola Wilcox's office was the 14-A floor. It was the 13th floor, but the company didn't want to identify a floor with that number, and so the level before the 14th was called 14-A.

As an unwritten rule, SBM human resources preferred bringing in ex-military personnel for the company's management positions. Leola Wilcox rose to her present position the old-fashioned way: she earned it. With no military background, Leola joined SBM as a first level programmer, receiving the highest performance reports each year until she now found herself having four program managers reporting to her.

Wallace exited the elevator and walked to the desk of Leola's administrative assistant. "Good morning, Mark…" Wallace didn't have to complete his statement.

"Glad to see you back, WC. Leola is waiting for you, so go right in."

Leola was sitting at the conference table in her office as WC walked in. She was reviewing several program spreadsheets that were all over the table. Looking over her half-frame reading glasses, she looked up at Wallace. "Well, I can see that you have already felt the pressure in the building." Wallace sat down at the conference table.

"How are you doing this morning, Leola?' Wallace replied. Leola put her highlighter down and pulled off her glasses. She stood up and walked to her desk, sat down, and opened a file on her desktop.

"Let me get to the point because I know you are eager to find out what is going on." WC got up from the conference table and took a seat in front of her desk.

"Somehow our billing department discovered that somewhere between 5 million to 10 million lines of software code got delivered to the Department of Defense. We have narrowed it down to the software delivered to the Navy in a two to two-and-a-half year period. We think those deliveries were made to as few as one or maybe spread out to four contracts. Where you come in is that you were the project manager of all the possible contracts." Leola handed the folder to Wallace. A label on the front of the envelope read: SBM Company Confidential. Wallace opened the envelope and read the names of the four contracts.

"I remember these. They were all software upgrades. Not one had to do with any new coding." Wallace sat in the chair with a puzzled look on his face as he thumbed through the material in the folder. Leola broke his concentration.

"The bean counters are talking about $1,000 per line of code. So we are looking at a lot of money that DTS wants to recover. About $50 Million dollars. The VP is hot, saying that one of our most experienced program managers should not have let this happen. Until the revenue is accounted for, he is out to have someone buried.

"In fact, he has started an internal investigation to see if any of SBM protocols were bypassed." Wallace looked up from the folder.

"You mean you want to see if I stole the money." Leola didn't say anything. She just made eye contact with Wallace.

"WC, I know you, but the VP reports to someone who reports to the board of directors, and when $50 Million dollars is at stake, the heat comes down like a snowball rolling downhill, getting bigger with each turn." Wallace stood up with the folder in his hand.

"Thanks, Leola. I get the picture. Do we still meet with the VP?" Leola reached into her purse, which was on the floor under her desk, and pulled out a pack of cigarettes. "No, that won't be necessary today. He's traveling and will not be back until next week." With the pack of cigarettes in her hand, she stood up and started for her door. Wallace followed her as they walked past the cubicles on her floor.

"I'm going downstairs for a smoke break. WC, you are good at what you do, and I know if anyone can bring this matter to a conclusion that will be beneficial for everyone, WC Barker is the person that can do it, as long as you have it done by next Monday when the VP returns. I know you understand my meaning."

Wallace knew what Leola was saying. SBM became one of the top software companies based on bringing in revenue. Everyone knew that heads were going to roll unless the contract recovered the money.

—

John F. Kennedy Aircraft Carrier.

Lieutenant Harding was on her way to the flight deck when she got the word that the skipper wanted to see her.

"Good morning, Skipper. You wanted to see me?"

"That's right, Harding. You are the only rated Joker pilot. They are upgrading the classification of the aircraft, so your own security clearance needs to be updated to stay in sync with the new classification of the plane. Check the folder for your email. Fill out the forms completely, copy me and send them off. Take care of that ASAP."

"Will do, Skipper!"

—

Flager Center, Jacksonville, Florida.

Jake Jefferson finished reading Elk's plan and looked at his watch. He was concerned about Brenda being so upset about flying to her parents. He checked his schedule and decided to go home and talk to her.

Jake and Brenda Jefferson had purchased a fixer-upper waterfront home on Fleming Island. They had been living there for the last eight years. The work on remodeling the house got completed two years ago. They were now working on finishing the boat house. From the boathouse, they could see planes landing and taking off from the Jacksonville Naval Air Station.

As Jake was turning into the driveway, Brenda was walking to her car. Jake finished parking, got out of his vehicle, and walked over to Brenda.

"I thought I'd come home for lunch so we could talk," Brenda smiled and kissed Jake. I was just leaving to get a few things. You can ride with me, and we can stop someplace for lunch."

309

They pulled out of their driveway and turned onto a rough two-lane road that led to the main highway. The drive from Jake and Brenda's house to the main road was about six miles. Just about halfway to the main road, there was a flash of white light followed by a horrible explosion. Jake and Brenda's car flew into the air, coming down in a ball of flames. A 100-yard area around the blast burst into flames, burning brush and trees that occupied the open field on both sides of the roadway. The Jefferson's were dead on impact when their car seats fell to the ground. Their seat belts were still securing their hot bodies in their seats

—

Montevilla Bartram Park, Gated Community, Jacksonville, Florida.

Finishing the telephone call with Tony, Eve placed a kiss on the phone receiver as she hung up. She put everything away in the kitchen and walked through her home, ensuring that every window and door were locked.

Eve turned on the security system, then went into the garage. She unlocked the door to the hidden room, stepped in and closed the door behind her. She then opened the second door, relocking the door behind her. Eve turned the light on. After her eyes had been adjusted, she looked around the room. Every wall was covered with newspaper clippings, pictures, both color and black and white, cut-outs from magazines.

Some of the journal clippings had turned brown from age. She then turned to a work table. Eve looked at every detail to see if there appeared to be the smallest indication of something being disturbed.

She then turned back to the door and cut on an exhaust fan and checked a thermostat, adjusting the cooling. Above the work table were two cabinets. Eve unlocked the cabinets and rolled out two large computer display screens with a keyboard. She clicked a switch; a smooth humming sound came from a 64 Terabyte server. Eve put a headset on, adjusting the microphone such that it was about a half of an inch from her month. The two 34 inch monitors were each showing four windows for a total of eight views. One set of windows were from the house security camera and showed a different view of the outside of the house every three minutes from all angles. Each of the other windows showed a different login reading: NSA, FBI, CIA, Pentagon, Interpol, Department of Defense, local agencies. Eve logged into each of the sites. After logging in, she began speaking into the microphone.

"Good afternoon, computer. Are you ready to do Mother's bidding?"

A computer voice spoke. "Good afternoon, Eve. I'm willing to answer your questions." Eve smiled.

"Computer, provide activity updates from all of the sites for the last 24 hours."

"CIA Field Agent Elkin Ardila purchased a ticket to fly from Jacksonville to Miami with a final destination of Brasilia, Brazil. No change in activity since your last login."

Eve picked up what looked to be a diary placed beside the keyboard. She made a couple of quick notes, then put it down and turned her attention away from the computer monitors and in the direction of the right side of the room. There, placed in the corner of the room, was a rocking chair. In the rocker was a mannequin dressed in women's apparel and a gray wig. The mannequin was wearing metal rim glasses.

"Mama, I talked to Tony this morning, and she told me to tell you hi and she sends her love."

—

Wallace C. Barker's Office, SBM.

Wallace finished his staff meeting with his section. During the meeting, he assured all the people who worked for him that there was nothing to worry about and no one's job was in jeopardy.

Everything was boiling down to a configuration management problem concerning software delivery, and Wallace announced that he and Felix would be working on the problem, and everything would be worked out in the next few days.

Chapter 31

WC walked back into his office, his thoughts on Felix. Felix did not conference call into the meeting. Wallace was just about to sit down when Alice called to him from outside his office.

"WC, Felix is on line three." Hearing Alice say that eased Wallace's thought process. He picked up the phone.

"Hello, buddy."

"WC, welcome back. I guess you have talked to all of the senior people upstairs. Leola is kind of cool, but the VP, I don't know about him. How did it go?"

Wallace opened his desktop calendar.

"Felix, we need to meet. Are you home? I'll pick you up, and we can talk while driving over to Anacostia."

"Yes, I'm home. Sure come by and pick me up. While you are here, I can show you that app I've developed. It's cool."

Wallace cut in. "Felix, we don't have time. I have 10 million lines of software code missing. We have first to find it. Second, we need to know who received the software code and then see that SBM gets their money." Felix didn't respond. Wallace continued. "So, I'll see you in about 20 minutes."

WC turned his attention back to his desktop calendar. There were two projects with in-process review pre-brief meetings and another one having a software walk-through. He emailed all of the leads on the projects that he would not be attending and to proceed without him. WC then sent an email to Leola indicating that he would be over at Anacostia for the remainder of the day.

Wallace pulled out of the SBM parking lot and headed for the Beltway. Someone once said that Washington DC is 200 square miles surrounded by reality. The beltway is the primary transportation vein to any location in the Washington DC Metro areas.

Felix lived in a four-story brownstone in the Kingman Park section of the District, or Ward Six. Ward Six is one of the closest neighborhoods to the Capital. Felix turned his house into one of, if not the most, technologically advance living structures on the planet. The energy was supplied to Felix's home by solar panels and the wind with excess power stored in a battery system set up that Felix designed and built himself. Felix's water supply was rainwater filtered with a backup system that produced water from the humidity.

Once Wallace picked up Felix, it would be less than a 15-minute drive to Joint Base Anacostia-Bolling, or what was once Bolling Air Force Base. The operating offices for four contracts that WC was the program manager of were located there.

Wallace's primary contact was the government program manager, whereas Felix interfaced on a daily basis with the senior and lead software developers on each of the contracts.

These were the people who would know about a delivery of software that wasn't scheduled within the statement of work. Wallace's concern was that, with what little knowledge he had on the delivery, he had to confront each of the program managers and their lead software developer about hiding a delivery of software, especially one so large.

WC pulled into Felix's driveway and looked up at a security camera that worked on facial recognition. If Felix had placed a picture of you in the security system folder, the security camera would compare your picture, and if it were a match, the garage door would open.

After parking his car, Wallace took the elevator to Felix's floor. He stepped into the hallway. "I'm in here. Come on back!" Wallace followed the sound of Felix's voice until he came to a closed door with a camera lens in the center of the door. Wallace stared into the camera, and the sounds of the door unlocking followed. He pushed the door open and walked in.

"Felix, what have you done, created another server room? Is this the third server room you have in this house?" Felix interrupted Wallace.

"No, it's the fifth. You are not counting the two in the basement. But those are old technology, and I don't use them anymore. WC, step over here so I can show you the new app I'm working on." Felix looked up from his keyboard, smiling at Wallace. "WC, I'm so glad you are back. Things were getting very dull around the office." Wallace was walking toward Felix's computer desk.

"Buddy, how can you say that? You haven't set foot in the DTS building in over four years."

Felix stopped typing on his keyboard for a second and said, "You're right, but I think it has been closer to six years since I walked into the building." Felix was such an unbelievable coder that SBM allowed him to work from wherever he wanted to work.

"Felix, power down. We need to get over to JBAB so we can catch those program managers. I need to clear this thing up before Monday." Felix raised his head and looked at Wallace.

"What's the connection with Monday?"

Wallace was now standing behind Felix looking over his shoulder. Pointing to the computer monitor, WC said, "Go to your line 3,042 and create a do-loop back to 2,001 and you will take at least another 88 seconds off of your processing time." Felix stopped typing to analyze what WC said.

"WC, you know something? You're right." Felix started making the suggested changes. While typing, he turned his head and looked up at Wallace. "WC, why is it you don't come back into coding? You know your stuff." WC smiled.

"We need to get going. I want to see each of these program managers today." Felix stood up from his table.

"The Joker." He started walking toward the bathroom and repeated. "The Joker."

Wallace stared at Felix, repeating what Felix said. "The Joker? What in the hell does that mean?"

Felix came out of the bathroom with a towel drying his hand. "The 10 million lines of software code got delivered to the Joker Project, but that program wasn't 10 million lines of software code. It was 8.5 million lines of code." Felix reseated himself at his computer desk and went back to his coding. Wallace stood beside the desk with his mouth open.

"Tell me, Felix, if you knew where the code got delivered, why didn't you say something?" Felix stopped typing and stared at WC.

"WC, no one gave any details. The DTS VP started the internal investigation, and the only thing they were doing was asking questions about you and your lifestyle but never trying to figure out what happened." Felix turned back to his computer and started typing again.

"It wasn't until you told me about the four projects and the timeframe for the delivery... I went into each of the company's databases, searched for a sizable delivery of between 5 million to 10 million software lines of code placed on their servers. You see, you can't add 8 million lines of code, and it goes unnoticed. Whichever company showed an increase of code on their server was the project where the software code got delivered." Wallace sat down on a stool next to Felix's desk.

"OK then, let's get over to JBAB and talk to the PM and software lead with the Joker Project."

Still typing code, Felix replied, "They won't be back in the office until tomorrow. Both of them are down in Jacksonville." Wallace looked at Felix with a puzzled expression.

"That's right. The upgraded software we worked on was installed on the one Joker aircraft that is assigned to the John F. Kennedy. As I recall, the Navy was still trying to get funding to install the upgrades to the rest."

Felix got up and walked across the room to a small refrigerator. He pulled out two Mountain Dew sodas, opened one and threw the other to Wallace.

"That's right. So pick me up in the morning. We'll get some breakfast and after that have a little talk with our Navy friends."

—

FBI Temporary Office, Jacksonville, Florida.

Faye entered the building. They had completed going to each of the disaster sites, taking over 130 pictures. She walked to her desk with a large envelope under her arm, the envelope filled with the images from all of the crime scenes where the explosions had taken place, and laid the envelope down. She then rolled a large corkboard from out of a closet, pulled a large box of pen-tacks from her desk drawer, and began to take out the pictures from the envelope, pinning them on the corkboard. She kept reminding herself to keep what Jake Jefferson shared with her in the back of her mind.

After pinning all of the pictures on the cork board, she arranged them in order by date from left to right on the board, beginning with the explosion at the Federal Building. Next, Faye sat down at her desk and started reading the eyewitness statements from each of the blast sites. As Faye went through the documents, she highlighted similarities as well as things that conflicted when compared to what some of the other eyewitnesses said.

Faye rubbed her eyes and stood up, stretching while looking at her watch. It was almost 8:30, so she decided to call home to talk to her son; but just as she started to dial the number, she realized what night it was. He was still at swimming practice. After putting the phone down, Faye's thoughts lingered on Agent Harris's daughter. Agent Harris's sister picked her up today, and they were flying back home. Agent Harris's daughter was in the same swimming class as her son.

Faye walked over to the soda machine, and as she was making her choice, she suddenly said out loud, "White light. All of the eyewitnesses saw a white light just before or at the same time of the explosions." She rushed back to her desk to verify her thought.

Sure enough, each of the eyewitness statements indicated that preceding the blast came a white flash of light. This information provided a connection with all of the explosions, but what was most important to Faye was that she did not have to rely on the association of the blasts with the CIA agents. Faye was relieved. She turned off the lamp on her desk and headed for home.

—

City Hall, Office of the Mayor.

Bubba Webb and Jerry Clark were working late into the night. Bubba was on his cell phone talking to his wife, while Jerry was sitting at the conference table going through prints, pictures, and an assortment of drafts of political advertisements in preparation for the upcoming election.

"OK, Honey. We won't be eating any fast food. In fact, Jerry just ordered two chicken salads and two bowls of soup that they should be delivered any minute now. Oh, and one other thing, non-sweetened iced tea. You see, I'm trying to eat better."

"All right, Bubba. The doctor should be coming to visit Joe in the next hour or so, and as soon as he lets Nancy know how he is doing and gives an update on the prognosis, I'll call you back. Love you."

"Love you too." Bubba placed his cell phone down on his desk and walked to the window to stare at the view of the city.

"Jerry, the city attorney is scheduled to meet with me tomorrow. I'd like for you to sit in. How's your schedule for 10:00 tomorrow?"

Jerry reached for his tablet and opened it to the calendar.

"Mr. Mayor, I'm supposed to meet with Terry and Faye, the FBI agent in charge of the investigation at 10:00. I think I should try to keep that appointment."

Bubba turned around and walked to the table and sat down across from Jerry.

"You're right. The outcome of your meeting will have a direct effect on what I'll be discussing at 10:00. You see, I'm pretty confident that we have at least three lawsuits filed against the city as an outcome from the disasters that we have experienced." Jerry Clark pushed a few draft campaign advertisement proofs in front of the Mayor labeled one, two, and three. Bubba had just picked them up when his office telephone rang.

After walking to his desk, he answered, "Hello, this is Bubba." It was the Police Chief. At the same time Bubba was answering the phone, Jerry Clark's cell phone ring. It was Kyle Martin.

"Mr. Mayor, we are pretty confident that we have another explosion very similar to the Federal Building, bus, and Danes Point Bridge blasts." The Mayor sat down at his desk. "OK, Chief. I'm sitting down now. Tell me the whole story."

"Well, Bubba this occurred between 1:00 and 2:00 this afternoon off Route 40 on Fleming Island. A 9-1-1 report got called in on a brush fire. When the Fleming Island Fire Department responded, they found one vehicle, a car, which had two bodies that were pronounced dead at the scene of the accident. The bodies were found, still in their seats, 200 feet from the blast, and with their seatbelts fastened. The Fleming Island Police Department is still conducting the investigation. That's all I have at this time, Mr. Mayor. Any questions?" Bubba was taking notes as the Police Chief provided the information.

"No, Chief, just give me an update as soon as the island police give you something. Thanks." Bubba hung up and looked over at Jerry, who was still talking on his cell phone.

"Kyle, you are only speculating, and you know more than anyone that I can't comment on that." Jerry looked in the direction of the Mayor.

"But, Jerry, you have to give me something. I helped you out, and so it's time to return the favor."

"Kyle I always repay my debts. As soon as I have a meeting with the Mayor, and we get an update from the Chief of Police, you will be one of the first people I call, even before we have a press conference."

"OK, Jerry. I will be looking for that call." Jerry hung up and placed his phone on the table, then repositioned his chair facing the Mayor.

"Well, Bubba, I guess you could tell from the call that was Kyle Martin and there has been another explosion."

Bubba and Jerry just stared at each other for a period that seemed like hours. Bubba spoke first.

"Wait a minute. I was just on the phone with the Police Chief. The Chief said that there was an explosion out on Fleming Island. Are you telling me that Kyle is associating an explosion on Fleming Island with what has happened in Jacksonville?" Jerry stood up and walked toward the Mayor's desk.

"I'm afraid so. At least, Kyle is *attempting* to tie the explosion on Fleming Island to the three blasts that happened in Jacksonville together."

Chapter 32

Langley, Virginia CIA Headquarters.

Roy Benning received the confirmation that Jake and Brenda Jefferson had been killed in a car explosion. He was on a conference call with the Director.

"I must pull Elk back from his trip to Brazil and put him in charge of the operation in Jacksonville. He is the most senior person down there now."

"Sure, that is the best course of action for the present, but get with the FBI Agent in Charge and bring them into the loop concerning our suspicions," the Director replied.

"Certainly, sir, and as a matter of fact, I'm thinking about flying down there and having a face-to-face with the agent." There was a long pause before the Director replied.

"That's your call, Roy. Just keep me in the loop." The call ended.

Roy turned back to his desktop computer and pulled up Elk's travel itinerary. He saw that Elk's plane would be landing in Brazil in another hour. Roy placed a call to Elk and left a voice message, then sent him an email and text message. As a backup, he called the U.S. Embassy, leaving a message for Elk to phone in as soon as he checked in.

Feeling that he had covered all of the bases for Elk to get his message and contact him, Roy pulled up Elk's personnel jacket. Even though Elk was the most senior agent, Roy remembered the conversation he had with Elk just before receiving his assignment for Brazil. It was emotional, but just the same Elk made a very threatening statement.

Roy was going through Elk's personnel jacket to find out the evaluation results on his last psychological screening. When an agent completed a field assignment, they were required to have a psychological screening. Most of the results would read just about the same: "Agent should be assigned to a desk position for the next sixth months and was not to be put in any life or death situations until fully rested."

Elk's reports were a little different. The last two screenings both indicated that he showed signs of depression with some erratic and inconsistent thought patterns. However, the Psychologist recommended that he was still fit to go back into the field after the typically six months stand-down.

Roy was just about to dismiss his thoughts that Elk could be the person behind these bombings when he saw a footnote in Elk's file. The reference indicated that Elk had signed for four cases of C-4 plastic explosives while on a mission in Central America. One box was missing.

In any other situation, this would not be a problem. In the business that they are in, ammunition, weapons, and explosives went missing on a regular basis. But considering Elk's skill set and experience, and the fact that all of the four Desk Chiefs and their wives got killed as a result of explosions, this single note sent up a red flag.

With a case of C-4 plastic explosives, Elk possessed all the skills necessary to execute all of the bombings. He had easy access to each of the victim's automobiles and complete knowledge of their habits, where they lived, daily calendar — even a fair amount of knowledge concerning the comings and goings of their wives.

Placing a time delay fuse with C-4 on the side of the engine block that could have been triggered by a cell phone call was child's play to a guy like Elk. Roy Benning knew that Elk had a passion for his job, which was the reason he desperately thought he deserved to be in the position of Desk Chief.

Roy placed a reminder note on his desktop to set up a meeting with both of the psychiatrists who evaluated Elk. He also sent an email to his administrative assistant to clear his calendar for the next two days and to get tickets for him to fly to Jacksonville and schedule a meeting with the FBI Agent in Charge of the Jacksonville Explosions.

But the real question was whether or not Elk wanted the job so badly that he would kill everyone until he got the position.

—

Silver Spring, Maryland, Wallace's Home.

After checking his mail, Wallace stepped into his townhome, walked to his refrigerator, and took out a bottle of water. He walked into his living room, turned on this television, and sat down to go through his mail. There were only a few letters, mostly advertisements, but Wallace knew that there was quite a bit of mail waiting for him at the post office. WC had stopped the mail delivery while he was on vacation with Eve. Wallace walked into his bedroom. He changed clothes, putting on a sweatsuit to do some running on his treadmill. Just as WC reached his closet, the telephone rang. A smile came across Wallace's face when he saw that it was Eve when he looked at the caller ID.

"Hello, lover. I wasn't sure that you would be able to give me a call tonight?"

"What would ever give you the idea that I wasn't going to call you? Besides, I needed to know whether or not to cancel my plane ticket. Remember we have tickets for the Berks Jazz Festival this weekend." Wallace quickly walked into his study and turned on his desktop computer to pull up his calendar.

"I'm glad you called and reminded me because, with all that has been going on at the office, it had completely slipped my mind. So when is your flight scheduled to come in?"

Now looking at his calendar, Wallace remembered when they had planned on attending the festival. Both he and Eve loved jazz, and the Berks Jazz Festival brought in some of the top stars in the business.

"OK then, I'll pick you up at Reagan National at 8:30. We'll have dinner, spend the night here, and drive up to the festival Saturday morning."

"That sounds good to me, and while we are driving to the festival, you can tell me what has been so pressing at work as to take your mind off our trip."

—

Joint Base Anacostia-Bolling, the next morning.

Felix wanted Wallace to stop for breakfast at the International House of Pancakes, WC was anxious to get to

Anacostia, so they compromised and used the drive-through at the local McDonald's to pick up some breakfast so they could get on base at 8:00 AM.

They were just finishing their coffee in Wallace's car when they stopped in a long line of vehicles at the security gate. A 100% ID card check was being conducted by security guards at the entrance to JBAB.

After clearing security, they proceeded to the parking area of the building where the offices of the Joker program manager and lead software developer were located.

"I am beginning to remember this project. Felix, they put us in those offices located two levels underground."

As Felix and Wallace were walking into the building, Felix replied, "You're good, WC. I remember the air conditioning system went out for two days; we almost lost the servers because of the heat."

After entering the building, they stopped at the main desk, presented their contract badges, and asked to see the PM of the Joker Project. WC picked up a strange stare from the receptionist when he requested to see the PM.

The receptionist asked Felix and Wallace to sign in and directed them to have a seat in the waiting area. Wallace took a place in the waiting area as Felix started browsing through some magazines that were on the table. Felix found a copy of *Wired* magazine, and picking up the magazine, he went over and sat by Wallace.

Felix was thumbing through the articles in the magazine when Wallace started talking.

"Felix you know the actual full name is the EA-21F Joker Electronic Attack Aircraft. This aircraft was built on a joint contract awarded to Raytheon and General Dynamics to build an airborne electronic attack fighter. The plane was based on the EA-18F Growler and the EA-6B Prowler. The concept of the design even included a laser weapon." Felix looked up from his magazine.

"You're good, WC. At first, the problem was finding the right combination of hardware material that could withstand the high-intensity heat generated by the laser." Before Felix could finish, Wallace interrupted.

"Yes, then somehow they found this substance... What is it called, Felix?" Both Felix and Wallace sat for a few seconds thinking.

Then Felix said, "Bauxite. The substance is called Bauxite, a little-known material that can withstand, but above all, hold heat at very high levels. I don't think that there is any documentation on how they found the right combination other than pure luck."

Wallace looked at Felix. "I don't remember how they stumbled into the Bauxite thing either but..." The sound of a voice pulled WC's attention away from the conversation.

"Mr. Barker, I'm Vickie. I understand that you wanted to meet with the PM of the Joker Project. May I ask you what this is about?"

Wallace stood up and faced Vickie, pulling out a business card, "Good morning. I'm Wallace C. Barker, and I work for SBM. I was the program manager over a software upgrade for the Joker Project two years ago. SBM delivered 8.5 million lines of software code to the project for which the government has not yet sent payment to SBM."

Vickie turned to the receptionist and asked if Wallace and Felix had signed in. Confirming that they had signed in, Vickie said, "Please come with me to my office." Vickie led WC and Felix to a door, where she placed her hand on the fingerprint recognition monitor giving them access to the secure office area.

As Wallace was following Vickie down the hall, he recalled the name of the PM of the project. "Is Andrew still working as the PM for the project?" Vickie didn't reply to WC's question. They reached Vickie's office.

"Please come in and have a seat." Vickie sat behind her desk with WC and Felix taking the seats across from her.

"I've only been on the project for about a week now. I remember from the project briefing update I had two days ago that SBM was mentioned, and there was some discussion concerning a delivery that was made. However, at present, I'm not at liberty to discuss it."

"Tell me this Vickie: is Andrew still the PM for the project?" Vickie quickly turned to the laptop computer that was next to her desk and started typing.

"Mr. Barker, I am sure that you are cleared for this information, but let me check." Wallace and Felix sat while Vickie checked Wallace and Felix's security clearance levels.

After Vickie had finished checking to see if WC and Felix had the Security clearance for the project, she picked up her telephone and pushed one button. "Alexander, can you come down to my office. I have two gentlemen sitting at my desk who have questions concerning that software delivered by SBM." Vickie placed the telephone down.

"That was Alexander Hill, the Director of Program Management for the government. He will be joining us shortly."

Wallace smiled, pleased to see that the level of importance had reached the Director level in the Government.

"Is Andrew still in Jacksonville? We were told that the PM was in Jacksonville this week."

Vickie looked away from Wallace. "I'll let Director Hill show you." Just after Vickie said that a very overweight man in his late forties entered the room.

"Good morning, good morning." Wallace and Felix stood up as, smiling, he said, "I'm Alexander Hill, the Director of the Navy's War Fighter Aircraft Programs here at JBAB. What can I do for you, gentlemen?" He was staring at Felix.

"Excuse me, but I think we know each other. You are Felix, correct? You may not recall, but two years ago we met at the Wire Head Tech show in Vegas." Felix smiled and looked at Wallace and back to the Alexander.

"I must admit that your paper on software file compression totally changed my approach to programming and program management."

Smiling, Felix said, "Well, thank you. I'm glad you enjoyed my paper."

Now looking at Wallace, Alexander repeated his question. "What can I do for you?"

"Still standing, Wallace said, "SBM delivered 8.5 million lines of code to the government for the Joker Project." After pulling a folder out of his briefcase, Wallace handed the envelope to Mr. Hill. "This folder contains SBM paying instructions for the electronic fund's transfer."

Alexander did not accept the folder. "Mr. Barker, I sorry but it's not that easy. The Joker Project has been reclassified to a much higher security level for national defense. SBM must first seek to get certified at that level and then submit your invoice through the proper channels."

Wallace looked at Alexander, thinking, "He didn't say that the government was not going to pay SBM." In a way, he had acknowledged the software delivery. All in all, Wallace figured he had gotten what he had come for.

"OK, Mr. Hill. Once SBM is certified at the new security level, I'll submit the invoice to Andrew, the PM."

"No, Mr. Barker. You'll present it to me. Andrew and our senior software managers were both killed in an explosion that occurred in Jacksonville, Florida last week."

Felix said, "Oh yes, I've read about blasts that have taken place over the last two weeks in Jacksonville." Everyone in the room stood in silence for a few seconds.

Alexander then said. "They were crossing the bridge, coming home from dinner, when it exploded. They were in Mayport for an on-site software inspection of the Joker on the John F. Kennedy Aircraft Carrier. Because everything has been reclassified, I'll be your point of contact. Here is my card."

Chapter 33

Kyle Martin's Office, WZXL, Channel Four Television News.

Kyle Martin was sitting at a large conference table with a stack of spreadsheets in front of her along with a laptop computer. Around the table were six student interns, also with a laptop computer in front of them and the same spreadsheets showing on the monitors. These interns were from the University of North Florida, Mass Communication Majors, who had received a three-month internship with WZXL Television.

Kyle shouted, "OK, everyone, what we need to do is find some type of link between the people who were killed in the explosions." One of the young interns raised his hand.

"Yes, what is your question?"

Intimidated by the status of Kyle, the student softly said, "What do you mean by a link?" Kyle looked down the table at the student, making eye contact.

"You have a list of 54 organizations that have made contributions to the Mayor's reelection campaign, including the names of the members. If you see that any of the members appear on the list of the people killed, mark it and let me know."

Kyle ordered pizza with soft drinks so the students could work through lunch. They were stacking the pizza boxes on the floor in one of the corners of the conference room as Kyle sat down at the head of the table.

"OK, let's see where we stand." Kyle pointed to each of the interns. As they gave their reports, she typed the results into a new spreadsheet.

Four organizations were prominent. Eight members of the Longshoremen Union were killed in the three explosions. The Longshoremen Union had contributed a little over $75,000 to the Mayor's reelection campaign. The Jacksonville Teacher's Union had five teachers that were killed. The Teacher's Union donated about $29,500 to the campaign. Five members of an organization named the Businessmen for the Development of Jacksonville showed contributions of $22,500 with five members going to their deaths between the three explosions. The last group that had members killed was a women's book club that identified themselves as the Jaguar Readers. Three members were victims, one in each of the blasts. The book club made a one-time contribution to the Mayor's reelection campaign of $11,800.

Reviewing the results on her computer monitor, a total of 21 people had something in common.

"What I want everyone to do is complete a full background check on each of these people. I want details, even down to how many bags of sugar they put in their coffee. Let's get started."

After giving these directions, Kyle turned her attention to going through each of the names to see if anyone stood out to her. She was ruling out the Longshoremen. Jacksonville was a port city, and one of the major employers for Jacksonville was the Port Authority. In Jacksonville, you probably couldn't walk 100 yards without running into someone who was connected to the Longshoremen.

Connection with the Teachers Union was a possibility, but the one organization that Kyle thought might produce the best connection was the Businessmen for the Development of Jacksonville. Kyle couldn't see any political power associated with the book club, and so that possibility was dismissed.

—

FBI Temporary Office, Jacksonville, Florida.

Roy Benning flew to Jacksonville in one of the CIA's Learjets. Meeting him at the airport was one of the administrative assistants from the Jacksonville CIA Field Desk. He was driven to the FBI temporary office for the meeting with Agent Faye Cook-Little.

Faye was sitting at her desk reading the Fleming Island Police report on the explosion that killed Jake Jefferson and his wife. Just the night before Faye had found a link that she thought would take her away from what Jake Jefferson shared with her in confidence. But with Jake and his wife being killed in this explosion and the only victims, everything was shifting back to the CIA link.

There was a knock on the conference room door where Faye set up the meeting, pulling her attention away from the reports. Standing in the doorway was Roy Benning.

Roy stepped into the conference room and introduced himself. After the introductions, they got to work. At present, Roy did not have any plans for sharing information concerning Elkin Ardila with the FBI.

Very meticulously, Faye laid a timeline of all four explosions, overlaying the tie-in of each of the CIA people who were killed. What nailed everything together was Agent Jake Jefferson and his wife's deaths. Unlike the other explosions that had collateral deaths, Roy and Faye came to the same conclusion concerning the Jefferson's death: it was a targeted bombing, maybe even an assassination.

Faye shared her information concerning the corroborating statements from the eyewitnesses of each of the explosions, all speaking of seeing a flash of white light just before the blast.

Hearing Faye's assumptions on the flash of white light linking the explosions together, Roy remembered that, after he had attended the classified working group briefing at Langley, he read an information paper that indicated that, by using Bauxite, the laser weapon produced a white light just seconds before the weapon hit its target. Once again Roy Benning held back from sharing this information with Faye.

Faye and Roy jointly concluded that the FBI would take over the full investigation of the four bombings. All local agencies would turn over their file cases to the Jacksonville FBI office. Faye and Roy also concluded that other investigative agencies would have no problem giving the lead to the FBI to reduce their case load. The problem facing them was the media. The media would need an explanation that would make sense and not give them any reason to keep digging.

Their dilemma was to find a reason that would not send red flags up. Faye and Roy quickly ruled out national security as the reason. Faye knew that someone like Kyle Martin would see through an explanation like that and keep digging to find out what security was being threatened

The solution they agreed upon was tying the explosions to the FBI and ATF raid on the MIE. The strike was initiated based on leads coming from the government of Brazil that the MIE was behind the assassination of the two security ministers. The bombings were planned to put pressure on the United States to support Essequibo's independence as a sovereign country. Because all the MIE members captured had been sent to Brazil, the US government was no longer involved.

Finally, Roy gave Faye the point of contact with the law firm that would be handling the collateral damage account. This was a bank account set up to pay damage claims to victims and victim's families filing claims against the Agency but, in this case, the city of Jacksonville. Because of CIA involvement, the Agency was assuming all liability claims. The law firm would be contacting Jacksonville's City Attorney.

The General Services Administration had already put out a request for proposals for two general contractors to rebuild both the Federal Reserve Bank and the Federal Building. Faye knew that this would please the Mayor and the city council. It would give the city the base funding to rebuild that section of the city.

After three hours, Roy and Faye had put together everything necessary to keep the CIA presence in Jacksonville a secret: a cover story, compensation for victims, the rebuilding of the two federal buildings, and the law firm to handle all of the legal paperwork. Roy sent a text message to the pilot of his plane indicating that he was finishing up and wanted to fly back to Washington in the next hour.

Roy stood up from the table and placed folders back into his briefcase. Faye looked around at all of the documents lying on the table.

"Roy, it's been great working with you today, but there is still one thing we have not figured out."

Putting on his suit jacket, Roy replied, "OK, Faye, what did we miss?" Faye stood, stretching her back.

"Roy, I still have to find out who is responsible for all of these killings."

—

Shands Hospital, Jacksonville, Florida.

Jerry Clark pulled his car up to the main entrance of Shands Hospital. "Thanks, Jerry. I just want to drop in a see how Joe is doing." Bubba stepped out of the car and walked into the hospital. He took the elevator to the floor where Joe Singletary's room was located.

"Look, Joe, Bubba is here." With a smile and sigh of relief, Bubba saw his best friend sitting up in his bed with his eyes open. He was forcing a painful smile. Bubba walked past Helen and Debra, going to his friend and giving him a big hug.

"Joe, I thought we were going to lose you. Man, I'm so glad to see you." Tears began to flow down Joe's face.

Bubba looked at Debra, who was crying and then at Helen. "Man, we have a lot to get done. As soon as you feel up to it, I'll have Jerry come by with some of the proofs we have been reviewing for the election." Bubba, full of joy that his best friend was recovering, was speed talking like he had never before.

The Mayor and his wife left Joe and Helen, and when they got to the lobby of the hospital, Debra said, "Bubba, I'm planning a memorial service for the book club members. Eve Harding is putting it together." A puzzled look appeared on Bubba's face. "Hopefully, we can have all of the arrangements completed before this weekend."

"Debra, I don't understand. Who is the memorial service for?" Now standing in front of the hospital, Debra turned to Bubba.

"Oh, I guess with so much going on you didn't know and I haven't brought it up. There were four members of our book club killed in the explosions. The first explosion took the life of Nancy Mansfield; Cathy Mills went in the second, Khristy Newborn in the third, and last week Brenda Jefferson." Bubba looked over his shoulder as Jerry Clark's car pulled up.

"Debra, somehow I could never figure why Eve Harding was in your group. I know she was a member, read the books, and attended the book club meetings but something didn't fit."

"What do you mean, Bubba?"

Bubba was opening the car door stepping in. "I can't really say. It's just a feeling." Debra stood on the sidewalk watching her husband drive away with Jerry, perplexed over what he just said.

——

Home of Wallace C. Barker.

Wallace pulled out of his townhouse garage, made a right turn, and proceeded to the beltway. Sipping a cup of coffee, his thoughts were on his mattress. He did not sleep well the previous night, tossing and turning before falling to sleep. Speaking to himself, he said, "I need a new mattress."

He knew that he was using his bed as a scapegoat for what was really troubling him. As he merged into beltway traffic, his thoughts began to focus on what actually caused his restless night.

As the program manager of the Joker Project, he had to sign off on every software delivery. SBM software delivery procedures were set in stone. No delivery could be made to a customer without the signature of the PM. On the other side, the process was that the customer was not supposed to accept delivery without seeing that name.

The next thing that was strange about the delivery was that there had to be a statement of work detailing what the code was designed to operate. If there were going to be any follow-up work, a statement of work had to exist somewhere.

Finally, at the end of the day, an SBM employee or employees had to take the statement of work, do the system engineering to design the scope of work, code the software, test the code, and make the delivery. As the beltway traffic came to a stop, using his hands-free device Wallace called Felix.

"What's up, WC? Are you headed to the office?"

"Felix, about that 8.5 million lines of software code. Can you tell me the scope of work that the software is performing and who signed off on the delivery?" The phone was quiet for a few seconds.

"WC, you know that is going to be hard. They have already compiled the software, so it's no longer in the source code. I have a few tools that I can use, but this is going to be 3:00 AM work when

331

everyone is at home sleeping. I'll get on it tonight. Check back with me in the morning."

"Felix, you're the best." WC was just about to hang up. "Wallace, let me ask you something," Felix quickly said before Wallace could hang up.

"Sure, buddy, what is it?"

Felix waited a long second. "WC, wasn't the Joker Project where you met Eve? She was working for that subcontractor, JBI…"

"You're right. I did meet Eve on that project, but what are you telling me, Felix?"

"Nothing. I've just been trying to piece all this together just like you. I mean, you should not limit your focus just on the SBM programmers. You know better than anyone else how many subcontractors we had on that project. Consider all of the programmers, even the government programmers."

Wallace thought about what his friend said. It made perfect sense. His focus was on SBM's coders. Wallace had five subcontractors writing code on the Joker Project. Wallace took the decision that, once he reached the office, he would review the work assignments given to the Subcontractors and compare that to the information Felix provided.

"I agree. I'll check out the duty logs when I get to the office and compare it to what you give me tomorrow."

It was evident to Wallace that whoever developed the code and delivered it to the government possessed complete knowledge of the SBM protocols and procedures for providing software products. What was also intriguing to Wallace was that a person or a group of individuals could produce such a high quality of code that it was apparently working correctly.

After another 20 minutes in beltway traffic, Wallace pulled into the parking lot of SBM. Walking toward the entrance of the building, he saw his manager just ahead of him. WC picked up his pace to a quick trot and caught up with her.

"Good morning, Leola. How are you doing?" Leola looked in Wallace's direction to acknowledge that he was there.

"Much better this morning than yesterday. I mean, I'm really glad that you're back. You just can't imagine the pressure that was coming down on me concerning the money that was a lost on that delivery. It was like a lawnmower cutting grass and going crazy, cutting everything down in its path." Wallace smiled. It wasn't often that Leola expressed genuine appreciation to her program managers.

They entered the office building and, after passing security, as they were walking toward the elevator, Wallace said, "By the close of business tomorrow I should have a firm handle on the full scope of work, of what operations that software is directing. I know that the EA-21F Joker is an electronic attack high-performance aircraft, and there have been some papers written concerning a laser weapons system being installed on the Joker." As they stepped into the elevator, Wallace pushed the buttons for their respective floors. Wallace and Leola were the only two people riding the elevator.

"WC, you know the Navy built five Jokers, but only Two are fully operational. I believe they are assigned to the John F. Kennedy Aircraft Carrier." Looking at Wallace, Leola continued. "As I recall, they shifted funding in their budget, halting the completion of four so that one could be completed. I haven't been able to find out an explanation for that decision."

Wallace added, "Yes. When Felix and I were at JBAB yesterday, Alexander Hall said that the project manager and the government lead software programmers were both killed in Jacksonville in some type of explosion. They were there to do an on-site software inspection of the Joker's operating software system." The elevator stopped on Wallace's floor. As Wallace was stepping off, he said, "I'll keep you updated as I get more information."

As Wallace was greeting everyone as he walked toward his office, he saw Alice get up from her cubical and begin walking toward him. As she got closer, she gave Wallace a signal for him to turn around and follow her to the break room.

As Alice and Wallace walked into the break room, Alice closed the door behind them. "WC, I've been trying to call you on your cell phone all morning. When I got into the office, this morning I got this call from corporate that two FBI field agents were in the lobby to see you, and I was to sign for them so that they could come up. We have no waiting area, so I told them to sit in your office until you arrive."

Wallace stood there for a few moments. He had no idea how any of this was tying together, but his gut said that this was a connection to the 8.5 million lines of software code.

"WC, did I do the right thing in signing them in and having them sit in your office. Wallace, please help me out here. I can't lose my job. What is going on?" Alice paused for a second, looking up into Wallace's eyes. "You told us that the whole problem was a configuration management problem and that you and Felix would have everything worked out by Monday. Now today FBI agents show up. I can't lose my job over some type of mistake."

Alice was shaking and sweating. Along with what Leola shared with him as they were walking into the building this morning, it was evident to Wallace the impact that this software delivery was having on everyone in the company.

"Alice, you did the right thing," Wallace said while reaching out and placing one hand on Alice's shoulder. "There is nothing to be worried about. I want you to sit in here, have a cup of tea, settle down, and get yourself together. In the meantime, I'm going to my desk to find out why they want to talk to me. I'm sure it's probably about some security verification or something."

Wallace left Alice in the break room and headed for his office. "Sorry to keep you waiting." Walking past the two agents who were sitting on the couch in Wallace's office, WC placed his briefcase on the floor behind his desk. Wallace then turned around, smiling, and reached out to shake their hands.

"Good morning, and please have a seat." As they were sitting down, WC said, "When I checked my calendar last night I didn't have any visitors scheduled for this morning." Although Wallace was told that the men were FBI agents, he wanted to be sure.

"I'm sure that you are aware that this is a classified site, can I see your ID?" One of the agents smiled and said, "I was waiting for you to ask." Reaching into their coat jacket pockets, they both pulled out black wallet ID covers, opening them while handing them to Wallace for inspection.

After reading their IDs, Wallace returned them to the agents and quickly said, "What can I do for you?"

One of the agents pulled out a folder while the other one began to speak. "Mr. Barker, we are just trying to close up a few open items that came across our desks regarding your holiday visit to Rio de Janeiro. The reason that you came up on the radar is that you and your friend, Ms. Eve Harding, were in Brazil at the same time when two ministers of security were assassinated: the Security Minister for Venezuela and the Security Minister for Guyana." As the agent was talking, Wallace's mind shifted back to the airport when he was taken into temporary custody because they thought he was some assassin.

"Stop! Don't go any further! I went through all of this at the FBI building when I got off the plane at Reagan National. I'm not an assassin. My full-time employment is with SBM as a program manager, and I'm a Major in the US Army Reserve and command a Special Forces A-team. If you did your homework, you would know that all of this is in my file. So I don't see where there are any loose ends to tie up."

Before responding to Wallace' outburst, the agents looked at each other, and then the agent with the folder continued.

"Major Barker, we apologize for what the Agency put you through when you returned to Washington DC. The loose ends that we are trying to resolve concern your traveling companion, Eve Harding. Were you aware that she had been to Rio de Janeiro before? She has also traveled to Venezuela and Guyana." Wallace was surprised by the question. This, he was not expecting.

"Eve has traveled a lot. She grew up in a military family, and being assigned all over the world is very familiar to a military family. I wasn't aware that she had been to Brazil nor to any of those other countries before. It didn't come up while we were planning our trip and I didn't see any need to raise the question of her past travels."

One of the agents was taking notes while Wallace was talking. The other just looked at Wallace. When Wallace finished, they looked at each other.

"One other question, Major Barker. Have you met Ms. Harding's family?" This was another issue that WC didn't anticipate.

"Where is all of this going? If you have something on Eve, all you have to do is fly to Jacksonville and ask her yourself!" Wallace stood up and walked toward the agents.

"Major Barker, once again we are very sorry for what you went through the other night at headquarters. You see, Lieutenant Harding's security clearance is being upgraded, and we need to conduct interviews with people who may know her to verify her status."

After hearing what the FBI Agent said, WC sat down. "You mean to check his status." Once again the two Agents looked at each other.

"Major Barker, I'm sorry, but could you repeat that?"

Looking at the Agent as he sat behind his desk, Wallace said, "You referred to Tony as a female by saying her. Eve has a son who is a Lieutenant in the Navy, not a daughter."

—

Office of Roy Benning, Langley, Virginia.

Roy was sitting at his desk immersed in the reports from the working group. The reports made it clear that whoever controlled the source of Bauxite controlled the future of laser warfare until another substance could be found. This meant the Agency was to maintain destabilization efforts in the region until a solution could be found. The job of doing this would rest on the desk in Jacksonville.

Checking his Blackberry and then his desktop computer, Roy saw that he had not received any messages from Elk. Six hours had passed since his plane landed in Brazil. Roy wasn't too concerned, but he was anxious to let Elk know that he would be assuming the position of Desk Chief at the Jacksonville office. Roy was going to let Elk decide whether to terminate the mission that he was on and come back to Jacksonville, sending another agent out to finish it up.

Elk's first job as the Desk Chief would be to do an assessment of what it would take to conduct the destabilization operation in the region. Roy knew that the Jacksonville office would need additional human assets to perform this operation as well as funding.

Personally, Roy did not care for destabilization operations. They are costly, burned up a lot of human effort, and the results were hard to measure. However, there was still a question of whether Elk had any involvement in the bombings in Jacksonville. Roy scheduled a meeting with the psychological counselor who interviewed Elk and wrote the last report.

—

WZXL Television News, Jacksonville, Florida.

In Jacksonville, Kyle Martin was working hard to develop any type of connection to each explosion that would lead to a meaningful story. She was leaving the WZXL office building to get some lunch. As she was walking out of the building, the same University of North Florida Intern who asked the question when they first started going through the casualty lists was also leaving the building.

Kyle didn't pay any attention to the young man until he called out to her. "Ms. Martin? Ms. Martin, may I have a word with you?"

Kyle stopped and turned around. "Aren't you one of my interns?"

Smiling, the young man replied, "Yes, ma'am, I am."

Kyle quickly snapped back, showing the irritation on her face said, "Can't this wait until I return from lunch?"

"Well, I guess it can but today is my last day of the internship, and I've been trying to see you all morning. I think I may have stumbled on a breakthrough for linking all of the explosions together."

Kyle stood in silence, then said, looking directly into the young man's face, "What makes you think you are so smart that you have come up with a connection and no one else has?"

This time, the young man was not going to be intimidated by Kyle. "Look, do you want to hear what I have found out or not? It's no sweat off my nose one way or the other. All I'm trying to do is the job that you hired me to do."

Kyle backed off and refocused her attention on the young intern. "I'm sorry. We've been going around in a circle, and I'm a little tired. What do you have?"

"Okay, if you recall, the Jaguar Readers book club had four members killed in the explosions. One club member died in each blast. Right? What I also discovered was that it appeared in each case that the husband and wife were killed together. There is not only a link between the women but also between the husbands. Three of the men came up as employees of the Federal Reserve Bank along with one of the wives. I believe that all of the explosions had some type of connection to the Federal Reserve Bank."

Kyle Martin liked what she was hearing from the intern. None of the other leads were making any sense. The fact that she could link four people who worked for the bank, and all were killed, could produce the story she was looking for, but she wanted more.

"Didn't you say that today was your last day as an intern?" The young man looked puzzled.

"Yes, our internship ends today."

Kyle quickly said, "Like hell it does. Get back in there and find the job descriptions for each of these people and get that to me as soon as possible. Your internship has just been extended."

The young intern quickly turned and started running back into WZXL office building, and Kyle, with a new burst of energy, turned in the opposite direction, headed to the closest Subway for lunch.

While walking, Kyle was contemplating calling either Faye Cook-Little or Jerry Clark. She figured if she called Faye, even if Faye had already discovered the connection between the people in the book club, Faye would probably deny the links; but even by denying the links, in a sense, Faye would be confirming that she was on the right track.

Jerry Clark would only be useful for establishing how the Mayor would react to the situation. Kyle figured that, since the people were federal employees, the Mayor really would not have that much interest in the case because everything would be handled by the FBI.

In Kyle's mind, the FBI handling all of the blasts would mean that she would be reporting on a story receiving national

338

coverage rather than local. This could possibly mean her break and the exposure she needed to be picked up with a national news bureau. As Kyle stepped up to the counter at Subway, she decided not to call either Faye or Jerry but to wait until her interns uncovered additional information on the book club couples.

—

FBI Temporary Office, Jacksonville, Florida.

After dropping her son off at school, Faye Cook-Little pulled her car onto Jacksonville's 295 Beltway to drive to the FBI temporary office on Blanding Blvd. Faye's thoughts slowly moved from what type of day her son would have at school to the biggest case she had ever had to handle. Faye felt like she was playing musical chairs. The music had stopped, and everyone had a chair to sit in except her.

The city of Jacksonville received a free get out of jail card with the federal government assuming liability for all damages in the area. The CIA field office would continue to be one of Jacksonville's dirty little secrets. As soon as the construction jobs started flowing, the four explosions would soon fall from the front page, moving further back until finally on the last page of the newspaper. Everybody had a chair except her. Faye was still stuck with finding out who had done this and why all of it had been done.

Chapter 34

As Faye pulled her car into the office building parking lot, she was considering moving her research on the investigations outside the Jacksonville area. Since she and Roy had decided on using the raid in Miami to connect the members of the MIE to the explosions, she had been thinking that just could turn out to be the real connection linking the bombings.

Faye's first step was to locate every piece of information on the MIE. Next, she needed to find out their connection to Venezuela and Guyana. What was also a puzzle was that the MIE members were captured in Fleming Island at Whitney's Fish Camp.

Whitney's Fish Camp was a very famous restaurant in the Jacksonville area. Faye, along with many of her friends, had dined there on many occasions.

As Faye pulled information off the web and the internal files of the FBI, she was becoming pretty sure that most of the answers to these questions would lead her back to the CIA's office in Jacksonville.

—

CIA Headquarters, Langley, Virginia.

Back in Langley, Virginia, Roy Benning was pacing in front of his desk while talking to the CIA psychological counselor who had written the last evaluation on Elkin Ardila.

"Roy, unless you have started an internal investigation concerning the mental health of Elk, you know that I cannot speak to the private information that Elk shared with me during our interview."

Frustrated a little Roy said, "This is the situation. In the last two and a half weeks, I've had four Desk Chiefs in Jacksonville blown up. I need to find out if Elk was in a state of mind that he would have had something to do with these explosions." The counselor did not reply for several seconds.

"Agency procedures clearly indicate that I must not share with anyone, I mean anyone other than the person I interviewed, the content of our discussion." The counselor stopped for several seconds, then continued.

"Roy you know this procedure probably a lot better than me. Start an internal investigation of Elk's mental competency, and once I receive documentation that a review board has been established, I will be at liberty to discuss this case. As long as there is no internal investigation concerning Elk's mental competency, everything that he said to me in confidence remains secret."

Roy knew that the counselor was right. It was a long shot he was taking in reaching out to the counselor. Roy thought that maybe the counselor would have his guard down and provide some useful information concerning Elk's state of mind.

The conversation ended, and Roy Benning sat down behind his desk. Roy shifted his thoughts back to Jacksonville. All of the explosions were still working cases being handled by the FBI office in Jacksonville. If the Jacksonville FBI office picked up something connecting the explosions to Elk, that would be the time to initiate the internal investigation.

Roy smiled while checking his Blackberry, looking for a message from Elk. After he didn't see any messages from Elk, Roy turned his attention to reviewing other human resources files of possible field agents who could be transferred to Jacksonville.

—

Shan's Hospital, Jacksonville, Florida.

While driving home from the hospital, Debra could not put the comment that Bubba made concerning Eve Harding out of her thoughts.

Debra trusted her husband's judgment. Bubba had made personality judgment calls many times over the lifetime of their marriage, and in most situations, Bubba would not make a statement, especially concerning one of her friends, unless he was sure about his call. However, what was different about this time was that Bubba did not give an explanation for what concerned him about Eve. In almost every case Bubba would follow up his statement with a reason and in some instances several reasons.

All of this was coming just at the time when Debra was trying to figure out how Eve knew about the deaths of three of their book club members. The list had not been published. Debra told Gracie about the members being killed in the explosions before she called Eve. Gracie said that she didn't talk to Eve before she came to the hospital to check on Joe and Helen. So how did Eve find out?

Debra thought maybe she was making too much of this. Why did it really matter how Eve learned about the death of their friends? So she dismissed the significance of this discovery and decided that, when they talked or got together for planning the memorial services for their members, she would ask Eve.

Debra could feel the fatigue coming down. She had been at the hospital almost as long as Helen had been there. Debra was looking forward to a hot bath and sleeping until Bubba came home from the office.

FBI Temporary Office, Jacksonville, Florida.

After arriving in her office, Faye decided to make a few calls before she started her research on the MIE. Her first call was to Terry Jackson.

"Terry, in reading the eyewitness reports, several of the witnesses said that they saw a white light just before hearing the explosions. Do you have any idea what they could be referring to?"

"Faye, I picked up on the same points. I did a search on explosions in our database. I'm sorry to say that this produced nothing. I also did a search on unexplained explosions, and once again I got nothing back from that search either."

With disappointment on her face, Faye thanked Terry. Faye's next call was to the FBI forensics team that had come down from Atlanta. These guys would have access to a much larger database field than the resources Terry could get into.

"Faye, we were not able to cross reference any known incidents with white light, but after analyzing the metal from several of the cars, we can say with certainty that the heat intensity was like nothing that we have ever seen." The forensics guy had just pushed something in front of Faye that she was not expecting.

"Please, clarify. Are you saying that you have never seen any explosion like this?"

"No, that's not what I'm saying. I've seen explosions something like this, but the heat intensity is at a far higher level than any of the other bombings I've investigated." Faye didn't comment, but then the forensic agent continued.

"You see, Faye, an explosion is a rapid increase in volume and release of energy in an extreme manner, usually with the generation of high temperatures and the release of gasses. Supersonic explosions created by high explosives are known as detonations and travel via supersonic shock waves." Faye cut in before the forensic agent could finish.

"Wait. Just tell me if you can give me anything I can follow to find out who is responsible for these explosions."

The forensic agent, apparently sensing the frustration in Faye's voice, calmly said, "I can tell you that all of the blasts were produced by the same source. That is, whoever did this was able to put together an exact set of procedure for each burst and deliver the blasts, in the same way, each time."

Faye completed her last note just when the agent finished. " I think you are telling me the same person set off all four explosions. Is that correct?"

The forensic agent quickly said, "Wait a minute. Let me check my notes, so I can be sure." Faye sat patiently while waiting for the forensic agent to reply.

"Faye, I know you are probably under a lot of pressure to bring closure to this case. What I'm about to say will read pretty much the same way in my official report, and that is that all of the explosions were produced in the same fashion in all four explosive devices and that all four are the same. What I can't tell you is what kind of explosive device did the damage."

The answer eased her level of frustration. However, Faye was no closer to finding a direction to focus her investigation on. The Forensic information provided the element that, once she had a suspect, could be used to either confirm or narrow a list down. Feeling bottled up in trying to find a motive for the explosion that could link all four together, Faye was looking at everything that was going on in the Agency leading up to the point when she received the assignment to babysit Agent Bo Brooks.

This was the first time Agent Bo Brooks had crossed her mind since the night she returned home from Miami. "I'm actually turning into the cold-hearted bitch who only thinks about becoming the first female Director of the FBI," Faye said to herself as she was pulling a notebook from her desk drawer.

Faye was working on 15 cases when she got assigned to Agent Brooks. She saw no connection with those cases and the explosions. Faye then checked out the local blotter reports, also finding nothing there that made a connection. She then moved on to the FBI register. The entry showed open cases by FBI regions.

After an hour and a half, Faye was just about to take a break before shifting her search to the Internet. She was giving up hope that her efforts would yield anything except more frustration. With a cup of coffee and a Danish, Faye returned to her tasks. Faye's Google searching was producing information, but she could not tie anything together.

"Bus loaded with tourists is held for questioning." This heading from a Brazilian newspaper article caught Faye's attention. Besides this article, she also found in additional two articles on the same subject.

Listed in these items was a mention of two people traveling on US Passports. Faye found a total of three reports of these people being married and the last as traveling companions.

Feverishly, Faye kept searching to see if they identified the couple by name. After multiple attempts, Faye could not find any information online that identified these tourists by name. She decided to contact the Brazilian authorities and requested to speak with the agent in charge of the investigation.

After several dropped calls, Faye made contact with the agent in charge of the investigation of the assassinations.

"Hello, this is Belo." Xoana Cardozo answered the phone with a calm, professional voice.

"Good, you speak English. I'm FBI Agent Faye Cooke-Little. I'm doing follow-up work concerning the MIE and their capture here in Florida. Hopefully, you will be able to assist me."

There was no answer. Fayre was just about say something when Belo spoke.

"Why, yes, I'm Special Agent Xoana Cardozo, but please call me Belo. I will assist you as far as I can."

Faye and Belo entered into a detailed discussion of what occurred in the holding of Wallace and Eve during their trip to Brazil. Belo also included their suspicions on the probability of Wallace C. Barker being the number assassin.

"Ms. Belo, I want to thank you very much for sharing with me so much information. What you have provided will be of some assistance in my investigation."

Faye sat back in her chair to think through the information Belo provided. What Belo shared really didn't take the case anywhere. Other than the fact that Barker and Harding were in Brazil during the assassinations, nothing else connected them to the MIE or the explosions in Jacksonville except the fact that Harding lives in Jacksonville and Barker lived here once before. Faye decided to follow the call up with a visit to Harding's home, if for nothing else than to get out of the office.

After unlocking the drawer where she kept her service weapon, she was just about to place it on her belt but began to listen to a conversation a couple of desks away. Two of the agents working a bank holdup had solved the crime. They had been working the case for several weeks.

"As we figured from the beginning, it was an inside job. They broke into the bank and moved the money to a different location in the bank vault. The money in that area of the vault was only counted once a month. Each day after the break-in they would take a little bit out of the bank with no one paying any attention."

Immediately, Faye sat down and began to look at the possibilities that the explosions could be connected to an inside bank robbery of the Federal Reserve Bank.

Chapter 35

Montevilla Bartram, Gated Community, Jacksonville, Florida.

Pulling into her driveway, Eve Harding checked the security cameras on the dashboard monitor before she stepped out of the car. Eve was in a cheerful mood, and as she unlocked the door leading into her kitchen, she was humming one of her favorite songs.

Eve had talked to Tony. Tomorrow she would be flying to Maryland to spend the weekend with Wallace and go to the jazz festival. Everything was going her way.

After entering the house, she did a walk-through to see if anything had been disturbed. After assuring herself that no one had entered her home, Eve sat down at the kitchen table and looked through her mail. When she saw that there was nothing of urgency in the mail, Eve decided to make some lunch and read the newspaper as she ate her meal. The front page of the paper referred her to the second page where there was a complete list of all of the victims killed in the four explosions.

Eve reached for her highlighter, carefully going through the list and marking the victims' names in yellow. She highlighted eight names.

"This is good. I must show Mama these and place this with the other news clippings." Eve smiled as she cut the clippings from the newspaper.

It had turned into a standard ritual for Eve Harding. On the third Saturday of every month, except for July and August, Eve would wait until it was midnight, turn off all of the lights in her home, check the security system and then go to her hidden room in the back of the garage.

After purchasing her home, Eve redesigned the house, adding the private room at the rear of her garage. Eve also upgraded the security system with technical enhancements for a high capacity computer server with other specialized equipment such as laser scanner and a 3D printer.

The walls of Eve's secret room told a story, a story that covered three generations of Harding's, a history that created the driving force for every decision that Eve Harding had made in her life. As you entered the room, a dark feeling came over you. A sense of hate, pain, suffering and sorrow unified into one emotion encircling deep into all of your sensitive cells. If someone were to visit this sanctuary, after their eyes adjusted to the light, that person would notice on the walls to the left, a genealogy chart of the Harding Family Tree. The whole story wouldn't become apparent until this intruder began to read some of the newspaper clippings.

The Harding Family was one of the richest families in the world. They made their money in Citrus Farming, growing, harvesting, and selling fruit, at one time controlling over 41% of the citrus market in America. In Florida, their farming empire stretched from the Panhandle to Key West. The Harding Farms also included citrus and other agricultural interests in Panama, Cuba, and Mexico.

Wauchula, Florida, was where the Harding's first citrus farm was started and where the corporate headquarters were located. Wauchula, Florida is in Hardee County. Hardee County gains its name from the Harding Family Citrus Empire.

The Harding Citrus Empire was always led by the oldest male of the family. Eve's great grandfather was in line to take over the company, but the Harding family believed in a Southern tradition that all male members of the family must serve their country in the military before he could run the family business. As the last remaining son, Eve's grandfather chose to join the Navy and became a pilot. He was the pilot of a B-26 Bomber.

On April 17, 1961, he was part of a flight of eight B-26 bombers that supported the Bay of Pigs invasion, the 1961 CIA-sponsored invasion of Cuba. In 1960, the CIA began to recruit anti-Castro Cuban exiles in the Miami area. The recruits received para-guerrilla and infantry training at a top secret location code named the Plantation. There were fewer than 1000 anti-Castro Cuban exiles organized into a brigade consisting of two infantry battalions and one paratrooper battalion. The codename for the CIA-sponsored group was Brigade 2506.

The CIA plan called for 26 B-26 bombers to support the invasion. Their mission was to bomb all of the Cuban airfields to stop the Cuban Air Force from providing air-to-ground support for the Cuban Army. Destroying the airfields along with the planes on the airfields was a major, if not the most critical, part of the invasion plan. Brigade 2506's key to success was a surprise.

The entire CIA operation was controlled by the CIA's South and Central American Desk located in Jacksonville. The Desk Chief of that office had full control and was making all of the decisions in the execution of the operational plan.

What had never been made clear was that 24 hours before the implementation of the invasion the Desk Chief changed the portion of the plan calling for aerial support. The Desk Chief reduced the number of planes supporting the attack from 26 bombers to eight.

Eve Harding's great grandfather, Flight Lieutenant Ronald Alexander Harding, was the pilot of one of the bombers to support the missions. Of the eight B-26 bombers, seven returned. One plane was shot down. The plane that did not return was piloted by Eve's great grandfather.

News clippings on the walls of Eve's secret room provided the history of the fall from riches to the poverty of the Harding Empire beginning with this headline: "Only Heir to the Harding Citrus Empire Dies in Mysterious Bomber Crash."

Eve's grandmother attempted to run the empire, but not having the business skills, she eventually lost everything and committed suicide.

Another pivotal news headline read: "The Harding Family Empire Declares Bankruptcy."

Eve's mother, the only child of Eve's grandparents, was placed in a foster home where she was raped and gave birth to Eve. Eve's mom told her the story of their family's history, planting the seeds of revenge.

For Sunday outings, Eve Harding's mother would take Eve to where the Harding Farming estate once stood. She drilled into Eve's mind each turn of events that resulted in the family losing their fortune.

Like her mother before her, Eve's mom committed suicide while in prison. Standing at her mother's grave, Eve vowed revenge on the people who made the decision that killed her grandfather and destroyed their lives.

Eve grew up homeless, became a child prostitute, and gave birth to a daughter she named Toni but intentionally spelled it, Tony.

Eve overcame her past and became an engineer; her daughter attended the US Naval Academy becoming a Navy pilot and the instrument of revenge.

Each phase of Eve Harding's life was built on the psychological and emotional indoctrination perpetrated by her mother. Eve's mom taught her that the position makes the person; the person does not make the Position.

After a person is placed in a position, all of their decisions are made based on what the Position dictates. If no one accepts a position, the position is vacant. Thus, no decisions are made because there is no one holding the position. As long as you have someone holding these positions, decisions will be made.

As an electrical engineer, Harding became a software programmer, mastering several software languages, developing into one of the top software designers in the information technology industry. Eve Harding was very strategic and systematic in identifying and selecting the software companies and projects that she worked on, picking only those projects that were in line with her objective, moving her closer to her goal. The same was true in raising her daughter.

After Eve Harding's mother had committed suicide, there was no family member with whom Eve could be placed. So the court system took over custody of Eve, and she was put in a foster home. Eve immediately disliked her foster family, and at the first opportunity ran away and decided that she was old enough and mature enough to take care of herself.

Eve traveled from city to city, mostly going with seasonal fruit pickers, sleeping anywhere she could, some nights in shelters other nights in group homes. For a period of time, she lived out of an abandoned car.

Occasionally the juvenile system would catch up with her. She would be placed back in a foster home, but only for a brief period of time. During that time Eve would attend school, maintaining the highest grades in her class until she saw the opportunity to run away from the foster home.

As Eve Harding grew older, she began to use her body as a means to provide money and shelter when she needed it, spending nights and sometimes as long as weeks with men whom she provided pleasure for and they, in turn, provided food and a place for her to stay. When Eve became pregnant, she knew that it was time for her to get focused and to develop a plan for revenge in her family's name.

Eve made the decision to have the baby, but Eve Harding knew that she was too young to have custody, and the child would be placed in a foster home and probably put up for adoption. Eve knew that it was a lot of things that she would have to do for her to keep her child.

In school, she was two and a half years behind graduating with her high school class. Eve also knew that she would not be able to obtain custody of her child until she had a job showing a steady income.

Eve entered Social Services and was placed in a group home. While in the group home, she re-enrolled in high school. Taking accelerated classes and testing out of certain courses, Eve Harding was able to graduate two weeks ahead of her class. The week after she graduated Eve gave birth to a baby girl naming the child, Toni but intentionally spelling the name Tony.

Eve Harding graduated at the top of her high school class as an honor student. Eve received several scholarships, and she made the decision to attend one of the state universities and major in engineering.

From the day that Eve entered Social Services, she made it clear that she wanted to have full custody of her child and asked what it would take for that to happen. The case worker that Eve was assigned saw a determination in Eve that she didn't typically see in her other cases. The case worker placed Eve's daughter in a foster home, delaying the adoption process to give Eve Harding the opportunity to complete college and obtain a job so she could show that she had the means and the stability to care for a child.

Eve Harding approached college in the same manner that she did in completing high school. Each semester Eve would take the course maximum load. She also accelerated her academic work by taking online courses while testing out all of the selected classes. In three years Eve Harding earned her degree in engineering.

Once again graduating at the top of the class, she was sought after by some of the top software design companies.

Eve was very selective in the companies that she interviewed with, and in each interview, she asked detailed questions far beyond the scope of the typical interviewer. Eve Harding was looking for the right company that would be suited to her plan.

—

FBI Temporary Office, Jacksonville, Florida.

As Faye Cook-Little walked out of the building, she made the decision to take her own car rather than driving one of the Agency cars. While sitting in her car, Faye went over what she was going to do for the remainder of the day.

First, drive out to Eve Harding's home for questioning, then pick up her son and take him to swimming practice. While her son was at swimming practice, she would do some shopping. Finally, she would take her son to dinner at his favorite seafood restaurant.

Faye began typing in the address of Eve Harding into her GPS telephone application. The screen indicated that it would be a 45-minute drive to Harding's home. Before hitting enter on the form, Faye pulled out her private cell phone, first checking on the phone to see if her son or housekeeper had attempted to contact her. After seeing that there were no missed calls or new text messages. Faye sent a text message to her son letting him know she would be picking him up and taking him to swimming practice. After waiting for a couple of minutes for a reply, Faye took the Agency cell phone, touched enter on the GPS application, pulled her car out of the parking lot and began to follow the directions of the GPS application.

The explosion case was never far from Faye's mind. She had received an email that the Mayor wanted to have a meeting tomorrow. The Mayor was looking for an update regarding how close the Agency was to solving the case. After four explosions in ten days, the city was on edge, wondering when the next one would occur. The regular school sessions would be starting soon so the other question would be if it were safe to open schools without having some idea as to who was responsible for the first four explosions.

Faye knew that she could go to the meeting and put together a good case that the MIE planned and executed the whole thing with the motive of robbing the Federal Reserve Bank to support their cause for the independence of Essequibo. That case scenario would not hold water when put before any experienced investigator, of course. The scenario would not stand for the simple reason that there had been four explosions when they only needed one to be used as a diversion to distract law enforcement and all other agencies away from the bombing at the Federal Reserve Bank.

Then there was another important question: by blowing up the Federal Reserve Bank, how would the MIE get the money? Faye considered this would be a reason to tie in the four CIA people who died in the explosion as being the federal employees who were the inside people working with the MIE. However, Faye knew that if she put out a possible scenario like that a real investigative reporter, someone like Kyle Martin would see through it in less than two or three Google searches.

Faye stopped at a traffic signal, waiting for the light to change so she could make a left turn and get on the Jacksonville 295 Beltway going south. Her personal cell phone indicated that a text message was downloading. The message was only one word: "HIE."

Faye smiled while clucking to herself. "We said that we were finished, and it was over. She is such a liar." She glanced at her watch while thinking about her schedule. It's not far out of the way, and I could always reschedule my trip out to Eve Harding's house or give some excuse that I decided to take a backup agent with me.

Reaching into the backseat of her car, Faye picked up a baseball cap and put it on along with a set of sunglasses. Faye exited the beltway and pulled into the drive-through of the liquor store. There was one car ahead of her. The car was served, and Faye pulled forward and ordered a fifth of Grand Marnier and four cans of Red Bull. Faye's mind was on drinking Geritol.

After paying, Faye pulled out of the drive-through and got back on the 295 Beltway. In four exits she left the 295, made a left turn at the end of the exit ramp, and proceeded east. After passing five traffic lights, Faye saw a sign that read Holiday Inn Express.

Faye pulled out her personal cell phone and replied to the message that read HIE with one word: Number? An answer quickly came back: 313. Faye exited her car, and after climbing the steps to the third floor, tapped on room 313.

The door opened, and Faye entered quickly, closing the door behind her. Standing in only her panties was Kyle Martin. Kyle and Faye fell into each other's arms, coming into a deep and passionate French kiss.

—

Maryland.

Wallace C. Barker pulled out of the Sterling Business Machine's parking lot, made a left turn, and started driving toward the beltway. Finally, after a ten-day vacation, Wallace had caught up with a lot of his work. The most important thing he had found was where the $50 million in software was delivered, which would probably lead to the government paying SBM for the delivery.

What was still hanging out there was finding out what the code executed. For certain, the Navy liked the software, and it was doing what it was intended to do. WC was coming to the conclusion that the code had to be written by more than one person. Although it was possible for one software coder to write a million lines of code, it was very unlikely. Possible but unlikely. The coder would have to be at the programming level of a Felix. Wallace didn't know of any programmers in the Washington DC area who had Felix's skill set.

After entering beltway traffic, WC contemplated the events of the upcoming weekend with Eve. A report came over the radio of a bombing outside the US Embassy in Venezuela followed by another report on shootings at the US Embassies in Guyana and Brazil. This caught Wallace's attention.

The reports said that a car was blown up in front of the Venezuela Embassy with no injuries. No one was injured in either of the shootings in front of the embassies in Guyana or Brazil either. Shots were merely fired into the buildings, only breaking windows.

When Wallace heard Brazil, he rubbed his face at the spot where Belo whispered in his ear at the airport when he and Eve were flying home from Rio de Janeiro. A group identifying itself as the Movement for the Independence of Essequibo, the MIE, took credit for the bombing and the shootings. They also said that there would be more attacks until Essequibo is a free and independent state. Wallace thought for a while whether this was the group that caused the trouble when he and Eve were in Brazil. WC quickly dismissed the thought, turning his attention back to the upcoming weekend.

Wallace still had not decided whether or not he was going to ask Eve to marry him. His emotions were all tied up between logic and just a gut feeling that something just was not right. WC was also wondering whether too much of his thought process was being influenced from the waist down rather than the neck up.

On their vacation in Rio de Janeiro, Wallace and Eve had taken their passion to another level. So for the moment, Wallace decided to put off making a decision on asking Eve to marry him and just have a good weekend at the Jazz Festival.

After making one stop to pick up some food along with wine and candles, Wallace drove into the garage of his townhome. Hearing his house telephone ringing, WC quickly placed the groceries on the kitchen table. The caller ID indicated that it was Felix.

"Hello, buddy. How was the traffic? I'm so glad that I don't have to get out in that mess every day," Felix said.

"It was just about the same as any other day. What's up, Felix? It must be substantial because we just talked a couple of hours ago?"

"WC, I just got some insider information. The Navy is putting out a sources-sought requirement tomorrow. They are looking for a company that has developed software for high intensive directed systems (HIDS). But get this: the company must have that new security classification."

WC quickly interrupted. "Isn't HIDS another name for programming for laser weapons?"

"You got it, buddy. We will be getting into some real star wars stuff."

Wallace smiled. "OK, Felix. We'll talk tomorrow when I get into the office."

Wallace placed the telephone receiver back into the cradle. Looking around his kitchen, his thoughts were on Felix and if there was another software programmer in the Washington area that was as talented as him.

WC knew that there was probably some little genius, writing software code in a basement or some garage, who could probably be much better than Felix waiting to be discovered. However, as of now WC did not know of any.

—

Jacksonville, Florida.

Meanwhile, back in Jacksonville, Faye Cook-Little was driving away from the Holiday Inn Express and her rendezvous meeting with Kyle Martin. She was lamenting the relationship they had and how it could be so exciting at one point, depressing at other times, and even confrontational.

Faye knew that the physical attraction they had for each other was one thing but that they were both using their relationship to further their career aspirations. They were women trying to survive and thrive in the male-dominated world. If the word would ever get out that their friendship went beyond being tennis partners, their whole professional careers would come crashing down on top of them.

Chapter 36

—

Jacksonville, Florida.

Kyle Martin would probably survive coming out of the closet in her profession more so than Faye. In a strange sort of way, it could end up being a boost for Kyle's career. In the media world, there is no such thing as bad publicity; keeping your name and image in the press in many ways keeps you in demand.

While pulling into her son's school to pick him up from his summer school program, Faye changed the radio to an all-news channel. Faye parked and turned up the volume on the car radio just when the announcer was reporting that the MIE was taking credit for the bombing and the two shootings. Faye could see her son walking toward the car. She quickly pulled out a cell phone and made a call to the office. No one was there, but she left a message that she wanted all the information concerning the bombing in South America and the shootings at the two embassies to be on her desk the first thing in the morning.

Faye was thinking to herself that, for the meeting tomorrow with the Mayor and the media, she had some definitive proof to tie the MIE to the explosions that had occurred in Jacksonville over the last 10 days. Faye felt that she would not have to consider, even mention, that four CIA agents were killed in the explosions. As Faye's son got closer to the car, Faye stepped out of the car to give her son a big hug and kiss.

"All right, my young man. How was school and where would you like to eat dinner tonight? I'll take you to your favorite place."

—

CIA Headquarters, Langley, Virginia.

At CIA headquarters in Langley Virginia, Roy Benning also heard the news concerning the bombings in South America. He had no news from Elk, and he knew Elk was on the ground somewhere in Brazil, Guyana, or Venezuela. Elk probably didn't know about the death of Jake and Brenda Jefferson, and Roy was sure he didn't know that the position of Desk Chief was his for the asking.

Roy knew that the MIE had a law firm in New York that worked for the group as a lobbyist at the United Nations. Standard FBI procedure was for the Agency to contact them and bring someone in for questioning. Roy sent an email to his FBI liaison and requested any notes from that interrogation.

It didn't take Roy long to consider how all of this was going to fit into Faye Cook-Little's investigation of the explosions that had taken place in Jacksonville. Roy felt that, with the MIE taking the blame for the embassy bombings and the two shootings and the FBI raid rounding up the members that were in the US, a tie-in could be easily made with the explosions without including that four CIA agents were killed.

To confirm that Faye Cook-Little had seen the accounts of the MIE bombing and the shootings, Roy noted on his calendar for the next day to call her to discuss how this latest occurrence could be used to their advantage.

After completing several emails, Roy Benning was just finishing locking up his classified material in his safe when he saw his secure cell phone number ringing. Roy could see that it was Elkin Ardila calling.

Roy was relieved to be receiving the call, but he quickly considered if he was going to bring Elk back to assume the position of Desk Chief or keep him on the assignment until they could close out the MIE case. This was especially important considering the bombing of the embassy and the two shootings.

"Hello, Elk. I guess this must be a good time for us to talk."

Roy had to re-adjust how he spoke to Elk. When agents are in the field, they assume a much different personality than how they present themselves at Langley or at their field desk. He couldn't really put a finger on why, but they did. Roy always thought of it as their survival personality. The more demanding the operation and the level of danger the darker the character would get. The assignments would range from being demanding purely from the importance of the information that was gathering, assignments that did not have any type of immediate danger, to the other extreme to where an agent was working on an operation with a high level of importance along with a high degree of risk.

From Roy Benning's years of experience, he could group, sub-group, and classify operational assignments into infinite numbers of categories. What it really came down to was that all operations and jobs were different, each with its own level of danger and excitement, along with their standard of importance.

"Roy," Elk said. "Is this a good time for you?"

"Go ahead, Elk. I'm listening." Roy noted a level of tiredness in his voice.

"Mission update report number one. This is an oral report. I arrived on station and did not report to the embassy. Security didn't seem to be up to standard." When Roy heard this, he quickly made a note. His intention was to follow up on this later in the conversation.

"Roy, all of the MIE prisoners that the FBI turned over to the Brazilian authorities have been taken to their maximum security facility. I did get word that an accident occurred, but everyone was recaptured with several losing their lives. I'm going to look further into this." Elk paused. Roy didn't say anything, just waited for Elk to continue at his own pace.

"I'm in the village where I first made contact with Ranuel and Krish. I'll start asking around tomorrow and give you an update by the end of the week if possible." Once again Elk paused.

"I've picked up a little chatter concerning the MIE claims, but most people haven't even heard of the group. Those who have heard of them only considered them as a group of politicians trying to get elected to some office either in Venezuela or Guyana. Just one last thing in this report: I sent Jake a full detailed report in my classified email. My operational money account has not been activated. I don't need any money now but remind him to see that it is turned on ASAP." Roy wondered if this was the right time to tell him about the situation in Jacksonville but decided to pass on doing that.

"OK, Roy. That's all I have. I will check back in with the Jacksonville desk later in the week. Signing off."

Roy replied in a serious tone. "Elk, outside of what you said, do you need anything? Is there anything I can do for you before you get back?"

358

"I'm just getting on the ground here. Let me make contact with my network, and I'll be able to give Jake a requirements list when I call with my next update." Roy thought for a second, but Elk's answer seemed like the proper response.

"Sounds good, Elk. We will talk again later."

After Elk had hung up, Roy started to fill in notes concerning Elk's report. What was of concern was Elk indicating that the security situation at the Embassy in Brazil was not up to standards. This had to be passed over to the State Department and the FBI. Roy Benning finished up his notes and decided to write up his situational report for the Director and the DDP the next morning. He had to come up with a solution to filling the position of Desk Chief in Jacksonville. Roy's thoughts were leaning in the direction of placing the next person in line as the interim Chief until Elk could close out the assignment in Essequibo, or at least until he could bring it to the point that it could be reassigned to another field agent.

Maryland.

The next morning Wallace had a million and one things on his agenda to accomplish before he was scheduled to pick Eve Harding up at the airport. He was thinking about picking Eve up and driving directly to Berk, Pennsylvania rather than spending the night at his townhouse and driving up the next morning.

Just as he was parking, the all-news radio station that he was listening to in his car gave an update concerning the bombing and the shootings at the two embassies. While listening to the news report, this time, WC recalled that several years ago his Special Forces Battalion was scheduled to take part in a South America joint special operation exercise that was going to be held in the jungles of Essequibo. The training was canceled because of budget cuts.

Stepping off of the elevator onto his floor at work, WC noted that everything seemed to be getting back to what he considered normal. As he walked toward his office, the noise level stayed just about the same. This was a far different atmosphere than the first day when he returned from his vacation.

Job security is a big thing in the software business. Co-workers are very sensitive about anything situational, especially an individual who can be pointed to who is placing the security of their job in jeopardy. It was a good feeling to WC sensing that his co-workers were comfortable that their careers were secure.

After logging into his desktop, Wallace searched for a request for proposals plus other announcements that would lead to business coming into SBM. It didn't take him long before he came upon the sources-sought announcement put out by the Department of the Navy.

It wasn't often that Felix was not correct when he said that he had insider information concerning government opportunities. Wallace was opening the announcement when his telephone intercom buzzed. It was his manager Leola.

"WC, how are you doing this morning? I was calling to see if you saw that announcement from the Navy on that sources-sought?"

Wallace replied, "Good morning to you. Why, yes, I'm downloading it along with the attachments…"

Leola said before WC could finish, "Wallace, you are right. I didn't see any attachments. Thanks for pointing them out. Anyway, when you are done going over everything, come up to my office so we can talk about it." WC watched his computer screen as the documents were downloading.

"Sure, Leola. Let me finish a couple of other things, and I'll be up to see you in about 20 minutes. Will that be OK?"

"Sure, Wallace, that will be OK. See you in 20 minutes."

The download completed, Wallace asked Alice, his administrative assistant, to make copies and provide one for each of his managers. He then typed up a memo and emailed it to his entire team asking everyone to review the documents and be ready for an afternoon meeting to go over possible approaches to winning the contract for SBM.

Now Wallace turned his attention to reading through the material in preparation for his meeting with Leola.

—

Jacksonville, Florida.

The same morning in Jacksonville, Kyle Martin walked directly into her editor's office without an appointment, closed the office door, and persuasively said, "We need to talk. I have a significant breakthrough on the explosions that have been taking place here in Jacksonville. It's strong enough that the networks will be all over it."

Kyle's editor was well aware of the bombings along with the shootings that had occurred in Brazil, Guyana, and Venezuela. What he did not know was how the incidents were connected to Jacksonville. Kyle powerfully closed the gap, connecting the dots.

"The MIE is the same group that the FBI conducted the raid on in Miami and captured some 23 members at Whitey's Fish Camp on Fleming Island." What Kyle's editor also didn't know was that all of the bombings were a cover-up for the primary objective of blowing up the Federal Reserve Bank and running off with billions of dollars.

Kyle proposed that the news team fly to Essequibo this morning and get as much background information on this historical battle over this small strip of land as possible. Besides gathering information on the MIE, she suggested they also possibly travel to Brazil to find out what happened to the men turned over to the Brazilian government to see if the person who shot the Ministers of Security for Guyana and Venezuela was among them. Finally, she suggested they have at least the beginning of the story ready for the six o'clock news and or the main story available for the 11:00 news the next night. Kyle's editor wasn't surprised at Kyle's request. Over the years, he had become accustomed to many such requests. In almost every case Kyle was right on target about landing a great piece of investigative reporting.

"Kyle, I have one question." A concerned look came over Kyle's face. "The Mayor and the FBI are scheduled to have a press conference this morning at 10:00. The purpose of the meeting is to bring everyone up to date concerning the explosions and what progress is being made to find out who is responsible and if the have any solid leads." Before Kyle's editor could finish, Kyle interrupted him.

"I have it from a very reliable source that the meeting for this morning will be canceled. My source also says that the press conference will be rescheduled for tomorrow afternoon at 5:00." Kyle's editor sat back down in his chair and opened the center drawer. He looked up at Kyle.

"What makes you so sure? To get you to Essequibo in time for all of this to happen, we will need to charter a private plane, put together our best film crew, and get you out of the door now! All of this is going to cost a lot of money. The problem is, if the Mayor and the FBI have their news conference before we are ready with the breaking news story, this will end up not being a breaking news story. I would have burned up a lot of resources that could have been used elsewhere. So, Kyle, before you answer, I want you to give me assurance that we will have time to break the story before the Mayor and the FBI press conference."

Kyle pulled out her notepad and thumbed through the pages as if she was trying to verify the information. She stopped at a couple of pages in her book, pulled a yellow highlighter from her pocketbook, and then began to highlight several lines in the notepad.

After thumbing through her notes, Kyle raised her head, looking her editor directly into his eyes.

"This is going to be the story that will get me promoted to a national news position. The Mayor and the FBI's press conference will not be held until tomorrow afternoon."

Her editor pulled out of the center draw of his desk the voucher notebook he needed to sign off on for the funding necessary for Kyle to leave for Essequibo.

On the opposite side of Jacksonville, FBI Agent Faye Cook-Little was ending her telephone conversation with Jerry Clark, the Mayor's Public Relations Director.

"Jerry, let's put it down for 5:00 or 6:00 tomorrow. I'm sure I will have all of the information I need from Washington FBI office and the US State Department to be able to give enough details at the press conference to satisfy your requirements and the Mayor's requirements."

"Faye, there is still one thing. I'd like to meet with you, let's say sometime this evening, which should give you enough time to have all of your information so I can provide any comments to your report from the Mayor's viewpoint. Is that possible?"

Agent Cook-Little pondered what Jerry was asking. The meeting would actually give Jerry a chance to get information so he could prepare the Mayor's talking points for the press conference. Faye also knew that Jerry was a good public relations man. In fact, Jerry Clark was one of the best. What Jerry really wanted to do was to have a chance to insert a word or a phrase that would send a good impression to the voting public so that the Mayor and the city of Jacksonville would be viewed in a positive light. Faye had not seen any figures, but it was certain that the four explosions had some effect on the tourists coming to Jacksonville.

"I'll tell you what, Jerry. Rather than going around and around about your place or mine, just come over to my office. We can talk here. I'll expect you at 9:30 tonight." Jerry agreed, smiling, as he hung up his telephone feeling like he had gotten the upper hand in the conversation.

Faye, on the other hand, was facing a lot of details that she had to put together before the press conference the following afternoon.

SBM Headquarters, Gaithersburg, Maryland.

Back at SBM, Wallace was walking up the steps to his meeting with Leola. He decided to take the stairs rather than the elevator to give him a last chance to think through what the Navy was asking for in the sources-sought requirement document that was just released.

As Wallace approached Leola's office, her young administrative assistance waved for WC to go directly in.

"Good morning, Leola. How are you doing today?"

As usual, Leola was sitting at her conference table going over spreadsheets of the contracts that she had responsibility for. Looking up over her half-frame glasses, she said, "WC, I know I've said this once, but I'll say it again. I'm sure glad that you are back. Somehow the contracts that you manage are always the ones I have the least problems with. You do excellent work, Wallace, so now tell me what you think of the Navy's request for a contractor to do HIDS?"

"Leola, I know that this may sound a little crazy, but I believe that the Navy wrote these requirements gearing the contract to be awarded to SBM." WC looked at Leola to get her facial impression.

"All right then, WC, give me the facts as to why you think this."

Wallace opened up his folder and pointed to pages and sections of the document he had highlighted in yellow.

Leola opened her copy of the Navy's requirement document, and they began to compare notes. For the next 20 minutes, they broke the material down section by section. They started to agree that a lot of what the Navy was asking for in the sources-sought SBM was the only software contractor that had the past experience to meet the Navy's requirement.

What was the standout condition was the Navy was seeking a company that had completed writing software code for the EA-21F Joker Electronic Attack Aircraft.

The Joker was the third generation electronic warfare and countermeasures attack aircraft, replacing the EA-18F Growler and before the Growler the EA-6B Prowler. Wallace and Leola knew that the weapons systems built into the Joker made the aircraft the most cutting edge electronic attack aircraft in the world and that no one company knew what all of those capabilities were.

The Navy did this by not awarding the whole job to only one contractor. The contracts to develop and build the weapons systems and capacities of the EA-21F Joker were broken down into so many subcontracts that no one company could tell what was being put together. It appeared now that the Navy was ready to bring everything together.

WC and Leola knew that the latest upgrade to the Joker's software systems was done by SBM less than two years ago. SBM was the lead and had six subcontractors working on several smaller modules in the project.

"As you can see, Leola, there are two requirements that a contractor must meet before they can even submit a bid. The first, which we have already completed, is to upgrade the company's security clearance. The second, which I consider a no-brainer, is to go to the pre-bid conference, which is a classified meeting, and receive the briefing on the EA-21F Joker. The meeting will be held on the John F. Kennedy Aircraft Carrier, which will be in Jacksonville, Florida." As Wallace was talking, Leola looked at her desk for her cigarettes.

"WC, I think you're right. When is this pre-bid conference?"

Gathering up his paperwork because he was sensing that Leola was planning to go downstairs for a smoke break, Wallace answered, "It's about two weeks before the pre-bid conference. I'll submit the forms to indicate that SBM will be attending and follow up with the travel request for Felix and myself before the close of business today." With her cigarettes in her hand, Leola started walking toward her door.

"OK then, WC, get all of the paperwork on my desk by the close of business today, and I'll sign off on it. Also, give me some idea of who may be our competition in this and who you will select as our subcontractors. I would guess you need to get started on lining up the contractors as soon as possible."

Following Leola to the door, Wallace replied, "You're right. My thoughts are to go with the same subcontractors that we won the upgrade contract with. Their past performance will speak for itself, I would think."

As Leola and Wallace walked toward the elevator, Leola said, "I wonder why they want us to go to the pre-bid conference on the John F. Kennedy?"

Wallace pushed the button for the elevator. He turned to Leola and said, "I could only imagine that they may have a prototype weapon system, and the Navy wants to do a demonstration. This way the contractor who wins the bid will have a good idea of what the Navy is looking for in a final laser firing weapons system."

Chapter 37

The Mayor's Office, the same morning, Jacksonville, Florida.

Henry Bubba Webb was on the telephone talking to his friend Joe Singletary. "Well, I really appreciate that, Joe." Bubba was smiling from ear to ear.

"Seriously, Bubba, Helen smuggled in my tablet, and I have been catching up on all of the news feeds. From the *Miami Herald* to the *Jacksonville Journal*, you have been covered and covered in detail. The story of what has happened in Jacksonville and how you have handled the situation has even been picked up by three or four major newspapers. There is a short read in the *Guardian* and the *New York Times*. They are covering the story, and all of what I have been reading has been positive news. This is great stuff, and you should be proud of what is going on."

Joe Singletary was sitting up in his bed at Shands Hospital, a couple of IV's still attached to him. "Just one last thing, Bubba, before Helen gets here. Helen has been getting on my back."

Bubba turned his attention to his office door when he heard someone knocking. It was Jerry Clark. Bubba waved to Jerry to come.

"Joe, guess who just walked in? Jerry, let's take a break so you can get some rest and we will talk later, maybe when I come over tonight. Take care." Mayor Webb hung up the phone and turned his attention to Jerry Clark.

"Was that Joe on the telephone?" Jerry Clark said as he took a seat in front of the Mayor's desk."

"Yes, it was Jerry. Joe said that you and he are supposed to get together this afternoon to discuss some of our campaign strategists, is that right?" Jerry Clark opened a notebook and looked at the Mayor.

"That's correct, Mr. Mayor. What I want to do this morning is go over some talking points that I plan to discuss with Joe, but before we do that, I wanted to talk to you about my telephone call with FBI Agent Faye Cook-Little." Bubba Webb stood up and came around his desk and sat down in the chair beside Jerry Clark.

"OK, tell me what you have."

The Mayor knew that press conference to give the media the update on the explosions had been canceled for that morning, but he had not been filled in on the details as to why.

Jerry Clark wrote in the details and went on to inform the Mayor about the meeting that he and Faith Cook-Little would be having that evening at the FBI's temporary office on Beach Boulevard. Jerry emphasized that his objective was to see exactly how Faye was going to present the details of the tie-in between the group that calls itself the Movement for the Independence of Essequibo and their objective to rob the Federal Reserve Bank. He also wanted to ensure that Faye presented everything in a positive light regarding how the Mayor, the Mayor's Office, and the Jacksonville government handled everything in a professional fashion.

Bubba Webb was pleased with what he had heard this morning from Joe Singletary and now from Jerry Clark. It seemed as if everything was falling into place for the Mayor's upcoming push to run for the highest office in the country. Funding was coming in, and his campaign bank accounts were filling up. He had people standing in the wings waiting to give him endorsements, individuals in positions that would pull other centers of influence into his team. These centers of power would translate into more dollars and more endorsements. Things were really looking up for Henry Bubba Webb and the city of Jacksonville.

—

SBM Headquarters, Gaithersburg, Maryland.

Wallace stepped off the elevator while Leola continued to the ground floor for a walk and her smoke break. When Wallace reached his desk, he quickly answered a couple of emails then turned his attention to completing the paperwork to let the Navy know that SBM would be coming to the pre-bid conference in Jacksonville and would be submitting a bid proposal for the award.

After completing the voucher requesting airline tickets and hotel lodging for himself and Felix for the trip to Jacksonville, he then emailed the paperwork to the SBM Travel Department with a copy to Leola for approval. Felix would be Wallace's senior software engineer and lead programmer on the proposal, but as the program manager, Wallace had to know as much about the project as anyone on his team.

WC was not the type of manager who just sat on the sidelines. So Wallace turned his attention to doing research on laser weapons, particularly how far the Navy had advanced on laser weapons systems and how much funding was allocated for lasers in the current budget.

Wallace told Alice to hold all calls and to take messages because he would be doing project research until it was time for him to leave for the airport to pick up Eve and he didn't want to be disturbed.

While just at the beginning of his research, WC saw that SBM would be competing against some of the best and biggest software and weapons system integrators in the business. IBM, CSC, Raytheon, Northrop Grumman, just to name a few. All of them had been experimenting and working to develop a laser weapon system that could be placed on a high-performance aircraft such as a jet fighter.

━

Jacksonville, Florida.

At the same time in Jacksonville, FBI Agent Faye Cook-Little was putting together the information she would need, for now, rescheduled press conference with the Mayor concerning the progress of the investigation into the Jacksonville explosions.

Faye logged onto the Agency system and begin to email to the Washington DC office to obtain all the information that could be provided concerning the MIE. She also looked up the name of the agent who was the lead on the bombing and shootings in South America. Just as Faye hit the enter key, she glanced at her cell phone and saw that Terry Jackson, the FBI forensic expert out of the Atlanta office, had sent her a text message. It only read "please call when you have a chance." Making a mental note, Faye continued to make the necessary arrangements to present the MIE as the primary suspects for the explosions in Jacksonville.

As information started to pour in, the likelihood that the MIE was behind everything was beginning to fit together — well almost together. Still, Faye could see that, for the purpose of satisfying the need to have a suspect to point to as well as to turn any attention away from the fact that four CIA agents were killed in the explosions, the MIE would do nicely for the present.

Faye heard a buzzing sound. It was her personal cell phone going off. She reached into a pocketbook and saw that it was a message coming from Kyle Martin. It read: "My editor bought off on my story. Flying to Essequibo and should be landing shortly. I will keep you updated on what I find. Love you, Kyle."

Normally, Faye would have been very upset about Kyle sending her a text message. Early in their relationship, they had agreed to only send messages when they wanted to meet at the Holiday Inn Express. But now, if things worked out the way that they had planned at their last meeting, Kyle would be moving to a larger city, a city where homosexual relationships are more acceptable.

Turning her attention back to the matter at hand, Faye re-read the accounts concerning the assassinations of the two ministers of security that took place in Brazil. Another small detail caught Fay's attention. According to the report, Eve Harding and Wallace Barker flew to Rio de Janeiro the day after the first explosion in Jacksonville. They stayed at the same hotel where both of the ministers stayed, and they arrived in the Jacksonville just one day before the last blasts that took place in Jacksonville. What also supported Faye's theory was that the Washington DC FBI office held Wallace Barker for questioning when he arrived at the Washington DC airport. Harding and Barker were becoming persons of interest.

Faye began to finalize her report and put it in the format that she would be presenting it at the news conference tomorrow afternoon around 5:00. Agent Cook-Little even had two persons of interest to add to the investigation. To get the approval she needed to send it to her direct supervisor and from there to the district office. If it were determined to be of a sensitive nature, the district office

369

would forward the report to FBI Headquarters in Washington. Just as Faye was about to hit the enter button on her keyboard, the telephone on her desk rang. Faye answered the call before she sent the document.

"This is FBI Field Agent Cook-Little. How may I help you?"

An unfamiliar voice answered. "Faye, this is Deputy Chief of CIA Operations South America Roy Benning. I'd like to talk to you about your explosions." Faye hesitated for a second. She knew a call like this would be coming, but the timing was a little daunting.

"Certainly. This is an excellent time."

Faye and Roy Benning discussed what had taken place in Jacksonville over the last ten days. Faye also talked about her theory concerning the MIE. Roy was relieved and agreed that it was a good way to stay away from any involvement with the CIA, both from the standpoint of an operational site being located in Jacksonville and the loss of four Desk Chiefs in the explosions.

Roy Benning approved of the approach Faye was taking and offered any assistance that she may need. Roy told Faye that there were probably some inaccurate points in the report, but that would be expected. If you presented an airtight case, it would smell of a conspiracy and the news media would be all over them and so it's best to have some inaccurate details they could punch holes in.

Faye thanked Roy Benning for his input and for offering any help. She ended the conversation by telling Roy that she would be in touch if she needed anything.

After reading over the report one last time, Faye hit the enter button and sat back in her chair to wait for the reaction from her supervisors. Picking up her personal cell phone, Faye did something that she seldom did, reply to a text message from Kyle: "Finished up everything on my end. Press conference is still scheduled for tomorrow at 5:00. Sitting here waiting for Jerry Clark to come by so we can go over what I will be presenting tomorrow. Love you too, Faye."

—

Parika, Essequibo, Guyana.

Krish was standing in the marketplace of Parika among some 500 merchant stalls where farmers, fishermen, and any other types of vendors were trying to sell their goods. It was a very busy place filled with the sound, smells, and atmosphere typical of any tropical marketplace. Hundreds of people were jamming the area, all trying to get a bargain on fish, fruit, clothing, and a thousand other goods or services.

With a shaved head, a full beard, and wearing a set of sunglasses, Krish had changed his appearance totally from when he was training at the Plantation in Florida. The market provided the ideal place for Krish to blend in and not be noticed.

Across from the market, on the northwest corner and just up the alley, was a small café, the Mermaid's Net. Since Krish had been back in Essequibo, he had discovered that both the governments of Guyana and Venezuela were aggressively searching for anyone associated with the MIE, arresting everyone they caught and immediately turning them over to the Brazilian government as an accomplice to the killings of the two ministers.

Through a friend of Krish's brother, Krish received a message that the few members of the MIE still in the area met at the café on the first Tuesday of each month. Krish couldn't be sure if the message was genuine and not the element of a plan to trap more members of the MIE. He had confirmed reports of other members of the organization being lured into traps set up by the government and captured. So he positioned himself in the marketplace at a location that he could clearly observe the front entrance into the Mermaid's Net.

This was going to be Krish's final attempt to make contact with the MIE in Guyana. If this did not pan out, he was going to Venezuela to see if he could have any better luck finding what was left of his organization.

Sometimes jokingly and at other times not as a joke, members of the MIE who lived in Guyana were referred to as the brawn of the MIE and the members who lived in Venezuela as the brains.

Krish's attention was pulled away from watching the entrance to the café to some commotion that was taking place at the opposite end of the marketplace. From his vantage point, he could

371

see a local news television van being parked and the crewmembers raising the satellite antenna. A small group of people began to gather around the truck. Although Krish was in a position where he couldn't hear what was going own, he could clearly see an attractive woman and two men with cameras step out of an SUV that pulled up beside the television van.

Immediately after stepping out of the car, one cameraman started photographing the woman and the other started taking shots of the crowd and surrounding area. Krish turned his focus back to watching the Mermaid's Net. Just as he did, he thought he recognized a member from the MIE entering the facility. Krish decided to wait for a minute or two before going into the café. As he waited, he identified a second member of the MIE, a man that Ranuel had introduced him to before they left for Miami.

In Krish's mind, he had seen one confirmed and a possible second member of the MIE entering the Mermaid's Net, which was enough for him to risk going into the café to see if he could speak with them. Krish walked less than ten feet when out of the corner of his right eye he saw the flashing lights of several police vehicles, and at the same time two unmarked cars pulled up in front of the entrance to the Mermaid's Net. Men with automatic rifles, some wearing assault gear, and others in civilian clothing, quickly jumped out of the vehicles and ran into the café. All attention in the marketplace turned in the direction of the alley and the Mermaid's Net.

Krish heard several flash-bang grenades followed by automatic and small arms fire. Smoke came rushing out of the front door of the café followed by several people running for safety and their lives. The policemen on the outside of the café were already putting up security lines restricting anyone from crossing. People from the marketplace and other areas of the square pushed their way up to the marked yellow lines, attempting to get a glimpse of what was going on. Krish walked within four feet of the yellow tape, close enough to hear several of the police guards talking. Krish moved a few feet closer to the policemen guarding the yellow taped off line limiting access to the alley where the café and the police raid were located.

"We only caught two. If we had waited for a for about an hour or so, there would have been more."

Krish was not surprised by what he was hearing. For sure, the Security Police had been watching the café for some time. Krish suddenly heard the voice of the news reporter who had rushed to the scene of the shooting from the other side of the marketplace.

"This is Kyle Martin of WZXL Television News bringing you this breaking news live from Parpkia, Essequibo, Guyana, Headquarters for the Movement for the Independence for Essequibo, or the MIE."

With smoke flowing from the windows and doors of the Mermaid's Net café in the background of Kyle Martin's broadcast, the scene gave the image of the full threat of the MIE as a terrorist organization. Kyle Martin continued to air as gunfire was echoing behind her.

"The Guyana's Security Police just conducted a raid, capturing at least two of the key leaders of this terrorist organization. You can still hear the gunfire as the MIE is putting up resistance until the end. The MIE is the same organization that the FBI identified as the terrorist group responsible for the four explosions that just recently took place in Jacksonville. Through unnamed sources, WZXL Television has learned that the MIE's motive was to use the explosions as a decoy while they robbed the US Federal Reserve Bank located in downtown Jacksonville, Florida."

Kyle Martin's live report, coupled with the background footage of the Guyana's Security Police raid, gave credibility to the allegations that the MIE was the terrorist group that is responsible for the explosions in Jacksonville.

From his right side, Krish felt a tug on his shirt. Slowly turning in the direction of the tug, he recognized a face he had not seen since they were arrested in Florida, a member of MIE. Krish could not remember his name, but he knew him. The man slowly spoke. "Follow me, and I'll get you out of here." Krish took a quick look around the area to verify that no one was watching them and followed the man back into the crowd and away from the Mermaid's Net café.

Kyle Martin lowered her mic and looked around the area. "Good job, everyone. I think we have enough. Let's get into the van so we can start cutting and putting our broadcast together as we drive to the airfield."

—

Sterling Business Machine, Gaithersburg, Maryland.

Wallace C. Barker was still looking over documents concerning the laser weapons program of the Navy and how far the development of the weapon had advanced. It was becoming clear that the contract that SBM was awarded four years ago may have been the stimulus to promote the progress of the system to where the Navy now believed that the weapon could be produced.

The breakthrough could have been the million lines of software code that was delivered to the Navy. The problem was that Wallace had no way to determine what was written in the code.

Wallace was pretty sure that the Navy knew for two reasons. First, because they were proceeding with a new contract for laser weapon development. Second, it seemed that the Navy was leveraging the contract such that Sterling Business Machine would be receiving the award. Wallace had found out enough to know that SBM needed to win the contract. His development group had to put together and present a winning proposal to the Navy.

It was almost lunch time, so WC decided to take a break, go to the gym for a workout and pick up a sandwich. It would be a few more hours before he would be meeting Eve at the airport.

At the health spa, Wallace's regular workout routine, after his warm up exercises was weightlifting, stationary bicycle, and a two-mile run, followed by 15 minutes in the sauna.

WC would then shower and pick up a sandwich or salad. Today he put a little extra into his routine. The weekend after he returned from the jazz festival he would be going to his Special Forces Reserve duty, but WC wanted to build up his blood flow and stamina for the anticipated sexual encounters that he would be having with Eve this weekend.

Setting a faster-running pace than his usual runs, Wallace visualized Eve's athletically well-defined body. As he circled the indoor running track of the spa, in his mind he could see himself touching each curve, sensing her responding to each touch with the sounds of pleasure. Sex was not a problem in Wallace's and Eve relationship. If Wallace could resolve those other unanswered questions, this could be the right woman for him.

After Wallace had a shower, he was walking out the door of the health spa when he ran into three JBI employees who had worked for him on the Navy's contract four years ago. Wallace thought that this presented an excellent opportunity to see if JBI would be interested in being a subcontractor to SBM on the future Navy contract.

JBI was a small software programming company that had carved out a place in the market by being a reliable subcontractor that produced flawless software code. They greeted each other and began to engage in small talk, slowly moving into the possibility of doing business with SBM again. Wallace thanked them for the great job that they did as subcontractors on the previous contract and assured them that he would keep JBI in mind if anything else came up in the future. Just as Wallace was about to walk away, one of the gentlemen asked about Eve Harding and how she was enjoying living in Canada.

"Eve didn't relocate to Canada. She moved to Jacksonville, Florida, and is teaching high school chemistry."

The guy who asked the question replied. "Oh, I guess she changed her mind. While she was with JBI, Eve would always talk about moving to Canada to make her home, even applying for dual citizenship."

Wallace said his goodbye and headed for his office. WC didn't think too much of what the guy said. It was not unusual for people to talk about the many places they that wanted to live.

—

Montevilla Bartram Park, Gated Community, Jacksonville, Florida.

Eve Harding was at home in her bedroom packing the last few items into a suitcase in preparation for her flight to Maryland. Her house telephone rang, and she saw on the caller ID that it was Tony.

Switching the button on the phone to the secure encrypted mode, she said, "Hello, my little darling. How are you doing?"

"Mom, you did switch the phone to the secure mode?"

"Of course, darling. We are so close to the end I would not want to make any mistakes." After a brief pause, Tony spoke.

"Just wanted to let you know that I transferred the money to close on the house from our Cayman Island account to HSBC. We should have a settlement in the next two or three weeks." Eve was smiling as she was listening to her daughter.

"That's so wonderful. Everything is going as we planned, but we must be careful. This is when the bottom could fall out, and we do not want that to happen."

"OK, Mom. I must go. I have to log some flying time. Love you."

With a mother's sadness in her eye, Eve replied, "Love you too."

Eve left the bedroom, checked the security camera's, turned on the security system, and went to the hidden room at the rear of her garage. Sitting down at her computer, Eve opened a file folder labeled "The Plan." She moved to a page that was titled checklist. Eve checked off four items on the list: money transfer, house settlement, closing, close out the account. Eve then saved everything into an encrypted file and logged off the network. She turned to the corner of the room and said, "Mama, you are going to be so proud of me when this is over."

Eve Harding went back into her house to complete the packing for her trip to Maryland to spend the weekend with Wallace. As she was leaving the house, sitting in her car in the garage, she typed a text message to Wallace: Lover, departing for the airport. Will be seeing you shortly. Eve.

Wallace was walking into his office after completing his workout at the spa. He heard the sound of his cellular phone signaling him that a text message had arrived. WC pulled out his phone and saw that it was from Eve. He sent a reply: Will pick up at curbside. Looking forward to a great weekend. WC.

Chapter 38

FBI Tempory Office Jacksonville, Florida.

Faye Cook-Little left her office and walked down the hall to the conference room, turned on the lights, and began to lay folders on the table. She was getting prepared for her meeting with Jerry Clark. Faye also intended for the meeting to be somewhat of a dress rehearsal for the press conference scheduled for the next afternoon. Faye was still counting on Kyle Martin's breaking news report being aired on television just at the same time or a few minutes before the press conference. Kyle's story coming at just about the same time as the news conference would give credibility to what Faye would be presenting.

Faye knew Jerry Clark. Actually, she knew him very well. Jerry was a very detail-oriented public relations manager, and she thought the Mayor very fortunate to have someone of Jerry's caliber working for him. But Faye knew that if someone could put a hole in her story, Jerry was the person.

—

Mayor's Office, Jacksonville, Florida.

Bubba Webb was driving home from the office, taking in the night skyline of his beautiful Jacksonville as he was on his cellular telephone talking to Jerry Clark.

"So, Jerry, are you sticking to your schedule to meet with that FBI agent tonight?"

Jerry Clark, still in his office and sitting at his desk, replied, "That's correct, Mr. Mayor. We are to meet at the temporary FBI office on Beach Boulevard."

Bubba Webb pulled into his favorite ABC Store. "Debra wanted me to pick up some of the wine she likes," Bubba said as he was stepping out of his car. "Well, I'll let you get on with your business, Jerry. Oh, one more thing. Joe Singletary will be coming back in another month or two. I think I'm going to let Joe go full time working the reelection except for emergency readiness. Let me know what you think about that sometime tomorrow."

Jerry was looking at his watch and thinking that he should leave for his meeting with FBI Agent Fay Cook-Little. "I have a good idea of what I'll tell you tomorrow, but I'll hold it until then."

"Jerry, that's fine. Think about it overnight, and we'll talk tomorrow, either before or after the press conference. Speak to you then."

"OK, Bubba. Have a good night, Mr. Mayor."

Jerry Clark started to clean off his desk. It was only a 10 to 15-minute drive to the FBI temporary office. He was looking forward to having a one-on-one conversation with Agent Cook-Little. After seeing what Faye was going to present at the press conference, if he could add a spin here and there that would let the viewing public walk away with a favorable view of the Mayor, which would be a victory for the upcoming campaign.

After turning everything off, Jerry Clark picked up his backpack, put his laptop computer in the bag, and headed for the City Hall garage.

—

Ronald Reagan International Air Port, Washington, DC.

Rather than picking Eve Harding up at the curb, WC decided to wait for her in the terminal. He loved to see Eve walk, especially when she was wearing high heels.

Wallace found himself standing in front of the information board just as her flight was landing. From where he was standing it was less than 100 feet from the security area and where she would be exiting from her gate. WC took a position a few feet from the exit gate such that he still would have a good vantage point when the area started to fill up with other family and friends to pick up and greet their arrival.

After checking his cellular telephone for any new emails or text messages, WC noticed a crowd coming down the exit way. A flight must have arrived. The flow began to increase, an indication that several planes had landed. The group of people walking past

WC had grown to the point where he was standing on his toes to get a good view and not miss Eve walking by. WC decided to call her, but just when he pulled out his cellular phone, he heard her voice.

"WC. WC, I'm over here." Wallace looked around until he was able to associate the sound and the direction. Eve was standing beside the baggage stall waiting. Wallace made his way through the people waiting to get their bags. Eve jumped into Wallace's arms, giving him a deep passionate kiss.

"Lover, its only been a week since we got back from our vacation, but it seems like years. I'm so glad that you came in to pick me up. How far do we have to go to get to the car?"

Smiling, WC looked for Eve's suitcase. "Oh, we are not that far from the terminal. Just a few feet after we get off the elevator."

WC held Eve's hand while pulling the suitcase behind them. "Eve, I have my things in the car, and I thought that we should get on the road now. We can catch the 10:00 concert tonight." They got on the elevator, and Wallace pushed the button for the floor where his car was parked.

As they stepped off, Eve squeezed Wallace's hand and said, "I have an idea. Why don't we pick up carry-out, go to your house, eat, get drunk, and screw?"

Wallace responded with a smile. "Sounds like a plan to me."

—

FBI Tempory Office Jacksonville, Florida.

Jerry Clark pulled into the parking lot. He parked, pulled down the sun visor, popped open the mirror and adjusted his tie. This was his first time going to the FBI's tempory office. Jerry thought to himself that this location presented a much better atmosphere than the downtown office. Every time he had to go there, Jerry would feel that he had to make sure that he was not under indictment for a crime. The atmosphere in this location was as if he was walking into an insurance company.

The front entrance was marked by a full glass door. On the other side of the door was a security guard sitting behind a desk. To gain entry Jerry Clark had to push a buzzer and the guard buzzed him in.

"My name is Jerry Clark. I'm with the Mayor's office, and I'm here to meet with FBI Agent Faye Cook-Little."

The man sitting behind the desk, without taking his eyes off Jerry, pulled a sign-in book from under the desk and pushed it in front of Jerry along with a pen. "Please sign in. Agent Cook-Little left the word to expect you. After you sign in, go through this door and up the stairs to the second floor. She is waiting for you in the conference room."

Jerry Clark thanked the security guard and headed for the door. As he walked up the steps, he began to focus on what he hoped to accomplish in the meeting.

Faye was walking from the break room holding two cups in her hands. "I see you were able to find us. We are still getting used to not being in that downtown Jacksonville environment. I have a cup of tea for you. I guess you still are drinking tea, not coffee." Jerry was at the entrance to the conference room, standing there watching Faye walk toward him.

"Why, yes, I'm still a tea person. Never been able to stand the taste of the coffee bean. You should switch over." Faye didn't reply. She just walked into the conference room and sat the cups on the table. She turned around to shake Jerry's hand.

"Have a seat, Jerry. As you can see, I've laid a lot of material on the table for us to go over. I also wanted you to see how I came to my conclusion concerning the Movement for the Independence of Essequibo."

After shaking Faye's hand, Faye sat down, but Jerry continued to stand, taking off his suit jacket while staring down her blouse. Faye very casually repositioned her clothing while pushing another folder over to the side of the table, pointing for Jerry to have a seat. Jerry smiled and hung his jacket behind the chair and sat down. He then opened the folder and began to thumb through the pages.

"Very impressive, Faye. It appears that you have really done your homework. There is a lot of information contained in these folders, so where do we start?"

Looking across the table into Jerry's eyes, she replied, "Like in any other process, we start at the beginning."

Faye started by educating Jerry about the little piece of land mass known as Essequibo and the 100-year dispute over the land between Venezuela and Guyana, which was now more valuable than ever because of the oil that may be located there. The Movement for the Independence for Essequibo grew legs out of this dispute.

Agent Cook-Little went on to tell her theory that the MIE needed money, a lot of money to finance the movement, and someone found out about the Federal Reserve Bank in sleepy little Jacksonville. The four explosions were set off as diversions to keep the police and all of the authorities running around in a chaotic situation and not focusing on the bank. While the police, FBI, and Homeland Security were conducting their investigation and trying to predict where the next bomb was going off, the MIE would slip into the Federal Reserve Bank and steal the money. Faye also speculated that more explosions were planned. What they didn't plan for was that another cell within the MIE would assassinate the Ministers of Security for Venezuela and Guyana in Brazil. The Brazilian government found out about the MIE and their training facility in Miami, made contact with State Department, and the rest was where they currently stood.

Jerry Clark raised his head from looking down at the folder while Faye was speaking. "Okay, Faye. All of that sounds good. But where do the Mayor and the Jacksonville Police Department fit into all this?"

Faye Cook-Little pushed another folder across the table toward Jerry Clark. "Jerry, remember I said earlier that more explosions were coming? Well, due to the investigative work of the JPD, those explosions did not occur because the Mayor directed the JPD to add more security at each of those locations. You see, the MIE was going to bomb City Hall, the Court House, and the downtown post office, but the Mayor and JPD's actions stopped all of that."

A big smile appeared across Jerry's face. "Good, very good. I like it; I really like it. Now at what point should we have the Chief of Police say something?"

Looking across the table into Jerry's eyes, Faye knew that Jerry had bought her story lock, stock, and barrel, everything she had laid out.

"Great question. What I figure is that the Chief would come after me and speak on continued security measures that he and the Mayor are considering, and what if any impact those measures would have on the community. What do you think?"

As Faye was looking at Jerry, he was going back through the folders as if he had lost something and was trying to find it. Faye began to feel nervous.

Jerry was fixated on his search, head down, moving from folder to folder. He was thumbing through pages, taking one or two pages out of each. Then, taking his pen, he underlined individual sentences, and sometimes entire paragraphs, and circled key words.

"What, Jerry? Did I miss something? Do you think the Chief should speak first or maybe the Mayor?"

Jerry stopped searching, sat back in his chair, laid his pen down on the table, rubbed his hands over his head and took a deep breath. Looking at Faye, Jerry said, "There is something missing, but I can't put my finger on it — and I'm not certain if it should be here."

Faye got up from her side of the table and walked around to Jerry's. She sat on the table looking down at the folders. Faye touched Jerry's hand while looking at the folders.

"Jerry, show me what you are looking for and maybe I can lead you to it so we can resolve whatever you are thinking about." The mood and atmosphere of the meeting changed. Looking into Faye's eyes, Jerry took a deep breath.

"Faye, whatever happened to us? Why is it that we didn't make it?" Still holding on to Jerry's hand, Faye stood up and walked back to the other side of the desk and sat down.

"Jerry, let's get back on point. After we finish this, maybe we can go get a drink and discuss that. We did have some good times, but do you see anything I need to change or adjust?" Jerry looked down at the folders and started to collect them.

"No, I think you have done an excellent job putting everything together. I really like how you have placed the Mayor and our Chief of Police in the position to take practical and decisive steps to head off any future explosions to ensure the safety of the

Jacksonville community. So no I have no other suggestions for the news conference. Where would you like to go to get that drink?"

Faye smiled, then said, "Why don't we go over to the Omni. They serve excellent Long Island ice teas. Let me put all of this away, and I'll meet you over there." Faye started putting all of the folders together.

—

The Townhouse of Wallace C. Barker.

In his house robe, Wallace was standing in front of his fridge with the door open, staring in. He raised his head and turned away from the refrigerator to look at the clock over his stove; it read 3:00 AM. WC was searching his fridge to see if there was still an energy drink left. From the upstairs bedroom, he heard Eve call out.

"WC, darling. When are you coming back to bed? I'm still hungry! I need you to come up here to fill my hunger with your hot passion." Just as the last words from Eve was heard, WC found the energy drink. He popped open the can, consuming the ice cold beverage as he was walking upstairs to his bedroom.

Walking into the bedroom, he disrobed and pulled the covers back off of Eve. As the covers were exposing Eve's body, Eve moaned and said, "Do me first, and then I'll do you; if you really give me a big one, I'll see that you get a big one too."

When WC woke up, the sun was piercing through the curtains in his bedroom. Eve was sitting in the chair across from the bed lacing up her running shoes. Eve looked over at WC lying in bed and smiled.

"I'm going for a quick run before we leave." Wallace sat up in the bed. "If you give me a minute to put my things on, I'll join you."

"Sure, I'll be downstairs stretching."

The bright morning sun along with a cool breeze made for the right elements for a pleasurable early morning run. WC didn't have the opportunity to stretch for they just started out running the minute he came downstairs.

"Let's do a couple of miles out and back. When we get back, we can change and leave," Wallace said as they started out. There was no response from Eve.

Just as they were topping the last hill headed back to WC's townhouse, Wallace said, "How is your daughter doing? Have you spoken to her since we returned from the trip?"

"Let's pick up the pace," Eve replied as if she had not heard him. "We need to get back so we can change and get on the road."

After showering and changing, they got on the road to the jazz festival.

Eve adjusted the car seat back and fell asleep. Wallace wanted the weekend to be fun, and he wondered why he asked about Eve's daughter. In a sense he wanted her to know that he knew, but he also wanted to know why she had not told him before. Wallace then thought back to Rio de Janeiro, when they were in the gift shop and on the beach, Eve using the cell phone when they had promised each other not to use any electronic devices until they returned.

While WC was driving, he looked over at Eve sleeping so peacefully. Wallace wanted to wake her up and get some questions answered. Wallace had a 30 thousand dollar wedding set, and before he made the decision to ask Eve to marry him, WC thought he deserved some answers.

Eve woke up as Wallace was pulling off the interstate. "What are you doing? This couldn't be our exit for Berk. We have another 45 minutes to an hour before we reach Berk?"

"I need to get some gas. The highway sign showed that a Texaco has some cheap gas." Eve rolled over on her shoulder with her back to WC, looking out the window.

After Wallace had completed filling the car, he stepped into the mini market and purchased two cups of coffee. When he got back to his vehicle, WC tapped on the window on the passenger side and Eve opened the window. Wallace handed her a cup of coffee.

"Thanks, WC. This is just what I needed." Wallace pulled back onto the interstate headed for Berk, Pennsylvania, and the jazz festival.

"I guess you aren't going to ask me how I found out that Tony was a girl?" Eve continued to sip on her coffee. Without waiting for a response from Eve, Wallace continued.

"My second day back in the office after our vacation, when I walked in I found two FBI field agents waiting to interview me. The purpose of the meeting was that Tony was up for recertification to have her security clearance moved to a different level. During the interview, they referred to Toni as she; when I corrected the agent who said this first and stated that Toni was really a female, they showed me your daughter's birth certificate and a picture." Slowly sipping the hot coffee, Eve continued staring at the road ahead. WC quickly turned his eyes to Eve and then looked back at the highway.

"You are always talking about our relationship and how we should be honest with each other. But it seems to be a one-way communication flow with you." It all began to come out, his qualms about all of the strange activities from Rio de Janeiro to the trip home to Jacksonville.

"I know I'm going all over the place, and everything probably has a simple answer. Sure you can accuse me of being insecure or anything."

All the questions Wallace had been putting off asking, he laid them out, starting from their vacation trip to Rio, the plane ride back to Fort Lauderdale, and why she did not disclose that her child was a girl.

Still looking at the window and sipping her coffee. Eve said, "There's the sign for a rest stop. Drinking all of this coffee, I need to go to the ladies room."

Wallace pulled into the rest area and parked. WC sat on the hood of his BMW waiting while Eve went into the ladies room,

In the ladies room, Eve entered a stall and pulled out her cell phone. She dialed a number. After two rings, Toni answered the call.

"Mom, something must be wrong for you to call me on our secure line. What is it?"

Whispering into the phone, Eve replied, "Why didn't you tell me about you getting a security clearance upgrade. They came to SBM and interviewed Wallace. With some further digging, they could discover the trail from you to me to JBI, the software code I developed and delivered to the Navy via SBM. If that happens, it wouldn't be long for them to see the connection to the Joker aircraft and the laser strikes."

"Get the VIN number of his car, and I'll take care of him," Toni said. "Next week I must fly to Andrew's Air Force Base in DC. The budget people would like to see the plane and ask the pilots some question. I'll do him while I'm in Washington and that will be the end of your boyfriend." Eve peeked through the stall door to see if any was within listening distance.

"I'll get the VIN number, that's not a problem, but hold up. I want to find out how much he knows. Remember, I'm the one who forged his signature on that software delivery four years ago." Toni and Eve agreed to wait the rest of the weekend before making the decision to kill Wallace, giving Eve additional time to find out if WC knew additional information linking them to the software.

After walking back to the car, Eve gave Wallace one of her best smiles. When she got closer, she said, "Did my lover wake up on the wrong side of the bed this morning? Sounds as if you had a pretty bad week. Do you want to talk about what's really bothering you or continue to accuse me of not being honest with you?"

She got back into the car, and as they left the rest area, Wallace backed away from asking Eve questions and began to talk about the million lines of software code that was delivered to the Navy. He didn't know exactly what the software executed, but it was interesting that the Navy put out a sources-sought request for companies with experience in developing software for HIDS. For the next 45 minutes, Eve listened to WC talk about his week. She only interrupted to give him a reassuring smile or to say something like "that's a shame."

Wallace had made reservations at the Hilton Hotel in Berks. Two of the concerts were in the hotel. The one they missed by staying at Wallace's house the night before and the second one that they would attend tonight.

WC got out of the car and walked into the lobby to register. After Wallace was out of sight, Eve got out of the car, walked around to the driver's side, and copied the VIN number of Wallace's car.

She then got back into the car, pulled out her cell phone, and texted Toni, giving her the VIN number along with a note:"Wallace has all of the pieces but is too dumb to put it all together. Proceed with elimination."

386

Chapter 39

Jacksonville City Hall.

The press conference was over, and everything had gone extremely well. Kyle Martin's story was broadcast about 15 minutes before the press conference started. The City Hall media center was too small to handle the crowds of reporters and media people who showed up trying to catch up with WZXL's breaking news story, which left all of the other networks looking like idiots.

Faye Cook-Little's report filled in the blank spaces that Kyle left out. Everyone was happy. The Mayor was seen in a very favorable light along with the chiefs of police and fire. The next question on everyone's mind was how the newspapers were going to run with the story the next day in the morning papers?

Bubba Webb invited everyone back to his private conference room for some down-home refreshments. While the selected group of invitees was coming off the elevators, Jerry Clark's cell phone rang. It was CNN. Jerry answered his phone, and as he was talking to the scheduling manager for the network, a second call came in from MSNBC. Jerry put CNN on hold and switched over to the call from MSNBC.

As the crowd was gathering in the conference room, Jerry could hear Mildred, the Mayor's administrative assistant, shouting from the Mayor's office.

"Jerry. Jerry Clark. I have the scheduling manager from *60 Minutes* on the Mayor's line. He wants to speak to you about doing a segment on Jacksonville and the Mayor."

FBI Agent Faye Cook-Little was still on the ground floor. Faye was just about to step onto the elevator to join the group in the Mayor's conference room when she answered her personal cellular phone. It was Kyle Martin calling from the plane bringing her back to Jacksonville from Brazil.

"Hello."

"Faye, did you see the broadcast?" Faye stepped back from the elevator, moving to a private location in the hall where the conversation would not be overheard.

"I saw the beginning but had to leave the office for the press conference. What I saw was great!"

Apparently, excited Kyle Martin said, "WZXL has already received a call from the network asking us to do the follow-up, but more important to keep me as the lead. It's to be something like a 25-minute piece."

"Oh, that's fantastic Kyle. It sounds like this could be your ticket to the majors."

"Faye, I surely hope so. I miss you. We are just coming back to Jacksonville to pick up some additional equipment and plan out the piece with my editor. Maybe you can come over after I land."

"Call me when you land, Kyle, and we'll see if we can make it happen." Faye ended the conversation.

When she got off of the elevator and started walking to the conference room, Jerry Clark was walking toward her talking on his cell phone. Jerry stepped in front of Faye, standing directly before her so that she couldn't pass. Jerry ended the call.

"OK, call me tomorrow, and we will finish the details." Jerry put his cell phone away as he smiled at Faye. Faye, gazing up into Jerry's eyes, returned the smile.

"Great job, Faye. Everyone seems to be pleased, especially the Mayor. Two of the major networks have lined up to do a spot on Jacksonville, and *60 Minutes* will be here next week."

"That's excellent, Jerry. I haven't heard anything from my boss, but that's a good thing. Say, I have an idea. I'm up for going to the Omni for more drinks sent up to our room. What about you?" Jerry Clark grabbed Faye's hand.

"Why do you think I stopped you. I was thinking the same thing. Off to the Omni Hotel we go."

CIA Headquarters, Langley, Virginia.

In Langley, Virginia Roy Benning was sitting at his desk writing notes from the Kyle Martin broadcast. The CIA media people made a tape of the show and were emailing it to Roy. Roy wanted to review the video several times before he took any action.

He had to be certain that there was nothing that would lead to discovering that the Agency had anything to do with the MIE. The email arrived with the attached video. Roy reviewed the video first by himself. Then he brought in all of his key staff, and they examined it together without Roy in the room.

When they reconvened, there were three points everyone agreed on. First, the MIE locations in Miami, both the headquarters and training center, had somehow slipped by the Agency. Second, the fact that the reporter connected the MIE people who were picked up by the local police at the trailer park were associated with the group responsible for the bombings and who would pull off robbing the Federal Reserve Bank was news to them. The final and third item was the last blast: it was in a remote section of the city, and only two people were killed, unlike the other three bombings. This was the weak point.

After over two hours of discussion, Roy and his staff concluded that there wasn't much they could do now. But the real question was who was actually responsible for the explosions? Roy made a note to call Faye Cook-Little the next morning.

—

Reagan National Airport, Washington, DC.

Wallace pulled his red BMW to the curb at the Southwest Terminal of Ronald Reagan National Airport. Eve quickly got out of the car and WC opened the trunk. Eve grabbed her suitcase, kissed Wallace, and headed for the security check. As she was walking away, Wallace stood by his car watching her sexy walk. He loved to see Eve walk in high heels, especially when she was wearing boots.

Taking the beltway route back to his house, WC opened up his car, driving 20 miles per hour over the speed limit. In his mind, he was recapturing the weekend. It was evident to him that, at this point in their relationship, sex was keeping them together. He was ending the trip without any answers to his questions. However, WC still had hope. He would be flying to Jacksonville on Tuesday to attend the pre-bid seminar for the Navy. He would only be in town for two days. They had agreed to see each other for dinner. Wallace thought about asking to stay at her house, but he didn't. SBM was paying the tab for the trip, so he decided to use the hotel, and besides, Felix would be traveling with him.

Back in the comfort of his townhome, Wallace was going over notes and other information he had gathered concerning lasers. WC had also collected research data on other countries' attempts to build a laser weapon system. Wallace discovered that a laser weapon had a firing signature unique to lasers. A few seconds before the laser beam hit its target, a flash of white light would appear. Wallace typed up a memo concerning the white-light signature preceding the laser hitting its target and sent it off to Felix, asking him to verify the research he had found. WC than decided to go to bed because he had an early morning appointment.

CIA Headquarters, Langley, Virginia.

Roy Benning arrived in his office 20 minutes ahead of his usual time. Just as he sat down at his desk, his secure telephone rang. It was Elkin Ardila. Roy picked up the receiver, but before he could say anything, Elk spoke.

"Roy, why didn't you tell me about Jake and Brenda Jefferson being killed in an explosion?' Roy wasn't surprised by the question. He knew that Elk would find out about the death of his co-worker sooner or later; he just didn't think that it would be this soon.

"Elk, I wanted to be sure that the Director would approve promoting you to the position."

There was silence over the telephone, then Elk replied, "So you have submitted the paperwork for me the take over the South American Desk in Jacksonville? Is that what you are saying?" Roy thought carefully about his next statement. He had not made a decision to give the position to Elk, even though Elk was well-qualified to assume the post. Finishing up the paperwork and forwarding it to the human resources department was not an issue. It would only take 20 minutes at the most, but Roy still had to give the Director and the DDP a heads-up about his decision. Roy didn't think that he would have any problems with the Director going along with his recommendation. However, the DDP was another matter. Just like before, however, if the Director gave the go-ahead to his decision for Elk to take the position, the DDP would have no other choice than to confirm Elk.

"Elk, the only other thing that must happen is for you to agree to assume the position of Desk Chief for South America Operations. Once I hear your agreement on assuming the position, then I can finish the paperwork. The ball is in your court, so what do you say?" Roy was surprised at what came next.

"Well, Roy, who will take over as the Lead Field Agent for Fertile Ground?" Roy Benning's face lit up before he answered Elk.

"As you know, Elk, that would be up to the new Desk Chief. The person in that position would make the recommendation, send the name to me for my concurrence. That's the way the process works."

"OK, Roy. In a couple of days, I have a meeting with Bartolomeu Donnachaidh." Roy cut in before Elk could finish.

"Elk, correct me if I'm wrong, but isn't he the head of the Secret Police in Brazil?"

"You are correct. Bartolomeu is the man who knows where all the bodies are buried. I am to meet with him and his number one field agent, Xoana Cardozo. They are to give me the inside information on the MIE."

"I know Xonana very well," Roy replied. "Not personally but from work she has done in Cuba. Xonana's cover name is Belo. A stunning lady as I recall."

"Yes, that's her. After I have this meeting, I'll fly back to Jacksonville and start organizing the office and select my replacement for Fertile Ground. My meeting with Bartolomeu and Belo will give me an idea of the real damage to the MIE and if it is still salvageable."

Roy Benning was satisfied with what he heard from Elk. Everything was working out. Roy ended the conversation with him and Elk scheduling to have a call later in the week after he had the meeting with Bartolomeu and Belo.

After making several notes concerning his call with Elk, Roy turned his attention to the next item that was on his calendar. Call FBI Agent Faye Cook-Little.

—

Jacksonville Naval Air Station.

The air traffic control tower at the Naval Air Station was buzzing with activity. The beginning of the week was always busy with training operations. The tower was changing flight operation officers from the night shift to the day shift. The day shift officer walked into the control tower. He looked at the situation board and then checked the logbook from the previous night.

Turning to the Chief Petty Officer, he said, "OK, Chief. How busy are we today?"

"Just about typical for a Monday morning, sir."

"Chief, who is piloting that Joker?"

"Flight Officer Tony Harding, call sign Junebug."

"Yes, I see on the board that she is scheduled for a quick run to DC and returns tomorrow. OK, everything seems to be in order. I'm going down for some coffee. Can I bring any of you a cup?"

From the air traffic control tower, Flight Officer Tony Harding was given clearance to take off.

"Junebug, this is ATCT. You are cleared for take-off. Have a safe trip and see you upon your return tomorrow."

"This is Junebug. Roger. Out."

—

Silver Spring, Maryland.

Later that morning, on Route 29 north of Washington DC, a red BMW Z4 was driving in the direction of Baltimore when a flash of white light was seen. The BMW exploded along with four other cars.

By the time the fire department, emergency medical team, police and highway patrol arrived at the scene, all of the vehicles were totally engulfed in flames. After the fires had been put out, the fire department announced that it would take another two hours for everything to cool down to the point where the police could start their investigation. All traffic was redirected to alternate routes.

Once the investigation began, the police found that all of the bodies were burn beyond identification. The cars' license plates were the only thing that could be used to identify who the drivers were.

—

SBM Headquarters, Gaithersburg, Maryland.

Having lunch in the company's café, Leola, Wallace's manager, was watching the television monitor. A banner at the bottom of the screen indicated that all traffic should avoid Route 29 north to Baltimore due to a fatal traffic accident blocking all lanes. Leola finished lunch and started back to her office. On her way she entered the ladies room, and standing at the sink was Wallace's administrative assistant, Alice. She was crying and extremely upset.

"Alice, what is wrong? Is there anything I can do?" Leola placed her arms on Alice's shoulders to comfort her.

"He's dead. He's dead. Wallace was killed in the accident on Route 29." Leola stepped back from Alice.

"No, Alice! No! That can't be? How did you get this news." Still sobbing, Alice attempted to answer Leola's question.

"The County Police called to ask if Wallace worked here, and I said yes. Then they asked if they could speak to him, but WC is out today. The officer said thank you, and we ended the call. Not long after that, my husband called and told me that Wallace was killed in the explosion on 29. He said that the call I got was to confirm if they had identified the right person." Leola quickly pulled out her cell. She called Wallace's cell and then his home telephone number. When she called the home number, a strange voice answered.

"Hello, this is Wallace Barker's home, and I'm Officer Kidwell of the County Police Department. May I help you?" Leola knew that what Alice told her must be true.

"I'm calling for Wallace. May I speak to him."

In a cold tone of voice, Officer Kidwell answered, "I am sorry to inform you that Mr. Wallace C. Barker was killed this morning in an automobile accident. I can take your name and telephone number, and once we have further details, we will contact you."

Chapter 40

Jacksonville International Airport.

Eve Harding was picking up her luggage at the Southwest Airlines baggage carousel. She heard her cell telephone ringing. When Eve looked down at the face of the phone, she saw it was Debra Webb. Eve hesitated for a moment while she considered what the call would be about.

"Well, hello, Debra. I'm at the airport. I just got back from Washington. Wallace and I spent the weekend at the jazz festival in Burke, Pennsylvania, and we had a lovely time. What's going on?"

"Well, darling, I guess you've forgotten that we were supposed to meet today to work out plans for the memorial services for our book club members. We decided to meet out at Whitey's Fish House on Fleming Island. We just arrived, and we haven't been seated as yet, so I was wondering whether or not you would still be coming to join us?" Still standing at the baggage carousel, Eve was collecting her thoughts and looking for her suitcase.

"Debra, I'm waiting for my bag, and for some reason, it hasn't come off the plane. I hope they didn't lose it. WC gave me this really cute little cup while we were at the jazz festival and I really wanted to keep it. You know it is just a momento, but it's the meaning behind it." Eve saw her bag coming on the carousel.

"It will take me about 45 minutes to an hour to get to Fleming Island from here, depending on the lunchtime traffic of course. So I don't want to promise you that I will be there. If I can't make it, I'll call you later tonight so you can bring me up to date on what we are doing?" It was a few seconds before Debra Webb replied.

"I understand, Honey. Take care of what you have to, and I'll call you tonight and tell you what we have planned and give you all the details. Hope you find your bag."

—

Jacksonville FBI Office.

FBI Agent Faye Cook-Little was finishing a telephone conversation with Jerry Clark.

"Sure, Jerry, that should be fun. I've never sailed before but always wanted to. I really appreciate you letting my son come with us. OK, I'll talk with you later tonight. Me too."

Smiling, Faye turned in her chair and caught several of her co-workers smiling at her. Faye quickly turned her attention back to her computer. Faye was trying to solve the question of who really did the bombings in Jacksonville. The phone rang, and Faye quickly picked up the receiver hoping that it was Jerry Clark calling back.

"This is Agent Cook-Little. How can I help you?" Faye was now looking at the caller ID, but she was pretty confident of who the caller was.

"Faye, this is Roy Benning. Is this a good time for us to talk?" Once again Faye surveyed the room and decided to go to a conference room to take the call.

"Roy, I'm going to put you on hold while I go to a secure telephone."

Faye and Roy talked for 20 minutes. Roy complemented Faye on coming up with the very good, believable story. He told her that it would not go unnoticed how she was able to keep the CIA out of the story. Roy asked whether or not it was just plain coincidence that the television news story broke just 15 minutes before she gave her press conference. He said that it could not have been planned better. Roy and Faye both agreed that the weakest point was the fourth bombing, which was not consistent with the other three, and they had to find out who the real bombers were. Faye told Roy that she had a lead. It was weak, just two people, one female, an Eve Harding, and one male, a Wallace C. Barker, a.k.a. WC, who were in Rio de Janeiro during the assassination of the ministers of security from each of those countries. One was currently living in Jacksonville, and the other was from Jacksonville but now residing in Maryland. They left Jacksonville the night of the first bombing, flying from Fort Lauderdale to Rio de Janeiro and returning to Jacksonville the night of the last attack. The male, Barker, was detained at the Washington FBI office when he arrived in Washington, suspected of being the "Number Name" international assassin, but he was released. They ended the call with Roy promising to do some checking on both of her suspects.

Faye left the conference room and went back to her desk. Before she could sit down, her office telephone was ringing. This time, Faye checked the caller ID before she answered.

"That was quick. You have something for me already."

With excitement in his voice, Roy Benning replied, "Faye, your person of interest was killed in a car explosion just a few hours ago over on Route 29. Three other cars were involved in the accident." Faye flashed back to when she was reading the eyewitness statements concerning the Jacksonville blasts.

"Roy, what jurisdiction is handling the accident?" Roy Benning gave Faye the name of the authority along with the point of contact that should be able to help her.

Faye then replied. "I'm going to give them a call. If they answer my question as I think they will, it will boil down to the same M.O. of the person or persons who did the bombings in Jacksonville."

—

Jacksonville International Airport.

Eve picked up her bag from the carousel and headed to the long-term parking lot. After paying the parking fee, with all due speed, she got on I95 South and immediately took the exit for 295 West.

While she was driving, Eve spoke aloud, as if someone was in the car with her.

"I can't wait until I get home. I'm going to tell Mama everything about those old hens. I can't stand any of them. There would not be a book club if it were not for me. Mama knows that I started the club for one reason and one reason only. Yes, Mama knows. Mama knows because she told me to do it… If those old bitches knew that I handpicked every one of them because their husband's worked for the CIA. Yeah, the Central Intelligence Agency. The same CIA that sent my grandfather to his death for the Bay of Pigs. Their husband held the same position of the men who killed my granddaddy, which led to my grandmother committing suicide and resulted in my mother getting sick and committing suicide too. They'll see that, if anyone takes that position, they will die because I'll see that they are killed."

Eve came out of her trance when she noticed how fast she was traveling. The last thing she needed was to be pulled over and get a speeding ticket. Eve could feel her heart pounding, and her body temperature was elevated. Eve glanced at her watch. Wallace and Eve had to get up early to get to the airport for Eve to catch her plane, so she only picked up a Danish along with a cup of tea at the airport. Coming up on an exit that would take her to a Panera Bread, Eve pulled her car off of I295 into a small mall where the Panera Bread was located.

Purchasing a salad, a bottle of water and a diet cola. Eve took a window table where she could see her car. After she was seated, Eve opened the bottle of water and consumed the contents just like she had finished running a 100-meter race. She took her pulse. Her heart was beating rapidly. Eve sat still for several moments, taking deep breaths to calm herself.

Eve Harding finished eating. She was sitting at the table thinking and drinking her diet soda when she began mumbling to herself in a quiet tone.

"It was so easy. I knew who drove what car. I always arrived at the meeting late. I would go to each car and write down their VIN number, and that would be it. None of the bitches knew what hit them. I sort of felt sad for Khristy Newborn for being the only woman to hold the position. But hell, shit happens. No one was feeling sorry for me when my grandmother committed suicide; no one was sad for me when my mother killed herself. No one reached out to help me when I had to sell my body so I could get money to eat and live." Eve was startled and looked up from staring at her plate into a smiling face.

"Excuse me, but are you finished? I can remove your plate." Eve nodded, got up and walked to her car.

—

Rio de Janeiro International Airport Brazil.

The Brazilian port authority was taking the applications for
baggage handlers for the airport. There were only 48 positions
available, but more than 100 people were standing in line in the
blistering sun waiting to fill out an application.

Krish had arrived at the airport employees' entrance gate just
a few minutes after 1:00 in the morning. Even at that time, some 50
people were ahead of him. Some had set up tents and were taking
turns standing in line while their partner got some sleep. The local
police showed up just around 5:00, and by that time the line had
doubled.

The MIE had dwindled to less than 100 members scattered
among four countries: Venezuela, Guyana, Brazil, and the United
States. Krish's task today was to gain access to planes as a baggage
handler. With what little money they had, the MIE had bribed one of
the employees of the Brazilian Airport Authority, a manager in the
human resources department, to hire a Julio Rivera. Krish had been
given forged documents identifying him as the man with that name.

—

Montevilla Housing Development, Jacksonville, Florida.

After pulling into her garage, Eve immediately walked into
her house and looked for her backpack. Just when she found it, she
heard her house telephone. The name on the caller ID was SBM.

"Hello?" Eve waited.

"Hello. Am I speaking to Eve Harding?" Eve didn't want to
answer too quickly, so she waited for a second or two.

"Why, yes, this is Eve Harding. To whom am I speaking?"

"My name is Leola Wilcox, and I work for SBM in Silver
Spring, Maryland. I'm WC's boss. Wallace reports to me."

"Why, yes, WC has mentioned your name, and in fact, he
speaks very highly of you. Why are you calling me? Has anything
happened to Wallace?"

Attempting to break the news about Wallace death as
sympathetically as possible, Leola went on to explain that she

received word that Wallace had been killed in a four-car crash on Route 29 just after rush hour that morning. Wallace had put Eve's name down to contact for any type of emergency.

Eve started crying, and while crying on the phone just said thanks, ending the call. After the call, Eve walked over to a cabinet, pulled out a bottle of gin along with a glass, poured herself a drink, raised the glass into the air, and said with a grin on her face, "No, Wallace C. Barker, I will not marry you."

Laughing out loud, then she said, "Especially since you are dead." She drank the entire glass of gin down in one swallow. "Toni really knows how to fly that Joker airplane." Now in a cheerful mood, Eve began gathering items, placing them in the backpack.

—

Mayport, Florida, USS John F. Kennedy Aircraft Carrier.

The pre-bid conference was about to begin. Three software development and integration companies were represented. The Navy set the bar extremely high for businesses to qualify to attend the day and a half conference.

Upon arriving at the carrier, everyone was ushered into a room to go through a security screening. Two forms of identification were required, one must have a photo. The companies were limited to only two representatives per contractor attending. After completing the security check, as a group, they were escorted onto the carrier.

The USS John F. Kennedy Aircraft Carrier is a nuclear-powered supercarrier, the best of her class. A ship's crew of 3000 with an air wing of 2,050 and approximately 108 planes, two of them EA-21F Joker Electronic Attack Aircraft, experimental. The Joker is the replacement, or the Navy is counting on receiving the funding for the Joker to be the replacement for the EA-6B Prowler and the EA-18F Growler. Aircraft carriers are the perfect platform to launch these aircraft to pursue their mission.

Once on board, the contractors were led into a flight briefing room. Captain Louis Wilcox, the manager for the Joker Project, opened the presentation. "Good morning, everyone. I'm the project manager for the EA-21F Joker aircraft. We have a very busy day for you. This morning you will receive our technical briefing. After lunch, you will have the opportunity to see the aircraft and speak with the pilots. With that said, we will start with our technical lead, Dr. Henry Smith."

As the morning progressed, the contractors received one technical presentation after another. They took a break for lunch, which was served on the carrier. One of the contractors' representatives stepped away from the group to make a telephone call.

"Hello, lover. I told you that I would be in Jacksonville this week." When Eve heard Wallace's voice, she had to sit down in the closest chair. She thought about how she should respond.

"Oh my God! Wallace is that you? Is it really you?" Wallace couldn't understand Eve's reaction to the call. "WC, your manager called me and said that you were killed in an accident on Route 29."

Wallace was shocked at what Eve told him. "Leola called you? Well, lover, I'm very much alive and was hoping that we could get together tonight. How's your schedule? When did you hear from Leola?"

"Less that an hour ago. As a matter of fact, I just walked in. Where are you staying, Wallace?"

"The Navy put us up at the Embassy Suites. I was expecting a Motel Six, but the Navy decided to spend some money, probably because only three companies made the cut and were allowed to come."

"WC, is that the Embassy Suite in Mayport or in Jacksonville?"

"Mayport, we will be finishing up here just around 6:00." Eve looked at her watch.

"Okay, I'll meet you at 7:00. I know an excellent seafood restaurant not far from the Embassy Suites."

"Sounds fine to me, lover. I'll be looking for you around 7:00."

After ending the call, WC quickly called Leola. Leola was happy to hear Wallace's voice.

"WC? Wallace? Wallace C. Barker? This is so wonderful! Alice received a call this morning telling us that you were killed in a

402

car crash over on Route 29. Something told me that they had gotten it wrong. Thank heaven you are OK. Where are you?"

"Well, boss, I'm fine. I'm in Mayport at the pre-bid conference for the Joker aircraft. Felix is here. How did the police determine that I was killed?"

Leola, breathing a sigh of relief replied, "Alice's husband told her that the crash was so bad that the only thing that could help the police to identify the bodies were the license plates." Wallace cut Leola off before she could finish.

"Leola, on my way to the airport I dropped my car off at the BMW dealer on Route 29 to be serviced. Sometimes, after the service, they take the cars out for a test run. I'll call the dealer to confirm that is what happened. But I'm OK. I must get back to the meeting. I'll send you an email tonight to bring you up to date on the conference."

Once the call ended, Leola quickly sent out an email throughout the company announcing the good news that Wallace was Okay, and he was at the Navy's pre-bid conference in Mayport, Florida.

Wallace made one last call before going back to the flight briefing room, to the BMW dealer where he left his Z-4 for service. It was just as WC had figured. The mechanic who serviced Wallace BMW took the car out for a test drive and was killed in the crash.

—

Eve Harding Home, Jacksonville, Florida.

Meanwhile, after Eve ended her conversation with Wallace, she had to work out her next step. Eve's plan from the beginning was to get sexually involved with Wallace so that he would be blinded by the sex and not pay any attention when she completed the coding of the software, forged his signature for delivery of the one million lines of software code to the Navy, and initiated her revenge plot. Eve knew that the odds were high that he would meet Toni at some point during the pre-bid conference since Toni was one of two pilots flying the Joker aircraft. WC was an intelligent guy, and Eve knew, when Wallace met Toni it will be the part he needed to start putting the puzzle together. Eve decided that, when she met WC for dinner, she had to find out if he had put everything together: from the breakthrough on the software code for the Joker aircraft to Toni flying the Joker and using the plane's laser weapon system to kill those people. If Eve confirmed that WC had put the plot together, she would kill him in bed, just after having sex.

On the other side of Jacksonville, FBI Agent Faye Cook-Little finished her call with the local authorities handling the Route 29 accident. Just as Faye was anticipating, her questions had been answered as she thought they would be. The people who witnessed the crash all spoke of seeing a white flash of light preceding the explosion. To Faye, that was enough to confirm that the bombing on Route 29 and the Jacksonville bombings was related. This information also moved Mr. Barker and Ms. Harding from a weak lead to persons of interest in the investigation. Faye decided to take a ride out to Ms. Eve Harding's home to have a face-to-face interview.

—

Rio de Janeiro, Brazil.

The mood in the country was uplifted when the news media announced that Brazil was among the finalists to host the next Olympics. Elkin Ardila was sitting in one of the most up-scale restaurants waiting for his guest to arrive and watching the special broadcast of the announcement. Every politician was taking credit for putting the proposal together, from the chairperson of the Brazilian Olympic Committee to the President. As the news reporters interviewed key figures in the government, it was evident that each was trying to get as much political mileage out of this announcement as possible.

Elk's attention shifted from the broadcast on the television monitor when he caught sight of an athletically built man and very sexy woman walking toward his table. He had never met either Bartolomeu Donnachaidh or Xoana Cardozo, Belo. He was identifying them from the photos the Agency emailed him.

Walking toward his table, Elk clearly saw that Belo was as beautiful as the image he had formed in his mind. According to CIA records, Bartolomeu was in his sixties but looked closer to a man of 40, maybe even 30-something. Bartolomeu was in top physical condition and looked like a man who could handle himself in a street fight. Elk stood to greet his guests.

After welcoming Bartolomeu and Belo, Elk kept his attention directed toward Bartolomeu, who was wearing double shoulder holsters, one under each arm holding a Glock 20 SF 10mm auto pistol. Seeing the type of weapon that Bartolomeu carried reinforced everything Elk read about him in the file the Agency sent to him.

Elk started out with light conversation, congratulating the country of Brazil on being among the finalists to host the Olympics. Belo stayed out of the conversation, only offering a casual smile or a nod of her head. Both Bartolomeu and Belo had a mastery of being able to focus on the conversation but continually watching the room, verifying every person in the restaurant while checking their memory banks for anyone on the list of people they could be looking for. Just after ordering their dinner, Belo finally joined the conversation. Elk thought to himself that Bartolomeu gave a signal to Belo to take over.

"Elk, you seem to have an above average knowledge about not only our country but also Guyana and Venezuela?"

Elk repositioned himself in his chair to look at Belo such that he could still see how Bartolomeu would react to his answer. Elk smiled before he spoke.

"That's a fascinating question. Why I think I have the same level of knowledge about the countries in the region as you, have about the United States. By the way, have you visited the States?"

Belo was just about to respond when the silence was broken by the sound of a cell phone. Bartolomeu reached into his jacket and pulled out his phone. He looked at the display and asked to be excused. He stood up and walked away from the table for some privacy. Elk's eyes remained fixed on him as he walked toward the entrance of the restaurant while Belo remained focused on Elk. Elk knew that you always wanted to know where a man carrying two Glock 10mm automatic pistols is located. After he could see Bartolomeu standing in the waiting area talking on his mobile, he turned his attention back to Belo.

"So where were we?"

Belo said that she had never visited the United States, but maybe one day she would. Bartolomeu finished his call, and upon returning to the table, stated that matters of state required that he and Belo leave. Elk stood, and they said their goodbyes. Elk then ordered a brandy along with espresso.

Drinking his espresso while sipping his drink, Elk concluded that the Brazilian secret police had not gained any information from the MIE captures that would associate them with the Agency.

Chapter 41

Temporary FBI Office, Jacksonville, Florida.

Agent Faye Cook-Little made a note on the network that she was leaving the office to conduct an interview with a person of interest concerning the Jacksonville bombings. It was common knowledge that the case had not been fully closed, but Faye didn't want to leave the impression that it was still being investigated. While driving, Faye called her housekeeper to let her know that she would be late coming home but to make sure that her son got to bed on time because they would be going sailing with Jerry Clark the next day.

While driving Faye was going over the elements that connected Eve Harding and Wallace Barker to the bombings. They left Jacksonville the night of the first bombing, flying to Rio de Janeiro where the two ministers of security were assassinated. Then they were back in Jacksonville when the next two explosions took place. Then Barker left Jacksonville just before the last bombing, and Barker himself was killed in a blast similar to the four that happened here in Jacksonville. If they are the bombers, what are they after? What is their motive?

Faye's cell telephone rang. Looking at the display, she saw that it was coming from the FBI forensics office out of Atlanta.

"Hello, this is Agent Cook-Little." A voice that Faye knew well started speaking with excitement.

"Faye, I found it. I found the type of device that produced the explosions in Jacksonville. It was a laser, a laser weapon of some sort with a very high-intensity heat signature. That heat signature produced the white light that all of the witnesses reported seeing." Faye pulled her car to the side of the road and pulled out a pad and pen.

"Slowdown a minute! A laser weapon? Do they exist, and who will have such a thing? The military?"

"Faye, there are a lot of high-tech companies currently working on laser weapons. Lasers are now being used in medicine, in particular, operations, cancer, and probably many other things that are still in development. But it's a big jump from using a laser to cut out tissue to blowing up a car." There was silence for a while. Then Faye spoke.

"OK then, give me the names of the top companies producing any type of laser machine."

"Faye, I thought that you would ask for such a list. I've emailed you a list of companies broken down into three categories: lasers for medical use, for military purposes, and for industrial applications."

Just on a hunch, Faye asked, "Is Sterling Business Machines, or SBM, on that list?"

"Why, yes, it is. How did you guess? SBM is one of the leading laser development companies in the military market. I take it that you must have something linking SBM to the investigation?"

Faye said with a smile, "Damn right, I do. Hey, thanks for the information. I know that you guys did a lot of hard work to dig this stuff up. I'm going to send you guys a bottle of Old Grand Dad."

"Faye, you don't have to do that. This is our job. It is always a pleasure when we can use our forensics expertise to help you guys in the field catch the bad guys."

Faye smiled as she completed making her last note in her small notebook, then said, "I appreciate that, but just the same, be on the lookout for a UPS package from me that will have a bottle, no two-fifths of Old Grand Dad." Faye laid her cell phone on the passenger seat, pulling her car back onto the highway in the direction of Eve Harding's home.

—

Mayport, Florida, USS John F. Kennedy Aircraft Carrier.

Back on the USS John F. Kennedy, the contractors were divided into two groups. Each group would get the opportunity to interview one of the Navy's officers assigned to fly the Joker aircraft. Because of security reasons, the pilot names were not disclosed, just their call signs. The group that Felix was in would be interviewing the pilot with the call sign Mad-Dog. Wallace's group would be talking to the pilot with the call sign Junebug.

Just as both groups were walking out of the briefing room headed to the flight deck, Wallace's group was informed of a change to the schedule. Flight Officer Junebug was called up to Captain Wilcox's office for a meeting. Everyone would be speaking with Flight Officer Mad-Dog.

In Captain Wilcox's office, Flight Officer Toni Harding sat in the small conference room waiting for Captain Wilcox to come in. Toni was trying to figure out why the captain had called this meeting. Mentally she was going through every step of her last flight with the Joker up to Washington, DC for the budget team to have some pictures taken of the plane. Toni knew that she took the proper approach into Joint Base Andrews. Harding heard her name called and quickly jumped to her feet.

"Yes, sir." Captain Wilcox came into the room.

"Have a seat, Toni. I want to speak to you concerning a couple of things." Harding waited until the captain took his place and then she sat down. Captain Wilcox opened what appeared to be Toni Harding's military personnel jacket. He pulled out a fountain pen, opened it, laid it on the table, then turned and smiled at Toni.

"Harding, you may not be aware of this, but I have held the position of program manager of this project for five years. Before coming here, I was commanding a squadron flying off the Kennedy. Once, returning from a routine mission when the weather turned bad, we ran into a low-level typhoon dangerous enough for us to have major concerns for night landings. Long story short; when I came in, my plane was hit by lighting, burst into flames, and went over the side. For some reason, and I'm still trying to figure it out what made me do it, I pulled my ejector and went up, directly above the deck of the flat-top. My chute didn't deploy, so I came down like a rock, breaking both of my legs. I was already on the promotion list, so when I got out of the hospital, they sent me to the program management course, and here I am." To Toni's surprise, when Captian Wilcox finished his story, he pulled out a pack of smokes and lit up.

"The reason I'm sharing all of this with you is that this project is about to move from concept to full production. Because of the top-gun flying you and Mad-Dog have done, this project is on the verge of placing into the Navy's flying arsenal the most scientifically advanced aircraft in the history of the Navy." The captain paused. "All of us had to undergo a security clearance upgrade. One thing came up on your background check. It seems your mother once worked for or is working for one of the contractors that are our leading company to win the contract. That company is SBM. My question is: does your mother work for SBM?" Inwardly, Toni took a deep breath before she answered.

"Captain Wilcox, my mother never worked for SBM. She worked for JBL, a company that was a subcontractor to SBM. However, she resigned from JBL four years ago and is a high school chemistry teacher here in Jacksonville." Captain Wilcox smiled while picking up his pen.

"I hoped you were going to say something like that. You see, we want SBM to get the contract for the Joker, and so we cannot go into this with even the appearance that SBM had any type of insider knowledge. So can you give me the name and a point of contact at the high school your mother teaches at so we get this verified."

Flight Officer Toni Harding provided the information to Captain Wilcox. After writing the information on a yellow note, he closed the personnel jacket, turned and smiled at Harding.

"Harding, the other thing that I wanted to tell you is that I was able to get a back door copy from a friend of mine who was on your promotion board. You will be receiving orders promoting you to Lieutenant JG, congratulations."

—

Rio de Janeiro, Brazil.

Krish was sitting in a chair on the balcony of his apartment. Because of the heat, he had taken his shirt off. He was writing a letter to his MIE contact in New York City. With all of the pressure coming down on the MIE, they were only using low-tech ways to transmit messages: mail, messengers, and carrier pigeons. No one could use telephones, mobile phones, or computers.

With the limited funds that the MIE had, Krish could only afford a one room apartment. The apartment was not air conditioned, so when the temperature was well over 95 degrees inside, and he was forced to sit outside to keep cool and deal with the heat.

He was letting his contact know that he was hired at the airport and would be starting his training the next Monday. Training was only a week. After the week of training, he would be assigned to a baggage handling team consisting of a baggage team leader, himself, and two other men.

At this point, he could not tell what airplanes he would be loading luggage on, but as soon as Krish was able to figure the system out, Krish said he would let the MIE know. Krish did not know what his assignment would be. He was thinking that at some point after he had been working at the airport long enough, he would be given a package to be placed on an airplane. The package would contain a bomb.

Krish finished the letter and put it in an envelope to mail the next morning when he left for work.

—

Montevilla Housing Development, Jacksonville, Florida.

Eve finished packing the backpack, then placed it beside the door leading to her garage. Rushing, she walked into her secret computer room located in the garage. She turned on her system to eavesdrop on the key government agencies she had hacked.

"Mama, it doesn't seem that they have caught on to anything that Toni and I have been doing. They are so stupid. They can create positions that get people killed but can't even figure out something as simple as what we have done. Revenge is sweet. We said that we would pay them back for what they did to us, didn't we Mama? And we have."

Eve moved her attention away from viewing the government agencies she had hacked into, looking at a folder labeled Finances. Located in this folder were all of her personal money accounts along with broker accounts. Over the last ten years, Eve Harding's net worth had grown to well over 2.6 million dollars, and she had about 1.1 million in liquid assets that she had the ability to move at any time she wished. It would take about five to 10 days to liquidate the

411

remaining 1.5. Eve made the decision that this was the time. Opening a notepad next to her keyboard, Eve turned to a page with username and passwords. As she entered the passwords, she transferred most of the liquid cash to a numbered account located in the Cayman Islands with a small portion of the money going to a numbered account in the Bahamas. After completing that transaction, she requested that the remaining 1.5 million to be liquidated and the funds be placed in a numbered account located in a bank in Switzerland. Eve Harding's eyes swiftly shifted to one of her security monitors. A car was pulling into her driveway. Eve completed her transactions, exited her secret room, and went back to the main house to greet her visitor.

The doorbell rang just as she entered her living room. Eve checked a monitor located by the door to verify if see knew the guest.

"Hello, may I help you?" FBI Agent Faye Cook-Little back was turned to the door when she heard the friendly voice greet her. Faye was looking at the surrounding houses. Faye turned around to see Eve Harding standing in the door.

"Hello, I'm FBI Agent Faye Cook-Little," she said, holding her FBI Badge in front of her so Eve could read it. " I'm certain that you are aware of the bombings that have taken place in Jacksonville over the last several weeks. I'd like to take a few minutes of your time to ask you some questions concerning a few of the victims who were killed in the bombings. Do you have a few moments to spare?"

Smiling, Eve opened the door wider to let Agent Cook-Little into her home. "Sure. It's not surprising that you would come. Please, won't you come in and have a seat over there." Eve directed Faye to the large sofa where Faye's back was to the doorway leading to the kitchen. Eve sat across from her in an armchair. Faye opened her notebook and began to give Eve a recap of the bombings.

"Ms. Harding, from what we have found out, you were in the same book club with four of the victims." Faye gaged Eve Harding's facial reactions and waited for answers.

"You know, I was making myself a cup of tea when you rang my doorbell. Would you mind waiting just a second to let me get my tea? Would you like to have a cup?"

Faye laid her notebook on the table and pulled out her cell phone. A text message was coming in.

"Yes, I'll have a cup. Just cream. I'll answer this text message while you are gone."

Faye began to type a reply on her cell while Eve walked into the kitchen. While in the kitchen making the tea, from a drawer Eve removed an eight-inch chef's knife. Holding it by her side, she walked back into her living room holding the cup of tea in her left hand and the chef's knife in the right hand down by her side, approaching Agent Cook-Little from behind.

As Eve was approaching, Faye said, "I'm just about finished with this text…"

Before Agent Cook-Little could send the message, Eve Harding, standing behind Faye, raised the chef's knife and thrust it down over the agent's head into her chest. The knife entered Faye's body just below the ribs and above the stomach, puncturing the heart. Blood streamed out of Faye's body onto the sofa and carpet.

Eve Harding walked around the couch and took a seat across from Faye. She drank her tea while watching Agent Cook-Little bleed out.

Eve looked at her watch, then looked at Faye. "Oh my, you took longer than I expected to bleed out." Still comfortably sitting across from her victim, Eve calmly finished her cup of tea, then left her living room to go to the secret computer room. In the hidden room, she began to destroy all of the hard drives on the desktop and the servers. After wiping all of the drives, Harding turned on a timer.

As Eve was leaving the room, she kissed the manikin, saying, "Well Mama, we did everything you told me to do. All of the people who were in the position of the same people that sent granddaddy to his death are dead. The Position has ended. I'm going to leave you now. I will always love you, Mama."

Back in the living room, Eve went through Agent Cook-Little's pocket book. Eve ensured that she had everything that Faye brought with her into the house. Harding then took her backpack along with Agent Faye Cook-Little's pocketbook and car keys. Eve put on a pair of rubber gloves and got into Faye's car and pulled out of the driveway. Eve read Faye's drivers license and set her GPS to Cook-Little's home address.

With traffic, it took Eve about 45 minutes to drive to Agent Cook-Little's house. It was a little past 7:00, just dark enough for a car driving on the same street could not see that Faye was not driving. Eve stopped at Faye Cook-Little's house just in front of the mailbox. Without getting out of the car, Eve crawled across the seat and placed both of the cell phones in the mailbox.

Eve Harding then drove to the Jacksonville International Airport. Before turning into the long-term parking, Eve pulled to the side of the road and put on a wig, sunglasses, and a baseball cap. After parking, she took the shuttle bus to the main terminal. Eve's cell phone rang. She ignored the call because she knew it was probably WC trying to reach her.

After entering the airport, Eve took out her boarding pass for a ticket that she had purchased two months ago. The ticket was for a nonstop flight from Jacksonville to Miami. After going through security, Eve was seated on a flight within 20 minutes. Just as the announcement was being made for all cell phones to be turned off or put in airplane mode, Eve used her mobile phone to activate the timers at her home. She then turned the phone off.

The nonstop flight would take an hour and 19 minutes. Eve's plane left at 8:20 pm. The timers were set to go off at 9:45 pm, about ten minutes after the aircraft landed in Miami. The only person who would be looking for her would be WC.

—

Market 32 Restaurant, Jacksonville, Florida.

Jerry Clark was parking and at the same time looking for Faye's car. He found a spot, parked, and checked his cell phone for messages, particularly anything from Faye indicating that something had held her up. It was just 8:45 and they were supposed to meet for dinner at 9:00. Jerry locked his car as he started for the restaurant.

Standing at the maître D's desk, Jerry said, "Dinner for two," as his eyes scanned the dining area first, followed by the bar, to see if Faye had taken a seat and he just missed seeing her car while walking from the parking lot.

"Just give me one moment, sir, and I'll be able to seat you," the maître d' said while he was scanning his seating chart. The maître d' raised his head, looking at Jerry. "Sir, would you prefer a booth or do you have a preference?"

Jerry smiled. "I prefer a booth." The maître d' reached his hand under the table and pulled out two menus, then signaled for a waitress. A young waitress appeared, took the menus from the maître d', then gestured for Jerry to follow her. Still searching the room to see if Faye had arrived, Jerry took a seat in the booth and checked his cell phone, looking for a text message.

—

Mayport, Florida.

At the Embassy Suites in Mayport, Wallace sat in the lobby checking his text messages while waiting for Eve. Eve Harding was late, but it was not unusual for her. Wallace sat patiently but lamenting the other occasions Eve left him seated in a restaurant for over two hours, and there was one time she didn't show at all and didn't even send him a message to let him know that she was not able to come. Once again Wallace began to question if this was really the right person for him. The sex was good, but there were too many other signals that indicated that something was not there. In a strange sense, Wallace felt relief. He felt like a weight had been lifted from his shoulders. This could be the sign that his and Eve's relationship was over.

—

Miami International Airport, Miami, Florida.

Eve's flight from Jacksonville landed, and with only a backpack, Eve moved through the airport crowd very briskly, following the signs leading to ground transportation. The line at the taxi stand was not as long as she expected. A buzzing sound was heard, and Eve smiled as she checked her cell phone. The buzzing sound was the signal that the timers had gone off igniting incendiary devices that Eve have placed all over her home, including the garage and her secret computer room. The blaze burned hot and completely melted everything in the house, leaving no verifiable evidence. The flammable solvent that Eve used was non-traceable because it was developed by Eve's high school chemistry class as a science project.

Eve stepped out of line and walked to a nearby trashcan. She disassembled her cell phone, smashing it to the ground and breaking the SD card into pieces. Then she placed everything in the trashcan.

After getting back in the taxi line, she got into a cab and gave directions to the driver. "Take me to the Miami Beach Marina on Alton Road."

Eve had rented a boat slip at the Marina, not under the name Eve Harding but as Jane T. Bush. Over the last four years, Eve Harding has taken private sailing classes, becoming an experienced, licensed, qualified sailor under her new identity, Jane T. Bush.

The cab pulled up to the Marina, and Eve, now Jane T. Bush, paid the driver in cash, including just the appropriate tip. Not too much or too little so the driver would not remember anything significant about the passenger.

Eve walked down the dock to a gate. She entered the security code for the gate and walked to the slip where her 45-foot catamaran, the Junebug, was berthed. Stepping on the deck of her boat, Eve opened the world of Jane T. Bush.

—

USS John F. Kennedy Aircraft Carrier, Mayport, Florida.

The next morning on the USS John F. Kennedy, Flight Officer Toni Harding was signing out for a four-day leave. As Toni was signing out, the Duty Officer said, "Do you have anything planned for your leave, Junebug?"

Toni finished signing out, then looking at the Duty Officer, said, "I plan to rent a plane and do some flying."

The Duty Officer, with a shocked expression on his face, said, "You know, Harding, you are the only pilot that flys all week, and when they take off, all the want to do is to pilot another plane. I don't understand it."

Walking up the ramp, Toni turned around to the Duty Officer and said, "One day I want to fly for one of the major airlines, and the more flying time I have on commercial aircraft, the better my resume will look."

At the Jacksonville International Airport, Toni rented a plane and filed a flight plan to fly from Jacksonville to the Miami International Airport. The trip would take a little over two hours. The trip went without incident until 15 minutes before Toni would be handed off to the air traffic controller at the Miami International Airport. The plane changed course, heading out to the Atlantic ocean. Once the aircraft is over water, it dropped below the radar. Forty-five minutes out into the Atlantic, the pilot sent a distress signal and then crashed into the sea. A 45-foot catamaran, the Junebug, rescued the pilot and pulled her safely aboard the boat.

After Toni dried off and changed in her cabin, she went to the galley. Eve was sitting at the navigation desk sipping a cup of tea while reading navigational maps. Toni poured herself a mug of tea, joining her mother at the table.

"OK, Mom, where are we headed? Have you finalized where we are going to lay low?" Eve looked at her daughter, giving her a big motherly smile.

"Honey, I think I've found the perfect place. A little spot where no one would ever think of looking." Toni looked down at the maps that were on the table.

"I currently have us on a course to the Bahamas. After we land, we will pick up some money and stay there for two days. When we leave, we'll island hop: Crooked Island, Turks, Dominican Republic, St Croix, Virgin Islands, down to Guadeloupe, St. Lucia, Trinidad, then to the little, unknown place that is between Venezuela and Guyana called Essequibo."

—

Jacksonville, Florida.

Back in Jacksonville, Jerry Clark was looking for answers. The FBI and the JPD found Faye's cell phones, but both of the phones had been wiped clean, all of the data on both phones erased. Nor had her car been located. She left a message on the network that

417

she was going to see a person of interest but did not give any details. The only other lead they had was that the forensics guys out of Atlanta said that Faye asked about Sterling Business Machines, and she seemed to have some interest in the company as a lead.

Bubba Webb could see that this whole thing about the missing FBI agent had his public relations director upset, and so he stopped by Jerry Clark's office.

"Jerry, I just wanted to come by and personally, tell you that the press release you put out concerning Joe Singletary and when he would be coming back to work hit the nail on its head."

Jerry Clark stood up. "Thanks, Mr. Mayor. I really appreciate you coming by to tell me that." Jerry was just about to sit down when Bubba Webb reached his hand out placing it on Jery's shoulder.

"Tell me, Jerry, any new information concerning that FBI agent? You know there's not much that happens around Jacksonville I don't know about, so tell me how you are doing and if there is anything that old Bubba can do?"

Looking down at his desk, Jerry replied, "Not much we can do. Everything is left in the hands of the FBI. Faye is a senior agent. People like her just don't make mistakes."

—

Montevilla Housing Development, Jacksonville, Florida.

The fire at Eve Harding's home was classified as being started in a suspicious nature, but Terry Jackson, Jacksonville Fire Inspector, had never seen anything like it. He knew that some type of incendiary was used to ignite the fire, but he could not get a chemical composition of the substance. Terry couldn't declare the fire an arson until he could positively identify what caused the fire. The only thing they had as hard evidence was that the homeowner, Eve Harding, was not at home. The neighbors said that the owner was friendly but kept to herself and traveled a lot.

—

CIA Headquarters, Langley, Virginia.

Roy Benning sat in front of his computer monitor reading field reports. The MIE had turned into a terrorist group. Since the raid in Miami, the MIE had claimed responsibility for two assassinations, four suicide bombings, and kidnappings the wife, who later turned up dead, of a Brazilian lower-level official. The word was out on the terrorist network that the MIE was trying to buy firearms, explosives, and equipment from any source that would accept their money. They were at the beginning stage of setting up a very sophisticated Internet network. Roy closed the computer folder, then reached for his secure telephone to call Elk Ardila.

"Elk, we have a lot of traffic coming in on the MIE. When can you break things off and take over your position back in Jacksonville?" Elk thought for a second.

"My meeting with Bartolomeu and Belo actually didn't produce any tangible results. I was planning on making one last swipe past my contacts in Essequibo, but I can see that everyone is keeping things quiet. I can take the tomorrow afternoon flight back to Jacksonville."

Roy made a note on his computer then said, "Good. I hoped that you would say that. When you get back to your office, and you get your desk organized, send me a plan of action on taking out the MIE." Elk said he would make up the plan and send it to Roy Benning.

As Elk was putting his cellphone back into his pocket, he said to himself. "I guess that is the way we work, build a group, turn them into terrorists, then hunt them down and kill them."

—

Rio de Janeiro, International Airport, Brazil.

Krish finished his week of training in luggage handling at the airport training center. He was assigned to a baggage team. Krish was given a secondary job. First, he would help to take the luggage off the truck and to place the bags onto the conveyor moving the luggage into the hold of the plane. At a point during that process, his

419

team lead would send Krish into the passenger loading door of the aircraft to retrieve carry-on and other baggage that would not fit in the overhead compartments of the plane.

In the terminal, an announcement was made for all Business Class Passengers flying to Jacksonville, Florida to please have their boarding pass and passport ready and to proceed to the gate for boarding.

This was Krish's first day on the job. His baggage team lead directed him to walk up the steps to the plane's business passenger entrance to pick up and tag the bags and bring them back to be loaded into the belly of the aircraft.

Krish walked the stairs up to the door of the plane. When he reached the top, he saw Elk Ardila in line with ten people in front of him. Krish pulled out a ballpoint pen and knelt to mark the bags that had been left. When Elk reached the door of the plane, Krish drove the point of the pen into Elk's neck, puncturing the jugular vein. By the time the airport paramedics arrived at Elk's side, he was dead, and Krish had somehow escaped.

When Roy Benning received word concerning the death of Elk Ardila, Roy stood up from his desk and shouted, "Someone has been killing my people, and I'm going to get the son-of-a-bitch and kill him."

—

Sterling Business Machines, Maryland.

WC was laying his notepad on the conference table. Felix was situated at the table playing a computer game on his cellphone. Felix coming into the SBM Headquarters happened very rarely. Leola was sitting behind her desk completing an email.

Looking over at Wallace as she hit enter on the keyboard, she said, "Wallace C. Barker, you look like shit. When was the last time you got some sleep, and I don't mean screwing either." Wallace rolled his eyes in Leola's direction.

"Don't give me that little boy look either. Now that we have won the Navy's contract, we need to get to work. OK, tell me how we are going to make the Navy the happiest people in the world?"

WC briefed Leola using the project plan he had developed. "The core of our work will start from this build." Wallace pointed to a binder on the table. "That's the million lines of code that we wrote and delivered to the Navy. I checked with billing and the payment was received yesterday." Leola smiled, but Felix reached across the table. Picking up the binder, he began to study the code. Wallace continued discussing the project plan, identifying some of the time spots in the plan that would require additional people to meet the delivery deadline."

Felix interrupted him. "We didn't write this code." Wallace stopped speaking and looked at Felix. "This software was developed by another company." Both Wallace and Leola looked toward Felix. Wallace knew that if Felix said the code was not designed by SBM, Felix was no doubt right, and he could tell who wrote the code.

"OK then, Felix, how do you know that someone else wrote the code? I suppose you can tell us who wrote the code?" Felix first looked at WC, then turned to look at Leola.

"These guys developed this code using API, Application Programming Interface. At SBM we use…" Leola, Wallace, and Felix all said it at the same time: "AOP." AOP is Aspect Oriented Programming.

Then Wallace said, "The only company that was a subcontractor with us on the upgrade project for the Navy that used API was JBL." Leola looked at Wallace.

"So, are we saying JBL wrote this software, gave it to you for delivering it to the Navy, and never billed SBM for the work?" Still concentrating on the code book, Felix raised his head.

"Leola, WC, give me a couple of days to really look at this in detail, and I think I will be able to tell you the names of the people who wrote this code." Leola got up from the conference table and walked to her desk, opened her pocketbook, and pulled out her cigarettes.

"Wait a minute. If JBL wrote this code, why didn't they bill SBM for the work? JBL is a small company that can't afford not to charge a large corporation like SBM for this amount of software code." Wallace reached across the table and pulled the binder away from Felix. He turned to the first page of the book to look at the delivery cover letter and software billing documents.

WC studied both documents carefully. Leola walked over to the conference table and looked over Wallace's shoulder. Felix, sitting across from Wallace, lean forward to watch WC's every move. Leola broke the silence.

"WC, do you see anything that could tell us what JBL is up to?" Wallace took a deep breath, then looked up at Leola.

"I didn't sign these documents. Someone forged my name and submitted this delivery. Somehow, someone got hold of our procedures book and the paperwork we use to make deliveries. They did a superb job forging my name and submitted the delivery to the Navy. This is what we are going to do. Felix, you take the book to see if you can find out who wrote the software code. I'll get the rest of the team working on my first deliverables for the Navy. I will also check my schedule to see where I was on the date that this delivery was made."

Leola looked at Wallace, then back to Felix. "OK then, let's just ensure that we stay on schedule for our deliverables to the Navy this time and keep a tighter watch on the security of our documentation."

Wallace and Felix left Leola's office. On the elevator, Felix agreed to call Wallace later that evening to give him an update on finding the people who wrote the software code. Wallace emphasized that he wanted to bring this to a conclusion before next week.

When WC was back in his office, Wallace went through his calendars to pinpoint exactly what he was doing on the date and time software delivery was made to the Navy. He was also considering who saw his signature enough to be able to copy it in such detail.

WC examined the delivery document with a magnifying glass. "Oh my gosh!" Wallace shouted and leaned back in his chair. Whoever did this scanned my signature and then produced both of these documents. All someone had to do was get hold of the clean delivery records, then get something of mine I had signed, a memo, performance appraisal, even a thank you note. The problem was that it could have been anyone in SBM, any of the six subcontractors used on the project. Wallace estimated any one of 83 people could have been the culprit when he combined the SBM staff and all of the subcontractors who were working on the project upgrade for the Navy.

—

Fort Meade Maryland.

Wallace's Special Forces Reserve unit was located on Fort Meade Military Base, which is about 15 miles north of Washington, DC. Once a month on weekends, the reservists would meet for training. During the summer, they would do two weeks of intensified training.

Since 9/11, Wallace's Special Forces brigade was putting in more hours than the typical Army Reserve unit. Because the active duty Army is much smaller, Army Reserve units, especially Special Operations units, such as Special Forces and Civil Affairs Military Intelligence units, are called up for mission critical assignments. The majority of these tasks assigned to the Reserve units were restricted to planning, logistical support, pre-execution support, operational support, and in some cases, post-operational support.

There was a time when Reserve units were referred to as weekend warriors. After 9/11 that phrase was no longer used because 40% of the military force serving overseas at any one time is made up of Army Reserve and National Guard units.

WC commanded an A-team. The team consisted of 11 Special Forces soldiers, each with a specialty, but also everyone in the team was cross-trained so if something happened to one particular individual there would be another soldier in the team with the training to step in and assume that person's responsibilities. Wallace's team had been together for two years. The primary area of operation was the Middle East. They had deployed to Iraq, Afghanistan, Pakistan, Oman, and even to Iran. In the Brigade, they were called the Hornets' Nest.

Wallace's drill weekends were divided into two four-hour training and preparation sessions. The first four hours the team conducted calisthenics, a two-mile run, and weightlifting, followed by a continuous 40-minute swim in the base pool. After lunch, training would shift to pre-mission and operational planning.

It was WC's first drill meeting since he returned from vacation. Wallace had kept himself in top physical conditioning while on vacation, but the two-mile run was still exhausting because the last 500 yards were uphill. Wallace and his men were doing a cool down walk just before heading to the weight room when the battalion's operation officer walked up to Wallace.

"WC, I hope you had a good vacation because we have a new mission for you and your team. Have your team assemble in the briefing room at 1300 hours to receive your operation orders."

At 12:45 Wallace and his team members walked into the brigade's briefing room. Seated in the front row were the entire battalion staff. At precisely 1300 hours the Brigade and the Battalion Commander, along with a civilian, who Wallace guessed was from Langley, entered the briefing room followed by the operation officer and the Battalion Command Sergeant Major. Everyone in the room stood up and snapped to attention.

The Brigade Commander walked to the center of the stage. "Take your seats, please." All eyes in the building focused on the commander.

"I'll be brief because you have a lot of work ahead of you. I picked this battalion to carry out this mission because, of the four battalions in this brigade, there is no doubt that you guys are the best and my number one Battalion. The other thing that I want to leave you with is that from this point own, everything that you hear is top secret and is not to be discussed with anyone outside of the room." The Brigade Commander paused and looked around the audience to ensure that everyone's eyes were directed at him. "Thank you very much, ladies and gentlemen. Good hunting and a safe return." The Brigade Commander left the briefing, then the Battalion Commander stood up and walked to the center of the stage.

"I would like to echo what the Brigade Commander said but add this. The Hornets' Nest A-team is the best A-team in this battalion. It is an honor to have such dedicated professionals in this command. I have no doubt that you will execute this mission in the tradition of the Special Forces motto: Anything, anytime, anyplace. I wish you the best of luck and good hunting."

A series of instructions were given by the following three staff officers that spoke. Wallace's A-team had ten days to get their

424

personal affairs and business in order, including providing their military orders to their employees. Those military orders are the federal government's legal document that releases the service member from their civilian jobs to go on active military duty.

On the 10th day, at 2200 hours, Wallace's A-team would report to Fort Meade with all of their equipment to be taken to Joint Base Andrews. At Joint Base Andrews they would be transported by air to the Plantation, Camp Blanding Florida, to receive further orders.

—

SBM, Gaithersburg, Maryland.

On Monday, Wallace arrived at work one hour before his usual time. Being called to active duty for 90 days during the beginning phases of the Navy's contract was going to send shock waves up at the top levels of the company. Wallace had been in this situation before, and his team still met all of the requirements of the contract, completing all of the work one week ahead of schedule.

Wallace had ten days to lay out every task that needed to be completed, to assign responsibility for the duties to be carried out by his managers. Looking at his watch, he knew that Leola should have arrived in the building and should be in her office. Wallace picked up the envelope that contained a copy of his deployment orders and started to Leola's office.

Leola was in the break room making coffee when she saw Wallace walk past the door. "WC, if you are looking for me, I am in the break room." WC turned around and joined Leola in the break room. When Wallace entered the room, Leola's eyes focused on the envelope Wallace was carrying in his hand.

"OK, Barker, where in the hell are you going this time? The only time you come to see me this early in the morning is when you have a piece of government paper in your hand."

Wallace and Leola made direct eye contact. Wallace could see Leola's eyes tearing up. Before WC could say anything, Leola took the letter out of Wallace's hand.

Chapter 42

"Barker, I know what you are going to say: if I tell you where I'm going, I would have to kill you." They both stood there looking into each other's eyes until Leola noticed that the coffee was ready. She turned her attention to the coffee, and with her back to Wallace, said, "You know what you have to do. Wallace, we thought we lost you once; let's not go for twice."

Back in his office, Wallace began to write down detailed instructions to his software developers on what he expected to be accomplished in the next three months. One thing still lurking in his mind was the unknown programmers who wrote the one million lines of code for the Navy. Felix was still working to pinpoint the individuals who were responsible.

The good part about being called up to active duty for three months was that Wallace knew he would not have any time to think about Eve Harding. It had been several weeks since he heard from her, and her house phone had been disconnected and her cellular phone mailbox messages were full. Wallace couldn't understand why Eve left so suddenly without saying goodbye. Wallace looked up from his work when he heard a door knock interrupting his train of thought.

Standing in his office doorway was Felix. Wallace checked his watch. It was only 8:30, and Felix was standing in front of his desk.

"What's up, buddy? Can I come in? Hope I'm not breaking in on you while you are working on something important." Felix walked in, closing the door. "I think we should talk in private. I'll leave it up to you who you share this with."

▬

MIE Training Site, Essequibo.

Word spread among the inner circles of the MIE that Krish had killed a CIA agent, but what was more important was who the agent was. Elk Ardila was the CIA person who the MIE had

426

identified as responsible for betraying them, turning their whole operation over to the Brazilian government that resulted in the capture of over two-thirds of their members. For Krish's actions, he was promoted to the head of commando operations.

Krish was taught well by the CIA. He utilized all the skills that he was trained in during the brief period with the Agency at the Plantation in Florida.

The MIE put out a five-figure bounty on the heads of every official in the Guyanan and Venezuelan government who didn't support Essequibo's demand for independence. Both governments at first didn't take the threats seriously, but within two weeks after the word got out, one Venezuelan minister was assassinated and one Guyanan minister, along with his entire family, was killed. The MIE claimed responsibility for both and said that there would be more if Essequibo were not given its independence.

Social media started to pick up chatter that lone wolves, people not associated with the MIE, were trying to locate political figures to take out to collect the rewards that the MIE placed on their heads.

With the media coverage that the MIE was getting, Kyle Martin's investigative report had taken on a life of its own. Kyle received the promotion that she worked so hard to get, moving up to the major network and working out of Washington, DC and reporting whatever she thought newsworthy in South America.

—

Jacksonville, Florida.

Every three weeks the Airport Authority compiles a list of the descriptions and the tag numbers of cars parked in airport parking lots for three weeks or longer. The list is sent to the Jacksonville Police Department. Once received by the JPD, the list is compared to the cars that the police are looking for. When the JPD compared this most recent list, they got a hit, a match on FBI Agent Faye Cook-Little's car. Once identified, Faye's car was towed from the airport long-term parking lot to the JPD forensic lab. There, the forensic team would go over the car to see if they could find anything that would give any indication of what happened to Faye.

Jerry Clark was sitting in Terry Jackson's office having lunch. They had picked up Subway sandwiches along with some chips and cokes. Jerry was trying to build a publicity story on the Mayor concerning his decision-making approach while handling the explosions in Jacksonville.

Terry and Jerry had known each other for a long time and so it didn't surprise Jerry when Terry said, "Jerry, I didn't know that you and Faye were dating?"

Terry paused for a while, then said, "You know there was some talk among the FBI guys that she was only seeing women." Jerry finished taking a bite out of his sandwich, and while he was chewing, he was staring at Terry. Jerry finished eating, laid the sub down on a napkin that he had placed on the top of Terry's desk, then took a big swallow of his Pepsi.

"Terry, if you paid any attention to all of the gossips around Jacksonville, you could listen to it for an entire year, and less than 2% of the stuff would be accurate." Just as soon as Jerry finished, Terry's telephone rang. Terry laid his sandwich down to answer the phone.

"Hello, this is Terry Jackson. How can I help you?" As Terry was listening, he set up in his chair, found a pen, pulled over the tablet that he had beside the telephone and began to take notes. Jerry Clark couldn't hear what Terry Jackson and the caller were talking about, but he could see from the expression on Terry's face that it was important. The conversation went on for several minutes without Terry Jackson saying too much during the conversation other than the occasional "you found that" or "yes I see." Terry finished the conversation and hung up the phone. He continued to write down his notes on the tablet.

Jerry Clark had finished his lunch and was standing up to put on his jacket and leave Terry's office when Terry looked up from his notes.

"Jerry, there is something that I think you should know. The JPD found Faye's car. It's been parked at the airport's long-term parking lot for the last three weeks. The forensics guys have just finished up the first sweep of the car. They found the same type of residue that we discovered in that house that burned down a few weeks ago. We still do not know what that residue is, but finding the same residue in Faye's car indicates Faye and the car were at the location where the fire occurred."

—

Wallace C. Barker's Office, Sterling Business Machine.

Surprised that Felix was standing at his door, he said, "Well, good morning, Felix, and sure, come on in and close the door behind you." Wallace picked up his desk telephone and called his administrative assistant to let her know he did not want to be interrupted.

Felix walked in front of Wallace's desk but then decided to sit at the conference table. At the table he opened a briefcase, taking out the binder that contained the one million lines of software code along with several other spreadsheets.

"WC, I want to apologize for taking so long to get back to you with this information. When I first discovered who wrote this code, in some ways, it didn't surprise me. So I went back through all my steps to ensure that I was identifying the right person."

Wallace was sitting across from Felix with a puzzled look on his face. "You see, Wallace, I first assumed that a group of people wrote this because it is such a significant amount of coding. As you know, when we assign coding tasks to our programmers, we typically break it down into 1000 lines of code per person. Then we give them about a week to complete the work before going to testing, and so it made sense to me that it had to be a minimum of five and maybe as many as ten people working on this vast volume of software code." Felix paused for a few seconds while he pushed two spreadsheets in front of Wallace.

"Now Wallace, you have seen the top sheet before, and if you look closely, you will remember who wrote this code. This was written at the beginning of that Navy contract when we were doing upgrades to their software." Wallace studied the spreadsheet, taking his finger and going down each line of code. When he finished reading the last line of code, he pushed his chair away from the table, stood up and walked to the other side of the room. "Oh my gosh!"

Wallace stood there in the center of the room for several seconds without saying anything. Wallace turned back around to Felix. "Felix, you are telling me that Eve Harding developed a million lines of code all by herself?"

Still sitting at the table, Felix looked up at Wallace. "Yes, Wallace, that is what I'm saying. It may sound unbelievable, but she did it." Felix stood up and faced Wallace. "WC, while we were on that upgrade contract for the Navy, I had to interface with Eve on several occasions. Every time I examined her coding, it was picture-perfect. I would go as far as saying she was a brilliant programmer. The approach that she used in putting this executable application together, I can only describe as genius, pure genius."

Wallace raised his hand. "Wait a minute, Felix. You said application. Do you mean that this code represents a separate application, an executable application?"

Felix repositioned his glasses before looking at Wallace. "Yes."

Wallace walked back to the conference table, sat down, and opened the binder. "Felix, the software is an application to do what?" Felix sat down across from Wallace.

"Eve Harding wrote the application for the complete acquisition of a target and firing of a laser weapon. As close as I can figure it, Wallace, Eve must have hacked into every company that has done any type of software development for a laser weapon and stole their software. Then, along with some off-the-shelf and some open source software, she just needed a minuscule amount of creativity to put this all together." Wallace opened the binder and read the coding language. Felix watched WC as he was completed reading a page and turned to the next.

"Felix, she designed the application to be installed on the Joker." Pointing at a line of code, Wallace said, "See, Felix, she locked the code in so that it would work only on one particular Joker aircraft. She designed it such that the whole application could fit on a one terabyte USB drive, small enough to be carried on the plane and plugged into the aircraft's weapon system through a USB port to fire the laser. When the plane returned, all the pilot had to do was

430

take the USB out, put it into his flight suit pocket, and walk away."
Both Wallace and Felix sat in silence. Wallace slowly looked up,
grabbed the binder, and walked over to his desk. Felix stood up
while closing his briefcase.

"OK, Felix, I'll get back to you if I need anything else."

Felix started for the door, then turned around and said, "WC,
I know you were thinking about marrying Eve, but things have a
way of working out for the best."

WC looked up at Felix from his desk. "Thanks, buddy."

WC turned to his computer and began to compose an email
to SBM Human Resources Department. Wallace requested the full
personnel files on all of the employees from one of SBM's
subcontractors: JBL. Wallace justified his requirement by saying he
was looking for a single programmer to be used on this contract. The
programmer had to have some very specific skills, and he said he
remembered that a person was working for JBL who may have the
skills he was looking for. Wallace's request was not unusual, coming
from a senior program manager such as Wallace. WC knew that if
SBM Human Resources Department did their job, the file that he
wanted should be in the folder.

Wallace turned his attention back to assigning tasks to be
completed while he would be away with his Special Forces A-Team
to his managers. A flag popped up on his monitor indicating that he
had an email from the HR Director. They wanted to know if WC
wanted only JBL current employees, and if not, how far back they
should go? Wallace clarified his request, making sure the dates he
gave included the period when Eve was working on the contract.
WC was just about to go to the break room for some coffee when the
HR email popped up with the attachment.

Wallace started going through the file. WC understood what
Felix meant when he said that her coding was brilliant. Eve
Harding's personnel file indicated that she was certified in just about
every software language currently being used. So she possesses the
skillset to create the code. The next question was why she created
the extra code and forged his name.

Eve's security jacket was part of her personnel file. The
jacket contains the detail information, where the person was born,
marriages, divorces, relatives, children and much more. This was the

personal information that was needed to obtain top security clearances. Eve Harding held a top secret security clearance. This approval gave Eve access to vital information concerning the contract and gave her authorization to submit software deliverables.

CIA Headquarters, Langley, Virginia.

Roy Benning was in the middle of a conference call with the Director, Assistant Director, and the DDP of the CIA. The DDP was speaking.

"Mr. Director, I think we should form a special working group to take care of this. From all that has gone wrong with operation Fertile Ground, I believe that if we let Roy Benning and his people continue working this action, it will be a disaster and we will end up doing a lot of damage control." No one on the conference call said anything for several seconds.

Then the Director spoke. "This is what we're going to do. Roy, when you identify the exact location of all the elements, we will use a contractor to execute. The DDP will put you in contact with a very reliable contractor we have used before. Unless someone has some additional comments, this will end our meeting."

After finishing the call, Roy looked over his calendar. It would be another five days before he had to travel. He made plans to fly to Jacksonville to reorganize the office after the death of Elkin Ardila. The Brazilian authorities had narrowed the list of possible persons responsible for the murder of Elk to a member of the MIE. They were fairly sure that it was the same person who escaped when the truck carrying the prisoners who were brought back to Brazil after the FBI raid in Miami went over a cliff and plunged into the ocean.

The Brazilian authorities didn't have a photo, just a composite drawing. For some reason, the personnel files of the baggage handlers were missing. That file would have held a picture.

Roy Benning received the email from the DDP giving him the name of the contractor that the Director recommended. Roy thought to himself when he saw the way that he had to contact the contractor that he had used him before. The Agency had always used contractors, but they were called upon more frequently since 9/11.

—

SBM, Gaithersburg, Maryland.

Over in Maryland, at Sterling Business Machine, Wallace raised his head from his desk. He had spent another night in his office working until he fell asleep. He finished the action plan for his team to do while he was gone. What was consuming him was the million lines of code and Eve Harding. Eve had programmed some very unique capabilities for the laser system.

Going line by line, Wallace found that the system was capable of acquiring targets by their IP address (Internet Protocol), and this was incredible. The Joker pilot could punch an IP address or several IP addresses into the plane's computer and make a surgical strike on any individual or even a network.

For Wallace, understanding the technology that Eve put into the software was, in a sense, the easy part. Because this was the woman he had fallen in love with and wanted to marry, he wanted to find out why she did it.

WC walked to the men's room to wash up. As he was walking back into his office, he heard his telephone ringing. As he approached the phone, he was reasonably sure that it was Felix. Wallace had sent Felix some lines of code to analyze.

"Good morning, Felix. Did you find out anything interesting?"

"WC, I said that Eve was a high-quality programmer, but the more I study her technique, the more impressed I've become."

Sitting down behind his desk, Wallace replied, "Felix, I totally agree with you. But what we must find out is not only how far this application will go, but and this is what is bugging me most, is why she did it? I don't see that it was for money." Felix cut Wallace off before he could finish.

"Wait! WC, we can't say that she hasn't sold this to another contractor or even another government." Wallace was quiet for a moment.

"Felix, I don't think so. The reasons I believe that is, if she was selling the application to other governments, why did she deliver it to the Navy?"

Felix agreed with Wallace and told him what he had found from studying the software code. Felix discovered that the application was capable of zeroing in on the computer chip that is located in a car if the IP address of the chip is known.

Wallace thought for a few moments on what happens when he takes his car in for service. The first thing that the car mechanic does is to connect the vehicle to the computer that does diagnostic tests.

"Felix, how hard would it be to get the IP address for a car's computer chip?" Felix didn't even have to think about it.

"WC, all you need is the VIN number. Hack into a dealership network, and you could get it. My thinking is that the firewalls protecting a car service records are probably not the best." WC agreed with Felix. Wallace was just about to say something when he heard Leola's voice.

"Barker, I've been getting reports from building security that my top program manager has been spending the last two nights sleeping in his office. Please tell me that's not true."

Wallace ended the call with Felix. "Leola, I've been analyzing that million lines of code. I think Eve Harding tried to kill me."

Trying to comprehend what Wallace just said, Leola backed away two steps from Wallace's desk.

Chapter 43

"Wallace that's a fairly serious accusation. You are talking about the woman you were planning to marry. How did you come to that conclusion?" Wallace told Leola everything that he and Felix had discovered concerning the code. Wallace was suggesting Eve Harding had taken a top secret government weapon system project and used it as a Saturday-night special in attempting to kill Wallace.

"I don't know, WC. That's a pretty big stretch. The big question is why. At this point, you can't prove anything has been compromised, and nothing has been stolen. She delivered the software to the Navy in compliance with the contract, and so the only thing that we can say is that she added a few enhancements. Also, remember, that SBM has been paid for the software. You don't have any tangible evidence that the Joker aircraft targeted your car."

WC didn't respond to what Leola said. He knew that Leola made good sense and was the perfect person for Wallace to bounce ideas off. How Eve Harding wrote the code gave it the capability to target Wallace and kill him. What he had to do was to put a Joker aircraft within 150 miles of Silver Springs Maryland and the dealership where he had his car repaired.

Leola said, "WC, go home, take a shower, and get some sleep. You only have five days before you have to leave for your Reserve duty, so I'm ordering you to leave this building."

Wallace left the SBM building. When WC got into the loaner car the BMW Dealership had given him to drive until the paperwork was completed by the insurance adjuster, he was just about to start the vehicle when Wallace thought that he could easily get the flight log records of both of the Joker aircraft.

There were only two Joker aircraft flying. Both were assigned to the US John F. Kennedy, located in Mayport Florida. All he had to do was send an email to Captain Wilcox and ask him to send the fight logs so they could do some repair calculations.

Before Wallace left the SBM parking lot, he composed the email on his Blackberry and sent it to Captain Wilcox.

—

Jacksonville, Florida.

The last of the funerals for the victims of the explosions were taking place this week. The Mayor had attended, or at least made an appearance, at almost all of the funerals. The city had sent flowers to all of the victims' families.

After the Jacksonville Police Department's forensic lab had completed the analysis of FBI Agent Faye Cook-Little's car, the car was turned over to the FBI so that they could run their own series of investigations. In the meantime, the FBI put out a nationwide search for Eve Harding as a person of interest in the missing person investigation of Faye Cook-Little.

Jacksonville Police Department closed out the investigation on the explosions, placing the blame on the MIE for an act of terrorism in an unsuccessful attempt to rob the Federal Reserve Bank. The federal government was paying compensation to the survivors and to the victims' families. The government also picked up medical expenses for the survivors.

Survivors and the victims' families had the option of rejecting the payout amount or proceeding to a court battle, which was sure to be very costly, complicated, and lengthy with no assurances of emerging from the fight with any compensation.

The city of Jacksonville received the first check for the rebuilding of the Federal Reserve Bank and the Federal Building. The city had to submit an action plan of how the city would rebuild the area of the town that was destroyed because of the bombing of the Federal Reserve Bank to the federal government.

Bubba Webb and the city council of Jacksonville were in lockstep concerning the Mayor's plan to revitalize that area of the city. Henry Bubba Webb's approval ratings for how he handled the situation during the explosion were at the highest level they had ever been. Bubba Webb had become a rising star in his political party. Mayor Webb had no problem seeking donations for his upcoming run to be the party's nominee to run for the President of the United States.

Joe Singletary's injuries had healed to the point he was no longer in a wheelchair. His physical therapy appointments still had him going to therapy three times a week, but he was using a walker to get around. As Henry Webb's campaign manager for his run for President, Joe Singletary was setting up an organizational structure like none Bubba Webb had ever seen before.

It was still several months before the primary season began, but Joe had already appointed a campaign organizer in every state. Joe Singletary and Jerry Clark came up with an idea for a book to be written about Bubba and how he handled the terrorist attacks in Jacksonville. They were interviewing ghostwriters to put the book together.

Jerry Clark was still holding out hope that FBI Agent Faye Cook-Little was still alive, perhaps being held someplace against her will. A day didn't go by that Joe did not talk to someone in the Jacksonville Police Department or with the FBI, exploring any theories that might explain what happened to Faye.

The JPD was trying to contact Eve Harding's next of kin, Eve's son, Tony Harding. The Navy's Criminal Investigative Service (NCIS) concluded the investigation into what happened to Navy Flight Officer Toni Harding. The NCIS investigation report's conclusion said that Flight Officer Toni Harding became disoriented on her approach to the Miami International Airport resulting in a navigational error that led to the Naval Officer flying her plane out into the Atlantic and crashing into the ocean after the aircraft ran out of fuel.

—

Townhome of Wallace C. Barker, Maryland.

When Wallace got home, he did exactly as Leola directed him to do. He took a shower, but instead of going to bed and getting some rest, he started packing his equipment for his upcoming deployment with his Special Forces A-team. WC had deployed so many times it didn't take him long to gather all of his equipment and put everything in his deployment bag.

After he had completed packing, he sat down at his desk, logged into his computer, and sent several emails. One was to the post office to have his mail stopped for the next 90 days, and another was to Felix, letting him know that he requested the flight logs of the Joker aircraft from Captain Wilcox.

WC was just about to take Leola's final advice to get some sleep when his computer signaled that an email had arrived. The email was from Captain Wilcox and had an attachment. Wallace opened the file, the flight logs of the two Joker aircraft.

The flight log is a chronological record of everything that happens to a particular aircraft. Everything that happens to that plane is documented in the register of flight: every takeoff and landing, landing locations, fueling, and maintenance. Digital records are also maintained on different components, systems, and subsystems of the aircraft as well.

Wallace opened the flight log for the first Joker aircraft. Reading the information on the first page confirmed all of Wallace's theories on Eve Harding attempting to kill him. The pilot of this Joker aircraft was Flight Officer Lieutenant JG Tony Harding, call sign Junebug. After reading Tony's name, Wallace flipped through the pages to the date that he put his BMW Z4 in the shop for maintenance.

At this point, it was no surprise to Wallace that on the same day that he put his car in the shop, Tony Harding had to fly to Joint Base Andrews located in Maryland and well within the programmable targeting range of the Joker's laser weapon.

After confirming that Tony Harding and the Joker aircraft were in a position to fire the laser weapon that exploded Wallace's BMW, Wallace began to go through the flight log to find out if he could identify any other dates that coincided with any type of explosion.

What was interesting was that, at the time WC and Eve Harding left for Rio de Janeiro, Tony Harding was flying the Joker aircraft on a training mission around Jacksonville. The next time Tony Harding was piloting the Joker was on the day that Eve and Wallace returned from Rio de Janeiro.

Wallace Googled both of the days to see if he could find anything significant that happened on either day. As Wallace pressed the enter button for his search to begin, deep inside he was hoping that he did not find any significant events that occurred on these dates.

The search results came back. On both dates, two massive explosions happened in Jacksonville, Florida. Both explosions together killed over 100 people, destroyed a major section of the Dames Point Bridge, and destroyed the Federal Reserve Bank and the Federal Building.

After reading the accounts of the explosions, Wallace knew he had to contact Captain Wilson and inform him that his aircraft was being used to destroy and to kill and that Toni Harding was the pilot responsible.

Wallace pulled out his Blackberry and placed a call to Captain Wilcox. Captain Wilcox's voicemail message indicated that he was unavailable and to leave a message. Wallace asked Captain Wilcox the call him as soon as he could because he had something of the utmost importance to talk to him about concerning one of the aircraft on the project. Then WC finally found his way to his bed and to some much-needed sleep.

A sharp pain pierced Wallace's head as he reached across his bed to the nightstand for his cell phone. Looking at the caller ID, he saw it was Navy Captain Wilcox returning his call. While answering the phone, WC got out of bed and started walking toward his bathroom.

"Good morning, Captain Wilcox."

"WC, I think you mean good afternoon. I got your message, but I was going to call you today. I have to give a briefing over at Langley, and I was wondering if you could attend the meeting."

Wallace checked the time on the wall clock. "What time is the meeting?"

"It is scheduled for 1600 hours. Do you think you could make it?" Wallace was standing in front of his bathroom mirror.

"Sure, I should be able to make it. Will I have to brief?"

Captain Wilcox quickly answered. "No, I just think that it would be good to have the project manager for the contract present just in case some questions emerge concerning the software. You can also tell me about the message you left for me."

WC and Captain Wilcox ended the call. Wallace shaved and got dressed. He had one stop to make before driving to his meeting at CIA headquarters. Wallace returned the loaner and picked up his new BMW Z-4.

—

CIA Headquarters, Langley, Virginia.

At CIA headquarters, Wallace had to wait in the lobby until Captain Wilcox came to escort him into the building. Even with Wallace's military ID and contractor's badge he still had to be escorted.

Captain Wilcox gave Wallace some insight concerning the meeting they were going to. Wallace was told that no questions would probably be directed to him but to keep up with everything being said so that, if something came up, he would be prepared to answer.

The meeting lasted for one hour. Captain Wilcox and Wallace stayed in the conference room after everyone else had left.

"OK, WC, you had something you wanted to speak to me about concerning one of the aircraft, and this is a perfect place for us to talk."

Wallace laid the software book on the table along with several other spreadsheets and the two Joker flight logs. As Wallace told his story, he got the impression that Captain Wilcox was not surprised by anything Wallace was saying.

The captain interrupted Wallace, walked over to a wall telephone, and dialed a number. "Roy, I'm down in conference room 4G7. I'm talking with the SBM project manager for our EA-21F Joker Software Upgrade Project. He is sharing some information that I'm sure would be of some interest to you. I'd like for you to join us."

A short time after Captain Wilcox made that call, Roy Benning entered the conference room. Roy introduced himself to Wallace but did not say what connection he had with the Joker Project. Wallace started his story from the beginning. When WC finished, Roy Benning looked at Captain Wilcox and said, "We'll talk later." He thanked Wallace and left the room. Captain Wilcox walked Wallace back to the entrance, thanked him for the information and said he could be contacted for some follow-up questions if necessary.

Driving back to his townhouse in Maryland, Wallace was so tired he couldn't even enjoy driving his new car. His concern was that he might fall asleep at the wheel and crash into some tree and become injured so he would not be able to go on his Special Forces mission. WC made it home without any incident. Once back, Wallace quickly changed into his pajamas and got in bed, but as soon as he laid his head on his pillow, his mind began to analyze the meeting he had with Captain Wilcox and Roy Benning.

Roy Benning looked familiar to Wallace, but he could not remember where he had seen or met him. What was more of a surprise to Wallace was that he sensed that both Captain Wilcox and Roy Benning either already had information or at least their suspicions concerning the new capabilities of the Joker and were waiting for someone to bring them the hard evidence. Either way, Wallace fell asleep knowing that a great weight had been lifted off of his back. He could now concentrate on his upcoming mission.

Chapter 44

The United Kingdom, Scotland.

In a villa on the coast of Scotland east of Glasgow near Edinburgh, a tall, athletic, well-built man stood on the balcony of this classic home smoking a pipe. He looked down at the shipping vessels as they passed through the narrow channel below headed into the North Sea.

His attention was taken from this view when he heard a voice from the computer that was located in his study: "You have mail."

Still puffing on a pipe, he walked into the study to his computer and clicked the mail icon to view his double-encrypted email message. The message read: "Twenty million dollars transferred to your Swiss account. Balance to be sent upon your confirmation of completion of operations. Detailed information to follow."

The man created a new file folder and labeled it Eighty-Four. The man then clicked the attachment icon and downloaded the attached file into the newly created file folder.

—

The Plantation, Camp Blanding, Florida.

A modified Hercules C-130 aircraft flew Wallace's A-team from Joint Base Andrews to the Plantation. The first sensation that everyone on the team felt was the heat and high humidity in Florida. All of the Hornets' Nest A-team's previous missions were to the Middle East. Because they were flown to Florida to receive their mission, the team was somewhat confident that their mission would be a location in the southern hemisphere, somewhere in South America.

The team loaded their equipment onto waiting trucks and got into the buses that would take them to the base camp. The buses and trucks bypassed the main post and drove the team ten miles from the main post to a training area of the Plantation that appeared to be on the outskirts of a swamp. Wallace and his men were told to unload and then set up a base camp in an area about 100 meters south of the point where they were dropped off. The team should be ready for their briefing at 0600 hours the next morning.

The A-team moved the 100 meters in short order, set up the base camp, established security, and began to check their equipment to ensure nothing was damaged during the flight to the Plantation.

The next morning Wallace's team members were drinking coffee when the Battalion Operation Officer, along with two staff officers and the same civilian that was at the initial briefing during the weekend drill, arrived to brief them.

When the group stood in front of the team, Wallace recognized the civilian, Roy Benning of the CIA. The Operation Officer introduced Roy Benning, but not as Roy Benning, as Jeff Mansfield. After the introductions, the CIA rep took over.

"Seventy-two hours from now, one section of your A-team will HALO from an altitude of 20,000 feet into a territory known as Essequibo. The other Section will arrive at the Georgetown International Airport in Guyana.

"Essequibo is a disputed region that is situated between Guyana and Venezuela. Your mission is to locate the training base of the group called the Movement for the Independence for Essequibo, or MIE. The MIE is a known terrorist group that has taken credit for the murder of the ministers of security for both Venezuela and Guyana, a CIA field agent, and two ministers of the governments of Guyana and Venezuela along with their families. The second part of your mission is to locate the commander, Krish and identify his movements. You have 90 days to complete your assignment.

"Section A will establish a base camp at this location. Section B will send two men each to these villages, Parika, Bartica, and Apotex, to obtain information. This section will communicate with the base camp any information they find out on a location for the MIE training camp. The base camp will check out this area to pinpoint the exact spot where they are located.

"Section B, this is your cover: you are a film crew looking for locations for an upcoming movie. The name of your company is the Trade Winds Filming Company out of Houston, Texas. All calls made to verify who you are will be routed through the official channels.

"If you meet all requirement before this period, you will be extracted. Your rules of engagement: only fire if you are fired upon. The packages you have been given contain all the necessary IDs associating each of you with the company. OK, what are your questions?"

Wallace looked around to see if any of his team had any questions. There seemed to be none, and so Wallace said; "How will we be extracted?"

Roy looked at Wallace and recognized him from the meeting he had with Captain Wilcox. "Major, haven't we met before?" But before Wallace could answer, Roy said, "Let's talk offline after this meeting.

"Both sections will be flown out from the Georgetown Airport. If things go south, you will E and E, escape and evade, to this location," he said, pointing to a spot on the map. "And a sub will pick you up. OK, that's it."

Wallace's men broke up into their sections to work on the details of the plan. WC walked over to speak with Roy Benning, AKA Jeff Mansfield.

Wearing sunglasses, Roy looked over the top of the frame as Wallace approached him. "When we met at Langley I had no idea that you were the commander of this team. You guys have an excellent reputation, and that's why your command selected your team." Wallace thanked Roy Benning for the compliment and then Roy continued.

"I think there are a couple of things you should know as a follow-up to the information you provided us about the explosions in Jacksonville. There is a nationwide alert for Eve Harding, and what we didn't tell you in that meeting is that her daughter, Flight Officer Harding, is missing and presumed to have died in a plane crash. A plane that she was flying ran out of fuel over the Atlantic just off the coast of Miami. The Flight Officer's body has not been found, just parts of the wreckage."

Roy Benning was quiet for a few seconds, then he ended by saying, "Major Barker, you've been around long enough to know that this will not be an easy mission. You can't plan for everything and need to be flexible. Once you find the location of the training camp, we have a private contractor who will pilot a drone over the area and destroy the camp. That same contractor will take out Krish. By the time that happens, you and your men should be flying out of the Georgetown Airport."

—

Essequibo.

Within the 72-hour period, Wallace's A-team had deployed to their mission sites. Wallace went with the section that Haloed into position in the jungle of the Essequibo Territory. The other section landed at the Capitol of Guyana, Georgetown. That Section picked up three SUV vehicles and started for the three assigned villages.

After establishing the base camp, Wallace didn't wait to hear from the Section that was trying to pick up information at the villages. Wallace sent out patrols each night to the locations he thought were good spots to set up a terrorist training base.

In all three villages, everyone knew of the MIE. Many people would talk openly about them but never gave any details. The Brazilian government placed a bounty on Krish's head, dead or alive for 500,000 U.S. dollars.

Eighty-Four arrived in Georgetown, picked up his equipment, and moved into a warehouse that was rented by the Agency as a USAID storage facility.

The Hornets' Nest A-team was ten weeks into the operation when they started to pick up chatter in one of the village's leading nightspots, a café' called the Mermaid's Net located in the town of Parika.

The chatter was that Krish's brother and his wife would be baptizing their youngest child on the first Sunday of the next month. Krish would be the godfather so it was expected that he would come to the baptizing. Almost at the same time, WC was leading one of the patrols when they heard gunfire. The patrol moved toward the sound and came upon the terrorists' training camp. Wallace and his men stayed in position and observed the camp for the next three days.

Wallace's section found that the camp was in a valley. The only reason they heard the gunfire was that the direction of the wind the night that they were on patrol enabled the sound to travel. The camp consisted of six buildings. After observing the training site for three days, Wallace concluded there were 65 men and women in the location receiving training.

When Wallace and his section got back to their base camp, they received the information concerning Krish. WC and his communications specialist were encrypting the message to be transmitted to Langley, and Wallace saw something in the report from the team in the village of Parika:

"Two beautiful women came into the Mermaid's Net. They appeared to be American. After asking around, we finally sat down with the harbor master for the village. After several drinks, he confirmed that they were Americans and were sailing a catamaran around the Caribbean. The name of the ship was Junebug."

When Wallace saw that the name of the catamaran was Junebug, there was no doubt in his mind that the two women had to be Eve and Toni Harding. All of the information was transmitted to Langley.

Roy Benning read Wallace's report, which included the information concerning Eve and Toni Harding. What Wallace didn't know was that both Eve and Toni Harding had been classified as wanted terrorists, and they were to be captured or killed. After reading the report, Roy transmitted a message to the contractor. The letter from Roy Benning to the contractor read:

"Confirmed location of the terrorist group. Enclosed is the confirmation of the site on the second targets. Positive identity confirmation by resources on the ground backed up by Satellite facial identification. Execute with extreme prejudice."

The Hornets' Nest A-team prepared to leave for the Georgetown airport. It was three days before Krish was expected in the village of Parika. Roy Benning wanted the team to be out of the country before that date.

Wallace got his men moving toward Georgetown. He then commandeered a motorcycle and told his people he would catch up with them in two days that he had something to take care of in the Parika Village.

Wallace wanted to find Eve Harding and ask her why? It didn't take long for Wallace to reach the village of Parika.

Luck was with him because, as WC was riding through the marketplace, he spotted Eve buying some fruit at one of the stands. Eve finished purchasing the supplies and started walking towards the Mermaid's Net Café'. Eve didn't see Wallace following her as she entered the café.

Eve looked around the cafe' to see if Tony had arrived. Eve and Tony had made plans to meet there after they had purchased supplies for the Junebug. Seeing that Tony had not come, Eve took a table at the rear of the café' in a place where she could see the entrance.

As she sat down at the table, she set the bag that had her supplies in it on the floor and put her pocketbook in the chair next to her.

After seeing Eve enter the Mermaid's Net, WC went to the rear of the café and came through the kitchen. From the kitchen's door, Wallace spotted where Eve was sitting. She had a good view of the entrance but not a clear view of the door that led to the kitchen.

Wallace picked up a tray, made his way to the bar, ordered a bottle of wine with two glasses. He then started walking through the crowd towards Eve's table.

Eve didn't notice the waiter carrying a tray with a bottle of wine along with two glasses walking in her direction. The server stops at the table. Standing on Eve's blind side, Wallace filled the glasses with wine. It wasn't until the waiter was taking the glasses of wine off of the tray and placing them on the table that Eve looked up. She was totally surprised to see that the waiter was Wallace and of his presence in Essequibo.

Wallace sat down in the chair facing Eve. WC was wearing civilian clothes carrying his 9mm automatic under the shirt he was wearing. With a spine-chilling look on her face, Eve Harding said.

"WC, you are worse than a bad penny, always showing up. Why can't you just die and go away." Not surprised by Eve's reaction, Wallace picked up a glass of wine and pushed the other glass across the table towards Eve. Keeping his eyes on Eve, he took a sip of the wine and sat the glass back on the table.

"Eve, I just want to know why? Why did you and your daughter kill all of those people?" Eve began to shout.

"You just don't get it. You really don't. I'll tell you, so you can die with the answer in your head. First, let's connect the dots. Dot one, remember the Bay of Pigs invasion of Cuba. Well, the CIA's plan called for sixteen B-26 Bombers to support the attacks. Got that! Now let's go to Dot number two. The Harding's Corporation citrus farming Empire. The third-largest citrus company in the world and the largest in the United States. That would have been my inheritance and my daughter's inheritance. WC, we were millionaires. More money and land than anyone in the state of Florida. Well at the time of the Bay of Pigs invasion, my grandfather was an Air Force pilot, and he was the commander of one of the B-26 bombers. The night before the attack, the CIA Desk Chief in Jacksonville, Florida, made the decision to reduce the number of the planes from 16 to 8. Not nearly enough to accomplish the mission. In effect, what the Desk Chief from Jacksonville was doing was sending the pilots to their deaths. Seven of the plane's returned, the one plane that didn't return was flown by my grandfather. He and his entire crew were killed. With his death, the Harding's Citrus Empire collapsed. My family lost everything. Both my grandmother and mother committed suicide."

Wallace sat up in his chair and said. "Eve that was a long time ago. You've carried that hate all of these years." Eve was reaching into the pocketbook she placed in the chair next to her.

"Lover, revenge has no expiration date. The CIA took everything from my family and me, so I had to get my revenge. Everyone who held the position of Desk Chief and anyone who was in line to get promoted to the position, I killed. I started that silly book club. When we had meetings, I would always arrive late, go to their cars and copy their vehicle's VIN numbers. Once I had the VIN, I hacked into the dealership network to obtain the IP address for the computer chip in their car. Once we had the IP address, Toni would fly a training mission, punch in the IP address, the Joker's plane's computer will lock on the car's engine and fire the laser from the Joker aircraft and the rest is history."

Eve pulled a .38 revolver from the bag and fired two shots at Wallace. Both of Eve's shots missed WC. Wallace pulled his 9mm automatic, firing one shot that hit Eve in her shoulder. Just as WC was about to fire a second shot Toni Harding came up behind WC and knocked him out.

With Eve bleeding, Toni carried her mother back to the Junebug. Someone in the café threw some water on Wallace, and he came to. WC saw that both Toni and Eve were gone. He left the restaurant, got on the motorcycle and headed for the airport. Wallace got back to his team at Georgetown, Guyana's airport, and the A-team flew back to the States that night.

During the flight back to the Plantation, Wallace typed up his report. His A-Team accomplished its mission in locating the Krish and the training camp of the MIE. As they flew, WC knew that the camp would be destroyed within the next 72 hours with Krish being taken out either at the camp or at a different location.

In a separate section of the report, WC included details of his encounter with Eve Harding. Wallace transmitted his report back to Headquarters.

It didn't take long before Wallace received replies to his report. First, from his Battalion Commander: "Major Barker, good show! You and your men have done great work. Because of your actions, you saved the lives of countless Americans. Safe flight home and see you upon your return."

Of the several replies of a job well done that Wallace received, the response that came from Roy Benning was the most chilling: "Acknowledged and confirmed. Thanks, Roy." Acknowledge and confirmed. The words stayed in Wallace's head as he drifted off to sleep.

—

Junebug, Parika's Harbor, Essequibo

When Toni got Eve back to the Junebug, she tended to her mother's gunshot wound. After she had dressed the wound, Tony pulled anchor to set sail; but when she turned the switch to start the engines, the entire boat exploded into flames, killing both Eve and Toni Harding.

Two days later, Krish was walking out of the church after the baptizing of his brother's son when he was shot in the head by a sniper's bullet. Later that night, an unmanned aerial vehicle destroyed the MIE's training camp.

—

Georgetown Section of Washington, DC.

Two weeks later, Wallace C. Barker walked back into a very exclusive jewelry store located in the Georgetown section of Washington, DC. The store clerk, Melvin, recognized WC as he entered.

As Melvin walked toward Wallace, he said, "Mr. Barker, WC, I remember you. I hope you have your receipt."

The End

Wilson Baker, Jr., who also writes as W.G. Goldstein, is the author of five Wallace C. Barker novels. A native of Jacksonville, Florida, Wilson now lives in Windsor Mill, Maryland.

Upcoming Wilson Baker, Jr. novels:

Murder On A Catamaran - Available Spring 2017

Bird Dog Six – Available Spring 2018

Official Website of Storyteller Wilson Baker, Jr.:
www.wbakerakawggoldstein.com

www.ingramcontent.com/pod-product-compliance
Lightning Source LLC
Chambersburg PA
CBHW051933090426
42741CB00008B/1164